May You Be the Mother
of a Hundred Sons

MAY YOU BE

THE MOTHER OF

A HUNDRED SONS

A Journey Among the Women of India

ELISABETH BUMILLER

RANDOM HOUSE NEW YORK

Library of Congress Cataloging-in-Publication Data
Bumiller, Elisabeth.
May you be the mother of a hundred sons : a journey
among the women of India / by Elisabeth Bumiller.
p.   cm.   ISBN 0–394–56391–3
1. Women—India.   1. Title.
HQ1742.B86   1990   305.4'0954—dc20   89–27120

Manufactured in the United States of America
Typography and binding design by J. K. Lambert
98765432
First Edition

For my mother

ACKNOWLEDGMENTS

THIS BOOK WOULD NOT HAVE BEEN POSSIBLE WITHOUT THE COUNTLESS people who helped me, encouraged me, taught me about India and invited me into their lives. A few deserve a special mention here.

In New Delhi, the wonderful, chaotic, loving Bissells and members of their extended family—Bim, John, William, Monsoon, Mrs. Nanda, Padma and Nisha—made India the extraordinary place it was for me; they will remain lifelong friends. Renuka Singh, my soulmate and collaborator in the search for Surinder Kaur, devoted weeks to that project and others, and gave me valuable suggestions after reading my manuscript. She, too, will remain a friend for life. The phenomenal P. J. Anthony of *The New York Times* New Delhi bureau selflessly helped me when he could have been doing something else. To me, he seemed like a gift dropped from heaven. Mani Mann provided much laughter, good friendship and a beautiful sari, and Ritu Menon lent invaluable insight and advice. In New Delhi, I would also like to thank Mani Shankar and Suneet Aiyar, Suman and Manju Dubey, G. Parthasaraty, Rama Mohan Rao, Richard Weintraub, Nilova Roy, C. P. Sujaya, Ella Datta, R. L. Verma, Sanjoy Hazarika and all of the fine people at 35 A/1 Prithvi Raj Road, particularly Abdul Toheed, Chunni Lal and the late Mohinder Singh. I also owe a special debt of gratitude to yet another member of the extended Bissell family, Mallika Singh.

In Calcutta, I am extremely grateful to M. J. and Mallika Akbar, Shekhar and Pakhi Bhatia, Rajbir and Meena Singh, and Shanti Bhattacharya, who fed me, entertained me and most of all guided me through the maze of their city. I would also like to thank Carolyne Wright for her permission to reprint her translations of Nabaneeta Dev Sen's poetry.

In Bombay, Vir and Malavika Sanghvi were like my home away from home. Both of them know how much they helped me, and how much their writing and thinking influenced me and this book. I also owe an enormous thank you to Bhawna Somaya, who is the person who made the chapter on film stars possible, and who became a good friend. I am grateful, too, to Vibhuti Patel for her time and energy in helping me to understand the workings of the Women's Centre, and to Siddharth Bhatia for his assistance in reporting.

In Madras, I would like to thank Jaya Gokulamani, who poured her heart and talents into our work in Salem District, and who literally helped nurse me back to health during the long drive back from Belukkurichi. I am grateful, too, to Jaya Arunachalam of the Working Women's Forum.

In Gujarat, I am appreciative to Ela Bhatt, Renana Jhabvala, Harish Khare, Anila Dholakia and all of the other people connected with the Self-Employed Women's Association. At SEWA Rural in Jhagadia, Anil and Lata Desai, Gayatri Giri and the other staff members taught me about health care for India's poor.

In Lucknow, I will always be grateful to our friend and teacher Dr. Surendra Singh, his wife, Reena, his mother and his remarkable daughters—Anu, Anju, Chotu, Rinki and Moon. Thanks, too, to Balraj Chauhan, who first led me to Dr. Singh. In Khajuron, I feel I can never repay the kindness and hospitality of Vindhya Devi, or Bhabhiji, and her late husband, Sheo Singh. I also owe many thanks to Mr. and Mrs. Shardul Singh, Amar Singh and Kitty Singh.

In Washington, I would especially like to thank my editors at *The Washington Post*—Ben Bradlee, Len Downie, Mary Hadar and Ellen Edwards—who thought it was a fine idea to send a Style reporter to India, and who cheered me on throughout my three and a half years there. Portions of this book were published in earlier versions in the *Post,* and I am grateful to the paper for allowing them to reappear here. I would also like to thank Kathy Sreedhar, whose help, expertise, friendship and tremendous enthusiasm kept me going, and whose work in India has been an inspiration for mine. I am indebted to Maura Moynihan for the priceless education she gave me about India, and for the laughter and friendship she brought into our home. Her mother, Elizabeth Moynihan, added to my education and set me on the right path that first week in Jhor. Marty Chen provided wisdom and advice, and Mahnaz Ispahani took time out from her own research to find material for me at the Library of Congress.

In New York, I am especially grateful to Peter Osnos, my editor at Random House, who has guided me and spurred me on since we started talking about this book in 1984, and also to my literary agent and friend, Amanda Urban, who was the one who thought I should write a book in the first place. Virginia Avery, my copy editor, did a superb job with the manuscript. Many thanks also to Ken Gellman for all his help at Random House. In Cincinnati, Barbara Ramusack provided fascinating material on Katherine Mayo, and my brother-in-law in San Diego, Dr. Michael Weisman, answered many questions about family planning. Ken Rice in Carmel did a beautiful job printing my photographs.

There are a few other friends I would like to thank as well. Many of them probably are not aware of their contributions, but it was in conversations with them about India and about women that I was guided to many of the thoughts and conclusions in this book. Geraldine Baum listened and encouraged, as she always has, but also offered insight into what it is like to be an American woman in the late 1980s. I am also thankful to Michele Slung, Susan and Howell Raines, Judy Gingold and David Freeman, Michael and Anne Mandelbaum, Daniel Yergin, Cristy West, Doris Reynolds, Dale Russakoff, Betsy and Victor Gotbaum, Mala and Tejbir Singh, Vikram and Tasneem Mehta, Sunil and Shalini Sethi, Amitav Ghosh, Raghu Rai, Vikram Seth, Elisabeth Bentley, the incomparable Harilal Dhingra, and especially Laura Richardson and Rone Tempest, our fellow travelers on a journey that ensured that we will always be part of one another's lives. The last friend I would like to thank is Dhiren Bhagat, who will not be able to read this book. Dhiren died tragically in a senseless car accident in New Delhi in November 1988, and since then I have often thought about the times he used to drop by our house Indian-style, unannounced, always ready for a piece of cake and a good argument about the inconsistencies of feminism. It was Dhiren who forced me to think through many of my easy assumptions, and I know we would have had lovely quarrels over this book. I will miss those, as I miss him.

Finally I am indebted to my parents, Gunhild and John Rose and Ted and Ruth Ann Bumiller, who have given me their love and support, and whose sense of adventure brought them to India and allowed me to see the country through new eyes. My father, especially, taught me how to travel; his films, from *By Jeep Around the World* to *Eternal India,* have guided and influenced much of my work. I am also indebted to my inspirational grandmother, Elizabeth Bumiller, who at the age of eighty-eight came to visit her granddaughter one insufferably hot summer in India. I also owe much to my equally intrepid and remarkable in-laws, Joseph and Etta Weisman, and my sisters and step-brothers—Trine, Karen and Jennifer Elken Bumiller, and Stephen, Michael and David Rose.

The last person I would like to thank is the most important. I think it is fair to say that this book could not have been written without my husband, Steve, who read the entire manuscript many times, believed in it when I did not, and whose support, patience and love were the source of my strength. This book is as much his as mine.

ELISABETH BUMILLER
Tokyo
September 1989

CONTENTS

May You Be the Mother
of a Hundred Sons

CHAPTER 1

ARRIVAL
AND
INTRODUCTION

THIS BOOK IS THE STORY OF AN AMERICAN WOMAN'S JOURNEY INTO WHAT for her was an unknown world, the lives of the women of India. It lasted almost four years, took me to most states in the country and forced me thousands of years back in history. I met and interviewed hundreds of women, although I am not sure that this number means anything. I learned the most from the handful of Indian women I counted as friends, and from the larger truths that came from the exploration of individual lives. Many of the Indian women I encountered led miserable existences, little better than those of beasts of burden. Others were among the most formidable people I have ever met. Almost all of them were inspiring. The story of Indian women is ancient, but it is also the story of the profound change, and contradictions, of the present day.

My husband and I first landed in New Delhi in the middle of a January night in 1985, and at the time it seemed as if we had flown the nineteen hours from our home in Washington, D.C., to a country that could not be part of the same planet. One of New Delhi's sodden winter fogs hung heavy over the runway, obscuring what little there was to see other than scrub and rocky soil. Later, I always thought it fitting that my first view of India should have extended no more than twenty-five feet in front of me.

I was twenty-eight years old and had traveled no farther from the United States than Europe. To prepare myself for India, I had dutifully read the recommended books and talked to numerous old India hands. *The Jewel in the Crown,* the public television series based on Paul Scott's Raj Quartet, was bringing magical scenes of Kashmir's Dal Lake and the golden desert of Rajasthan into American living rooms at the time; I had been moved by the film *Gandhi* a few years before. None of that seemed to have anything to do with the India I first encountered, and no book or person could have described the physical sensation of simply breathing the air. This was before the completion of the modern Indira Gandhi International Airport, so our arrival was not sanitized by a sealed walkway into a brightly lit terminal. Instead, we stepped out the door of the plane and were instantly assaulted by the overpowering smell of a Delhi winter night—smoky and sweet and overripe and utterly foreign, with a promise of adventures to come. Later I discovered the odor was from the smoke of the cow-dung fires that people built to cook food and keep warm.

I was shaking as I walked down the steps and onto the tarmac, feeling like an innocent unworthy of what was before me. As we waited under the belly of the plane for a rattletrap bus to take us to the terminal, I stared through the mist at the Arabic letters on a parked 747 that had arrived that night from the Gulf. We had flown over Saudi Arabia on our way, and it took me a moment to readjust to my new place in the world; the Middle East was now west. The fog and my fatigue gave everything an amorphous, dreamlike quality, as if India had no edges and no point of penetration. It was the first of many times I would feel as if I were free-falling in space, with nothing to hang on to and no point of reference.

I had come to India because of my husband. I still don't like to say it that way, but it is one reason, I think, that I wrote this particular book about India instead of another. For the past five and a half years, I had been a reporter for the Style section of *The Washington Post,* and Steve, my husband, had covered the White House for *The New York Times.* We were married in 1983. A little more than a year later, Steve joined the foreign staff of the *Times* and accepted New Delhi as his first assignment.

I knew almost nothing about India. My father had spent three months there in 1956, while making a film about traveling by jeep around the world, and the image I had of the country, to the extent that I even thought about it, had come chiefly from one scene in that film that had stayed with me for years. It was of Hindu worshipers on the bathing ghats, or steps, leading into the waters of the Ganges at Benares, one of the holy cities of India. People swarmed into the river, gulped mouthfuls of fetid brown water, and stood knee-deep in silent meditation as they cupped their hands in prayer toward the sun. The shot had a beautiful amber light, which I now recognize as the color of dawn on the Ganges. But it all looked so inaccessible to my world.

Yet I had always wanted to report from overseas, and once I got used to the idea of India, I developed, along with my nervousness, a lot of romantic notions about the passage ahead. Our first day in Delhi, however, did not distinguish us as intrepid travelers. We were cosseted several centuries away from Benares at Delhi's Taj Mahal Hotel, a luxury high rise with a white marble lobby filled with the scent of fresh tuberoses and a powerful disinfectant. We had checked in at five in the morning but were awake at eight. Steve, with great trepidation, parted the heavy curtains to peer out at India. Beneath us lay a mist-shrouded expanse of trees and foliage that looked like an ominous South Asian Sherwood Forest. Above it, floating languidly on the morning breeze, were enormous birds reminiscent of pterodactyls. "I'm supposed to cover this country," Steve said, only half joking, "but I'm afraid to go outside." I later learned that we had been gazing down on cabinet ministers' gardens, which make up some of the most expensive real estate in the country.

New Delhi at eye level later the same day presented other surprises. The city had been described to me as a gracious capital of broad streets lined with mango trees and gardens bursting with dahlias in the cooler months. That is true, especially on a clear day in early spring, but what my new eyes first focused on is also true: a rundown metropolis in various stages of urban expansion and decay. The fog gave everything a gray, gritty cast. There had been fifteen different cities built on and around New Delhi, spanning the eleventh to twentieth centuries, but this last one looked as if it hadn't been finished. Graceful white-columned "bungalows" sat behind big brick walls, but outside there were no sidewalks, just rubble and dust. Many of the bungalows were streaked with black water stains from the years of monsoons. A few glass-and-steel skyscrapers rose assertively out of the small business area

of central New Delhi, but everything else was in dire need of maintenance, or at least a fresh coat of paint. And that was the "new" Delhi
built by the British. When we drove to the markets of the old city,
we were hit by a rock-video kind of intensity: hawkers, jostling
crowds, blaring Hindi film music, pigs, cows, goats, chickens, parrots,
diseased dogs, bicycle rickshaws, one-armed lepers, legless beggars,
ragged children. On the streets surrounding Jama Masjid, the largest
mosque in India, the smells of incense, jasmine and sewage mingled
with the delicious aroma of Indian bread puffing up in the oil of a
frying pan. Photographs and films cannot completely capture the
sensory overload. Until then, I had always been slightly disappointed
to find the foreign countries I visited in some way shadows of what
I had imagined. In India that first day I was incredulous.

Trying to establish a bit of my old Washington routine, I went for
a run that first morning in Lodi Garden, a lovely park of well-worn
lawns and crumbling fifteenth-century tombs left by one of the city's
invading dynasties. There I came upon one of my first Indian women.
She was following a bullock across the grass and collecting the animal's
warm steaming dung with her hands. She put it in a basket and headed
home, I later learned, so she could mix it with straw to make little cakes
for cooking fuel.

The first week we moved into a house on Prithvi Raj Road, an
address that sounds as lyrical to me now as it did then, in the heart
of the "forest" we had seen from our hotel room. Among our neighbors were diplomats, Prime Minister Rajiv Gandhi's cabinet members
and Indian industrialists. Our house, which the *Times* had rented for
a dozen years, was an undistinguished one-story white stucco with a
pretty garden and four bedrooms. All of the rooms had ceiling fans
and most opened onto a central veranda where I later hung a big brass
birdcage with two noisy green parrots. I put grass mats and dhurrie
rugs on the floors and re-covered the furniture in Indian handloom.
The house came with a cook and a housekeeper and a part-time
gardener and laundryman, an absurd infrastructure for two people to
inherit, but standard help for affluent Indian families. Toheed, the
cook, had worked for the *Times* for more than a dozen years. Mohinder, the driver at the *Times* office, had been there for twenty.

As the days passed, a pattern of relative normalcy began to assert
itself. I took Hindi lessons in the mornings, then settled in to work.
The Washington Post already had a Delhi correspondent, but I had
made arrangements with my editors to write longer feature stories

about social issues and culture. I also thought I would try to write a book, although I was not sure about what. Several people had suggested it should be about Indian women, but I resisted the idea because it seemed a marginal concern compared with the more important problems—poverty, overpopulation, threats to national unity and religious violence—facing India. Besides that, I was already sensitive about my status as "the wife" who had followed her husband halfway around the world. I certainly didn't want to write the predictable "woman's book."

This is not to say that I didn't consider myself a feminist, but my feminism, such as it was, consisted of an unformed, conventional belief in equal rights and the self-absorbed determination to have a career. I was born in 1956 in Denmark—my mother is Danish and my father, an American, met her on a ferry to Copenhagen during his round-the-world jeep trip—but I came of age in Cincinnati in the mid-1970s. The women's movement had fought many of my battles for me, and to a large extent I reaped the benefits. My family naturally assumed I would have a profession. I went to Northwestern University's journalism school, then to the Graduate School of Journalism at Columbia, and at neither place did I encounter any overt discrimination. My first year at Northwestern I had taken a course in women's history that included Betty Friedan's *The Feminine Mystique* and Simone de Beauvoir's *The Second Sex,* but I had never joined a women's organization or written exclusively about women's issues. Washington is a town run and dominated by men, but there my most impassioned feminist emotions centered on the kitchen, in arguments with my husband over who should cook dinner and clear the table.

Before moving to India I had had little exposure to poor people. I had written stories about migrant farm workers on the Gulf Coast of Florida when I worked for *The Miami Herald* for one year in the late seventies, and I had delivered meals to the homeless every other week the last two years that we lived in Washington. These activities served chiefly to relieve my conscience. I was a registered Democrat with vague concerns about the poor and the homeless, but I had never confronted poverty on a massive scale and had never been forced to think about the system that creates it. In truth I had spent considerably more time writing about the rich than about the poor. When I started at the *Post,* I covered Washington parties—political fund-raisers, art openings and the occasional White House state dinner—and also interviewed such swells as Cornelia Guest, the debutante turned aspiring actress. When Ronald Reagan became president I graduated to writing profiles of a number of the staff people who ran his administration and chronicling some of the first-term excesses of Nancy Reagan and the new California money that had arrived in town. The truth is, I was hesitant to write a book about Indian women because I was intimidated by the subject.

So for my first two years in India, I did not pursue "women's issues" in particular. I wrote instead about Calcutta's writers, painters and filmmakers, and how their work reflected one of the most ruinous but creative cities on earth. I wrote about the legacy of the British Raj, focusing on a group of Indians who belonged to a curious anachronism, the Royal Bombay Yacht Club. Later that year, I went to the fiftieth anniversary of Rajiv Gandhi's prep school in the foothills of the Himalayas, using the event to explore the sensibilities of Rajiv's affluent school chums, the "computer boys" who had joined his government and were advising him how to haul India into the next century.

And yet, it was the stories I wrote about women that touched me the deepest. At the beginning of my second year I met a bride, the wife of a scooter-cab driver, who said her husband had set her on fire because she had not brought enough dowry to the marriage. She had spent three months in a hospital and had been discharged with scars over 60 percent of her body. Rippled, splotched skin was still visible on her hands and neck, and later she showed me the horrible scars on her stomach and calves. She was one of the lucky ones. There are more than 600 bride burnings, as these attempted murders for dowry are called, in New Delhi each year. Most of the women die.

I had also spent the previous summer listening in amazement as college girls informed me they would be happy to marry a stranger of their parents' choice. I remember asking a twenty-year-old student in economics at Delhi University, Meeta Sawhney, if she loved the childhood friend her parents had decided she should marry. "That's a very difficult question," she answered. "I don't know. This whole concept of love is very alien to us. We're more practical. I don't see stars, I don't hear little bells. But he's a very nice guy, and I think I'm going to enjoy spending my life with him. Is that love?" She shrugged.

Women, I was beginning to realize, were my window into the Indian interior world, and into the issues of family, culture, history, religion, poverty, overpopulation, national unity—indeed, the very problems I had earlier thought were unrelated to the concerns of women. By this time, too, I had begun to make friends with several Indian women. One was an academic, working on her doctorate. Another was a journalist, and a third designed Indian clothes. They had seemed, at first, so much like me. I soon learned that they were but they weren't, and the differences opened the window a little bit more. There are many ways "in" for an outsider in India, of course. I knew Americans who studied Moghul water gardens, classical Indian dance or the cult of the god Krishna. I knew other Americans who wrote reports on the government's health care system or raised chickens. I knew reporters who covered political developments in Delhi and terrorist attacks in Punjab. All are ways of illuminating at least a pocket of a seemingly unfathomable civilization, and I am not sure that raising chickens is much less revealing than an interview with a member of Rajiv Gandhi's opposition. Women were my way "in," in part because they were the most natural, familiar path.

I cannot pretend to have included every kind of Indian woman in this book, nor can I claim that the women I have chosen are a representative sampling in a country as diverse as India. Most of the women in this book are Hindus, representing the country's majority religion, although I have included Muslims, Sikhs and Christians as well. I selected the women because they interested me, like Aparna Sen, the Calcutta director who made a beautiful and controversial film about an upper-middle-class housewife who commits the unforgivable sin of having an affair. Others are here because they inspired me, like Ela Bhatt, the quiet revolutionary who organized thousands of illiterate women vegetable vendors, quilt makers and trash pickers into powerful trade unions, changing the definition of "work" and also the way a woman looked at herself. Some are here because their lives illustrate important issues, like A. P. Christian, a village health worker who worried that her pay would be docked if she didn't produce her yearly quota of couples for sterilization operations. Many are here because their stories need to be told. In the state of Rajasthan, in September 1987, an eighteen-year-old widow named Roop Kanwar was burned alive on her husband's funeral pyre. No one will ever know whether an educated young woman committed sati willingly, or was pushed. In south India, I met Muthaye and her husband, Mohanasundaram, poor farm workers who said they had been forced to kill their day-old infant daughter because they couldn't afford the cost of her dowry. In their part of the country, it was something that people did, although no one liked to talk about it. In Bombay, I met Assumpta

D'Sylva, a middle-class Roman Catholic woman who was undergoing a test, called a chorionic villus sampling, to determine whether the baby she was carrying was a boy or a girl. She already had two daughters, and if this child was a girl, she would have her aborted. The state government made testing for this purpose illegal a year later, but at the time Assumpta D'Sylva was relieved she could do it. It wasn't that she and her husband didn't have the money for a dowry. It was simply that India was a country where the birth of a girl was often viewed as a calamity, and where almost every woman had heard the Sanskrit saying "May you be the mother of a hundred sons." It was a well-known blessing, given to a Hindu woman at the time of her wedding, which I eventually came to see as a curse. "Our society makes you feel so bad if you don't have a son," Assumpta D'Sylva explained. "Especially when I go out for parties, people say, 'How many children?' and I say, 'Two girls,' and they say, 'Oh, too bad, no boy.'"

It is often said of a country as complex as India that for any one statement made, the exact opposite is also true. Certainly most declarations of fact must take into account conflicting evidence. Economists in and out of the government, for example, believe that the gap between the rich and the poor is growing. But they also know that India has abolished the old specter of famine, and that most Indians are generally better off now than they were at the beginning of independence from the British four decades ago. Women are in an especially paradoxical situation. The country that is home to hundreds of millions of illiterate and impoverished village women is also the nation that produced Indira Gandhi, one of the most powerful women in the world. Most Indian women may belong to what one government report calls the country's "single largest group of backward citizens," who suffer double discrimination because they are both female and poor, but in the larger cities highly educated women are beginning to transform modern Indian society. Indian men may beat their wives, but they worship goddesses; some of the mightiest deities in the Hindu pantheon are women, like Durga and the especially monstrous Kali, who murdered her victims and then gorged herself on their flesh and blood. The condition of some Indian women is so wretched that if their plight received the attention given to that of ethnic and racial minorities in other parts of the world, their cause would be taken up by human rights groups. And yet, in the tradition of great visionaries like Mohandas K. Gandhi, the "Mahatma," or "Great Soul," whose principles of nonviolence inspired political change throughout the world, there are also Indian women who are doing such innovative work among the poor—especially women—that they are bringing about radical change in a peaceful way.

The "typical" Indian woman, representing about 75 percent of the four hundred million women and female children in India, lives in a village. She comes from a small peasant family that owns less than an acre of land, or from a landless family that depends on the whims of big farmers for sporadic work and wages. She can neither read nor write, although she would like to, and has rarely traveled more than twenty miles from her place of birth. In many cases she does not know who the prime minister of India is and cannot identify her country on a map. Sometimes she does not know about the existence of her own village panchayat, or governing council, but even if she does, she is rarely aware that there is a place reserved for a woman member, because only men attend the meetings. She does not own land in her own name, or even jointly with her husband. She believes that she catches colds and fevers from evil spirits that lurk in trees. Her occupation is field work, chiefly harvesting, planting and weeding, for which she often receives less than fifty cents a day—in many cases, half the wage that a man receives for the same amount of work.

She has to juggle this labor with her other full-time job, the care of the house and the children. Her husband does not help her; indeed, he does not even consider what she does at home as work. No American woman who struggles with family and career can completely imagine what this means in India. A village woman starts her life from scratch every day. Even a single chapati, the Indian flat bread, has behind it a chain of drudgery that has not changed in thousands of years. To make a chapati, a woman needs water, which is often several miles away by foot. She also needs wheat, which she must harvest by scythe, under a blazing sun, in a back-breaking bent-forward motion, and then grind by hand. To cook the bread she needs fuel, either firewood, which she collects herself, or cow-dung cakes, which she makes herself. To get the dung she must feed the cow, and to feed the cow she must walk several miles to collect suitable grasses. (This assumes that the family is lucky enough to even have a cow; many do not.) The bread is at last prepared over a small mud stove built into the dirt floor of her hut. While she cooks, she breast-feeds one child and watches three others. If she fails in any of these tasks, or performs them too slowly, her husband often feels it is his perogative to beat her. And yet invariably she considers her husband a god and says that she loves him. I used to ask village women exactly why they loved their husbands, a question that always confused them. "I love him because he gives me food and clothes" was the usual answer. My favorite response came from a thirty-year-old village woman named Malti Devi, who in a leap of logic explained that she loved her husband "because if I don't, he will beat me."

Such a woman rarely has control over her own fertility, despite the Indian government's commitment to the present five-year, three-billion-dollar family-planning program. At the time of her menstrual period she is considered impure, and in one isolated part of India I discovered that women were made to sleep outside their family homes until the bleeding was over. That was in the village of Malapatti, in the southern state of Tamil Nadu, where one night I met a thirty-year-old field laborer named Bommakka who was about to lie down in some clumps of dried tree roots and dirt, which had been designated as the spot where the women of the village should sleep during their periods. Bommakka was convinced that if she returned to her home she would go blind or eventually be punished—perhaps her husband or son would fall sick, or the harvest would fail. "Whoever comes to tell us that this is not true," she said, meaning me, "we will not listen."

A woman like this may begin producing babies as early as the age of fourteen. She delivers them on the floor of her hut, usually with the help of her mother-in-law or a dai, an untrained village midwife. There is a good chance the child will grow up malnourished, with iron and vitamin A deficiencies, and without basic inoculations to protect against polio, typhoid, diphtheria and tetanus. One in ten children in India will not live to be a year old. If the child is a girl, there is an even smaller chance that she will survive, even though girls are biologically stronger at birth than boys. This is because the girl will often be given less food and care than her brother. Assuming she lives, she may go, erratically, to a one-room village school but will be pulled out whenever her mother needs help with the other children and the chores in the house. Her education is over when she is married off as a teenager to a young man she has never met; from then on, she will begin a new life with her husband's family as a virtual beast of burden. "I am like an animal," Phula, the forty-year-old wife of a farmer, told me in a village in India's northern plains.

So pressing is the problem of women that the World Bank has now cited it as one of the most urgent tasks it must face. As Barber Conable, the president of the World Bank, said in his 1986 inaugural address in

Washington: "Women do two-thirds of the world's work. They produce 60 to 80 percent of Africa's and Asia's food, 40 percent of Latin America's. Yet they earn only one-tenth of the world's income and own less than one percent of the world's property. They are among the poorest of the world's poor."

Steve and I spent some time living with a village family our last year in India, and not once do I remember seeing the woman of the house, Vindhya Devi, or Bhabhiji, as we called her, pause for a moment in a never-ending cycle of cooking and cleaning. She was awake long before I was up, getting the fire started in her mud stove at the first light of dawn, and she went to bed long after I was asleep. Her evenings were spent at the same stove as she waited for the men to finish gossiping under the big neem tree outside. Her husband and his friends liked to sit on string cots under the branches, talking about local politics as twilight arrived. In the winters, they built a small fire to keep warm. I loved sitting with them in its warmth, reveling in the sense of space and release I felt when I looked up at an entire galaxy of stars. Bhabhiji could never be part of this. As a woman of one of the village's highest castes, she had to live in purdah, or seclusion. Although she was spared from field work, she never ventured farther from her front door than the well that stood fifty feet away. Her husband finally came in to dinner late, but she did not eat until he had finished, and then only what was left. Most of her adult life had been spent entirely within the mud-and-brick walls of her home. Showing her face in the village would have hurt the reputation of her family. Her purdah was a mark of status for her husband; it proved that he was prosperous enough to provide for her and that he had a possession that had to be kept safe from the other men. At the end of my day in the village, when the worst of the heat was over, I used to look forward to walking to an old bathing pool at the edge of the fields and watching the sun go down. It was a five-minute walk from the house, but I don't think Bhabhiji, in thirty-three years, had ever been there.

And yet, today, India has a scattered though vigorous women's movement with the growing power to bring about some measure of reform. In 1988 in the Indian Parliament, women accounted for 10 percent of the members, whereas in the United States Congress, women represent 5 percent of the membership of both houses. In India, women have become doctors, lawyers, judges, scientists, business executives and airline pilots. Many married women with children have consuming careers; their lives and problems are not radically different, on the surface at least, from those of their American counterparts. They receive master's degrees, work in the offices of advertising agencies and worry about getting their children into the right schools. They go to the beauty parlor, follow national politics and resent it when their husbands' friends ignore them at parties. The Indian Constitution guarantees them complete equality under the law. Hindu women may divorce; they may inherit nearly as much property as their brothers do. Indian women won the right to abortion, without a fight, in 1971, a year and a half before *Roe v. Wade* legalized abortion in America.

In New Delhi, the Indian government is investing millions of dollars in new programs aimed specifically at rural women. The results have been mixed. But most important, in a revolutionary change from a decade ago, these programs have shifted their approach from welfare to training. Feminists have lobbied the government to treat the poor village mother not as a passive beneficiary of a handout but as a potential resource who can be taught a skill, like raising cattle, that will help in the development of India itself. Studies in Indian villages have shown that raising a rural woman's income will usually increase the household income, but raising her husband's earnings generally will not. Women tend to spend all of their wages on their families, while men buy liquor, cigarettes and other treats for themselves. Increasingly, women are seen by development specialists as the real agents for change in rural India. As Gotz Schreiber, a senior economist in the World Bank's Women in Development Office, explained to me, "If we're serious about giving the next generation a better life than this one, it requires giving the mothers sufficient control over financial resources."

Former prime minister Rajiv Gandhi, who infuriated feminists in 1986 by siding with Islamic fundamentalists on a bill that in effect prohibits divorced Muslim women from demanding alimony payments, nonetheless appointed more women to cabinet and sub-cabinet-level positions than did his own mother, Indira Gandhi. He was also the chairman of a national advisory committee on women. Women who worked for him, who admittedly had to be allowed a considerable degree of sycophancy and enthusiasm, used to say they had never seen another minister in the government, even a woman, who took such a personal interest in women's programs. This simply may be because Gandhi reflected, as the forty-six-year-old product of elite English-language schools and Cambridge University, the evolution in thinking about women that has occurred among his generation and class. During an interview I had with Rajiv Gandhi in August 1988, he himself brought up the name of Germaine Greer, the feminist, although he admitted he did not have "a strong reaction either way" to her work. "Our society is still very much a male chauvinistic society," he told me. "It comes out every day." We were sitting in a conference room at the prime minister's residence on Race Course Road, and although it was hardly an informal chat, Gandhi, as much as the situation allowed, became discursive. "I mean I have meetings with ministers, with very senior officials," he said, "and suddenly, you know, they say something and I say, 'Look, you're being totally chauvinistic. How can you say that?' " He told me about a recent meeting in which he and several ministers were discussing employment for women in such fields as teaching, village work and the police. "And suddenly," the prime minister complained, "they come out with, 'Well, how can a woman do this sort of thing?' Of course it's not true, a woman can do it."

Fifteen months after I left India, Rajiv Gandhi was defeated for reelection by a coalition led by his former finance minister, Vishwanath Pratap Singh, who had broken with Gandhi over the issue of government corruption. Singh's party, the Janata Dal, or People's Front, drew its base of support from the conservative "Hindi heartland" of the north, where women have had a more difficult time entering politics than in other regions of India. In the weeks after the election, Singh appointed no women to his senior cabinet; the highest-ranking woman in government was Maneka Gandhi, Rajiv Gandhi's estranged sister-in-law, who became a minister of state for environment. Her biggest issue was not women's rights but animal rights. In Parliament, the number of women was greatly reduced from the previous record level of 10 percent of the membership. The situation was hardly encouraging. And yet my feeling—and the feeling among people I spoke to in India—was that even if programs and policy for women did not make further progress under V. P. Singh, at least there would be no retrenchment. The gains in the past decade had made it difficult to turn back.

Certainly the history of India's women is not one of unrelieved misery. It is believed that the status of women deteriorated only in relatively recent times, the past two thousand years or so. Before this, some historians have theorized, there was an ancient "golden age," sometime around 1000 B.C., in which Indian women were considered the equals of men, or at least had a higher status than they did in the later millennia. Scholars have based this belief on evidence left by the

Aryans, the seminomadic tribes who wandered into India from Central Europe around 1500 B.C., establishing the beginnings of Indian culture as it is known today. (Although the Aryans are thought to have been somewhat lighter-skinned than the indigenous tribes already living in India, "Aryan" is a linguistic rather than an ethnic term. The Aryan tribes spoke a language that was the ancestor of, among others, Latin, Greek, Persian, Sanskrit, English, German and Italian—all members of what scholars call the Indo-European or Aryan family of languages. The Aryans were determined to keep themselves separate from India's indigenous tribes, and scholars believe this eventually led to the Hindu caste system, which segregated all Hindus into rigid hereditary social classes.)

It was the Aryans who left the first written record about life in the subcontinent, the *Rig Veda,* a collection of 1,017 Sanskrit poems that with later literature forms the basis of historical reconstruction of the era. The works describe a society in which women married relatively late, at sixteen or seventeen, and did not live in purdah. They took part in gatherings of the clan and had prominent positions at religious rites. Most important, they were in charge of cattle-raising, the chief occupation of the Aryans, and made bows, arrows and other weapons for the men when they went to battle.

No one is quite sure why, but over the next two thousand years, the position of women gradually eroded. Girls were married off at a younger age and were barred from religious rituals. Widows were not permitted to remarry. Sometime between the years 200 B.C. and A.D. 200, the upper-caste law codifier known as Manu produced the first compilation of Hindu law, which assigned to women the status of chattel. "Woman is as foul as falsehood itself," Manu wrote. "When creating them, the lord of creatures allotted to women a love of their beds, of their seat and ornaments; impure thoughts, wrath, dishonesty, malice and bad conduct." A woman had no hope of an autonomous life. As Manu stated: "From the cradle to the grave a woman is dependent on a male: in childhood on her father, in youth on her husband, in old age on her son."

Manu is seen by some feminists today as the chief culprit in the history of the subordination of Indian women, but Manu's compilation of the law does not explain the steady decline in the status of women that had occurred before his time. Many historians have come to believe that what happened to women in India was what happens to all women as a society evolves from wandering, pastoral clans into sedentary groups that make their living by agriculture. In a tribal society, women are more involved in the means of production. In a settled society, where there is relatively more leisure and less fear of enemies, the roles of men and women become increasingly demarcated. Men tend to assume a superior position and women a secondary one. The "golden age" for women, a notion many historians believe was promoted by nineteenth-century Indian nationalists eager to find a utopian past, may have been nothing more than a stage in the development of Indian society. Manu may well have been a misogynist, but the society in general was probably motivated by other stresses. As the Aryans spread geographically, they came into contact with other cultures, particularly the darker-skinned Dravidian tribes of the south. In the opinion of Romila Thapar, a highly respected historian and a supporter of women's causes in India, the oppression of women developed hand in hand with the idea of preserving caste distinctions. Manu's code of law, which first set down the rules of caste in India, is in her view an illustration "of the need to rigidly define caste society," to create rules that keep the outsiders, the people viewed as "pollutants," in their place. Consequently, there are elaborate rules in Manu's code governing precisely who may marry whom. "To avoid pollution, you must control birth," Romila Thapar explains. "But you lose control over birth if you lose control over women."

The next historical decline in the status of women is popularly believed to have come at the time of the sixteenth-century Moghul invasions. Although there had been earlier Muslim invasions, the Moghuls brought Islam to India on a large scale, and with it, at least in the view of many Hindus, the regressive attitudes toward women that spread the practices of purdah and sati. Others are less sure of the Muslim role in the decline of women. Romila Thapar says there is evidence of the seclusion of upper-caste women and of sati before the Muslim invasions. Whatever the case, it was not until the nineteenth century, at a time when sati and purdah showed no signs of abating, that the first impetus for reform began among the middle class in Calcutta, at that time the capital of British India. The reformers were opposed to sati, purdah and child marriage. They promoted education for women, a wife's limited right to property and the right of widows to remarry. This movement, which later spread to the western states of Maharashtra and Gujarat, was inspired by far-thinking male reformers like Rammohan Roy, who founded the Brahmo Samaj, a reform sect of Hinduism, and other men genuinely troubled by the condition of women. Recent historians, however, have concluded that another major impetus for what is considered the first phase of the Indian women's movement came from the desire of middle-class men to make themselves more socially acceptable to the British imperialists, who employed the men as junior administrators in the bureaucracy and as brokers in the East India Company. The woman in the Bengali middle-class household—unseen, uneducated, isolated—clearly did not conform to the English model of what, for the time, was considered a proper wife. She was not, for example, educated even to the extent of the colonial wives, who knew how to run competent households and assist at social functions in the furtherance of their husbands' careers.

Yet the reform movement, at least in the early part of the century, was a theoretical reform falling far short of revolutionary change, "a safe issue," as the scholar Meredith Borthwick has written, "that did not present a vision of imminent social chaos." The women were to be educated only to enhance their roles as wives and mothers. While the men argued the issues of reform, the women stayed home, most of them unaware that they were the subjects of so much debate. It was not until the second half of the century that some of the reforms were made law—widows were allowed to remarry in 1856; sati was banned in 1859—and even then, the laws had limited impact. What did change was the standards by which Bengali middle-class women were judged. By the dawn of the twentieth century, a new woman had emerged, one who, in Borthwick's words, "appeared in mixed social gatherings, and was a member of various philanthropic and social women's organizations." This woman "had received a basic education and read improving literature—domestic instruction manuals and 'refined' fiction." The new woman represented the values of "cleanliness, orderliness, thrift, responsibility, intelligence," and had "a moderate interest in and knowledge of the public world of men. These were added to, rather than substituted for, the traditional virtues of self-sacrifice, benevolence, devotion to the husband, respect for elders, and household competence."

It was this new middle-class woman who responded to the upheavals that began in Indian life with the birth of the nationalist movement at the end of the nineteenth century. Women's emancipation was one of the goals of the nationalists, and by 1905 the men were encouraging women to participate in the Swadeshi movement to boycott foreign goods. Within the next twenty-five years, three major women's organizations were founded, the first of them with links to the British movement for women's suffrage. The most influential of the organizations, the All India Women's Conference, began in 1927 as a forum that met to discuss women's education but soon expanded into a group that worked to stop purdah, child marriage and the other problems first tackled by the nineteenth-century reformers. This time, however, it was women who discussed women's issues, and it was women who determined that these issues should not be separated from the larger concern of India's subordination to England.

The women had their first chance to prove themselves on a massive scale in 1930, when Mahatma Gandhi launched the first of his civil disobedience campaigns. The British responded by arresting most of the nationalist leaders and throwing them into jail. Jawaharlal Nehru, India's founding prime minister and a leader in the civil disobedience campaign, recounted what the women did to keep the movement alive in *The Discovery of India,* a book he wrote largely in jail: "Most of us menfolk were in prison," Nehru explained. "And then a remarkable thing happened. Our women came to the front and took charge of the struggle. Women had always been there, of course, but now there was an avalanche of them, which took not only the British government but their own menfolk by surprise. Here were these women, women of the upper or middle classes, leading sheltered lives in their homes— peasant women, working-class women, rich women—pouring out in their tens of thousands in defiance of government order. . . . It was not only that display of courage and daring, but what was even more surprising was the organizational power they showed."

The women had been in large part inspired by Mahatma Gandhi, who saw women as autonomous, independent people, and also as an important social base for the movement. No man before or since has done so much for women's rights in India. In summoning the masses of women into the freedom struggle, Gandhi told them they must no longer be "dolls and objects of indulgence" but rather "comrades in common service" with their husbands. "Man has regarded woman as his tool," Gandhi wrote. "She has learnt to be this tool and in the end found it easy and pleasurable to be such, because when one drags another in his fall the descent is easy." In 1925, Gandhi had chosen Sarojini Naidu, one of the leading women freedom fighters, as president of the nationalist Congress party. In 1931, largely as a response to women's participation in the civil disobedience campaign, the Congress party passed a resolution endorsing political equality for all women, regardless of qualifications. This was at a time when women in some European countries had not yet won the right to vote.

Gandhi did have his limitations as an emancipator. The role of women in the freedom struggle was for the most part supportive and auxiliary, limited to spinning, picketing, distributing literature and attending meetings. Gandhi himself saw women as long-suffering vessels of self-sacrifice, who should neither earn the principal wages in a family nor disrupt the balance at home. But he nonetheless moved a large step forward from the nineteenth-century reformers by seeing women as active participants in their own progress and not, in the words of the feminist Madhu Kishwar, "as helpless creatures deserving charitable concern." Certainly Indian women responded to Gandhi in a way they never had to any other male leader, a phenomenon that has always interested Romila Thapar, who believes the psychological connection between Gandhi and the masses of women has not been adequately explored. "There's something about him," she told me, "that makes him very much like us." Erik Erikson, in *Gandhi's Truth*, the Pulitzer Prize–winning psychoanalytic study of the Indian leader, suggests what that might be. Gandhi, Erikson argues, believed in the "natural superiority" of the self-sacrificing woman but could not tolerate this notion "without a competitive attempt at becoming more maternal than the most motherly of mothers." Gandhi thus saw himself as a "mother" to his mother, his father and India "herself." (Erikson, in one of his most seductive meditations, also explains his belief that India is essentially feminine, or, more precisely, that "Father Time in India is a Mother." Indians, Erikson says, live in "a feminine space time," a world in which they feel enveloped and carried along as participants in a larger continuum.)

The next major development in the history of Indian women did not come until the mid-1970s, after the government released "Towards Equality," an explosive, far-reaching report on the status of India's women that revealed that conditions for many of them had actually regressed in significant ways since independence. It is this report which serves as a basis for the current women's movement in India, although feminists prefer to categorize the present movement as the natural "third stage," after the nineteenth-century reform in Calcutta and women's participation in the freedom struggle. Historically this view is correct, but it is also a way for Indian feminists to distinguish themselves from the Western women's movement and to emphasize their often-repeated point that feminism has a different context and set of goals in India.

THROUGHOUT MY JOURNEY, I WAS ALWAYS AWARE OF AN OUTSIDER'S limitations in a foreign country. I struggled daily with the problem of what standards to apply. There have been Western journalists who romanticized India, and there have been others who saw in it only those things that reinforced their own sense of cultural superiority. One member of the latter school was Katherine Mayo, a reform-minded American free-lance journalist who wrote a book called *Mother India,* which included many chapters on the condition of Indian women. It was published by Harcourt, Brace in 1927, to an explosion of criticism on the subcontinent, and it quickly became a best-seller in England and the United States. India was then struggling for independence from the British, but Mayo came to the conclusion that the Indians were not ready to rule their own country because, among other things, they overindulged in sex. She asserted that all of an Indian's woes—"poverty, sickness, ignorance, political minority, melancholy, ineffectiveness" and the "subconscious conviction of inferiority"— could be blamed on the effects of widespread child marriage. Mayo argued that men ineptly raised by child brides were physically feeble, given to unrestrained sexual appetites and of morally "bankrupt stock" at an age when "the Anglo-Saxon is just coming into full glory of manhood."

Mayo reserved some of her most graphic prose for accounts of the methods used by dais, the village midwives, to deliver babies. She described the first dai she encountered as having a "Witch-of-Endor face," "vermin-infested elfs-locks" and "dirty claws." Citing doctors' reports, Mayo wrote that if a delivery is delayed, the dai "thrusts her long-unwashed hand, loaded with dirty rings and bracelets and encrusted with untold living contaminations, into the patient's body, pulling and twisting at what she finds there." If the delivery is difficult, "the child may be dragged forth in detached sections—a leg or an arm torn off at a time."

Sixty years later, Indians still revile Katherine Mayo, although, interestingly, there has been an American radical feminist reinterpretation of her work. Mary Daly, in her 1978 book, *Gyn/Ecology,* wrote that Mayo "shows an understanding of the situation which more famous scholars entirely lack. Her work is, in the precise sense of the word, exceptional." Mayo, in her own way, was a feminist, and although her observations often reveal more about her than about India, many of the conditions she reported still exist. Village dais, though not nearly so malevolent as Mayo described, have helped to keep India's maternal mortality rate one of the highest in the world, even though the Indian government has attempted, with mixed success, to train the dais to give up dangerous medical practices they have followed for thousands of years. When I went to a meeting of dais organized by government health workers in a tribal region of the western Indian state of Gujarat, I learned that many of them still push on the mother's stomach during labor, risking rupture of the uterus, and cut the baby's umbilical cord with an old knife or a stone. On the wound they sometimes put cow dung, which they believe is an antiseptic.

Katherine Mayo, as egregious as her views were, held a certain fascination for me. She had done, after all, what I was trying to do. There is little written about her, but one line in her entry in *Notable American Women 1607–1950* says a great deal: "Katherine Mayo's moral indignation at the sexual exploitation of women had long been an unrecognized concern of her own life, an anxiety she could confront openly only in writing about distant places and alien cultures." She came to India for only three months, relied extensively on British government statistics and met no women leaders of the nationalist movement. Her larger failure, of course, was the lack of balance she displayed in making judgments about a society that was less developed—and held different values—than her own.

But how does an outsider measure India? When one assesses the government's village health care system, should India be admonished for inadequate facilities and the lack of medicines at its clinics, or should it be praised for at least creating an extensive rural health care network? Where does one strike the balance between criticism of a five-thousand-year-old civilization and forty-year-old nation always at risk of disintegrating into religious and ethnic violence, and admiration that it has at least remained a democracy, if only on its own terms, at a time when one neighbor, Pakistan, has mostly been a military dictatorship and another, Nepal, a monarchy? For Katherine Mayo, these questions were easy. She judged India by rigorous Western standards, dismissing those before who had "swathed the spot in euphemisms."

I embarked on my own journey with open eyes, and in my encounters along the way I tried to understand before I judged. The first half of this book is an exploration, through the lives of certain women, of the problems that plague most other women in India. In the middle of the book is a chapter about the current feminist movement and how it is struggling to solve those problems. The last part of the book is a look at some successful Indian women: Indira Gandhi, women in the Indian Parliament, three creative women of Calcutta, the film actresses of Bombay, a policewoman and a New Delhi housewife. One of the last chapters considers India's attempts to control its population. This is the nation's biggest challenge, and women remain the key to the population-control program's success.

Throughout my journey, I came upon some highly sensational and disturbing aspects of Indian society—female infanticide, for example—but the material in this book is not designed to shock. I have arranged the issues more or less in the order in which I encountered and understood them. One woman led me to another, and one topic drew me into the next. I often felt as if I were traveling from the most evident to the most elusive.

A journey like this suggests some kind of personal transformation, but I am not sure that people really change in their basic character. It is probably true that they simply become more intensely themselves, or what they were meant to be all along. But certainly the balance of a person's views can change. Although I am still learning exactly what my experience in India meant to me, I do know that it transformed much of my thinking. It was in India that I had some of the most moving experiences of my life—seeing the birth of a baby in a village, or the quiet dignity of two young boys who waited outside a Calcutta crematorium with the body of their dead grandmother, her face shrunken but peaceful amid the tumult of the city.

At the very least, my journey forced me to question assumptions about mortality, religion, duty, fate, the way a society governs itself and the roles of men and women. It deepened my feminist convictions and made me realize how individual, yet universal, is each woman's experience. In the beginning, there were times when I felt that what I was exploring had little consequence for the lives in the world from which I had come. But slowly I realized that the way Indian women live is the way the majority of women in the world spend their lives; it is Americans who are peculiar. Ultimately, I realized my journey to India was a privilege. Rather than going to the periphery, I had come to the center.

WEDDING FIRST, LOVE LATER

Arranged Marriage Among the Educated Classes

DURING WEDDING SEASON IN NEW DELHI, IT IS POSSIBLE TO SEE THREE, four, sometimes even five nervous bridegrooms riding through the streets on white horses toward women they barely know but will marry that evening. The little wedding parties are hard to miss: the groom, wearing an elaborate brocaded suit and a headpiece with streamers covering the embarrassment on his face, is escorted on his ride by a phalanx of relatives and a ragtag, improbably named "disco band" playing tinny, off-key marching music. The Hindu priests have deemed it an auspicious night, and it is easy, after stopping in traffic to let a few of these processions pass, to become carried away and imagine the thick Delhi air redolent with hope and fertility. Each procession can take half the evening to reach the site of the wedding, usually a home or, if the family has recently come into money, a big lawn at one of the new luxury hotels. The groom is often several hours late, which greatly annoys the bride's family but is not a catastrophe. The bride, meanwhile, has been closeted with her mother, aunts and close friends, monosyllabic and nearly immobile under a gaudy red silk sari so extravagantly trimmed with gold that it can weigh fifty pounds. This is just as well, because she is meant to be a passive presence at her own wedding, with her eyes demurely cast down, like a silent maiden from an Indian miniature painting. Her preparations have taken all day and are a ritual in themselves. Flowers have been woven into her hair, small jewels applied over her eyebrows and an intricate lacelike design painted in henna all over her hands and feet. Afterward, she usually says she can remember very little of what happened that day.

One of my pastimes in India was going to weddings. People were always inviting me, thinking that an American woman would enjoy the spectacle. In three and a half years, I think I went to nine as an official guest. Other times I would stumble into a wedding at one of the big hotels, and if I peered in long enough, the parents would usher me in to congratulate the bride and groom. In India, a wedding is a chaotic pageant that can last until six in the morning, and more and more has become a public validation of a family's status and wealth. If a family is rich, it is not unusual to have a thousand guests. Even a working-class family will put on a feast for two hundred, ensuring crippling debt for the next decade. (At a wedding in the alley behind our house, the father of the bride, who made $800 a year driving for the Vietnamese embassy, paid $3,200 for the lunch party and dowry.) I went to Hindu weddings, Sikh weddings, and a Muslim wedding. Two of the weddings were given by noble families of the former princely states; at one the groom arrived in a silver horse-drawn chariot and at the other by elephant. At some of them, particularly one in a lush, plant-filled courtyard at midnight during a break in the summer monsoon, I was transfixed by the sweating faces of the bride and groom, who sat cross-legged in front of a sacred fire while the priest chanted Sanskrit prayers and poured sandalwood powder into the flames. There is a sensuousness to Indian weddings absent from the cool churches of the West. Others were gaudy celebrations at Delhi's first-class hotels, part of what Indira Gandhi once derided as "five-star culture," and were distinguished by melting ice sculptures and the video camera recording an event that would keep Delhi's old families fussing for weeks about all the new money in town. There was one thing, though, that marked almost every wedding I attended: the look of dazed terror on the bride's face as she began the rest of her life with a man who was little more than a stranger to her.

In India, an estimated 95 percent of marriages are still arranged, including the majority of those among the educated middle class. As with so many other statistics in India, no one is certain of the accuracy of this estimate, and in fact many sociologists and much of the general public believe the percentage of arranged marriages to be even higher. When I first came to India, this astonished me. I knew arranged marriage was standard among villagers and the rural poor—in other words, most of the country—but I did not expect that an Indian man who had lived in the United States would come home after years of dating American women to marry someone he had met only three times. I did not expect college women in the big cities to gladly give their parents the task of finding them good husbands. I was more amazed when some would say yes to a prospective groom after a half-hour meeting. "I could decide maybe in a day," a twenty-year-old New Delhi commercial-arts student told me. Then she thought a minute. "Well, maybe that's a bit rushed. Maybe in a week."

Marriage for love exists only among a very small slice of India's urban elite. Rajiv Gandhi has a love marriage, as do most of those in the younger generation of Delhi's fashionable circles. Almost all of our friends had love marriages, although I used to suspect that a few had been more arranged than the couple let on. (Often if two people started dating seriously, which could have hurt the reputation of the girl and prevented her from finding a good husband later, the parents quickly moved in and mobilized for a wedding to save themselves from neighborhood gossip.) Outside the big urban centers, attitudes are changing as well. In a 1973 survey of college men and women in the south Indian city of Hyderabad, two sociologists, Prakasa and Nandini Rao, found that "an overwhelming majority of the students wanted more freedom in selecting a future spouse" and concluded that "the forces of modernization are resulting in liberal attitudes toward mate selection among the college students." But in that same study, more than a third of the students said they did not think it was necessary to know a spouse before marriage.

Arranged marriage is not unique to India and has in fact existed in some form in most societies throughout the world. In the West, only in the last three hundred years has love come to be seen as a part of marriage at all—a development that academics theorize evolved from the concept of courtly love in the Middle Ages and also from the impact of Christianity, which is thought to have deepened the bond between husband and wife by likening it to the relationship between man and God. Much later came industrialization, which increased social mobility and broke down the extended family, a change that is just beginning in India.

Arranged marriage survives among the Indian middle class partly because a new kind of system has emerged. (The term *middle class,* as it is used in India, refers not to those in the middle economic group but to the people in the top 10 percent, who can afford to buy consumer products and live what the West would consider a semblance of a middle-class life.) A generation ago, a bride and groom rarely spoke to each other before the wedding. In many cases they had never even laid eyes on each other. They had no veto power over their parents' choice, and if the marriage was miserable, so be it. Even now, for the majority of Indians, marriage still works this way.

But these days middle-class couples are allowed to meet several times before making a decision, and a few can go out once or twice alone. Although most marriages are still arranged among members of the same caste, engagements may last six months and more, and women may reject the choice of their parents. This is considered a substantial breakthrough, and some families insist the result is not an arranged marriage at all. Leila Seth, a socially progressive mother who is one of only ten women among the four hundred High Court judges in India, told me, "Frankly, I don't think it's such a bad system." The prevailing opinion among the middle class is that not only do these marriages work, but they are more successful than those in the West.

In the summer of 1985 I set out to write a story on arranged marriages in the middle class. There had been a number of articles on the subject by Western correspondents, but most had focused on the entertaining pages of matrimonial ads in the Sunday newspapers. They do make for good reading. From *The Hindustan Times:* "Alliance solicited from industrialist/businessman of Delhi for graduate, 21, slim, fair, beautiful daughter of Delhi-based Brahmin industrialists. Write Post Box No. 5729." From *The Times of India:* "Intelligent, well-read, beautiful, home-loving, English-speaking girl preferably from liberal-minded Christian family for extremely weil-placed senior government executive, good-looking, late forties, must be willing to settle in North America, religion and caste no bar." But I was more interested in discovering if there was something in arranged marriage that really did "work." These were my early days in India, when I was filled with a newcomer's enthusiasm and a determination to break away from my Western judgments. In retrospect, I realize there was something else going on. My own parents had been divorced, as had some of my friends. I think I was searching for some kind of a "secret" to marriage that the Indians had and Americans did not.

Arun and Manju Bharat Ram were recommended to me as the ideal couple, an example, their friends said, of how arranged marriage functions at its best. It turned out they were neither typical nor middle-class: Arun Bharat Ram, a prep-school classmate of Rajiv Gandhi, was heir to one of the largest industrial fortunes in India. Indira Gandhi and fifteen hundred others had come to his wedding. Maybe the "secret" to the success of the marriage was simply money and connections. On the other hand, their families were prime examples of the highly Westernized industrial society in which parents still see marriage, at least for some of their children, as a business alliance. There were also love marriages in Arun's family, and he himself had dated American women while studying in the United States. In the end, I found no one who better illustrated how Indians could turn what I thought was the relationship between marriage and love upside down.

The Bharat Ram house was an expanse of marble, with modern Indian art and security guards, set behind gates in one of Delhi's leafier neighborhoods. It was August and insufferably hot, but in the Bharat Ram's VCR-dominated study, I sank into the leather sofa and froze happily in the blasts of the best air conditioner I ever encountered in India. I sat there once to talk to Manju, then returned, feeling perversely like a marriage counselor, to put the same questions to Arun. He was forty-five, slight, and had a handsome, delicate face; dressed in a sport shirt and slacks, he looked as if he had just spent a pleasant morning on the golf course. He had the social ease and upper-class distance that marked a lot of Rajiv Gandhi's school chums. Manju was traditional and more accessible. She had a pretty, warm face and wore an expensive silk sari. Her hair was in a long braid down her back.

They first met in 1967, the year Arun had come home to New Delhi after graduate school at the University of Michigan. He was twenty-six and about to start work in the family's textile business—high time, his mother said, that he found himself a wife. Seeing no movement on the part of her son, she took matters into her own hands and began an all-points search. But Ann Arbor had changed Arun. Although he still felt "truly very Indian," he also felt "a contradiction, coming back from the West, that I shouldn't be getting into an arranged marriage." Finally, he agreed to see a prospective bride, "with no strings attached," just so his mother would stop pestering him.

That was Manju, a twenty-two-year-old graduate of a home economics college and the product of a conservative middle-class business family that never dreamed their daughter might marry a Bharat Ram—even though traditionally the bride's family marries above itself on the economic scale. (Sociologists say that marriage with a bride of lower status assures the groom's family that their new daughter-in-law will be sufficiently dependent on them.) Both Manju and Arun belonged to the prosperous Bania subcaste, which falls within the larger Vaisya, or merchant, caste. In India, arranged marriages both reflect and reinforce the caste system, which remains especially rigid among the rural poor. But unions like that of Arun and Manju prove that caste is still important among at least some sections of the upper class.

A marriage broker hired by Manju's parents had introduced the two families, but Manju was no less reluctant than Arun was to take the next step. Even though she had always known that her marriage would be arranged, she shuddered when she remembered how a relative had been made to parade before her future in-laws and then quote from Shakespeare. "They discussed her coloring as if she weren't there," Manju remembered. "It really was like a girl being sold."

Arun and Manju's first meeting was over tea with their parents at a luxury hotel. Manju was so scared that she dropped her cup, but everyone quickly assured her this was a sign of good luck. Arun, meanwhile, still had stiff legs from sitting cross-legged during his sitar lesson that day, but all Manju knew about his limp was that she was about to be married off to a man who might not be "normal." The only impression she made on Arun was that she was "a pretty girl" and "very quiet." After the meeting, Arun told his mother, "I've done you your favor; now leave me alone." But his mother persisted, and Arun agreed to see Manju again.

This time they went to dinner together and left the parents behind. "That was when I talked to her for the first time," Arun remembered, "and I felt she was quite interesting." Manju decided the same thing. "We had a lot of things in common," she said. "He was always soft-spoken. He never tried to show off his family and his background. He always made me feel like an individual."

They saw each other two more times, but with chaperones. At this point, the courtship had gone on long enough and a decision had to be made. Manju had already told her parents she would marry Arun if that was what his family wished—she had no major objections, she liked him, and that was enough. A few days later, Arun's mother came to the house. "We want her," she said. Immediately the massive wedding preparations got under way.

"Obviously, I wasn't in love with her," Arun told me matter-of-factly about the days after the engagement was announced. "But whenever we met, we were comfortable. According to our tradition, that would lead to love. I was willing to accept that." Manju felt the same. "At the time, I didn't love him," she said, "but it was very exciting for me. Suddenly, I was very important. All of my parents' friends were a little envious about the family I was marrying into." The wedding took place six months later, followed by a honeymoon in southern India, where the two spent their first extended time alone. "We had always had people around us," Manju said. "This was awkward and difficult. One didn't know how much to give." She missed her parents and called them every day.

Afterward, she began a slow adjustment to life within a family that was much more sophisticated than her own. "These people were more aware of things happening around the world," she said. "At times, I felt as if I were stupid. But I learned how to cope with it. My husband helped." When they moved to their own house five years later, there was another adjustment. "It was a frightening experience, living by ourselves," Manju remembered. "There were times when we didn't know what to do with each other." She kept reminding herself that her mother always said a woman has to compromise a lot. "She also used to say, 'If you're unhappy, unless it's really bad, don't tell me.' "

By the time I met them, nearly two decades and three children later, the Bharat Rams had long since adjusted to married life. It is always impossible to know what is really going on in someone else's marriage, of course, but the Bharat Rams said they were happy, and I believed them. "I've never thought of another man since I met him," Manju told me. "And I also know I would not be able to live without him. I don't think I've regretted my marriage, ever." Arun echoed his wife. "It wasn't something that happened overnight," he said. "It grew and became a tremendous bond. It's amazing, but in arranged marriages, people actually make the effort to fall in love with each other."

It was a curious love story. As far as I could tell, they had it all backward. I had been raised on one of the favorite themes of Western literature, that of star-crossed lovers like Romeo and Juliet whose love is a force that exists on its own, a magic that defies the constraints of society. But here the Bharat Rams were telling me that love can be concocted simply by arranging a marriage between people of common background and interests. In middle-class India, where the family is still more important than any of its individual members, love is believed to flow out of social arrangements and is actually subservient to them. "True love" is possible only after marriage, not before.

Middle-class India defines love as long-term commitment and devotion to family, which can be developed only with much patience and time. In their view, Americans instead define love as passion—which inevitably leads to disappointment in marriage after the glow of those first romantic years wears off. This reasoning always seemed to me a striking example of the Indian belief in their moral superiority over what many of them see as the decadent West, with its dismal record of divorce. Americans just give up, Indians believe, when the marriage hits the rough spots and falls short of an unattainable ideal. Sudhir Kakar, one of India's foremost psychoanalysts, put it this way: "Americans have too great an investment in marriage. The peculiar part is that you think any human institution should satisfy so many different needs. Americans say there should be romance, a mother for the children, intellectual stimulation also. For two people to be all that to each other is a bit much."

Many of the young women I met dismissed "falling in love" as something for teenagers and bad Indian films. A few said they had experienced "puppy love" with a boy at school but assured me they were too grown-up for that now. One of these women was Meeta Sawhney, the twenty-year-old Delhi University economics student who had convinced me that women would be my window into the Indian interior world. As she had explained to me: "When my friends who are in love talk to me, I think they sound silly." She had become engaged that summer to a childhood friend her parents had chosen for her. We had been talking for an hour in her bedroom when I finally asked if she loved him. "That's a very difficult question," she said. "I don't know. This whole concept of love is very alien to us. We're more practical. I don't see stars, I don't hear little bells. But he's a very nice guy, and I think I'm going to enjoy spending my life with him. Is that love?" She shrugged, indicating no worries about her future. "I know this is going to work. I know everything about him. I know his family. On the other hand, if I were in love with this guy, I would be worried because then I'd be going into it blindly."

I thought this was madness, or a good job of brainwashing, but later decided Meeta Sawhney was simply rationalizing what she had been dealt in her life. What choice did she have? Only women from the most Westernized families have the luxury of falling in love before marriage, and even they had best do it only once. In America, a young woman can move on after her first, intense love affair fizzles, but an Indian woman risks gossip that might ruin her chances of a good husband later. One very Westernized couple I knew had dated quietly for a year and a half. At that point, the man's mother took him aside and told him that since the woman was from a good family, he could no longer risk her reputation by stringing her along. He had one of two choices: either cut off the relationship or make her his wife. He did the honorable thing and married her.

Most teenagers are still not allowed to date, so parents think their children will have no experience on which to make an intelligent decision about a lifelong mate. One of a mother's biggest fears is that her carefully penned-in daughter will make a getaway one day and fall for the first rogue who comes along. I remember the ruckus in one Indian family I knew when their beautiful niece fell for a handsome Mexican exchange student. I was rooting for her, but alas, one of the interloper's old girlfriends turned up and whisked him off to south India, breaking the niece's heart but averting a family crisis. Most girls are more docile and have come to believe what they have been told from childhood: that they will love the husband their parents select. "From the beginning, my mind was set that my parents were going to choose the right person for me," explained Rama Rajakumar, a thirty-four-year-old Brahmin from the south Indian state of Tamil Nadu. Brahmins are the highest caste in India. I spoke to her in Delhi, where she was visiting on a break from her job as a supervisor at the World Bank in Washington. She had been living in the United States for sixteen years. One evening in 1971, when she was just starting out in Washington as a World Bank typist, she had gone to a friend's house and met a man—a Tamil Brahmin, as it turned out—who was studying at the University of Texas. He seemed like "just another guy" to her. She heard nothing from him until two years later, when he sent a letter to the friend saying he wanted to marry Rama. She was not as thunderstruck as might be imagined. It was important to Rama that she marry a man of her own caste, and it was probably no less important to the groom. Tamil Brahmins are hard to come by in the United States, so it was not extraordinary that an eligible one would be interested in Rama. The friend quickly took on the role of marriage broker and wrote to both sets of parents in India.

First, the horoscopes of the prospective couple were exchanged. "They matched perfectly," Rama told me. The parents exchanged further details on family background and education. Then photos were mailed. A few months later, Rama's parents declared themselves pleased. Rama, who was twenty-two and had not had a date with anyone in the four years she'd lived in America, told them she'd marry the man. "I didn't know him at all," she said. She had not seen him since the meeting two years before, but she was certain that her parents knew best.

The wedding took place in 1973 in India. When I asked Rama if she had worried beforehand that she might not fall in love with the man, she gave me a puzzled look. "No," she said. "I just thought, He is my husband, and I love him. He is going to be everything to me from now on." Apparently he had been. After twelve years of "very happy" marriage, she said, "I still think he's a better husband than anybody I could have asked for."

I remember coming home stunned from interviews like this, mystified by what was going on in the minds of these women. They had seemed so much like me at first. What I did not understand at the time was the powerful sense of fatalism that Indian women have. Strict Hindus believe that their present lives have been predetermined by their karma, the accumulated sum of all good and bad actions from their previous lives. These beliefs are so central to the religion that they influence even the casual Hindu today. Women routinely told me that they had decided to marry a man half an hour after the first meeting because they felt it was "meant" to be. "It's the biggest gamble of one's life," said Ritu Nanda, the thirty-seven-year-old director of one of India's most successful home appliance companies. "So why not just leave it to destiny?" A traditional woman believes that she was married to her husband in her previous life and will remain married to him in the next. The women I interviewed were too sophisticated to endorse that view, but nobody dismissed it as nonsense, either.

This brings me to Meena, whose name I have changed for reasons that will be obvious. She, too, felt that her marriage was predetermined—but I'm getting ahead of the story. I first met her one summer, at the home of a friend. She was twenty-five, pretty and stylish, proud of being a "modern" girl who worked in her father's laboratory supply business. She was from a middle-class family, was ambitious and assertive, and spoke rapid, idiomatic English. She and her parents had been engaged in an active search to find her a husband. "My parents are going about it in a very scientific way," she said. That meant they were checking the matrimonial ads and alerting relatives and mutual friends to be on the lookout for prospects. "I have already been shown several boys," she told me. (In arranged marriage parlance, men and women are "boys" and "girls." During the introductory family get-togethers, boys and girls are not said to meet but rather are "shown" to each other. This is in fact the most accurate term for the excruciating event.)

None of the boys had been up to Meena's standards, and she had rejected them all. "One of them didn't even have the guts to finish his own pastry," she said. "He had to ask his mother first. So I said, 'Good-bye.' " She had asked the boys who were businessmen detailed questions about their accounts, because "being in business myself, I want to know." She seemed to be in the market for a chief executive officer rather than a husband. I didn't have much hope that she'd find either one.

I was wrong. Seven months later, I got an invitation to her wedding. She had found herself a young doctor, her sister-in-law's brother-in-law, a plump twenty-eight-year-old with a soft, sweet face. She had first met him at her house, where both sets of parents made awkward conversation over tea. Then she and the boy went to her room alone for twenty-five minutes. She found him "very nice to talk to" and was "indifferent" to his looks; he was a big improvement over her previous prospects. "There were one or two cases where the guys physically repulsed me," she said. That evening his parents called and said the boy wanted to see her again, so the two met alone for coffee the next day. After that there was a month of silence. Then one day the boy's mother called Meena's mother, and the two women got down to business. The boy's mother wanted to know if Meena had become engaged to anyone else, and when Meena's mother said no, the boy's mother said the family would like to ask for Meena's hand. Meena's mother said she would check to see if her daughter was still interested and call back.

Meena thought about it for a moment, then said yes. "I was very indifferent, frankly," she explained to me later. "I used to always judge any proposal that came my way on the specific merits." Since the boy had good credentials and she had no major objections to him, she instinctively felt that the marriage would be right. She knew his family was more conservative than hers, but she did not expect that to be a problem. "I was very fatalistic," she said.

The two went on three dates before the wedding—once, shopping, followed by lunch at Pizza King; another time to a movie; and then to an expensive dinner at the Taj Mahal Hotel. Afterward they sat in the lobby and watched the foreign tourists go by. It was all very glamorous. Meena had been spending her days shopping for saris and linens, helping with the guest list, and discussing the new Maruti car her parents were going to give her as a wedding present as the major part of the dowry her parents had promised her in-laws during the prewedding negotiations. Fortunately, Meena was discovering that she liked the boy "tremendously." The idea of a husband thrilled her. "I was excited about having a man around, living with him, and having all the frills and fancies," she said.

Her wedding started "on time," a mere two hours behind schedule. I arrived only a half hour late, thinking this would be socially correct, and found myself alone with the caterer. This gave me a chance to look around. The wedding was to be held in a large grassy area, open to the sky but enclosed on four sides by circus-style canvas fencing. Inside, rows of metal chairs sat facing a center platform with two red plush-covered thrones for the bride and groom. Waiters were still setting up a buffet of heavy chicken and lamb curries in a tent lit by fluorescent lights. Skinny men were hanging strands of marigolds from the canopy under which the religious ceremony would take place. It all had the feel of a small-town fair. As I watched the preparations, the hot afternoon gave way to a pretty orange sky and then a cool March evening. The grass smelled fresh, and Delhi's traffic rumbled in the background.

Meena finally arrived, looking predictably dazed, and was immediately ushered to a room in a little building near the wedding enclosure. The women of the family surrounded her, offering bits of advice. Her wedding dress was a heavy silk in hot pink, and her nose ring, similar in style to an enormous jeweled hoop earring, hung from one nostril all the way down to her lips. This made talking difficult, although she giggled a lot. I gave her a bouquet of sweet peas and wished her good luck.

At last the groom pulled up on his white horse and things got under way, in a manner of speaking. There is a certain aimlessness to Indian weddings that is confusing at first. Most of the guests ignored the religious ceremony, talking among themselves and wandering around while children chased each other through the grass. A rigid row of aunts had already positioned themselves near the food. None of this was considered impolite. Wedding ceremonies usually drag on for hours and only immediate relatives are expected to endure watching them without interruption. But I loved much of what I saw. As a priest chanted Sanskrit prayers, Meena and the groom sat under the canopy in front of the sacred fire for several hours, the glow from the flames reflected in their faces. Toward the end, after Meena's father had slipped the priest some rupees to hurry things up, as fathers of Indian brides often do, Meena and the groom rose to circle the fire, the groom leading Meena slowly in a clockwise direction. The couple took seven steps, each one representing a blessing: food, strength, wealth, happiness, progeny, cattle and devotion. After the seventh step, the marriage was irrevocable. The priest sprinkled holy water on the couple, and soon they took their seats on the two thrones as the flashes from the guests' cameras exploded in their faces. Meena said afterward that her mind was a blank.

When it was all over around midnight, she said good-bye to her family and, like most Indian brides, broke down in tears. I had long since left, but I had seen these melodramas before. They are the crucial hysterical conclusion to any Indian wedding. From that night on, the bride is no longer considered a daughter in her parents' home. Instead she will move in with her husband and in-laws and begin a new life among a household of strangers. Indian brides handle these partings with great theatrics, often wailing uncontrollably, which I eventually decided was the only rational response, given what was in store for many of them. The bride's mother and sisters wail along with her, and so does her father, as she is slowly pushed through the crowd and into the car that will take her away. The first time I saw this I didn't even know the family, but I found it so wrenching that I cried too.

Meena spent her wedding night tossing nervously in a bedroom with her mother-in-law and several other women she did not know. In conservative Indian families, this is traditional; the new husband and the men sleep elsewhere. It was not until the next night that Meena was allowed to sleep with her husband, and then was relieved when he didn't want to make love. "That was rather nice of him," she said. "Normally, a boy just pounces on the girl." Both she and her husband were virgins. The marriage was finally consummated the following night, an experience Meena described to me as quick and physically "very painful." Neither husband nor wife talked much about what was occurring between them, although the next morning Meena noticed that her husband seemed glad that "he had got through it—no disaster had happened."

At first I heard from friends that Meena was ecstatic about her new life. Then I began hearing that she was fighting with her mother-in-law. That seemed routine, so I didn't give it much thought. But then, not quite a year later, I was told she had moved back with her parents and that the marriage was over. I was surprised—not by a marriage that had turned out badly, but by Meena's return home. Ten years ago that would have been impossible for her; her parents could not have endured the scandal and she would have had to stick with a miserable marriage for the rest of her life. So I guess this was change. I went to see Meena a few days after her first wedding anniversary, on a depressing, already hot March afternoon. I sat with her for two hours, in a darkened upstairs flat with a view through the chick blinds of children playing in the dust of a dried-out park. She was thinner and looked badly shaken, and she cried as she told me she would probably get a divorce. It was awful for her. No matter what all the Indian magazines said about the increasing divorce rate among the middle class, the truth was that for women it was still considered shameful. Meena would have trouble marrying again. Her husband would not.

At first the marriage had been "okay," Meena said. At her in-laws' request, she had given up her job and was helping around the house, cleaning and cooking, primarily. She claimed she had no trouble filling her days, even though she could no longer go out and see friends as freely as before. "When you have time on your hands," she said, "you make things in the kitchen that don't need to be made, or eat things you don't need to eat." But she was eager to be a good Indian wife and so was willing to compromise. That especially applied to sex, which had not improved since the first night. Her husband was often impotent, and on the nights when he wasn't she found she still didn't enjoy "the act itself." Her mother-in-law, meanwhile, had been keeping a close watch on the time the newlyweds spent in their room alone.

After the first month, Meena felt her husband was withdrawing from her. Then he stopped talking to her altogether. Two silent months later he finally admitted that he had made a mistake and that his mother had pressured him to marry her. He no longer came to their room, sleeping on the terrace instead. "It was horrible," Meena said. "I was shattered." She decided that he must have "homosexual tendencies" or other "physical problems." Her mother-in-law, she believed, was "filling his ears with lies" about her. Another problem was the Maruti; the car delivery had been held up by the company, yet Meena's mother-in-law was demanding to know where it was. By midsummer Meena had moved back with her parents—"I would have committed suicide if I hadn't come home"—and was taking daily tranquilizers and sleeping pills prescribed by a psychiatrist. She had seen the doctor only once because he would not treat her unless she and her husband came in as a couple. Then, that fall, her mother-in-law suddenly called to ask her back. By this time, Meena had found a good job in advertising, and her parents, more concerned about their daughter's happiness than what the neighbors might say, told her not to go. But off she went, determined to give it one last try. The reconciliation lasted a week, and after a fight with her in-laws, Meena was back home.

Who knows what the other side of the story was. I didn't have it in me to track down Meena's husband and present him with her charges just as the family was beginning divorce proceedings. Maybe Meena was impossible to live with. Maybe she had been too "modern" and aggressive and had made her husband feel inadequate in bed. I guessed he had been telling the truth when he said he had been pressured into marrying her. He probably was not so awful, although I suspected her mother-in-law was. The point is that Meena's experience, from the bride's point of view, was not at all unusual. Certainly her sexual problems were not.

In theory, during the first phase of an arranged marriage, a bride has tremendous seductive power over her husband. The first few years are meant to be spent in sexual passion, but when things cool off, as expected, then parents believe it is fortunate that they had the foresight to match up two compatible people who can settle down to the everyday business of life. "Love is fine," Usha Seth, a forty-one-year-old New Delhi housewife, told me. "But after the first few years, that's when you realize how important it is that a person is considerate and kind." Parents are also aware of the all-consuming lust that can rage between a young man and woman who have never had sex before. This is sometimes cited as one reason that the bride spends time away from her husband during the first year of marriage, usually in long visits to her family. Mahatma Gandhi says in his autobiography that it was this custom that helped keep him from drowning in sexual obsession during the first year of his arranged marriage, when he and his wife were thirteen. Every few months, his bride's parents would summon her home. "Such calls were very unwelcome in those days," Gandhi wrote, "but they saved us both." (The Gandhi biographer and psycho-analyst Erik Erikson, however, sees something more significant in Gandhi's admission of adolescent lust. "How 'passionate' such a boy or man really is becomes a moot question, for we can only know of the quantitative threat which he feels the need of confessing," Erikson writes. "But one thing is devastatingly certain: nowhere is there any suggestion of joyful intimacy." Erikson argues that Gandhi in fact harbored "some vindictiveness, especially toward woman as the temptress," which in his later years made him attempt, at first with mixed success, a life of celibacy.)

Whatever may be true of Gandhi, the common reality appears to be closer to what Meena experienced. The psychoanalyst Sudhir Kakar, in a 1987 lecture delivered at the University of California at Berkeley, spoke of the "widespread sexual misery" among all classes in India. "Even discounting the sexual woes of a vast number of middle- and upper-middle-class women who come for psychotherapy as an unrepresentative example," he said, "there are other, direct indications that sexual misery is equally widespread in the lowest castes." The standard notion in India has always been that very poor and very rich women enjoy sex because they live free of repressive middle-class morality. But Kakar cited interviews with Harijan, or "Untouchable," women in Delhi—members of the lowest of castes—who described sexual intercourse as "painful or distasteful or both," portraying it "as a furtive act in a cramped and crowded room, lasting barely a few minutes and with a marked absence of physical or emotional caressing."

This does not surprise the country's growing band of "sexologists," as sex therapists in India are called. A foreign traveler cannot help but notice the advertisements for aphrodisiacs, sex "cures" and special medicines on billboards across India. "Most Indian men, whether rich, poor or middle-class, use their wives as sleeping pills," Prakash Kothari told me. "They do not know that foreplay and afterplay are important ingredients in the sex act." Kothari, the country's best-known and most publicity-conscious sexologist, a professional who should not be confused with the "doctors" who advertise on billboards, runs a thriving high-priced practice among the middle class of Bombay. He has done some serious research, yet has an unfortunate style that gets in his way. He autographed a copy of an American pornography magazine and gave it to an Indian woman journalist I knew; for me he brought out his collection of seventeenth-century miniature ivory penises and breasts from Rajasthan. Less flamboyant is R. H. Dastur, another Bombay sexologist and author of the best-selling *Sex Power,* a how-to book now in its sixth printing. In interviews that Dastur's researchers conducted with 695 middle-class women from 1983 to 1986 in Bombay, Dastur found that only 10 to 15 percent said they reached orgasm during intercourse. The rest, Dastur said, "merely submitted to sex and went through it mechanically with the idea that it was their duty in order to have a male child." Significantly, there is said to be no word in any Indian language specifically for "orgasm." Non-English-speaking women use words loosely translated as "happiness" or "perfect satisfaction."

Dastur is an internist who fell into sex therapy as a sideline after his patients began bringing their problems to him. Most were young men consumed by guilt over masturbation or convinced that it would lead to insanity. Other men were unsure about how to perform intercourse. Before marriage, said Dastur, "the large majority of the middle class has had no sexual experience whatsoever." The most common problem among the married couples Dastur treats is premature ejaculation or impotence, which Dastur says the husband often blames on his wife. In one case, the impotence had lasted for seven years from the day of the wedding. Kothari claimed he knew of cases of impotence that lasted twenty years. Sudhir Kakar goes a big step further in *The Inner World,* his psychoanalytic study of Indian childhood, when he writes of the "ubiquity" of male impotence in India, blaming it on a "vicious circle that spirals inward in the Indian unconscious." Kakar's theory is that women are sexually threatening to Indian men, which causes "avoidance behavior" in sexual relations, which then causes frustrated, lonely women to "extend a provocative sexual presence toward their sons." Certainly, Indian mothers make a huge emotional investment in their sons. Kakar believes this is a human reaction to the distance from her husband that a woman feels in a typical arranged marriage. Her son may well be the first male with whom she has had any sort of deep and satisfying relationship. This ultimately produces adult males, Kakar believes, who are afraid of being overwhelmed or "devoured" by their mothers. Thus, to complete the cycle, they fear the sexuality of mature women. Mama's boys and the Oedipus complex are of course not unique to India, but the intensity and pervasiveness of the cycle may be.

In India, it is common for boys to sleep with their mothers until they are five years old. In Calcutta, I knew of a woman who still slept with her seventeen-year-old son. A psychoanalyst there told me that was not unusual. In 1961, a study of a community of business families near Delhi found that more than half the men described themselves as being closer to their mothers than to their wives. Another woman I interviewed, a government researcher whose arranged marriage had split up, told me the relationship might have worked if she had demanded that she and her husband not live with his family. "But it's too much to ask of a boy," she said. "If he leaves his family and joins his wife, it's sort of a crime. He's known them all his life and he's only known me for three years."

Social historians say that procreation and duty were traditionally more important in Indian marriage than sexual satisfaction. Husband and wife have never been regarded as equals. Two thousand years ago, the upper-caste law codifier Manu wrote that a husband, "though destitute of virtue, or seeking pleasure elsewhere, or devoid of good qualities," must be "constantly worshipped as a god by a faithful wife." Only the lower castes married for sexual pleasure, according to Manu. Khushwant Singh, a historian, journalist and social observer, is only half joking when he says that "all of the violence in this country comes from repressed sexuality."

These views are hard to reconcile with the extraordinarily rich tradition of love and passion that is India's heritage. The *Kama-sutra* is probably the most famous poem ever written on the finer points of lovemaking, and the erotic temple sculptures at Khajuraho still startle Westerners. The Indian gods copulate blissfully across the pages of the great epics, and every schoolchild knows the love story of the god Krishna and the beautiful milkmaid Radha. She was no worshiping doormat but rather a proud, passionate woman who cried out to Krishna that "my beautiful loins are a deep cavern to take the thrusts of love." Those words were written in the twelfth century, in an erotic, lyrical love poem called the *Gitagovinda* that is still performed and sung throughout India.

Today, the legend of Krishna and Radha remains one key to understanding the relationship between marriage and love in India. The *Gitagovinda* made them the most popular couple in the Indian pantheon, coinciding with the Bhakti movement in Hinduism, which emphasized an intense personal devotion to a god, almost like that of a lover and beloved. Today, rural women in particular worship Krishna almost like a movie idol. Anyone who doubts that need only see the frenzy that occurs on his birthday in Brindaban, a village in the north Indian plains where thirty-five hundred years ago he is said to have seduced Radha and a bevy of equally inflamed milkmaids. Every year, tens of thousands of villagers and pilgrims mob the temples for the ritual darshan, or viewing, of the Krishna idol, typically a life-sized plastic doll hidden at the back of the temple behind wooden doors. One September I watched the steadily rising fervor of the crowd in the sweltering, hour-long buildup before the doors were opened. Drums were beating, and devotional music was slowly building in intensity. Finally, when Krishna was revealed, the women moaned and cried out, throwing money, Indian sweets and strings of jasmine flowers at the idol. The writer Ruth Prawer Jhabvala develops this desire beautifully in her short story about a widow, Durga, who was married off at a young age to an impotent old man. He has left her with money but also with the vague sense that "somehow, somewhere, she had been shortchanged." One day an old aunt, Bhuaji, begins to tell Durga the stories from the Krishna legend, and soon Durga's life changes: "Sometimes—when she was alone at night or lay on her bed in the hot, silent afternoons, her thoughts dwelling on Krishna—she felt strange new stirrings within her that were almost like illness, with a tugging in the bowels and a melting in the thighs. And she trembled and wondered whether this was Krishna descending on her, as Bhuaji promised he would."

The point is that the Krishna love story is about an adulterous affair, not marriage. Radha had a husband, whom she returned to. Krishna himself is said to have had 16,108 wives, one of the more amusing statistics I came across in India. But not one of those wives ever measured up to Radha. As for the *Kama-sutra,* it was an encyclopedia of erotic education meant largely for the aristocracy. The Khajuraho temples are more puzzling; no one has ever been sure why they were built, but they appear to have been enjoyed chiefly by the king and his court. For the large majority of Indians, love and passion have never been synonymous with marriage.

In that sense, the "new" Indian arranged marriage is something of a breakthrough after all. The middle class has essentially created an odd hybrid by grafting the Western ideal of romantic love onto the traditions of Hindu society—yet another example, perhaps, of the Indian talent for assimilating the culture of a foreign invader, much as the country absorbed Persian and Moghul art, architecture and language. In the end, the result is something completely and peculiarly Indian, including the notion that it "works." It is of course possible to match up two people of common backgrounds and interests and then watch as they fall in love. What are the American personal ads and dating services, after all?

The Indian idea that you can make two people fall in love, mostly because they think they are going to, at first seemed to me interesting and in its own way romantic. It was part of the "secret" I was looking for, I suppose—that compromise and perseverance can be as important to a successful marriage as love. Certainly no marriage in the West remains the same as it was on the wedding day. In the end, I came to see that Indians do have important insights into marriage and love. And yet, I saw too many husbands and wives in India who seemed unconnected to each other, as if the invisible thread that you can sense between a happy couple had never existed for them. They had nothing in common but the social class into which they were born. Most of the marriages I knew were not disasters, but many of the couples didn't seem to be friends. There seemed to be an intimacy missing in Indian middle-class married life, partly because few people expect it.

And then there was Meena. "You know," she assured me, after tearfully finishing the story of her wedding and impending divorce, "arranged marriages do work."

CHAPTER 3

FLAMES

A Bride Burning and a Sati

WHEN HINDUS LOOK AT FIRE, THEY SEE MANY THINGS BEYOND FLAMES. The little blazes that accompany all religious rituals and rites of passage are also an earthly embodiment of God, both comforting and all-powerful. Ten days after a baby is born, God is in the fire at the ceremony in which the child is given a name. At marriage, a bride and groom must take seven steps around a fire, and at death, during the Hindu cremation rites, the body is consumed by the sacred purifying force with a life of its own. One year during the spring harvest festival of Holi, when I was staying with Bhabhiji and her husband in the village of Khajuron, I went to the traditional bonfire on the eve of the holiday. Logs and bundles of straw had been piled near the village temple, not far from the bathing pool where I liked to walk in the evenings. It was early March, so the night was still cold, and a full pale-yellow moon had appeared from behind a cloud. A little group of women sang strange high-pitched love songs of Radha and Krishna as the villagers arrived with bundles of wheat to singe, for good luck.

One man brought a bull with a bad leg. Just before the fire was lit, he led the animal seven times around the pile, in hope of a cure, then turned his back with the rest of the crowd while Pandit-ji, the village holy man, started the blaze. Watching the leaping flames would have been inauspicious, so I turned my back, too. When it was safe to look, I turned to see the flames roaring up into a starry sky, hot, seductive and frightening. I remember watching the villagers with their bundles of wheat silhouetted against the blaze and feeling as if I had wandered into a harvest festival from a thousand years before.

Fire is also a special presence in the lives of Hindu women. From earliest childhood, little girls are told the story of Sita, the paradigm of the loyal, long-suffering wife, who threw herself onto a burning pyre to demonstrate her purity. In the classic text of the *Ramayana,* the great Hindu epic, Sita was the submissive wife of Rama, the hero and god. One day in the forest, Sita was abducted by the demon king Ravana, who dragged her off to his kingdom in what is today Sri Lanka. After a great war, Rama defeated Ravana and rescued his wife, only to reject Sita as the spoiled goods of another man, "a sacrificial offering polluted by a dog." As Sita listened, horrified, Rama told her, "I undertook the effort of war only to clear my name and that of my family. I am not able to stand your presence, even as a man with sensitive eyes cannot stand the light."

Sita insisted that she had remained pure. "I am not what you take me to be," she implored. "Ravana's body touched mine as he carried me off, but am I to blame for that?" She requested that a funeral pyre be built, but when she threw herself into the flames, the gods miraculously rescued her. This was divine proof of her innocence.

Sita's ordeal has left an indelible mark on the relationship of Indian women to fire, which remains a major feature of their spiritual lives, a cause of their death and a symbol, in the end, of one of the most shocking forms of oppression. What follows is the story of two Indian women, Surinder Kaur and Roop Kanwar, both of them victims of fire and Hindu tradition. One of them is lucky to be alive, the other is dead.

Surinder Kaur is a Sikh, illiterate, the mother of two, from a working-class neighborhood on the outskirts of Delhi. In 1983 she almost burned to death in her own home and accused her husband and sister-in-law of setting her on fire deliberately. She lived to tell her story, but like most personal tragedies in India, hers remained largely unknown; no famous lawyers or outraged women's groups came to her side. At her request I have changed her name.

Roop Kanwar was a member of the traditional warrior caste of Rajputs, with a high school education, from a small village in Rajasthan. In 1987 she died in the flames of her husband's funeral pyre. Her death shocked the nation, was deplored by the prime minister, and was partially responsible for the ousting of the chief minister of a state government.

In both cases, I spent weeks trying to learn what really happened to cause the violence but finally had to accept that the truth could probably never be known. Surinder Kaur may have been burned by her husband and sister-in-law, or she may have immolated herself. Roop Kanwar may have been forced to her husband's pyre, or she may have chosen to die. Whatever the case, both were victims of a society in which women are not only burned to death but are raised to see self-immolation as their only escape from miserable marriages—or, worse, as an act of courage and religious inspiration.

———————•——————

ON AUGUST 12, 1983, ON A GRAY, SWELTERING DAY AT THE END OF DELHI'S monsoon, Surinder Kaur, the thirty-year-old wife of a scooter-cab driver, was doused with kerosene and set on fire. The burning occurred at her home, in a small, dark entranceway leading from her front door to an inner courtyard. She ran screaming out into the street, her clothes on fire, and threw herself into a pool of water that had collected there from the heavy rains. Her husband lifted her out of the gutter and drove her in his scooter-cab to a nearby hospital, where she was admitted with burns over 60 percent of her body. In India, with wounds like these, most people die. Remarkably, Surinder lived, although she would have deep, permanent scars on her legs, arms, neck, upper chest, stomach and back. Only her breasts and face were untouched. These facts, at least, were not disputed. Beyond that, the stories wildly diverged.

Surinder claimed that her husband and his sister had tried to burn her to death. They were angry, she said, that she had not brought more dowry to the marriage. "My husband was holding my hair, and my sister-in-law poured the kerosene on me," she told me angrily. Then her husband guarded the door while her sister-in-law lit the match. Based on this account, the police charged Surinder's husband with assault and her sister-in-law with attempted murder. The case has languished in New Delhi's Sessions Court for years.

But the husband and the sister-in-law maintained that Surinder's burns were self-inflicted and that she had framed them as revenge for her unhappiness in the house. The sister-in-law said she was having tea upstairs when she heard screams from below. "She was shouting, 'I'm burning, I'm dying,' " the sister-in-law told me. The family had never asked her for any dowry, Surinder's husband and sister-in-law said, and in any case, she had brought them nothing.

My search for Surinder began during my first year in India. That summer I had come to my benign conclusions about arranged marriage, yet I sometimes wondered if I had too tolerantly interpreted an essentially repressive tradition. My editors in Washington, familiar with reports about "bride burnings" in India over the last several years, gave me a chance to explore the darker side. They asked me to find a woman who had lived through a bride burning and was willing to tell her story. Their request turned out to be more difficult to fulfill than I expected, simply because most women who are victims of bride burnings in India do not survive. If a woman does not die right away, she usually succumbs to infection in a substandard hospital a few days later. The police say the low survival rate helps to make the practice a popular form of murder. Bride burning is also grimly expedient. Guns and knives are expensive, but kerosene exists in every Indian household and rarely leaves a trail of solid evidence. Prosecutors find it difficult to disprove the usual argument made by the in-laws, who testify that the burning was a stove accident or a suicide. Since it has taken place behind closed doors, there are no witnesses. Usually the burning occurs in the first year of an arranged marriage, after it has become clear that the bride's parents will not meet the demands of the in-laws for more wedding gifts. Once the woman is disposed of, a new bride, who presumably will fulfill the dowry demands, is found. Sometimes in-laws ask for cars, videotape recorders and thousands of dollars.

It was not until the late 1970s that the terms "bride burning" and "dowry death" came into use in India, when a handful of feminists began protesting against the occasional case that became known to the public. One of those early activists was Subhadra Butalia, a college lecturer in English literature, whose life changed in October 1978 when she witnessed a bride burning across the street from her home. "I had just finished lunch when I heard screams coming from the opposite house," she told me calmly one evening as we sat in her living room. "There had been a quarrel going on before." She looked into the large glass windows of the house—it belonged to a rich industrialist—and saw the flames. "It was like a pyramid of fire," she recalled. The woman was taken to the hospital, and she gave a statement that her husband, her mother-in-law and her grandmother-in-law had burned her. She died fourteen days later. Subhadra Butalia testified for the prosecution at the trial, but a murder conviction by a lower court was overturned on appeal. "I was very disturbed," she said. "I used to see this girl. Sometimes you establish a communication with a person without talking to them. She had a small baby. I thought that I should talk to the colony people and do something about it, but everyone was very indifferent. They said it was a domestic matter." Frustrated, Butalia decided to write an article that would help publicize the case and discovered, while checking through back copies of newspapers, that an ominous number of women had been dying in "stove accidents" each year—in 1975, almost one a day in New Delhi alone. Dowry, Butalia wrote in the subsequent article, was "a social malaise that has assumed alarming proportions." By 1983, the number of deaths in New Delhi had nearly doubled, to 690, catching the attention of the Western news media. The CBS program *60 Minutes* turned up to report on the phenomenon. In 1987, the government released figures in Parliament that showed that the cases of registered dowry deaths nationwide numbered 999 in 1985, 1,319 in 1986 and 1,786 in 1987. These figures almost certainly do not reflect the actual number of dowry deaths in a country where most people do not report domestic violence. In India, violent deaths are common, but the dowry death statistics are especially startling because they are even higher than those for deaths caused every year by terrorist activity in Punjab, which is considered the most serious threat to Indian national unity.

Feminists and police officials could not determine whether the number of dowry deaths was increasing or whether more were being reported. There was also debate on whether dowry alone was the reason for the murders. Dowry seems to have been an Indian tradition since ancient times, although in the Sanskrit religious texts there are only perfunctory references to parents who gave away daughters "decked with ornaments" at the time of marriage. Indian historians say dowry coexisted with the custom of "bride price," which was a relatively small sum of money paid by the boy's family to the girl's parents as compensation for the loss of their daughter and also as the price of her labor in the house and fields. Bride price was generally favored by the lower castes, particularly in northern India, while dowry became the preferred practice among the upper castes. Gradually, dowry spread to almost all castes, whereas the custom of bride price was generally confined to tribal groups. Indian social historians attribute the spread of dowry to the desire of the lower castes to emulate the upper castes, and to the spread of prosperity. As a village family's wealth increased, it became a matter of prestige to keep women off the land. In such a family a woman, who had once been an asset, involved in harvesting the family fields, became, like Bhabhiji, a virtual shut-in—a liability who had to be unloaded for a price.

Ironically, education and affluence encouraged rather than discouraged the practice. A college boy, instead of adopting what the West would call an enlightened view, came to see his diploma as a sign of increased worth, enabling his parents to demand more dowry for him. Young men in the elite Indian civil service generally commanded the highest prices, followed by the sons of prosperous business families. Dowry was outlawed by Parliament in 1961, but the law failed miserably in trying to eradicate the practice. In the last two decades, fueled by a consumer boom among the new Indian middle class, dowry has spread like an epidemic to communities that never practiced it before. And its purpose has changed. No longer is it seen as a collection of wedding gifts to help a couple start a new life; instead, it is a way for the groom's family to elevate its economic status. In three and a half years in India, I asked women and men all over the country about dowry, and the answer was almost always "No, we didn't have dowry until the last few years." As Shanmugam, a village weaver in the state of Tamil Nadu, explained: "Some of the people in the area have started private businesses, and they are a little bit more well off than the others. These people demand dowry from the bride's parents. Seeing this practice, others also demand."

In order to find a bride burning survivor I could talk to, I set out one January morning in Delhi with Renuka Singh, a good friend who was working on her doctorate in sociology at Jawaharlal Nehru University. Her dissertation was about the status of women among different castes, income groups and religions in Delhi, so Renuka had contacts with feminists and the social welfare organizations in town. A lawyer she knew had given her the name and address of Nirmala Kumari, a young woman who he said had survived a bride burning. The lawyer told Renuka that the woman had just been discharged from the burns unit of Safdarjang Hospital and was now recuperating at home.

We followed the directions to a complex of three government-built concrete high rises, all of them overlooking a landscape of scrub brush and dust, and began searching for sector IV, flat 42. We soon realized that the address we had didn't make sense, and decided we would have to knock on the door of flat 42 in each of three buildings. We spent most of the next hour roaming the stairwells. We passed hanging laundry, breathed in the smells of cooking oil, and startled children, who stared at us as if we were a pair of visiting seals. Renuka, in her deep-red wool shawl and delicately tailored Indian tunic and trousers, called a salwar kameez, was almost as much of a curiosity as I was. The first of the three flats was dark, tiny and cold. No, the woman said, she didn't know Nirmala Kumari. As we headed for the second number 42, I wondered if Nirmala Kumari's face would be scarred, and imagined her coming to the door with a baby on her hip. I pictured her as thin, shy, with a dupatta covering her head. But no, said the second woman, there is no Nirmala Kumari here. The people in the third number 42 had never heard of her either.

Out of flats but with most of the morning still ahead, Renuka and I drove to Safdarjang Hospital to see if Nirmala Kumari was still there. The government-run hospital, which had one of the biggest burns units in the city, handled a large number of dowry cases. Renuka and I walked into the general ward of the burns unit, dingy under the glow of dull fluorescent lights, and found bed after bed of men and women, but mostly women, with hideously blackened faces, swollen and distorted beyond recognition. Some did not look human, and many were completely wrapped in bandages. The most serious cases were lying naked under what looked like inverted metal cradles that had been covered with blankets. People who are burned very badly cannot withstand even the weight of a sheet. I wondered how many of the women were dowry cases, but they were much too sick for me to consider approaching them.

Renuka and I found the nurse on duty, and I asked why so many women were in the ward. "Not all of them are dowry cases," she said, "but there are so many, so many." We inquired about Nirmala Kumari. "I remember her," the nurse said right away. "She was in bed forty-eight." Renuka and I were startled. After our hunt at the apartment complex, we had begun to wonder if Nirmala Kumari even existed. It was quite possible that Renuka's lawyer friend had given us the wrong name. Here was the first proof. The nurse flipped briskly through her record book, a ledger with entries written entirely by hand, and soon found what we wanted. "Nirmala Kumari," the entry said. She had been admitted on November 16, 1985. She was twenty-five years old, and had been burned over 55 percent of her body. I followed her entry across the page, to the right-hand column and saw this: "Expired 25/11/85, 6:20 P.M." Renuka and I were looking for a woman who had been dead for five weeks.

We stood there in silence. Nirmala Kumari had lived only nine days in the burns ward. "How did she die?" I finally asked the nurse, who by that time had become very nervous. She referred us to her supervisor, who referred us to the hospital's administrator, and at that point Renuka and I decided it was time to go home. "I felt as if I knew her," Renuka said in the car on the way back. I felt the same. It was a tenuous connection, of course, and mostly imagined; I didn't even know for sure that Nirmala Kumari had lived in the housing complex where we had knocked on the three doors. But she probably lived in a building that was something like it, and I knew she had been in severe pain during her last nine days in the burns ward. The morning had provided a glimpse of something that at least resembled her life.

Renuka's lawyer friend had given her a second name, Surinder Kaur, although all he knew was that she was a young woman who had been burned by her husband two years before. This woman lived in Raghubir Nagar, a lower-middle-class housing colony on the outskirts of Delhi. Renuka and I drove there a few days later. The neighborhood was one of the haphazard settlements that had been multiplying on the far edges of Delhi, representing the hopes of hundreds of thousands of people who had left their villages to find work in the big city. A lot of scooter-cab drivers lived in Raghubir Nagar, and their little three-wheeler taxis were parked at crazy angles along the muddy lanes. The houses were small brick-and-cement blocks, all with balconies and flat rooftops providing excellent views into the neighboring homes. This guaranteed entertainment during slow afternoons and ensured that one person's business was everyone else's. The address the lawyer had given us was incomplete, but people we asked in the streets said they had heard there was a girl burned somewhere in the area a few years back. They knew her at the medical dispensary, too, where she had gone to have her bandages changed. After some twists and turns, an old man finally led us to Surinder's house, a cement box that looked like all the others. A woman sitting on a string cot outside the front door directed us upward. "Surinder is very sad," she said. "She paces back and forth and cries all the time." We walked up a narrow staircase and out on a roof to find a young, pretty woman standing in the fading light of the cold winter afternoon. At first I thought she might be Surinder. "I am her sister," the woman said shyly. "Surinder isn't home." The two of them lived up there, in a small shed that had been built in a corner. Inside, the shed was dark and cramped and filled with the greasy smell of fried food. A string cot took up most of the room; another leaned upright against the wall. There was a small burner on the floor and pots and pans stacked nearby. In a corner were a few vegetables and bottles of milk. Along one side of the room was a black-and-white television set. The sister told us that Surinder lived on the twenty-five dollars a month that the court had ordered her husband to pay her. It looked like a grim, lonely existence. We told the sister why we wanted to meet Surinder and arranged for a time to come back. Before we left, the woman on the string cot downstairs asked a question as if she were my conscience speaking out loud. "What good will writing do?" she wanted to know.

Surinder wasn't there when we returned, and Renuka and I assumed, correctly, that she was avoiding us. But when we arrived unannounced at eight in the morning a week later, we found her there, brushing her teeth just outside the door of the shed. She was a tall, slender and pretty woman, thirty-three years old, with pale brown skin and large dark eyes. Her hair was pulled back in a bun, and she wore a cotton salwar kameez with an old cardigan for warmth. Her face was clear of any scars, but I could see rippled skin on her hands and neck. She was angry that we had tracked her down, and she had no intention of spilling out her life to two strangers. She had told her story to Renuka's lawyer friend once already, and that had not changed anything. "I'm fed up with telling my story," she snapped.

But Renuka began speaking to her in Punjabi, the language of the state of Punjab and Surinder's mother tongue. Renuka was always a comforting presence. She listened well, and people told her things. She was also a Sikh, like Surinder, and soon Surinder loosened up. We talked that first morning, and then again a few days later, sitting on the floor of the shed. I asked the questions, Renuka translated, and Surinder told us a story that was, in many ways, remarkable only for its ordinariness. Most Indian women are not set on fire by their husbands, of course, but the life that Surinder described leading up to the burning could have been that of any poor Indian woman raised to be no more than chattel in her in-laws' home. Surinder cried when I asked about her treatment there, dissolving into silent tears as she stared dully at a Hindi movie on the television set. "I'm unlucky that I'm still alive," she said. "I wish I were dead."

What follows is her side of the story, or the story, at least, that she chose to tell us. I have changed the names of her husband and sister-in-law.

She was one of several children—it was never clear how many—born into a poor farming family that struggled to make a living on the dry north Indian plains. Her parents could not afford to keep her, so at the age of four Surinder was sent to live with her uncle in Delhi. He had settled in one of the little boxes in Raghubir Nagar and had become, like his neighbors, a scooter-cab driver. In a good month he brought home one hundred dollars. The uncle was willing to accept the added expense of Surinder because he needed someone to look after his widowed father, Surinder's grandfather, who lived in the house. Surinder did as she was told. Throughout her childhood, she cooked the meals, cleaned the house, washed the clothes and attended to her grandfather's needs. There was no time for her to go to school, and she never learned to read and write. She claimed she didn't mind. She lived there because her grandfather needed her, not to go to school or advance herself. In the evenings, she went to the neighborhood Sikh temple to listen to the religious songs. She told us this was the only time she left the house. She had no friends, and no other contact with the outside world.

And yet Surinder had come to see this life as satisfying. After all, she knew nothing else. "I was never so happy in my life," she told us. "My grandfather took care of me. There was no worry. I ate, I wore nice clothes, I lived well. It was a very secure life."

Her happiness ended with her marriage. When she was twenty, Manjit, a distant relative she had never met—he was the brother of the wife of one of her uncles—came to the door with a group of friends to invite the family to his wedding the next day. But when Manjit and his friends saw Surinder, they decided she would be a better wife than the bride who had been arranged. Manjit quickly backed out of the marriage and the next day spoke to Surinder's grandfather about marrying her. At first I thought this tale was too bizarre to be true, but it makes sense if one thinks of a bride as a commodity that can be quickly exchanged for a better deal. It mattered not at all that Surinder objected and spoke of her "bad feeling" about the groom. The family insisted it was high time for a twenty-year-old woman to be married.

The wedding took place on September 30, 1979, ten days after Manjit had come to her door, at Surinder's grandfather's house. By Indian standards, it was a modest lunch for two hundred people, with meat, under a big tent. Surinder's dowry—furniture, a television set, a refrigerator, jewelry and cash—was loaded on a bus and taken to her in-laws' home that night. The next morning, Surinder said, "the whole drama started. When the family saw the dowry they said, 'You've hardly got anything.'"

As Surinder recalled, they harassed her day after day. Sometimes they would go to her uncle's house and demand large sums of cash. If they didn't get it, they beat her. They beat her again when her first child, a girl, was born, because she had not given birth to a boy. She was lighter-skinned than the other women in her in-laws' extended family, which she said made the resentments worse. "My color mattered to them," she told us proudly. "They were jealous because I was beautiful." They treated her as a virtual slave in the house, forcing her into a cycle of constant cooking and cleaning. "Sometimes they even locked the refrigerator so I wouldn't be able to drink anything," she said. Two years after the wedding, her mother-in-law was hit by a truck and killed. Surinder's father-in-law had died much earlier.

Although the deaths might have brought some peace to Surinder's life, instead she was even more threatened by the other women in the house. She became convinced that her husband was sleeping with the wife of his older brother. He himself had told Surinder there were others. "He told me he would only come to me when other women weren't available," she said. "I didn't enjoy sleeping with him." She became angrier when she discovered that her husband was giving money to the older brother's wife, and also to his own sister, Amrita. The sister had recently come back to live in the house because her own marriage was ending and she needed financial and emotional support. Soon Surinder was certain her husband was sleeping with his own sister as well. Although she may well have been irrational at this point, her suspicions are not necessarily unfounded. In India, psychologists say, affairs with relatives are not unusual. The psychoanalyst Sudhir Kakar, who has a middle- and upper-middle-class practice, once told me that of his patients who were having affairs, most were involved with extended family members.

By August 1983, the tension in the house had become unbearable. During one fight, the husband and his sister had thrown kerosene on Surinder, and she was sure they were going to kill her. At the time, talk of dowry deaths was everywhere. A few months before, a New Delhi judge had caused a sensation in India when he handed down an unprecedented death sentence for a husband, mother-in-law and brother-in-law charged with the murder of Sudha Goel, a young woman who was nine months pregnant. Neighbors had testified that Sudha Goel's parents had been unable to meet demands for a refrigerator, motor scooter or cash after the wedding, and that the three defendants had dragged the screaming wife into the garden and set her on fire. In a statement made before she died, Sudha Goel said her mother-in-law had ripped off her jewelry just before lighting the match. (The husband, mother-in-law and brother-in-law were acquitted on appeal.)

On August 12, 1983, Surinder was at home with her two-year-old daughter and one-year-old son feeling weak and feverish. Her husband and his sister were there too. Around two-thirty in the afternoon another fight erupted as the husband and his sister began beating Surinder. Suddenly her husband grabbed Surinder to hold her still. His sister threw the kerosene, and Surinder fell to the floor. Then her husband went to guard the door as his sister threw the match. Surinder told me later she didn't remember where it hit or how it ignited. All she recalled was that she ran, flaming, past her husband at the door. "He just let me go on," she said. "When you're burning, nobody wants to touch you." She threw herself into the gutter. On the way to Ram Manohar Lohia Hospital she was still conscious. "My husband told me that if I blamed him, he would kill all my uncles," she said.

A short time later, Renuka and I went to see Surinder's husband. He still lived in the house where the burning occurred, a large, run-down, two-story home on a dusty alley closer to the central part of town. The husband, Manjit, turned out to be a slight, sad-eyed Sikh with a turban and a medium-length black beard. Sometimes he was so passive that he seemed uninterested; at other times tears came to his eyes and he asked why his life was destined to turn out as it had. "My faith has been totally broken," he said. "I just want to die." His sister, Amrita, was a tiny woman with a little-girl voice and a forceful manner; she often took charge of the conversation. We talked in a dark bedroom that opened onto the central courtyard, where two women in the family squatted on the floor over a lunch of rice and lentils. Surinder's two children lived there but had been sent away to boarding school, which Manjit claimed he could hardly afford. He was also upset that he had no one to cook for him. He and his sister had been in jail for more than a month before they were released on bail, and when they finally came home, his neighbors told him his children had been eating from the gutters in the streets.

This was his version of the story:

The problems, Manjit said, began right after the wedding. "She used to get angry about every little thing," he said. His new wife had brought no dowry, and yet he had not complained. "We knew she was poor," he said. He thought she would be happy in the house, the same one he had been born in thirty years earlier. It was old, but much larger than the house where she had lived before. And it was close to the large markets of Karol Bagh, where women from all over Delhi came to shop. Manjit's father had worked in those markets as a vegetable salesman; he was an immigrant who had settled in Delhi after the 1947 partition of the British Empire into India and Pakistan drove him from the border state of Punjab. It was a move that would instill in his offspring, as in millions of others, a feeling that they were refugees in their own land.

Manjit's new wife was soon complaining all the time, even though she was not treated as a slave, Manjit said, like most new brides. After Manjit's mother died, Surinder had to cook only for her husband and two children. His two brothers and their wives kept to themselves upstairs; his sister, Amrita, came by only for visits. And yet his wife became very jealous of his relationship with his sister, even though he was just trying to help Amrita out. She had left her husband, and she desperately needed money. But Surinder hated her husband's giving cash to his sister. "She wanted to control my brother," Amrita said. As it was, Manjit was working night and day, trying to make one hundred dollars a month for his own wife and children. He was never unfaithful. "I treated her as nicely as possible," he said. But still she would get angry. One night when he came home at eleven for dinner, she gave him cold vegetables and bread. When he told her to heat it up, she became furious. What kind of a wife was this? Sometimes after their fights she would go to her uncle's home. Manjit began to wonder about the two of them. Was it her uncle she wanted? Had there been a relationship before the marriage? He began to think about it all the time.

In August of 1983 there was another terrible fight. Surinder had been behaving strangely—beating their small daughter and once even threatening to burn the child. But this time, Surinder poured kerosene on herself and said she wanted to commit suicide. "Then she called her uncle," Manjit said, "and told him that I had poured kerosene on her and was trying to kill her." Some days later, on August 12, Surinder was at home feeling weak and feverish after donating blood for a relative. Manjit had gone to the hospital to pick her up and had found her there in the relative's room, whispering in a corner with her uncle. When the two saw Manjit they stopped. "Why did they stop whispering when I got there?" he asked us. This was the proof he needed. He was now almost certain there was something between them. At home that day, his wife was even angrier than usual. Manjit felt he could no longer control her and grew more and more worried that she would try to kill herself. Finally, in desperation, he left the house and went a few doors down to an old family friend. He wanted to ask her what could be done for his wife. It was there that he heard the screams.

When he reached the hospital with his wife, the doctors wanted to know what had happened. "Whatever I tell you," he said, "you won't believe it."

I had gone to see Manjit only out of a sense of responsibility, because I wanted to write a fair story for *The Washington Post*. There had been no doubt in my mind that he was guilty, but now I was confused. I assumed Manjit was lying about certain parts of his story, but I knew Surinder had not told the entire truth either. For one thing, she was not now as impoverished as she said; Renuka and I discovered she had recently had a job inspecting clothes at a garment house. I had also never been comfortable with her claim that this was a dowry case, simply because she had been burned nearly four years after her wedding. Bride burnings over dowry usually take place in the first year of marriage, before there are children. It was clear that there were more serious problems in Surinder's marriage than a lack of wedding gifts. Kanwaljit Deol, the woman who ran the New Delhi police department's antidowry division, told me that parents of burned women frequently cited dowry as a reason for the burning because they knew it would guarantee more police attention. Deol said her statistics proved that suicides by burning were more common than clear-cut dowry deaths, and that sometimes a woman made miserable in her in-laws' house burned herself to get back at them. "Women are very smart," she said. "We've had cases where a woman would put kerosene oil on herself, then run to the police station. It's really crazy. Sometimes when I'm talking to women, they'll say, 'Well, if there's nothing to be done, I'll just kill myself.' " In Deol's view, the story of Sita and the tradition of sati had been reinterpreted by the desperate twentieth-century bride. "Fire in particular has had this significance," she said. "When all of us are small children, we hear these stories." Later I mentioned Deol's remark to Subhadra Butalia, the women's activist who had witnessed the bride burning. "Why should a woman burn herself to commit suicide?" she responded, infuriated. "Why torture yourself like that?"

Whatever the truth, Surinder had never mentioned that her in-laws were harassing her for dowry in the two separate statements she made to the police in the hours after the burning. She also had not blamed her husband. During her first night in the hospital, she told a police investigator and then a court representative that her husband had beaten her but had left the house before the burning occurred. Her sister-in-law, she said, acted alone. This was why her husband was charged with assault and her sister-in-law with attempted murder. Renuka and I asked her why she had changed her story for us. "My husband told me on the way to the hospital that if I blamed him, he would kill all my uncles," she said. This certainly fit a pattern. One reason there are so few convictions in dowry deaths is that women are often afraid to implicate their husbands, or are simply reluctant to do so. Judge S. M. Aggarwal, who handed down the death sentence in the Sudha Goel case and has ruled on dozens of others, told me that even if a husband has tried to kill his wife, she may still feel it is her duty "to serve him, and not cause him any harm."

The police investigation itself was of little help to me. Judging from the reports I saw, there appeared to be no direct evidence to support either side of the story. Not much was listed as evidence: A swatch of the clothing worn by Surinder the day she was burned was sent to a police lab for analysis and was found to contain kerosene. And on August 11, the day before the burning, Surinder had gone to the neighborhood police station and lodged a complaint that her husband was beating and starving her. It appeared from the inspecting officer's report that the police did not interview neighbors or witnesses at the scene, and from the court file I learned that investigators apparently did not collect evidence at the house. A police photographer, however, did take some pictures of the interior. And yet the investigation took four months—a month longer than the maximum allowed. Subhadra Butalia had told me about these delays. "The police take their time and wait for the accused to bribe them," she said. "The courts insist upon evidence, but without it, the court must give the benefit of the doubt to the accused."

The first hearing in Surinder's case against her husband and sister-in-law was on June 3, 1985, almost two years after the burning. Surinder herself did not testify until April 1 of the following year. The trial was still not over when I left India more than two years after that. Court cases in India are notorious for their Dickensian delays. Testimony is never heard without interruptions: Two witnesses will testify, for example, but because a third has failed to appear, a judge will stop the proceeding and adjourn the case to the next available court date, sometimes six weeks later. Judges do not usually issue arrest warrants if a witness fails to answer a summons, at least the first or second time, so it is not unusual for a case like this to dribble on for a decade. Problems in the Indian courts are so legendary that the Indian government lawyers representing India and the victims of the 1984 Bhopal chemical gas leak argued that the case against Union Carbide be tried in the United States, where they thought they could get a faster and more generous settlement. The Indian government's own brief admitted that even routine Indian court proceedings "turn into such protracted odysseys that it is not unusual for litigation to long survive the litigants themselves." To back up their argument, the lawyers quoted a 1976 decision by the Indian Supreme Court in which a justice sarcastically noted that the case had passed its "silver jubilee," but that "at long last, the unfortunate and heroic saga of this litigation is coming to an end."

Surinder's trial was but one small scene in the immense tragicomedy of the Indian criminal justice system. On April 1, 1986, she took the stand in a dilapidated courtroom, in the middle of a long morning of other cases, and calmly stuck to the original story she had told to the police, but not to me: that her sister-in-law acted alone after Manjit left the house. The case was adjourned to May 1, when Surinder identified the sandals and shawl she was wearing on the day the burning took place. The police inspector who recorded her statement in the hospital and the constable who sent the evidence to the lab also took the stand. The case was adjourned to July 8.

By this time I had written the *Post* story and was working on other assignments, but I employed a Delhi lawyer, R. L. Verma, to keep track of the rest of the trial for me. After each hearing he sent me reports, which grew increasingly farcical. On July 8, another inspector testified; then the case was adjourned until August 8, at which time K. K. Sud, the defense attorney for the husband and sister, refused to cross-examine Surinder because her uncle, whom he considered crucial to the case, was not present. The case was adjourned until October 27, but on that day the uncle once again did not turn up. At the next hearing, on December 11, a doctor from the hospital testified about the nature of Surinder's burns, but the cross-examination could not take place because Surinder herself failed to appear. The next hearing was set for February 11, 1987. This time Surinder appeared, but her uncle did not. Even if he had, nothing would have happened because there was a lawyers' strike that day. The next hearing was set for April 1, when Amrita sent a medical certificate saying she was ill. Under law, all court proceedings have to be held in the presence of the accused, so nothing happened that day, either. On the day of the next hearing, May 18, the lawyers were once again on strike, this time over the lack of court fee stamps. Court fee stamps, which look like little postage stamps, have to be put on all motions, briefs, and other documents filed in the courthouse. For some reason, the courthouse clerical staff had run out of them, and all legal activity had ground to a halt.

After six more months of similar delays, the judge finally lost his patience. On November 11, he wrote out a detailed order asking that the cross-examination of Surinder be closed, and then set the next date for December 10. But on that date, the defense moved an application that Surinder be recalled for cross-examination after all. Verma, who had been following the case for one year and nine months, could not resist some editorial comment of his own. "So the rigamarole has started all over again," he wrote. "And this is only the trial court. Years will roll until the matter reaches the Supreme Court."

The delays continued into June of the following year, when the presiding judge was transferred to another job. The case was then sent to a different court. Surinder showed the burns on her arms to the new judge, who adjourned the case until September 14. I was back in the United States when I got the next letter from Verma, who informed me that on September 14 the judge had abruptly adjourned the case until after the first of the next year.

I tried to see Surinder before I left India in the summer of 1988, but I learned that she had moved to Punjab. Verma was able to talk to her when she appeared at her hearing in September, though, and he wrote me that she planned to remarry. She told him that her husband had already "remarried"—even though there had been no divorce—and that the husband's new "wife" had given birth to a daughter. The second wife apparently was caring for Surinder's children as well. Surinder asked Verma if she needed to file a lawsuit if she wanted to legally divorce her husband. "In fact, she was probing me for legal advice," he wrote to me. That afternoon, she turned up unexpectedly at his office with more questions about her case. This didn't surprise me. In two years of sitting in on Surinder's hearings, Verma had grown increasingly sympathetic to her; Surinder was clever enough to recognize a well-connected lawyer who could help her.

What really happened on August 12, 1983? Is it possible, as Surinder maintained, that the family's resentment against her had been building for years—first because the dowry wasn't enough, then because her firstborn wasn't a boy, then because of false suspicions of an affair with her uncle? Did the husband and sister-in-law want to get rid of her so they could control the house—and find a new bride with a large dowry? Or, as the husband's lawyer maintained, had Surinder planned to burn herself only a little bit and then blame her husband and sister-in-law? Is that why there were no burns on her breasts and face? Did she become horrified when her plan got out of hand? Sometimes I have thought it might have been a combination of both scenarios. In the fury and confusion of the fight on August 12, maybe Surinder did pour kerosene on herself, did threaten to commit suicide—and then, in a rage, her husband or sister-in-law threw the match. Or did they pour the kerosene, and did Surinder then light the match?

To this day I still wonder what happened and I suppose that I always will. If I were forced to decide, I would have to agree with the defense lawyer, as odious as that is to me, and say that her burns were self-inflicted in an attempt to frame her husband and sister-in-law. But my judgment is based on instinct, not evidence. My guess is that the husband and sister-in-law will be convicted, and then the appeals will go on for years. "In burning cases, usually the sympathies are with the wife," explained K. K. Sud, the lawyer for Surinder's husband and sister-in-law. "The presumption is that a woman would not want to burn herself, or to disturb her home and children, by making a false accusation against the husband."

The truth is that I never really trusted Surinder. In the beginning I felt so sorry for her that I gave her some clothes and a little money, but gradually I began to feel manipulated. She begged me to find her a job, but I discovered she had one already. She told me one story and the police another. She said she couldn't read and write, but Verma told me he had seen her engrossed in a Sikh religious book while she waited for her case to be called. A lot of the neighbors complained that she was a troublemaker. Certainly she was physically aggressive, and she boasted that she won her frequent fights with her husband. "After two slaps from me," she said proudly, "he couldn't even get up off the floor."

None of this disproved her story, of course. Nor did it prove that her husband and sister-in-law were telling the truth. Surinder Kaur, however unlikable, and no matter what happened, was a casualty of the centuries-old custom of dowry, dangerously transformed by the forces of urbanization and a consumer society. Rather than eliminating dowry, modernization had instead made it lethal. In essence, Surinder Kaur was forced to live in several centuries at once—with the result that she nearly lost her life. It was something I understood better when I encountered the story, and the growing legend, of Roop Kanwar.

ON SEPTEMBER 4, 1987, UNDER A BLAZING SUN IN THE VILLAGE OF Deorala, Roop Kanwar, the eighteen-year-old widow of an unemployed college graduate, was burned alive on her husband's funeral pyre. That much, at least, is not disputed. Beyond that, the story has taken on the proportions of myth. The people of Deorala and Roop Kanwar's family and in-laws said that the young girl, who had been married only seven months before, deliberately committed sati. Roop Kanwar sat calmly on the pyre with her husband's head in her lap, they said, chanting Hindu prayers and showering blessings on the crowd as hundreds, perhaps thousands, of villagers watched. They tried to dissuade her, they said, but God had called her and she would not listen.

Urban women's groups, stunned by the first successful sati in many years, countered that this was preposterous, and that no educated woman would choose such a gruesome way to die for a man she hardly knew. Roop Kanwar was forced, they said, or drugged with opium. Whatever the truth, the dusty little mound where she had died quickly became a place of religious pilgrimage. More than five hundred thousand people, including local political leaders and a state official of Rajiv Gandhi's Congress party, came to worship there in the first two weeks after the event. Roop Kanwar became a goddess, revered for her courage, and funds were collected to build a temple in her honor on the site. Seven months later, Deorala was still attracting four hundred visitors a day, including those who believed that offering a prayer at the scene of her death would cure cancer or allow a childless woman to conceive.

I first heard of the young woman eight days after her death. On September 12, 1987, I opened up *The Times of India* and saw a front-page story that seemed incredible. Under the headline THE SPIRIT OF SATI LIVES ON, a *Times* reporter in the newspaper's Jaipur bureau,

Shabnam Virmani, had written this lead: "Deorala is a village without remorse. Not a tear glistens in any eye—just the dull gleam of religious fanaticism." The story recounted how a young Rajput girl, Roop Kanwar, had been inconsolable over her husband's sudden death. After his body was brought to her, she had put on her wedding dress, walked to the cremation site with the funeral procession, arranged herself on the pyre with her dead husband's head in her lap, then asked her brother-in-law to light the fire. The police did not turn up until five hours after the burning. The story stated that it was "unlikely" that Roop Kanwar had been coerced into sati by her in-laws because she was an educated girl who presumably had a mind of her own. The rest of the article centered on the excitement building in anticipation of September 16, when the chunri ceremony was to take place. The flames, kept going after the cremation, would be doused with milk, and one of Roop Kanwar's chunris, or shawls, would be draped on the ashes. It was the final rite in honor of the sati, and more than one hundred thousand people were expected to attend.

Sati had once been common in India, particularly among the Rajput feudal warlords who built the palaces and forts that still rise from the rocky landscape of Rajasthan. Scholars are not sure of the origin of the practice, although there are early references to it in the historical accounts of the ancient Greeks and Scythians. In India, references to sati first appear in the Hindu epics, dating from about two thousand years ago. Five of the god Krishna's wives were believed to have immolated themselves on his funeral pyre; four of Krishna's father's wives had done the same. The custom is named after Sati, the wife of the god Shiva. (She is no relation to Sita, the wife of Rama, who had to undergo the fire ordeal.) In the Hindu myths, Sati's father refused to invite her husband to a sacrificial feast, which greatly mortified her and was apparently an acceptable reason for her to burn herself to death. Shiva pulled her corpse from the fire and carried it on his head as penance. But the god Vishnu, afraid that this act would somehow give Shiva great power, cut Sati's body into bits. It fell to earth in either five, fifty-one, fifty-two, seventy-two or one hundred eight pieces, depending on the version of the myth. More than a thousand places in India claim to have received a bit of Sati, usually her ears, breasts or sexual organs. Although she did not actually burn herself on her husband's funeral pyre, the term *sati* has come to be used for all widows who immolate themselves.

By the first century A.D., sati began to gain the support of some of the Hindu law codifiers, who described it as an act of great honor. It was generally practiced by the upper castes and reflected the belief that a man's possessions—and his wife was his chief possession—could be sent with him into the next world if they were burned along with him. It was also considered a better alternative for a widow than facing a miserable life of abuse from her in-laws, who frequently blamed her for her husband's death, made her sleep on the floor and kept her isolated from the rest of the family and all social functions. Many widows were beaten, denied food and forced to beg in the streets.

It was the Rajputs of the old princely states that made up the region of Rajputana who glamorized sati in the legends that mothers told their little girls. It became customary for not only wives but also concubines, sisters, sisters-in-law and even mothers to hurl themselves on the pyres of their dead men. Many historians claim—and the Rajputs believe—that the practice became widespread during the Muslim invasions of five hundred years ago, when an entire clan of men could be lost in a single battle. Rather than submit to the conquerors, the women killed themselves in mass immolations. Whether it is fair to blame the Muslims is a matter of emotional debate in India today; recent historians say sati was prevalent long before the Moghul invasions. In any event, today there are stones and temples that stand in honor of the dead women across Rajasthan, romantic memorials seriously at variance with historical accounts by European travelers who wrote of widows who were drugged, tied down to stakes or pushed back on the pyre with poles. In 1829, the British outlawed sati, and in recent years the few widows who attempted it were stopped by the police. At the time of Roop Kanwar's death, the belief among the elite in India was that sati had all but died out.

How, then, could an educated woman have committed sati in the India of the late 1980s? Even if the sati had occurred—and I was still not certain of that—I could not imagine a celebration such as the one the *Times* was describing. The villagers seemed to be living in another century. Was the newspaper story true? Who was Roop Kanwar, really?

Three days later, Steve and I were heading toward Deorala, a village of ten thousand people about a five-hour drive southwest from Delhi. Our plan was to see the chunri ceremony and to talk to the villagers and Roop Kanwar's parents and in-laws. Steve thought the immolation might make a story for *The New York Times,* and I thought that the incident, however atypical, might be included in this book. We had with us a young Indian couple from the nearby city of Jaipur to help us with the local dialect.

What happened during those next forty-eight hours was almost surreal. Deorala was in the grip of a sati fever that defied the notion of India as a modern, secular state. It was the first time I had so directly felt the power of religious fundamentalism. I never would have believed it had I not seen it with my own eyes.

We parked the car on the grounds of Deorala's secondary school, a run-down brick building on the dirt road leading into the village. As long as we were there, we thought we should drop in on a teacher to find out what the educated people of the village were saying. The excitement in the village had emptied the school's classrooms, and we found Madan Lal Gupta, an English teacher, sitting in a little office with nothing to do. We asked him about the sati. Yes, he said, it had occurred on September 4 at one-thirty in the afternoon. He and the rest of the school first heard about it a half hour later. Did Roop Kanwar die voluntarily? "She herself was willing," he said with authority. "Nobody forced her to die." We asked him what he thought of this. "No doubt it is not a good thing in this modern age," he began sensibly enough. "But now there may be some miracles, and many big, good things may come to us." It turned out that Madan Lal Gupta, an educated man who was imparting wisdom to the next generation of Indians, perfectly reflected the feelings of the rest of the village.

That became apparent as we left the school and began the walk toward the center of Deorala. Along the road dozens of little souvenir shops had sprung up, offering grotesque color photo montages of Roop Kanwar supposedly burning on her husband's pyre. The most popular one used pictures of Roop Kanwar and her husband, apparently cut out from snapshots taken on their wedding day, superimposed on a picture of fire so it seemed that Roop Kanwar was smiling serenely as she went up in flames with her husband. The boy peddling the picture wanted thirty-five cents. By the day of the chunri ceremony, the pictures were selling briskly at four dollars each, nearly a week's wages for a farm laborer.

By the time we arrived in the center of Deorala, we were part of a festive wave of revelers pouring in by truck, bus, tractor, camel cart and foot. The men wore the scarlet-and-yellow turbans of Rajasthan, and the women came in bright red full-length skirts, short overblouses, glittering veils, large nose rings and thick silver ankle bracelets. Hindi film music and popular religious songs blared from loudspeakers.

Nobody seemed to notice the demonlike sun and the dust that swirled in hot, thick clouds. Roop Kanwar's death had occasioned a carnival, and it appeared that no one within a hundred miles intended to miss it.

Steve and I followed the crowd to the sati site, a hard little mound of dirt with a low circle of bricks surrounding the place where the burning had taken place. In the center of the brick circle was a small fire, left over from the sati and fed continuously with dried coconuts; around it were piles of incense sticks, and over it was a crooked wooden scaffolding. On the day of the ceremony it would hold a gold-and-fuchsia canopy decorated with strands of marigolds. Young men from Rajput youth groups marched in a clockwise circle around the fire, wielding swords as they chanted "Sati Mata ki jai"—"Glory to the Sati Mother"—in order to guard the place from magic that might have taken away the power created by Roop Kanwar's immolation. Pinned to the young men's breast pockets were little cloth tags embroidered in neat Hindi letters that said MAHASATI ROOP KANWAR—the Great Sati Roop Kanwar—and beneath, DEORALA. In an outside circle, the crowd pressed forward to get a look, although they were hindered by camel carts lumbering through with leaking barrels of drinking water. In the middle of the confusion, an old, skinny woman knelt in the dust, flailing her arms wildly. People told us she had been possessed some time back, and that she had been brought to Deorala in hopes that the evil spirit would leave her.

Steve and I fanned out into the crowd, looking for people who could tell us about Roop Kanwar. The few women I found who were willing to say they had seen the event—and they were growing fewer by the hour as the police pressed their investigation—assured me that Roop Kanwar had acted willingly. The sati had made her a saint in their eyes. "If we had known she was going to do this, we would have touched her feet," said Kamal Kunwar, a housewife. "Now I will give her a place in my house and worship her every day." Yet most women said that they themselves were not courageous enough to commit sati. "Sati is not possible for all women, but only those who are very blessed," said Ratan Kunwar, a fifty-eight-year-old mother of two from a nearby village. "Now I have come here for the blessings from this holy place." Other women had made their way over to the home of Roop Kanwar's in-laws, where her room had become a shrine overnight. I pushed my way forward, then peeked in through a window with the rest of the crowd to see the bed she had shared with her husband. The brick house was clearly that of a well-to-do village family. In one corner of Roop's room was a television set, a symbol of their affluence.

I was finally able to find Roop's parents and in-laws in a nearby tent, where they were participating with Hindu priests in a religious ceremony in honor of the sati. When it was over, I approached them. Roop Kanwar's mother, who seemed dazed but not stricken, told me that her daughter used to read the *Bhagavadgita* during her childhood; her father, Bal Singh Rathore, a big man in a disheveled turban who lived in Jaipur, told me that Roop was "very religious" but admitted that "no one could have imagined this." Amazingly, he had not found out about his daughter's death until he read about it in a newspaper the day after it happened. Like his wife, he seemed more stunned than anything else. "The sati lives," he assured me. "She is not dead, she is alive. Just as we bathe in water, she bathed in fire." I kept pressing him, and finally he cut me off. "Just as you know English and have your own traditions," he said, "we have our own traditions. The loss has made me sad, but there is grandeur associated with sati. My family's name will be famous all over."

Roop's father-in-law, a Hindi teacher at a secondary school, was more talkative, even though the police had arrested his younger son, Pushpendra Singh, on a charge of abetment to suicide for lighting the funeral pyre. The rumors were that Roop's father-in-law would be next. Steve and I sat down with him for almost an hour. What follows is his version—and Deorala's version—of what happened.

Roop Kanwar grew up as the youngest of six children in a working-class family that had recently settled in Jaipur, the modern capital of Rajasthan and once one of India's most glittering princely states. Gayatri Devi, the jet-setting former maharani, still lives there in a chintz-filled house on the grounds of her onetime home, the Rambagh Palace. Roop Kanwar had no contact with Jaipur's old nobility, but the city she lived in was hardly a backwater. Her father, who ran a trucking company, had seen to it that his daughter had finished ten years of school before her marriage was arranged. Roop Kanwar did not appear, at least from her pictures, to be a traditional Rajput girl. In her wedding photos, she did not veil her face and stare at the floor like a proper bride; instead, the camera caught the unashamed smile of an exceptionally pretty young woman with large, sensuous eyes. Newspaper reports, quoting villagers, described her painted nails and the colorful polyester salwar kameezes she wore—all marks of a modern girl. Roop's family insisted, however, that she was devoutly religious. One village woman claimed that she prayed for four hours a day. For part of her life, Roop had lived in the eastern state of Bihar, next door to a temple honoring Sati, the goddess who had committed suicide. She continued to worship Sati when she came to Rajasthan. She read the Hindu religious epics every day and fasted on Tuesdays, also in accordance with Hindu traditions.

In January 1987, an auspicious time when the streets of Jaipur were already bursting with hundreds of wedding processions, Roop Kanwar married Maal Singh, a fellow Rajput and high school graduate who was then looking for a clerical job. She had met him only once before. In his wedding pictures, he looks worried and ill at ease with the celebrations around him. But the couple settled into an apparently peaceful marriage, at the home of the groom's parents in Deorala, about a two-hour drive from Jaipur. By Indian standards it was a prosperous, developed village. *Manushi,* India's leading feminist magazine, reported that in most families a husband, brother or son worked in the towns nearby, usually in government offices. About 70 percent of the village was literate. Almost all of the houses, like that of Roop Kanwar's in-laws, were made of brick and cement. There was electricity and tap water. Many families owned television sets and motorcycles.

Seven months after her marriage, Roop Kanwar had just returned to Deorala after a visit with her family in Jaipur when her husband became ill. The next day, after a night of vomiting and stomach pains, the family took Maal Singh to a hospital in a nearby town, where he seemed to improve. Roop Kanwar and her mother-in-law returned from the hospital to Deorala that night, but at eight the next morning, September 4, 1987, Maal Singh suddenly died, apparently of a burst appendix. The doctor did not tell the family the cause of death, and the family said they did not ask. The body was brought back by jeep to Deorala at ten in the morning and was placed before Roop Kanwar.

At this point, Roop's father-in-law claimed, he fell unconscious, conveniently remaining that way until the sati was over. (Numerous villagers, however, said they saw him at the burning pyre.) Roop, who was praying, announced to the family that her soul should be united with her husband's and that she planned to commit sati. When people in the family tried to dissuade her, she replied that a curse would befall anyone who tried to stop her. As the word of her decision spread through the village, holy men came to see her to make sure the true sati spirit was within her. Once they determined that it was, her in-laws gave their blessings. She changed into her wedding dress, led the funeral procession through the streets of the village, circumambulated the pyre for fifteen minutes, then climbed onto it. Her husband's head was laid in her lap. Maal Singh's fifteen-year-old brother lit the pyre, but it didn't catch; at this point, according to an anonymous eyewitness quoted by the newsmagazine *India Today,* Roop Kanwar fell off the pyre with her feet scorched and had to be helped back on. By this time nearly every Rajput household in the village had brought pails of ghee, or clarified butter, which they threw onto the wood until it burst into flames. *India Today* described the crowd, which various accounts estimated at five thousand, as "cheering," "applauding" and "frenzied."

At the time, as unthinkable as it seems now, Steve and I did not completely discount this version of events. We felt this way partly because we had spent an entire day talking to villagers who assured us, one after another, that Roop Kanwar had been willing to die. An entire village seemed to have its story straight. We also could not imagine that anyone was capable of an act of such enormous cruelty as pushing a young girl onto a funeral pyre. Our theory was that Roop Kanwar, an impressionable young girl, had been so shocked by her husband's sudden death that in the confusion and delirium of the moment she had succumbed to the pressures of others to observe a tradition that had been instilled in her since birth.

This view was enforced for us that evening back in Jaipur, when we met Sushil Kumari, an elegant fifty-four-year-old Rajput woman, a relative of one of Rajasthan's royal families, who had come to the city that day to join the women's organizations in a demonstration against the sati. Protesting in the open was a giant step for her. She had only recently begun to leave her house after thirty-two years of purdah, and the demonstration would be the first time she had publicly denounced such a central part of her heritage. Ever since childhood, she had been told there was no higher achievement for a woman than sati. "It is very, very ingrained in the Rajput psyche," she said, sitting before dinner in a dimly lit living room in one of the big houses on the Civil Lines road. "It is glamorized, it is eulogized. It is drilled into us, whether we are educated or not, that the husband is a god figure. It is the ultimate achievement for a girl. We heard about it all the time. In fact, in 1955, a few months before I got married, a cousin became a sati. We were always told that no matter what your husband was like, you should never, ever think of leaving him." Only 150 years earlier, in her in-laws' family, one or two of the six wives of every husband routinely committed sati. Many of the women left their handprints along the walls of the house before leaving for the pyre, and these could still be seen. Committing sati, Sushil Kumari said, guaranteed that a woman, her husband and seven generations of the family after her had a "direct passport" to heaven and would be released from the painful cycle of birth and rebirth.

Sushil Kumari seemed to us a traditional but sophisticated woman. After all, when her father had refused to let her go to college, she had gone on a one-week hunger strike and had won the right for herself. Yet I had learned in India how deceiving a cosmopolitan exterior could be. So I asked her if there was a part of her that still felt sati was an honorable thing. To my surprise, she came at my question from the opposite direction; it turned out that she was in fact ambivalent about her public protest. "I will be very frank and say that a part of me, when I heard about the sati, felt very, very sad," she said. "I will be very frank and say: I don't believe in it. But it is a very hard thing for me to say."

Afterward, at a dinner with some friends, we met an American woman visiting India who scolded us for taking such an isolated, unrepresentative event as a sati and sensationalizing it for American readers. Why didn't we write about the good things in India, she asked, such as all the marvelous textile exports? I was irritated, but not as much as I might have been. In this case I was afraid she might have a point. Maybe we were making too much of a weird little incident.

The events of the next day erased my doubts. Roop Kanwar's death may have been an aberration, but the mob of two hundred thousand that swarmed into Deorala the next morning for the chunri ceremony was a shocking statement on the status of women in rural India. The chunri ceremony had been scheduled for noon, but the villagers, fearing interference from the police, held it at seven in the morning. By the time Steve and I arrived, the crowd seemed right on the edge of hysteria and was hostile to outsiders like us. Tens of thousands were still straining to see Roop Kanwar's silver-and-scarlet shawl draped over the ashes. I tried to fight my way through the crowd to get closer to the immolation site but was stopped by overwrought teenage boys belonging to the Rajput youth groups.

The day before, the Rajasthan state authorities had banned any attempt to "glorify" the immolation, a vague ruling that was not enforced. I saw no police at the immolation site on the day of the chunri ceremony, although police did stop buses several miles away from going into Deorala. This had the effect of easing traffic and probably ensured that more people, not less, got to see the final rites. By the time of the ceremony, a half million people had already visited Deorala, and donated twenty-five thousand dollars to a newly formed sati committee for the temple construction. *India Today* reported that among those who came to receive the sati mother's blessings were a joint secretary of the Rajasthan state committee of the ruling Congress party, an opposition party leader and two opposition members of the state assembly.

In the weeks that followed, the odd little event came to be seen among India's urban and educated elite as a national disgrace. It plunged the country into months of debate over the condition of women, the failures of education and the rise of religious fundamentalism. The story of what "really" happened to Roop Kanwar changed every day. Numerous English-language newspapers, citing anonymous "eyewitnesses," began reporting that Roop Kanwar had been coerced. *The Sunday Observer* in Bombay quoted an unnamed farmer who said that Roop Kanwar had tried three times to get off the pyre but was pushed back on by the crowd. *The Telegraph* in Calcutta quoted "some Deorala women" who "hesitantly and reticently" admitted that Roop had tried to escape by hiding at the Deorala home of her aunt. The Women and Media Committee of the Bombay Union of Journalists sent a fact-finding team to the village and then published a report citing an unnamed Congress party worker who said Roop Kanwar had to be dragged out of a barn and forcibly placed on the pyre. When she screamed and tried to escape, the report said, she was surrounded by Rajput youths with swords. *The Hindustan Times,* under the front-page headline IT WAS "NOT" VOLUNTARY, quoted village "sources" who said the husband, Maal Singh, was under treatment for impotency, shock and depression at the time he was married to Roop Kanwar, and that since her marriage she had spent less than three weeks at her husband's house. She lived there for ten days after the marriage, the sources said, and then returned to Jaipur, where she became involved with another man. Based on such a piece of evidence, *The Hindustan Times* concluded: "The sources said this truly knocked the bottom out of the theory of her voluntary 'sati' since there was clearly no great attachment between the young girl and her husband."

The Indian Express seemed to speak for most of the English-language newspapers when it attacked the immolation in an editorial as "barbarous and primitive," but at least one newspaper in the more widely circulated and traditional vernacular press defended the sati and redefined the debate as a class war of the irreligious minority against the religious majority. *Jansatta,* a leading Hindi-language daily, berated Westernized, secular India, which it presumed did not believe in reincarnation, in an editorial that stated that "the people who consider this life to be a beginning and an end in itself will never understand the custom of sati." Sati ought to be reconsidered, the editorial said, "but the people who do not know or understand the customs and convictions of the common people of India have no right to do it." The editorial concluded that "Roop Kanwar did not commit sati under threat from anyone. She had such a terrible disappointment in her own life that she had no alternative but to be burned with her husband . . . and if this self-denial of hers should become a center of reverence and worship, it is but natural." The next day, the editor of *Jansatta* was besieged in his office by fifty outraged feminists.

Under increasing pressure, the police finally arrested Roop Kanwar's father-in-law and five other members of his family soon after the chunri ceremony. But the charge was abetment to suicide, not murder. The police also began rounding up other villagers from Deorala on the new charge of "glorification" of sati. But it was not until September 27, eleven days after the chunri ceremony and more than three weeks after the immolation, that the prime minister himself publicly reacted. In a letter to Rajasthan's chief minister that was released to the press, Rajiv Gandhi termed the immolation "utterly reprehensible and barbaric," adding that "all right-thinking people should speak out against this and those who are glorifying the murder of a young woman." When I asked the prime minister a year later why he had taken so long to react, he put the blame on Rajasthan's chief minister, Harideo Joshi. "I had talked to the chief minister a day after it happened," he said. "I told him he must take some strong measures, and I didn't want to interfere in what's really a state government area. When we found out that he was not doing something, then I thought we just had to step in." But it was hard to see why a condemnation of the immolation could not have been more swiftly issued from the prime minister's office even if the chief minister had handled the situation well.

Whatever the case, Harideo Joshi's difficulties in managing the aftershocks of the burning led in part to his ouster by the central government four months later. Steve and I had gone to see Joshi the evening before the chunri ceremony, when he seemed at a loss to handle the crisis he had on his hands. He was under enormous pressure, from women's groups, the press and especially New Delhi, to stop people from attending the chunri ceremony, but he seemed confused about whether the government could ban people from assembling for a religious purpose. The Rajputs claimed that the chunri celebration was a religious rite and a vital part of their traditions. Rajputs, as it happened, were a crucial part of Joshi's constituency. "I had advised them they should not permit people to go there," Joshi said. "But the difficulty is that they take it as a religion, not backwardness."

This also became a significant point of debate. Writing in an issue of the journal *Seminar* that was devoted entirely to sati, the historian Romila Thapar suggested that religious traditions such as those the Rajputs were claiming "often arise out of contemporary needs but seek legitimation from the past." The editors of the feminist magazine *Manushi* came to the same conclusion. In a revealing article that examined the influence of the Rajputs in the chunri ceremony and the pro-sati campaign that had simultaneously sprung up in Jaipur, Madhu Kishwar and Ruth Vanita reported that the leaders of the pro-sati cult were urban, educated men in their twenties and thirties, newly prosperous, with property and family connections. The secretary of a new pro-sati group in Jaipur, for example, ran a thriving leather export business; his wife was the graduate of one of Delhi's most elite colleges. Kishwar and Vanita found that the phrases shouted at the sati site by Rajput schoolboys were modeled on election slogans rather than religious chants and that the song sung at the daily evening worship there was similar to a popular Hindi film tune—which was not of Rajasthani origin, and had nothing to do with sati. Kishwar and Vanita concluded that "the sati cult in its present-day form is primarily the product of a phony religiosity that is the accompaniment of newfound prosperity, harnessed by political leaders for their own vested interests." The Rajputs appeared to be using the sati issue to shore up their sagging political power. (The Rajputs had once been the dominant caste in Rajasthan, but outsiders had moved in and were now running the state government.) As Romila Thapar asserted in *Seminar:* "The Rajputs therefore seek to demonstrate their solidarity and status through other kinds of actions. One mechanism is to choose a ritual which is controversial and insist on supporting it."

Three months after Roop Kanwar's death, the Indian Parliament passed a tougher law banning sati, which some feminists argued was not really needed; an adequate law existed, and both murder and suicide were already illegal. But the government had to do something. The fact remained that in the India of 1987, hundreds, if not thousands, of people had stood and watched a young woman die. Why did not one person try to help? Roop Kanwar's in-laws claimed that they tried to dissuade her. How was it not possible for several of the grown men in the family to physically keep an eighteen-year-old woman away from a funeral pyre?

As in the case of Surinder Kaur, I will always wonder what really happened. But if I were forced to decide, I would theorize that Roop Kanwar was pushed. Certainly she was worth much more to Deorala dead than alive. Again, my decision is based on instinct, not evidence. All I know for certain is that I thought one thing in the beginning, as I did with Surinder Kaur, but came to a quite different conjecture in the end. India seemed to have a way of making me do that.

The larger tragedy for both women, of course, was their profound powerlessness to control any aspect of their lives. So many words were spent debating whether or not Roop Kanwar died voluntarily, and yet in an important way they were meaningless words. What freedom did an Indian woman have to decide anything in her life?

As *Manushi* asked: "If a woman does not have the right to decide whether she wants to marry, and when, and whom, how far she wants to study, whether she wants to take a particular job or not, how is it that she suddenly gets the right to take such a major decision as whether she wants to die?"

CHAPTER 4

BEYOND THE VEIL

The Women of the Village
of Khajuron

THE VILLAGE OF KHAJURON LIES DEEP IN A POCKET OF THE FERTILE GANGES
River plain, part of the "Hindi heartland" of northern India where
some ways of life have not changed in thousands of years. Most of
Khajuron's farming families still live in mud huts, segregated, like their
ancestors, into neighborhoods by caste. They draw their water from
wells, cook their meals over fires made from cow-dung cakes and go
to the village sorcerer for magic spells when their cattle fall ill.

Over the course of a year, I lived in Khajuron during a half dozen
visits, and sometimes at sunset, when I walked through the smoky,
hazy light along the dirt road leading out of the village, I saw men
crossing the fields, carrying their wooden plows home on their shoulders. I felt as if I had been dropped into a distant century. On one
religious holiday, I watched as the head of a family, my host, put
turmeric paste on a goat's forehead and a hibiscus blossom on its head.
He then slit a bit of the goat's ear and threw the blood into a sacred
fire as an offering. In the evenings, jackals howled in the surrounding

fields. Later at night they stopped, but then I was kept awake by the snorts of the water buffalo tethered near my bed.

Khajuron is the village where I stayed with Bhabhiji, an upper-caste farmer's wife who lived in purdah. My purpose in Khajuron, which should not be confused with Khajuraho, the site of the erotic temple sculptures in central India, was to interview women of all castes in one village over the period of one year so that I could write about how they managed their lives. But I also wanted simply to live in Khajuron, to sleep, eat and work there, so that I could experience, to the extent that a foreigner could, a little bit of how most Indians live. Three fourths of the world's population live in villages; one seventh of the world's population live in the 560,000 villages in India. Khajuron lies almost in the dead center of the enormous Indian state of Uttar Pradesh, which has a population of more than 120 million. As a separate entity, U.P., as the Indians call it, would rank as the eighth largest country in the world. The ways of the 1,000 people of Khajuron are the ways of most of humanity.

One of the most important events that I saw that year, an event that in its own way revealed the true condition of the women of Khajuron, was the election of the village chief, who is called a pradhan. The campaign was in its final days when the summer monsoon arrived, forcing the six candidates on the last weekend before the Tuesday election to canvass through rain and the powerful kind of mud that sucked sandals off your feet and squished up cold and clammy between your toes. The battleground areas of the campaign were the outlying village hamlets, clusters of mud huts poking up from the flat fields, and the voters who lived in them had been subjected to the noisy candidates' processions all weekend. On Sunday at seven in the morning, Arvind Kumar Awasthi, a thirty-four-year-old Brahmin, was the first candidate through the hamlet of Ranjit Khera, leading his band of supporters in a chant of "Vote for the chair!" A few hours later, the dirt footpaths of Ranjit Khera were filled once again, this time with the supporters of Rameshwar Prasad, a sixty-year-old leader of Khajuron's Harijan community, who shouted "Vote for the tractor!" The tractor was his campaign symbol, and the chair was Awasthi's. The incumbent was represented by a camel. The symbols, which had been assigned to the candidates by the local election authorities, appeared on the ballot and enabled illiterate people to vote.

The night before, I sat under the neem tree outside Bhabhiji's house and talked to the village elders about campaign developments. A few of the candidates had turned up to lobby for support and be interviewed by the press, which was me. I asked them about their qualifications, their platform and the issues, such as they were. Arvind Kumar Awasthi, the Brahmin candidate, said he was running against the incumbent, a middle-caste farmer named Shri Ram Choudhary, "because he harbors feelings of hatred toward Brahmins." He complained that when electricity was brought to the village, "persons of influence" had determined the site of the poles carrying the wires, and thus the Brahmin section of the village had no light. Shri Ram Choudhary, the incumbent, chose to ignore such allegations and merely said he was running on his record, which he considered impressive. "Whatever I have done in the past," he said, "I will do again." Rameshwar Prasad, the Harijan leader, told me the next day that he was running as a champion of the oppressed. "Always there is a fight between the rich people and the poor people in this village," he said. "I am the symbol of the poor people."

At the end of each interview, I tried asking each candidate a question he had never before heard in his political career: "What are you going to do for the women of the village?" This was clearly a misguided inquiry, and most of the candidates dismissed it. "The women of this village are not educated," said Choudhary, the incumbent. "Therefore whatever you tell them goes in one ear and out the other." As he answered, Choudhary pointed to his ears with great exasperation. His audience laughed appreciatively. Two to three years ago, Choudhary continued, adult education was offered for the women, and yet they weren't interested. "They were ashamed that they were so old and they couldn't read," he said.

PARTLY, I HAD BEEN MOTIVATED TO LIVE IN AN INDIAN VILLAGE BY reading the accounts of a few other Western women who had done the same thing. Sarah Lloyd, a British landscape architect, had lived in villages in Punjab and written *An Indian Attachment* about her experiences there. It was a curious book, derided by Delhi's intellectuals, who found her account of her relationship with an uneducated opium-addicted Sikh both bizarre and condescending; I thought the story of "Jungli," the Sikh, was weird, too, but was impressed with Lloyd's unsentimental descriptions of village families in Punjab. "There was a superficial contentedness about the restful rhythms of their daily tasks and the constant chattering between neighbors which belied the bitterness and resignation often smouldering underneath," she wrote. "And somehow the conversation within families—and not just Jungli's family—seemed to lack the real friendship and understanding that is not uncommon in the supposedly arid family life in the West. Not once did I witness positive abandoned joy: it was as if there were wires straining at their hearts." Another English woman, Sarah Hobson, had written *Family Web,* a compelling account of the life of one Indian family in the southern state of Karnataka. Hobson, like Lloyd, discovered the tensions underneath the façade of simplicity.

But my real inspiration was Victor Zorza, an expert on Soviet politics and a former Washington columnist who had left his old life as a celebrated Kremlinologist to live in a remote Indian village high in the Himalayas. Zorza's five years there had been the basis for newspaper columns in *The Washington Post, The Guardian* and *The Times* (London). I interviewed Zorza in India in 1986 for a profile about him for the *Post,* and it was he who taught me the importance of living in a village rather than dropping by for the day. Villagers may be uneducated but they are extremely clever, he said, and very good at telling an outsider what they think she wants to hear. The truth about a village, Zorza believed, could come out only slowly, with time—time for trust to build between the villagers and the outsider, and time for the outsider to peel away all the layers to get at the truth. "Some of the things I'm writing now are the very opposite of what I used to say before," Zorza told me. "The people who in the past I regarded as good I've found are baddies, and vice versa." Zorza, who had undertaken his columns as a mission to explain the despair of the world's have-nots to the haves, was determined to involve his readers on an emotional level, to prove that the illiterate poor are rich when it comes to the complexities of emotion.

That said, I did not have five years. But I was able to spend as much as six days at a time in Khajuron, and during the course of a year I lived there for a total of three weeks. I was there for the blistering heat of May, the cold days at the end of December, the spring harvest festival and the July election for headman. When it was hot, I slept outside under mosquito netting on a charpoy, or string cot. When it was cold, I slept inside a brick-and-mud shed. I brought in my own water but ate Bhabhiji's chicken curries and rice sitting on a mat on the mud floor; not once did I have the stomach problems I frequently suffered after eating at restaurants and hotels. I took baths in a dark little room off the central courtyard, dipping a small urn into a cold bucket of well water and pouring it over myself. In the winter, the air inside the little room was so chilly I could see my breath. In the summer, it was so humid that the bath made no difference. I used the family latrine, a mud hut with a straw roof over a hole in the ground, built a few hundred feet away from the main house. At night, bats flew around in the hole or flapped overhead. And yet Bhabhiji and her husband were fortunate. Most families had no room for a latrine and had to make a long trip into the fields.

I spent my working hours in long interviews, sometimes two hours at a time, with what eventually amounted to twenty-five women from the highest to the lowest castes. By the end of the year, I came to two unqualified conclusions: First, both men and women struggled in the village, but the women, because of their gender, struggled and suffered twice as much as the men. Second, the women of Khajuron had one of two lots in life, defined entirely by caste. If a woman belonged to one of the upper or middle castes, she was virtually a hostage, confined within the walls of her home to isolation and demanding housework, which her husband did not consider work. Many men said their wives did "nothing" all day, even though most women never stopped working at physically exhausting household chores. If a woman belonged to the lower castes, she was free to leave her house, usually to work at seasonal labor in the fields for less than fifty cents a day. She was of course expected to handle all the housework and child care as well. It may be too strident to say that a woman in Khajuron was either a prisoner or a slave, but whatever one wants to call her, she could never hope to escape from her fate nor determine it herself.

Susheela Bajpai was one of the first women I met. She was the wife of a Brahmin landowner, plump from prosperity, with a round, soft face that had been spared the effects of the sun and worries about feeding her two children. She left her house only about once a month, usually for shopping or to see friends in Lucknow. She covered her face with her sari until she was beyond the limits of Khajuron and the neighboring village down the road. Only outside this limit was she freed by her anonymity. The rest of the time, Susheela stayed inside, confined to several small rooms and a central courtyard. Admittedly, it was one of the best houses in Khajuron, with a courtyard made of brick instead of the usual mud and a television set that kept her caught up with the programs from Delhi. On Sunday mornings, she and her husband invited in about thirty people, all from the upper castes, to watch the exploits of Ram and the anguish of Sita in the *Ramayana,* a popular television series based on the great Hindu epic. The first time I went to see Susheela, she gave me tea and cookies under her ceiling fan and assured me she was happy with her life. "I don't want to go out any more than I do," she said. Her husband, who had insisted on listening, then spoke up. "I am a social person," he said. "I am a man. She is a woman. So she cannot go anywhere. This is my rule."

At the other extreme was Sudevi, a fifty-year-old widow from one of the lowest castes. She worked in the fields whenever one of the big landowners would hire her and on other days received a few rupees from the rich families for pulling water out of their wells. She never made more than fifty cents a day and was lucky if she could find work fifteen days a month. Her husband had died fifteen years earlier from tuberculosis, leaving her nothing. Many days she was forced to beg at the big landowners' houses. When I first went to see her, in her mud hut with a caved-in wall, she was embarrassed that she was wearing no blouse underneath her rough cotton sari. She had only one, and she had just washed it; I could see it hanging to dry in the sun. She was bony and leather-skinned and told me she was living on flat bread and salt. She owned no land and said that as a widow she was sometimes called bad names. Her twenty-three-year-old son was living with her, but he had no work either, and his wife was eight months pregnant. "My boy doesn't have enough food," said Sudevi. "When I feel hungry, I drink water."

Between these two extremes was Asha Devi, the twenty-year-old wife of a son in a prosperous middle-caste farming family. She neither enjoyed the status of Susheela Bajpai, the Brahmin landowner's wife, nor suffered the widow's miseries of Sudevi. Yet in some ways, her life combined the worst of both worlds. She had married into a hardworking family that was on its way up, and its members kept her in purdah to further enhance their position in the community. Keeping women off the land had always been a mark of distinction; in Khajuron, as soon as a family could afford it, the women were brought indoors. Predictably, it was often these striving middle-caste families, the ones with the most to lose and the most to gain in their precarious new positions within the village hierarchy, who secluded their women the most rigidly. Asha Devi led an even more cloistered life than Susheela Bajpai, and with none of Susheela's relative luxuries as compensation. Asha Devi left the house only two or three times a year, to see her mother. The rest of the time she lived as a virtual servant in her in-laws' home. At the age of sixteen, she had been married to a man she had never seen before, and since then she had been cooking and cleaning for his parents, his three older brothers and their wives. She was up at six, in bed at midnight, and ate only after everyone else in the family had finished. I spoke to her on the top floor of the house but during the entire conversation never even saw her face; she had pulled her sari completely over her head, as a sign of deference, and probably of terror. I asked her what would happen if she walked out into the village. "My mother- and father-in-law would scold me," she said, "and my husband would also scold me." I turned to her mother-in-law, who was listening to every word, and asked the same question.

"If she went out," decreed the mother-in-law, "we would not get respect."

———————————•◦•——————————

I FOUND KHAJURON BY MAKING CAREFUL PLANS THAT DISINTEGRATED, AS they always did in India, into fate and serendipity. Since our first year in Delhi, Steve and I had been thinking about living and working in a village together. I wanted to use the material for this book, and he wanted to write a series of articles for *The New York Times* about life in one village in India. We talked about it on and off, finally deciding that no village in India was big enough for the two of us. We had covered the same story a few times in India in the past, and predictably *The New York Times* and *The Washington Post* had squabbled over turf and quotes. This time I wouldn't be writing for the *Post,* but nonetheless I wasn't in the mood to turn up at the door of a woman's mud hut and discover that the most interesting event of her week was that the *New York Times* reporter had been there the day before. And yet I did not want to go alone. Finally, Steve and I decided that a pair of villages within walking distance of each other might work.

We then settled on Lucknow, the capital of Uttar Pradesh, as a base. Lucknow had once been the center of a brilliant and then decadent Moghul court, but more important for us, it was in the heart of a vital northern farming belt and only a fifty-minute flight from Delhi. The people there spoke a Hindi that was similar to what we were learning in Delhi. We surmised, incorrectly, as it turned out, that therefore the Hindi spoken in the villages around Lucknow would be like our own.

One morning in May I landed in Lucknow as a one-woman advance team in search of two villages. My only contact there was a friend of a friend, who directed me to Lucknow University, where I was eventually sent to the office of Dr. Surendra Singh, a professor in the school of social work, who had done extensive research in the state's rural areas. (Readers may at this point be wondering why so many people in India are named Singh. *Singh* means "lion," and it is helpful to remember that all Sikhs use the name Singh, but not all Singhs are Sikhs. Dr. Surendra Singh was a Kshatriya, a member of the Hindu warrior caste, which had traditionally owned large tracts of land in Uttar Pradesh and frequently used Singh as a last name. In Rajasthan, many Rajputs also used Singh as a last name.)

I found Dr. Singh behind a large desk, surrounded on three sides by the usual gaggle of tea-drinking colleagues, students and hangers-on. I told him what I wanted: two predominantly Hindu villages, with a range of castes, each with a population of about one thousand, both of them a one-to-two-hour drive from Lucknow and a short walk apart. Dr. Singh, a round but compact man in his mid-forties with a cherubic face, thin mustache and courtly manner, was amused. Even then, I was aware that I was rattling off my specifications as if he were a short-order cook, but Dr. Singh made some notes and said he would consult the census. The next day he presented me with a list of a half dozen villages that met my requirements, but before I had a chance to be elated, Dr. Singh politely informed me that working in any of them would be nearly impossible.

"You are not known in these places," he said. "No one will trust you or tell you the truth. It would be better to live in my brother's village, where I could properly introduce you." Dr. Singh's elder brother, Sheo Singh, the husband of Bhabhiji, had stayed back in the village, to manage what remained of the family land. Dr. Singh had left years before. It was the story of independent India, an illustration of how land reform had shrunk the once-large holdings of feudal landlords in rural India and compelled their sons to seek education and make their living in the burgeoning cities. Dr. Singh's story was also proof of the close ties to the land retained by the first generation of urban Indians, and why so many had kept to the ways of the village— arranged marriages, for example. Dr. Singh had distinguished himself from the millions of others by the remarkable success he had made of his life. Educated in village schools, he had gone on to Lucknow University, where he now was in line to become head of his department.

Dr. Singh's village turned out to be Khajuron, of course, an hour's drive from Lucknow. A twenty-minute walk from Khajuron was Gurha, a larger village, where Steve could work. I went with Dr.

Singh's wife, Reena, and his eldest daughter, Anu, to take a look at both the next day. As we headed south from Lucknow on one of the major arteries of central U.P., a two-lane paved road that led across fertile plains of wheat and under shady groves of enormous gnarled mango trees, Anu, a nineteen-year-old college student, quizzed me about America. She had been up all night studying for an English exam on Shakespeare, Browning and Auden, which she had taken early that morning. (One of the questions was "How much was Lady Macbeth responsible for her husband's death?") But now Anu wanted to know if we had a caste system in the United States and whether everyone was rich. Her state was one of the poorest in India, but the soil in that particular area was fed by canals, the land was benevolent, and the poverty not too wretched. We passed people on motor scooters, bicycles and horsecarts. Most of them seemed to have things to do and places to go.

· At the town of Bachharawan, chiefly distinguished by dust and a chaotic roadside bazaar where bananas and tin pails were for sale, we turned east, onto a smaller paved highway, and came to the edge of Gurha. From there we turned right onto a bumpy dirt road that crossed marshy land and more fields. This road was only a mile long, and toward the end I could see Khajuron rising up as a little mound, surrounded on all sides by the plains. Within minutes we reached the outskirts—mud huts with thatched roofs, barefoot children, women breast-feeding babies on string cots, cows tethered near piles of long grasses. The car lumbered its way through, climbed up a small hill and came to a stop under the neem tree in Bhabhiji's front yard. To the right was the low-lying brick-and-mud shed where Steve and I would later sleep; in front of me was the main house, a large, weathered two-story brick structure with an open central courtyard and enormous double doors of heavy, rough wood that you opened and closed by pulling on brass rings. To me, the house looked like that of a prosperous farmer from Saxon times in England. I later learned that it was 150 years old and had changed little from the day it was built.

Bhabhiji and Dr. Singh's brother came out of the house to greet us, Bhabhiji smiling shyly, Sheo Singh talking nonstop. He was, in fact, the exact opposite of his brother—a tall, large, loud, boisterous man with a white mustache and skin darkened by the sun, who liked to smoke a hookah. Bhabhiji, slender and barefoot, was wearing a simple cotton print sari, red glass bangles, a nose stud and toe rings. She had gray hair, lovely dark eyes, workworn hands and a kind, comforting face. She gave us tea, and then Anu took me on a tour of Khajuron.

By this time I had been in enough villages in India to know that they are generally not quaint places brimming with interesting mud architecture and picturesque women in colorful saris. Most are depressing little collections of uncharming shacks, plagued by dust, heat, flies, open sewage and disease. Khajuron had all of that, too, but the upper- and middle-caste parts had meandering lanes, old brick houses with carved wooden doors, and pretty views looking out toward the green fields of young wheat. By Indian standards, Khajuron was poor but not desperate. It lay in the political district that had been represented for years by the Nehru dynasty, including Indira Gandhi when she was prime minister. Unlike other villages, Khajuron did not suffer from lack of water. In fact, the village had such access to irrigation canals that its surrounding fields suffered from the opposite problem: a poor drainage system, flooding and excessive salt deposits caused by water-logging. There were hand pumps, and one tube well which pumped water from below the ground. Electricity had come five years earlier, and three of the 250 families now had television sets. Three farmers had tractors, and two had licenses to grow poppies for opium, which they sold at enormous profit to the government for medicine. People assumed they made even larger profits on the black market. On the edge of the fields there was a tall, narrow temple to the god Shiva, and a two-room brick schoolhouse stood nearby. On the Gurha side of the village lay a large pond, covered during parts of the year with white flowers. The bathing pool where I walked in the evenings had been built of brick by a Brahmin landowner more than a century before, but its two pavilions still stood and were reflected in the cool water below. I don't want to romanticize, but in truth, especially during the few temperate months of the year, Khajuron, for me, was a pleasant place to live.

The physical plan of the village was an indication of the complex social structure that lay underneath. The most powerful landlord, a mild-mannered college-educated Kshatriya farmer named Shardul Singh, lived in a large brick house on the highest spot in the village; around him were clustered tiny communities of houses belonging to the different castes and subcastes. There are four main castes in India, the highest being the Brahmins, who were traditionally teachers and priests. Next are the Kshatriyas, the warriors. Below them are the Vaisyas, who were traders and merchants, and after them come the Sudras, the farmers. The Harijans have no caste at all—hence they are

considered outcastes. For thousands of years they were called Untouch-
ables, but during the independence struggle Mahatma Gandhi gave
them the name Harijans—"Children of God"—which paved the way
for reform, including affirmative action quotas for Harijans and other
low castes in jobs and education. Harijans, however, are still among
the most impoverished and degraded people in India.

Within each caste are hundreds of subcastes, which change from
region to region, and, like the main castes, were originally connected
with specific professions. The Indian Constitution did not abolish caste,
but it did outlaw discrimination on the basis of caste. In the cities, caste
is to some extent disappearing, and people generally do not have to
make their livings according to the accident of birth. But in the
villages, caste was as insidious as ever and in large part predetermined
the course of a person's life. The education of the younger generation
was only slowly changing things.

The subcaste of mustard-oil makers in Khajuron, for example, lived
together in their own little grouping of mud huts and still, for the most
part, made oil from mustard seeds. The clay-pot makers still made clay
pots and lived in a little community near one of the village hand
pumps. The Kurmis, or large farmers, lived in relatively sizable houses
not far from Shardul Singh's gates; most of them still worked the land
for a living, although some of their sons had found jobs in Lucknow.
The Pasis, who traditionally had been pig tenders, were farmers, too,
although with smaller holdings. They were one group whose occupation had changed, yet their former calling would forever classify them
as Harijans. This had not prevented them, however, from creating
castes within their outcaste. Those Pasis who had been born in Khajuron—the old families—lived in the heart of the Harijan section, called
Pasitolla; those who had arrived only in the last few decades lived on
the outskirts of the village, closer to the dirt road. The two Pasi groups
did not mix much and even supported different candidates in the
election for village pradhan.

Steve and I arrived in Khajuron to begin our work in September
1987, four months after I first met Dr. Singh. (A year later, even after
sharing a shed with him, and putting our charpoys side by side under
the stars, we never called him anything but Dr. Singh. We were always
"Mrs. Elisabeth" and "Mr. Steve.") Dr. Singh and three of his daughters stayed with us at the home of his brother, who turned out to be
the second-largest landowner in the village. Without our ever request-
ing it, the entire Singh family had become involved in our project.

There were, I think, several reasons for this. Most of all, Dr. Singh wanted to make absolutely certain that his American guests were comfortable and stayed out of trouble. But I also think our research interested him and gave him a fresh glimpse of his roots.

Unfortunately, staying with the Singhs aligned us with the upper-caste landlords in the eyes of the rest of the villagers, and in the beginning I had trouble talking with some of the Harijan women because of our living arrangements. Rameshwar Prasad, the Harijan leader and, I later learned, a blood enemy of the landlords, actually went so far as to report Steve and me to the local police as possible American spies. It is difficult to know what the CIA might have learned in Khajuron, and, needless to say, nothing ever came of Prasad's harassment. Yet I fretted about our decision to live with the village landlords, even though I never figured out an alternative. Living with the Harijans would simply have aligned me with them, against the landlords, whose good graces I needed to remain in the village. Beyond that, it was unrealistic to think of living with anyone but a family that had space for us and could afford to feed us. Eventually it worked out. In the end, I was able to talk with plenty of Harijan women, I made peace with Prasad, and Bhabhiji and her husband could not have been more generous hosts.

Their house was one of the largest in Khajuron, built so that all family activity occurred in the central courtyard open to the sky. Once a week, the mud floor was smoothed with fresh greenish-brown cow dung, believed to be a disinfectant. In the hot weather, Bhabhiji and her husband slept on their charpoys in the courtyard; in the cold weather, they slept in one of the enclosed storage rooms off this courtyard, which contained five-foot-tall mud urns that held wheat and rice. Bhabhiji's mud stove, or chulha, was built into the floor of the courtyard in a protected corner. There was no electricity, and at night we ate by the light of an oil lamp.

In the mornings after breakfast (fried Indian bread and potatoes for Dr. Singh; omelettes and white bread for us, because that is the sort of breakfast Americans were supposed to eat), Steve would leave with Dr. Singh for Gurha. I would go with one, two or three of Dr. Singh's five daughters—different ones came along on each trip—to begin my interviews in Khajuron. My Hindi was passable for Bhabhiji's house, but the lower castes spoke a local dialect and could scarcely understand me. I had an easier time understanding them, but I still needed Dr. Singh's daughters to translate. I selected the women by caste, so that

I would have a representative sampling. I would arrive at a woman's house, tell her I was writing a book about women in India and ask if she would answer a few questions for me. The "few questions" claim was not exactly accurate, but I needed to get my foot in the door. The truth was that I had prepared a somewhat nightmarish list of 193 questions with my Hindi teacher in Delhi, covering work, education, living conditions, family relationships, health, education, religion, politics, popular culture and knowledge of the world outside Khajuron and India. Only rarely had I written out questions for interviews before, but then, I had never tried to interview so many uneducated women, in a foreign language, and in depth.

Every single interview was excruciatingly slow and difficult. Many lasted for two hours, the limit of my patience, and considerably beyond the limits of patience of many of the women. Although a few were amazed that someone was actually interested in their opinions, and appeared ready to talk all day, most were shy and nervous. Many times a woman had to breast-feed her baby and peel potatoes while she was talking to me. Sometimes her husband would try to speak for her, although I usually asked the husbands to leave. Other times friends would wander in and offer their opinions, or a swarm of kids would stand around giggling. They called me "the Ameriki poochnee wallee," which means "the American question-asking woman." The weather was usually suffocatingly hot, and flies buzzed incessantly around my head.

At times I lost heart and decided the questionnaire was a bad idea and was not getting me anywhere. I knew a lot of the answers were made up, and that the artificial situation I had constructed—an interview—was not the best way to learn the truth about rural women's lives. And yet it was a beginning, a way of getting to know them. The interviews allowed me to sit in their houses for hours. I watched them knead the chapati dough, saw how they massaged their babies with mustard oil and listened to them fight with their mothers-in-law. The women were poor, but this did not mean they all had inhibited personalities. When I asked the village pradhan's daughter-in-law, Santosh Kumari, if she had any say in her arranged marriage, she laughed and gestured toward the mud floor and crumbling brick walls of her home. "If they had asked me, I wouldn't have come to this house," she said. "I would have gone to a much better place." When I asked if her mother-in-law treated her well, she laughed again. "If my mother-in-law is bad," she said, "will you bring me a nice one?"

People I knew in rural development had advised me to be as specific as possible in my questions. I would get nowhere, they said, dealing in abstract concepts like fairness and equality. So I devised my questions as simple building blocks on basic themes. For example: "What is your education?" "Would you like to know how to read and write?" "Why did you not go to school?" "Do your children go to school?" "Who is it more important to educate—your son or your daughter?" Invariably, the sons were sent to school and the daughters stayed at home.

I also asked the women to tell me precisely how they had spent the day before, from the moment they got up to the time they went to bed. The minutiae always led me to the same conclusion: the women worked harder than the men. Phula, for example, was forty years old, a mother of four, the wife of a prosperous Pasi farmer who had lived in Khajuron all his life. He grew sugarcane, potatoes, rice, coriander and wheat. During the harvest, he employed up to fifteen people a day, and he made close to $1,000 each year. In the government census, a man like Phula's husband would be listed as the head of household, which he was, but a wife like Phula would be considered a nonworking dependent. And yet consider what she did all day: "Yesterday I got up at five in the morning," she told me as we sat in a dark, cramped room off her central courtyard. After rising, Phula walked half an hour into the fields, because the family had no latrine, then half an hour back. When she returned, she cleaned the pots used for the meal the night before. Soap was a luxury, so she used mud and water, scraping with her bare hands. She swept the floor of the house, squatting over a short-handled broom, then walked back to the fields to collect tall grasses for her cows to eat. This took several hours because she had to remove all the thorns. She fed the animals, then went into the house to make lunch for herself and her husband—the lentil stew called dal, and chapaties and rice. She rested during the heat of the afternoon, then got up to wash the pots before dinner. A dozen times during the day she had to fetch water from the well outside her house; she also had to make cow-dung cakes for fuel. And this was a leisurely time of year. In a few weeks, when the wheat was ready for harvesting, she would have to spend most of her time in the fields, managing her household chores in between. She felt her husband treated her well, although he was, after all, entitled to certain rights as the head of the family. "Sometimes he beats me if I make a mistake, or if I forget to give fodder to the animals," she said matter-of-factly. Phula had been married at seven and had begun living with her husband at fourteen. She had never learned to read and write because her parents had not sent her to school. "If I had been educated," she said, "I would have done some work." By "work" she meant paid work; she did not take into account the hard physical labor that she did all day.

Of the twenty-five women I interviewed, nineteen had never been to school. The other six had at least a grade-school education; three of them were Brahmins, and three were from prosperous middle-caste farming families. Almost all of the men had more education, however rudimentary, than the women, which meant they could at least read the local Hindi newspapers and participate in discussions about politics and other issues affecting their lives. It was almost always the men who went shopping, either by foot or bicycle, at the wooden stalls that lined the main road through Gurha, and so it was the men who dealt quite literally in the ideas of the marketplace. Even the lower-caste women who ignored purdah rarely went to the market. When I asked why, they usually said they did not want to go, either because it was too far, or because they did not like the way the men treated them. Whatever the reason, it further isolated the women from society, and from each other.

Almost every illiterate woman I spoke to said she would have liked an education, and when I took that a step further and asked each woman what she thought an education might have done for her, a large number firmly believed that schooling would have pulled them out of the village and saved them from a life of drudgery. "If I had been educated, I would be a big person and I would not be doing all of this," said Sada Vati, the forty-year-old wife of a middle-caste farmer. I asked her what a "big person's" job would be. "Service," she replied, which was the village description for work in government service in an office in a town or city, perhaps even Lucknow, typically as a low-level clerk behind a desk with a salary guaranteed for life. In the village, any work that did not involve hard physical labor was considered almost glamorous. "I want to sit on a chair and do work," said Rajban, a tailor and the mother of five. It was naïve, of course, for the women to think education would have guaranteed them a job. One of India's biggest problems was its millions of young men with high school and college educations who could not find work.

The one encouraging sign was that the women of Khajuron were beginning to send their daughters to school, however sporadically. There were ninety-three boys and eighty-eight girls registered at the village's two-room schoolhouse. "At first, girls were not educated," Cheta Lal, the headmaster, told me. "But now they are coming a little bit more." That was just grade school, however; 80 percent of the boys went on to the high school in Gurha, but only 20 percent of the girls did. And although almost every woman I spoke to said it was important to educate sons and daughters equally—I am sure they said this because they thought it was what I wanted to hear—the reality, when I pressed, was that the boys were sent to school more often than the girls. It was practical economics in a country with no social security system. When money was scarce in a family, it made more sense to educate the boy, who would remain with his parents and support them in their old age. A girl was a wasted investment because she would leave her parents after her marriage and live at her in-laws' house. As Sada Vati, the farmer's wife who wanted to do "service," explained about her son and daughter: "The boy will live here, but my girl will go." Sada Vati had complained about her lack of education, and yet she was not sending her seven-year-old daughter to school, just as her mother had not sent her.

One of the more serious problems of the women in the village was their lack of access to adequate medical care. Although there was a government-trained midwife assigned to the village, she lived in Gurha and was so overburdened with her work there and in one other village that she rarely got to Khajuron. Only a third of the women I interviewed used her, even though her services were free. Most of them went to a Dr. Kamlesh in Gurha, who charged more than one dollar— two days' wages for field work—per visit. On his wall he displayed a photograph of himself standing next to a cadaver in medical school. Those seriously ill had to go all the way to Bachharawan, or even Lucknow. Most women delivered their babies on the floors of their huts, and at least half had lost one or more children during childbirth or in the first few years of the baby's life. Three women I interviewed admitted they were trying to limit the size of their families, but two of them were doing it by only now and then taking birth control pills. The other woman, a Brahmin, had been given an IUD by a doctor in Bachharawan after the birth of her fifth child. The average number of living children per family appeared to be three or four, but Sheela, the thirty-year-old wife of the village silversmith, had eight. She was more than ready to stop, but her husband refused to allow her to have a government-funded sterilization operation. "There is no need," he insisted. Sheela, who was sitting on a nearby charpoy, just shrugged. "He is afraid it will make me weak," she said.

Not surprisingly, the women knew almost nothing about the village council, or panchayat, although they generally voted in elections, following their husbands' instructions. Seven claimed never to have heard of the panchayat. Of those who had, about half said it did some good. The rest complained. "There is no justice," said Rama Devi, a Harijan woman who served as one of the village midwives. "Only the rich people are given the facilities and we are not." Although the Uttar Pradesh state government had reserved places on every panchayat for women, the provision was widely ignored. As elsewhere, no woman served in Khajuron, and no women went to the meetings. But the women were clearly aware of where the real power lay in the village. When I asked who was the most powerful person in Khajuron, only one said it was Shri Ram Choudhary, the incumbent pradhan. Almost everyone else said it was Shardul Singh, the largest landlord. When I asked why, the answer was simple. "He has the most money and the most land," said Vidhya Devi, a thirty-five-year-old field laborer.

A number of women had never heard of Rajiv Gandhi, and of those who had, there was some confusion about who he was. Most identified him not as prime minister but as Indira Gandhi's son, and most were unable to say whether he was good or bad. Indira Gandhi, however, was widely viewed as good. "She helped the poor people," several women told me. Some clearly identified with her as a woman and said that being a woman helped her become a good leader.

At the end of each interview, I asked each woman what her biggest problem was. The answers included not having enough money, worries about marrying off a daughter, needing a better house and fears about a husband's illness. Many women complained that the water from the wells and hand pumps was brackish, which it was, and that they did not have enough land. Only one woman owned land in her own name. The rest did not even own it jointly with their husbands. The pradhan's daughter-in-law complained that she did not have enough nice saris. Susheela Bajpai, the Brahmin landowner's wife, wanted better schools for her children. Sudevi, the widow, said she did not have enough money. But by far the most obvious, pressing problem, more than education and medical care, was lack of paid work. The women had no way to earn a living, no skills, no training. At the most, they could find field work only six months of the year. Every single woman I interviewed wanted to be taught a skill, but there was no factory near Khajuron, and no accessible market for goods she might produce in her home.

I also asked each woman this question: "If you could be anyone in the world you wanted, or have any job that you wanted, what would it be?" This stumped everyone—it was one of those abstractions I had been advised to avoid—but I was curious, and the answers were revealing. The immediate response of almost every woman was, "But I am not educated, so I cannot do anything." Then I would say, "No, imagine"—and "imagine" was the difficult word—"that anything is possible. What would you be?" It was nearly impossible for the women to make that leap. Finally, after prompting, a woman usually said she would like to be a teacher. It was one job they knew about. Teachers were usually Brahmins, and respected. Susheela Bajpai, the Brahmin landowner's wife, wanted to be a teacher, and so did Sudevi. Three women wanted to be doctors, and two wanted to do sewing at home. My favorite answer came from Phula, the prosperous Pasi farmer's wife. She wanted to be the village pradhan, which I took as a sign of great progress.

I often went back to the women who had been the most receptive to me and talked about other things. Susheela, the Brahmin land-owner's wife, always liked to hear the news from Delhi and insisted I sit with her and have tea. Unlike the others, Susheela could talk to me about Indian film stars because she saw three or four movies a year during her trips to Lucknow. Sudevi, the widow, had never seen a movie in her life. When I went to see Sudevi again during Holi, the spring harvest festival in early March, she was in the middle of her hut, up to her knees in mud, at last repairing the crumbling wall of her house. The more exciting news was that her daughter-in-law had given birth to a little boy, who was now four months old. Amazingly, he looked plump and healthy. I asked Sudevi and her daughter-in-law to come outside with the baby, and I took a picture of all three of them in the afternoon light. I promised I would bring them a copy on my next trip.

At the end of each day in the village, just as it was getting dark, I would walk back to Bhabhiji's house, completely exhausted. Bhabhiji always gave me a cup of her sweet, milky tea and invited me to relax on the charpoy near her mud stove. So much smoke came out of it that I found it difficult to breathe—I suppose Bhabhiji, in all her years of cooking, had somehow become used to it—but I would sit there anyway, watching as she chopped onions for dinner on a small wooden board on the floor. As the guest, I was never allowed to help, but Bhabhiji was always interested to hear about my day. So I told her, and related just a little of what the women had said. I think she found my compilation of the obvious details of the women's lives quite odd; she must have wondered what possible use it was for me to know that Phula had spent several hours collecting fodder for her cows that morning. I imagined reversing the situation: Bhabhiji's daughter (her only child, who was married and living in another village) turning up at my mother's house in Cincinnati and interviewing my mother's friends about how long it took each of them to drive to the supermarket.

As Bhabhiji and I talked, her husband was outside supervising either the slaughter of the chickens or the plucking of the waterfowl that had been shot in a nearby marshland that afternoon. I never learned what kind of birds they were. Every time I asked, I was told they were "local birds," and from what I could see, they looked to be about the size of pigeons. Bhabhiji's husband brought them in, their bright red flesh all cut up, and Bhabhiji put them in a brass pot of onions, mustard oil and spices simmering on the stove. The spices—cinnamon, coriander, red chilies, bay leaf, cloves and cardamom—had been ground by one of her servants that afternoon. Because she was the wife of Khajuron's second-largest landowner, Bhabhiji had two or three servants who turned up a few hours each day to help her wash clothes, clean pots and, in this case, grind spices by crushing them with a cylinder-shaped stone used like a rolling pin over a flat slab of rock. It was miserable work, and Bhabhiji rarely did it herself. She made certain, however, to select the combination of spices for each meal herself.

While Bhabhiji cooked, the men gathered under the neem tree for the evening's conversation. Steve and Dr. Singh were usually back by this time, exhausted, too. Dr. Singh would go into the house to get a cup of tea from his sister-in-law, and Steve and I would go into the shed to compare notes on the day. Often we were overcome with frustration. "This is the hardest thing I've ever done," Steve said every evening. He was collecting, at what seemed to him a glacial pace, material for what eventually became a five-part series on caste, village politics, family planning, religion and the pressures of change in Gurha. I usually complained that I had just spent six hours in three interviews and had uncovered nothing more startling than the fact that my subjects had all eaten chapaties for lunch. On other days, Steve and I could only marvel at the elliptical evasions of the villagers. In one typical exchange, a man told Steve and Dr. Singh that he had no wife and children, but then excused himself a short time later because he said his wife and children were waiting for him at home. Steve pointed out the discrepancy in English to Dr. Singh. "Yes, first he was saying one thing," Dr. Singh said diplomatically, "and now he is saying this thing." That ended the discussion. Dr. Singh was above all an eternally polite man, who in any case had learned that there were some things in villages that took too much effort to understand.

By twilight the men had built the fire under the neem tree. It was by far the most pleasant time of day. Sometimes, when we sat around the fire, Dr. Singh would tell us a little about his childhood growing up in the village, including the story, my favorite, about the monkey that kidnapped him. When he first told us, we laughed, but Dr. Singh swore it was true. When he was a baby, he said, a female monkey had grabbed him from the house and escaped all the way up to the top of the neem tree with him in her arms. The family was beside itself. "They called to the monkey but she would not come down," Dr. Singh said. "Fruits and allurements were given, but still she remained in the tree." Finally, after some time, the monkey relinquished the baby, returning him safe and sound on her own. "Yes," said Dr. Singh, pleased and amused, "she loved me." On other nights, the village pradhan from Gurha turned up, full of questions about the United States. "Are widows allowed to remarry in your country?" he once wanted to know. "Do villages in America have electricity? Do the rich people exploit the poor?" Dr. Singh had some questions of his own. "In America," he asked, "if a person is a cobbler"—cobblers in India were Harijans—"and he makes a lot of money, is he respected, despite his profession?"

If the conversation lagged, or bogged down too heavily in Gurha politics, I would go into the house to see how Bhabhiji was doing with dinner. One of Dr. Singh's daughters was always helping her, usually by rolling out the chapati dough. About nine or ten, we were called in to eat. Dr. Singh, Steve and I sat cross-legged on a grass mat in the middle of the courtyard while Bhabhiji and Sheo Singh served us bird, chicken or goat in little bowls. There were steaming chapaties to scoop up the sauce, and rice on the side. It was hot, spicy and utterly delicious.

———————————•-•———————————

KHAJURON COULD HAVE BEEN MISTAKEN AT FIRST AS A VILLAGE WHERE people led troubled but essentially simple lives away from the complications of the modern world. It turned out, of course, that the people in Khajuron were like people anywhere else—they resented rich landlords, fought with their neighbors, channeled their ambitions into their children, looked down on those they considered beneath them and had emotional problems they were unable to solve on their own. For such anxieties they needed Phula's husband, who moonlighted as the village sorcerer. People came to him, about ten to twenty per month, when they were ill or felt they had been possessed by evil spirits. Ramjiai, a twenty-five-year-old vegetable picker and mother of two, went to him one day with a stomachache, which she was sure she had picked up from the evil spirits in the fields. Phula's husband held a clove in his hand, recited to himself a special mantra he had learned from his guru, then blew away the clove. Two hours later, Ramjiai's stomachache was gone. "And yet there are no evil spirits," Phula's husband explained to me. "There is only disease. But people think there are evil spirits, so when I say the mantra, people think the evil spirit is gone. They believe they are cured—and they become cured." Phula's husband reported a 90 percent success rate.

The more serious conflicts in the village centered on the violent feuding that had split the landlords and the Harijans over several generations. It was an epic drama, with roots in ancient history, but forever altered by Indian independence and the upheavals of modern land reform. Decades after these events, it was still affecting the election for village pradhan.

The land on which Khajuron had been built lay in the great cradle of Hindu civilization. In the *Ramayana,* the hero-god Rama ruled these plains from nearby Ayodhya, one of India's seven sacred cities. All of the farmers in Khajuron felt a certain pride in cultivating "Ram's land," as they put it, and it was no surprise to me to see how crowded Susheela Bajpai's house was every Sunday for the *Ramayana* television series.

But in truth, during the last few hundred years, the real rulers of the land had been the zamindars, or landlords, who had grown rich under the system of sharecropping, in which peasants cultivated the landlords' land but were permitted to keep only a small portion of the grain for themselves. The landlords built spacious houses and lived on the scale of small-time kings. It was not until 1952, five years after India's independence, that the new government abolished the zamindari, the landlord system, forcing the landlords to give up most of their huge holdings. It was the end of a feudal order and the beginning, or so it was hoped, of modern times.

One of those suddenly forced to live in the new world was Babu Achal Singh, a Kshatriya, who was the largest landlord in Khajuron at the time. Once Babu Achal Singh's estate had stretched for two miles in one direction and three miles in the other, taking in sixteen villages and earning him enough to keep twenty servants in his sprawling brick house overlooking the fields. After land reform, his holdings were reduced to sixty acres, which in itself was bad enough for him. Much worse was the ascendancy of Rameshwar Prasad.

Prasad was a low-caste Pasi, born and raised in Pasitolla, with a high school education, political ambitions and a lifelong hatred of the landlords. They had exploited his people for too many years, and now, with independence and the coming of land reform, he was at last in a position to do something about it. In 1948, he reported Babu Achal Singh to the local authorities for allegedly celebrating the assassination of Mahatma Gandhi, who had championed the rights of the lower castes no less than the cause of independence. Singh said he was just handing out sweets to celebrate the installation of a village sugarcane press, but he wound up spending fifteen days in jail. Prasad's real rise began the following year, when the predominant lower castes elected him as the pradhan of Khajuron in the first village elections held in independent India. For the Harijans of Khajuron, this was an astonishing turning point. After centuries of degradation, one of their number now had political power, and perhaps their lives might finally change. Prasad quickly consolidated their support. In 1952, the year the zamindari was abolished, he was elected to the state legislature on a Congress party ticket.

For Babu Achal Singh, this was the last straw. He became convinced there was no place for a man like himself in the new India, and three years later, he was dead. His land was left to his two sons, who had recently returned to the village from the nearby city of Allahabad. One of the sons was Amar Singh, and the other was Shardul Singh. It was a terrible time for them. They were young and inexperienced, the price of grain was low, and Prasad taunted them publicly. One day in the village he called them two little chicks, boasting that he would soon pluck all their feathers. In 1959, when the government began consolidating landholdings—through an elaborate system of reassigning land so that a family's holdings would be in a single block rather than in scattered parcels—Prasad, in the landlords' view, seized this as an opportunity for more power. The landlords charged that Prasad, in a further attempt to reduce the landlords' holdings, set up stooges who claimed that a parcel of someone else's land was theirs.

By 1961, the landlords became convinced that tactics like these were

alienating Prasad from other villagers as well. Tired of feeling power-
less, Shardul and Amar Singh put up a washerman and a few others
for the 1961 village panchayat elections. Enough of their candidates
won to encourage them to challenge Prasad for his seat in the state
legislature the following year. They did so by putting up a Pasi, hoping
that someone from Prasad's own caste would cut into his vote base.
Then the landlord brothers launched an all-out assault. They ran a
bicycle courier service to all parts of the constituency, keeping track
of developments in 165 villages. They enlisted seventy volunteers, and
Amar Singh campaigned for six days by elephant. Prasad was defeated,
and power returned to where it had always been, in the hands of the
landlords.

The reestablishment of the landlords did not, however, bring peace.
The warring continued and soon deteriorated into violence. First some
of the landlords' men murdered one of Prasad's supporters, spreading
tension in the Pasi community. The next year Shri Ram Choudhary,
the middle-caste farmer who was the incumbent pradhan during my
year in Khajuron, plotted further revenge with Bhabhiji's husband and
two other men. One night at sunset, they set upon Prasad while he was
walking home from his fields and threw him down. Bhabhiji's husband, Sheo Singh, our host in the village, cut off most of Prasad's nose
with a knife.

In the hospital, Prasad's nose was reconstructed with plastic surgery,
but it never looked right again. It was crooked, and the tip was too
bulbous. Shri Ram Choudhary had not wanted to kill Prasad. He just
wanted to humiliate him, and that he had done. "They were fed up
with my policies, so they attacked me personally," Prasad told me,
with only mild anger, two decades later. The police investigated, but
under pressure from the landlords nothing ever came of it. With Prasad
defeated, the feud settled down, and in 1973 Shardul Singh was elected
as a local district leader, in charge of Khajuron and fifty other villages.
From then on, Khajuron was relatively peaceful, although village
politics continued to seethe with rivalries and resentments.

Which brings us, finally, to the campaign of July 1988. I had been
coming to Khajuron for more than a year, and the race for pradhan
fell during my sixth, and final, trip to the village. The leading candidates, once again, were Shri Ram Choudhary, the incumbent, who had
the support of the landlords and was fighting to retain his seat, and
Arvind Kumar Awasthi, the young Brahmin, who was a strong challenger. The other leading candidate was Rameshwar Prasad, the Pasi

and deposed former pradhan. "I was controlling this village," Prasad told me, "but my power was distributed hither and thither. Now I am going to collect my power back."

THE WOMEN ALL POURED OUT OF THEIR HOMES ON ELECTION DAY, A GRAY and muddy Tuesday, when the rain at last had stopped. I was surprised to realize how many of the women I knew. For a year, I had been sitting in their houses, but since so few of them went out, I had never seen them together as a group. Now here they all were, lined up in front of the schoolhouse to vote, peeking out from the saris covering their heads. They waved to me or said hello. Most actually seemed happy to see me. For the first time in Khajuron I had a small sense of success, or at least of completion. Adding to that was the presence of my father, who had come to India that summer to make one of his travelogues. The film he had taken of the bathing ghats at Benares before I was born had been my first look at India; now I had brought him to Khajuron on this last visit so he could get some footage of an Indian village election. When I looked over at him, he was busy filming close-ups of the chair, tractor, camel and other symbols that appeared on the ballot. The monsoon light was drab, but otherwise it was a good scene for a filmmaker: children darted between the lines of voters, screaming happily, and the voices of the adults buzzed excitedly. Thirteen hundred people were registered to vote, a figure that included the population of the hamlets, and turnout was expected to be 70 percent. Election day was yet another festival in Khajuron, an excuse to take the morning off from the chores and the fields.

The candidates' campaign workers were clustered in tiny little knots on the sidelines, going over the big books of voting rolls and sending out messengers to get people down to the polls. The only unhappy people were the candidates, who moved nervously through the crowd and then went into huddles with their advisers. Arvind Kumar Awasthi looked the most nervous of all. Not only was it his first election, but he had spent the night before trying to control damaging scuttlebutt that he had been bribing poor people for their votes with the promise of dhotis, the sarong-style cotton garments worn by the men. "This is a rumor," he said, looking worried. "It is all wrong."

The only person I didn't see was Sudevi, the widow, even though I had been looking for her all morning. I wanted to say good-bye, and also to give her the photograph of her grandson that I had taken in

March. It was a nice picture: Sudevi was on the right, peering shyly out from her sari, while her daughter-in-law stood on the left, proudly holding her firstborn on her hip. In the photograph the baby looked pudgy and healthy, a four-month-old in a pink-and-green wool sweater and a little cotton hood. Under his eyes were dark smudges of kohl, a black powder that Hindus believe wards off evil spirits. I scanned the crowd for Sudevi once again. At last I saw her, standing in one of the long lines of women waiting to vote. I waved to her, and she waved back. I hurried over to give her the picture.

She took it in her hand and looked at it for a long time. Finally she sighed.

"The baby died at the end of March," she said quietly. There was no shock in her voice, just sad resignation. Babies died all the time in Khajuron. "For four or five days he had fever," she said. She and her daughter-in-law took the baby twice to see Dr. Kamlesh in Gurha, who gave him medication for double pneumonia. They thought the baby was getting better, but one day, suddenly, he died. "We were not thinking that the boy would die of fever," Sudevi said. She had buried her grandson in the fields. Hindu custom calls for young children to be buried, not cremated.

The day after the election, Arvind Kumar Awasthi, the Brahmin challenger, was declared the new pradhan. He won with 389 votes, compared with 278 for Prasad and 254 for Shri Ram Choudhary. Though the landlord-backed incumbent had been defeated, it was not really a surprise. No pradhan in the history of Khajuron had ever been reelected. Arvind Kumar Awasthi had won with the support of Khajuron's large Brahmin community, as well as some middle-caste voters and a few Kshatriyas who had split with the other landlords. Although I never learned if the charges of vote-buying were true, Awasthi was clearly a young man in a hurry who had run an energetic campaign.

But when I asked him what he intended to do for the women, his answer was hardly the voice of a new generation. "The ladies in this village don't want to do anything," he informed me. "Even if an effort is made, they still won't do anything. They are very traditional in their attitudes."

I don't suppose it would have mattered, though, if the new pradhan had by some miracle been enlightened regarding women. As it was, a village election like this barely touched the lives of the women. They heard some news from their neighbors, but they did not participate in the campaign and always voted as their husbands did. The women were like shadows, irrelevant to village debate and the shaping, such as it was, of the future. Their lives, as Simone de Beauvoir wrote in *The Second Sex,* were concerned not with the transcendence of existence, but with the repetition of life—with babies born, and babies who died, and babies who grew up and married to begin the cycle anew. The labor they performed in this pursuit was essential to life itself but was largely invisible. All of them accepted this; only one woman I spoke to came anywhere close to seeing it as unfair. "Men are not smarter," said Sheela, the silversmith's wife. "But they have been educated and go outside. Women stay in the house."

As I left the village for the last time on election day, I had the feeling that I had just begun. It was as if I had peeled off one and a half layers of fifty, and what I had learned was only an early glimmering of truth. After all, it was not until the last time I had tea with Susheela Bajpai, the day before the election, that she finally admitted what had been apparent all along, despite her earlier denials: she did not like purdah. "I would like to go out and meet people," she said. "But I can't. People will talk, and say, 'Why are you starting this thing?' "

More than anything else, my experience in the village taught me firsthand about the most fundamental centuries-old problems of women in India. I left Khajuron wondering if change would ever come, and if it was even possible for the government or a feminist movement to significantly affect their lives. I also left in awe at the women's resilience and strength. Without them, and especially without Bhabhiji, who taught me the most, I would have missed the most troubling, and inspiring, part of my journey in India.

CHAPTER 5

NO MORE
LITTLE GIRLS

Female Infanticide
Among the Poor of Tamil Nadu
and Sex-Selective Abortion
Among the Rich of Bombay

IF YOU GAZE DOWN AT THE VILLAGE OF BELUKKURICHI FROM THE ONE-thousand-year-old Hindu temple that sits on one of the higher surrounding hills, the valley below takes on the lush, whimsical character of an illustration from a book of fairy tales. Clusters of coconut palms sprout up from the land, and little cars motor purposefully along roads that bisect the radiant green fields of cassava and sugarcane. Belukkurichi lies deep in the interior of the south Indian state of Tamil Nadu, far from the plains of Khajuron, and the moist landscape seems to have given the village a softness around its edges. At this distance, the scene appears serene, and the life within it benevolent. If you come down from the temple, what you see at first does not entirely change that impression. Although the drab little mud huts are clustered on reddish dirt lanes strewn with garbage, most have electricity and two dozen of them have television sets. Many of Belukkurichi's three thousand villagers appear almost plump, and you understand why when you see them eat with great enthusiasm the mounds of rice that they mix with cool yogurt. Even the Harijans seem reasonably well fed and do not have the sunken, defeated look of those in the north.

As you approach the town, you soon come upon the signs of a healthy village commerce: bicycle-repair shops, sweet crackers for sale in glass jars, pigs rooting through fruit peelings, clumps of red bananas hanging from tea stalls. The village even has a small library, a primary school and an old movie theater. As you walk through, your ears are filled with the usual film music blaring from unseen radios. The literacy rate of the women who come to shop here is higher than the national average, and they do not veil their faces with fear and embarrassment before strangers. Both young girls and grown women pin strands of cream-colored jasmine blossoms in their hair.

And yet, in this valley and another beyond it, I learned, families sometimes poisoned their newborn daughters. In August 1987, I met four couples, all poor farm laborers, who told me that the hardships in their lives and the astronomical expense of marrying off daughters had forced them to murder their infant girls. "I don't feel sorry that I have done this," Mariaye, one of the four mothers, told me quietly. "Actually, I think I have done the right thing. Why should a child suffer like me?"

The four couples described the practice as not uncommon in the area. No one knew for certain, however, how prevalent female infanticide really was. Certainly it was not the custom of the majority, and most of the people in the valleys around Belukkurichi considered it wrong. But the phenomenon was sufficiently widespread so that government-employed midwives who lived in the area told me they feared for a newborn's life if it was so unfortunate as to be the third or fourth girl born into a poor family of farm laborers. Such a family could not possibly afford the price of another girl's dowry, a custom which in Belukkurichi had spread to lower castes that had not observed it even a decade before. The birth of a daughter had become a devastating blow, one that a family believed could threaten its survival. At best, a family saw a daughter as an investment with little return. She would never earn as much in the fields as a son, and her small contribution from day labor would end when she left her family after marriage. To some villagers of the valley around Belukkurichi, "putting a child to sleep," as they called it, seemed their only choice.

In some ways, female infanticide was the poor woman's version of another phenomenon among India's upper classes—the use of prenatal tests to determine the sex of a child. Statistics in India showed that after such a test, if the fetus turned out to be female, most women decided to abort. Obviously, both sex-selective abortion and female infanticide represent a kind of extreme behavior, and my reaction to both was revulsion. I have decided to explore them here because I think they are revealing, if shocking, symptoms of the larger problem facing women in India.

I learned just how deep-rooted that problem was during my stay in Belukkurichi, when I witnessed the birth of a baby. I had been interviewing families in the area with Jaya Gokulamani, a community-development worker from the state capital of Madras. Although Jaya had lived in Belukkurichi on and off for a year and a half, she spoke an upper-caste Tamil, the language of Tamil Nadu. She had to remember to switch to the looser, less imperious local dialect when working among the villagers, for reasons that became apparent the day the baby was born. That morning we were near a government health center, a primitive building of concrete blocks squatting in the red dust. Midwives who worked in the health center told Jaya that a mother who had walked in an hour before was about to give birth, and they invited me, the foreign visitor, to watch in the delivery room. Never before had I seen a baby born, and when I saw the fat little eight-pound boy on the delivery table and then heard him cry out, I was moved to tears. For the first time in my life I understood something I had heard for so many years—that the birth of a child is both the most ordinary and the most extraordinary event in human experience. As I watched the midwives wash the blood off the baby, I marveled that such a healthy, perfectly formed creature had been produced by a poor village mother, a woman who had been deprived of proper nutrition and modern medical care. In this village especially, the birth of the baby seemed no less than a miracle.

A moment later, I was brought back to the realities of India. The health workers told the woman her baby was a boy, but when Jaya came in a few moments later, she smiled and congratulated the woman on her new pillai—the word in Jaya's upper-caste Tamil for "boy." But in the local dialect, *pillai* meant "girl." The woman now thought she had given birth to a daughter and was shocked.

"You told me it's a boy," she said accusingly from the delivery table to the midwives, who were tying up the baby's umbilical cord. "Are you lying to me?"

One of the midwives held up the baby for her to see. The mother smiled, relieved. "No one is lying to you," the midwife said, and then explained the different meanings of the word.

Afterward, the midwives told us that they knew for certain that the woman had murdered her second daughter. If the newborn had been a girl, they said, she would also have been killed.

IT WAS THE BRITISH WHO FIRST DOCUMENTED THE PRACTICE OF FEMALE infanticide in India in the late eighteenth century, chiefly among upper castes in the north. In some areas, officials reported discovering entire villages without even one female child. Lalita Panigrahi, in her book *British Social Policy and Female Infanticide in India,* recounts the experience of James Thomason, a British official who in conversation with a group of landowners in eastern Uttar Pradesh in 1835 happened to refer to one of them as the son-in-law of another. "This mistake raised a sarcastic laugh among them," Panigrahi continues, "and a bystander briefly explained that he could not be a son-in-law since there were no daughters in the village. Thomason was told that the birth of a daughter was considered a most serious calamity and she was seldom allowed to live. No violent measures were however resorted to, but she was left to die from neglect and want of food." Panigrahi says that a chief reason for the murders was the exorbitant cost of dowries among the upper castes. Many families also faced enormous difficulties in finding their daughters good husbands from a limited supply of suitable bridegrooms. Not marrying off a daughter was unthinkable and brought disgrace on a family.

The British outlawed infanticide in 1870, and a century later, educated Indians believed that the practice, like sati, had all but died out. That assumption was shattered in June 1986, when *India Today* published an explosive cover story, "Born to Die," which estimated that six thousand female babies had been poisoned to death during the preceding decade in the district surrounding the town of Madurai in Tamil Nadu. Although it was impossible to know how accurate this estimate was, the magazine reported that the practice of female infanticide was prevalent there among the two hundred thousand members of a poor subcaste called Kallars, who fed their infant daughters the lethal oleander berries growing in their fields. "There is hardly a poor Kallar family in which a female baby has not been murdered sometime or the other during the last ten years," an agricultural worker named Muniamma told *India Today.*

People were stunned by the *India Today* story, although perhaps they should not have been. After all, neglect of girl babies was commonplace. Studies have consistently shown that girl babies in India are denied the same food and medical care that boy babies receive. They also suffer more from severe malnutrition. Girl babies die more often than boy babies, even though medical research has long found that girls are generally biologically stronger as newborns than boys. The birth of a boy is a time for celebration, but the birth of a girl is often viewed as a crisis. "The women of the family spread the news rather like a family illness or calamity," the social worker and women's activist Tara Ali Baig wrote in her book *India's Woman Power*. In India, she observed, the belief was that boy babies "should want for nothing. They should be fed when they howl, be dandled and coddled by everyone in sight and when ill be surrounded by acute feminine anxiety." This pattern of discrimination continues through a woman's life, making India one of the few nations in the world where men outnumber women, and where the ratio of women to men has declined since the turn of the century. In 1901, the Indian census reported that there were 972 women for every 1,000 men; by 1981, the figure had fallen to 933 women for every 1,000 men.

After the *India Today* story appeared I decided I would try to investigate the subject myself. Female infanticide, however, was clearly so sensitive an issue that I knew I was undertaking an ambitious and probably unrealistic task. When I called *India Today,* staff members confirmed as much and told me there had been such an outcry from the Kallar community in Madurai after the "Born to Die" story appeared that the magazine had been burned in the streets. They believed that no one would talk to me if I went there, and they suggested that I go to another area in Tamil Nadu where female infanticide was suspected, taking along a person who was known and trusted by the local people. (Female infanticide was not unique to Tamil Nadu. In October 1988, just a few months after I left India, *India Today* reported that in a cluster of a dozen villages in a remote western corner of Rajasthan, an estimated 150 newborn daughters were put to death each year; among the area's 10,000 people, there were said to be only 50 young girls.)

The *India Today* correspondent in Tamil Nadu gave me the name of Jaya Gokulamani, the rural-development worker, who he thought might be able to help me. I looked her up at her apartment in Madras and found a forty-four-year-old widow, a Brahmin, tall, commanding and softhearted. When I met her, she was working two afternoons a week as an announcer at the local racetrack. Her knowledge of the villagers in Belukkurichi, about an eight-hour drive from Madras, came from her role as a consultant to a Danish government health project in Salem District, of which Belukkurichi was a part. For a year and a half, Jaya had lived off and on in a two-room house in Beluk-kurichi, where her job had been to assess the work and the living conditions of the Indian government health workers in the area, and also to help the villagers administer a newly created "community welfare fund" that would pay for such things as roads and public latrines. It was not the sort of life she ever would have imagined for herself, but in a sense it was a modern interpretation of the widow's lot in India. Jaya would never remarry—it was not part of her culture, she said—but instead would devote herself, if not to charity, then at least to useful work. I also think the Brahmin in her—and there was a lot of it—enjoyed the power she had to change the villagers' lives.

Jaya told me she was convinced that female infanticide occurred regularly in the area around Belukkurichi, and that she would be happy to take me there and work as my go-between and interpreter. (Tamil, one of the fifteen official languages of India, has no resemblance to Hindi.) It would be difficult but relatively well-paying work for her, but I think the real reason for her enthusiasm was that she saw the potential for the exposure of a social evil in whatever I might write. A month before in Belukkurichi she had seen a ten-day-old baby girl die, and she was haunted by the knowledge that she had been unable to prevent it. "I want people to know about this," she said firmly. The mother of the baby had herself died during childbirth, and the relatives had brought the healthy newborn to Jaya. She took care of the child for six days, but on the seventh day the mother's sister asked for the baby back. Jaya had been in the area long enough to fear the worst, so she told the woman she had some friends who could bring up the child. The woman said no, the baby belonged to her family. Jaya, with great misgivings, handed the child over. Three days later, she saw the baby again—but this time the infant was blue and suffocating on the examination table of a local doctor. The child's two grandmothers had brought the baby in, saying the girl refused milk and was having difficulty breathing. The baby died as the doctor examined her. "The child had been so beautiful," Jaya said. "She looked like a doll. If she had been a son, it wouldn't have happened like that."

To reach Belukkurichi, Jaya and I drove southwest from Madras into the interior of Tamil Nadu, past soft green rice paddies and a roadside temple where Jaya stopped to offer a prayer to the south Indian goddess inside, Adhiparasakthi. The south has its own deities, languages, foods and customs. I am not the first to observe this, but the entire region really always seemed to me a different country from the north. Not only was the south cleaner, tropical and more luscious, but the people themselves seemed to reflect the gentleness of the landscape. Close up they appeared physically smoother and somehow sweeter than the villagers struggling with a harsh existence in Uttar Pradesh or Bihar. Historically, the south never had to defend itself from the waves of invaders like those who crossed the mountains from Central Asia into northern India. South Indians believe this has made them less aggressive and kept their culture "pure."

At the end of the day, Jaya and I reached the town of Salem. We checked into a hotel and the next morning made the one-hour drive to Belukkurichi, where we spent our days for the following week. We returned to the hotel in Salem every night, but we had lunch every day at the home of one of Jaya's friends in Belukkurichi, a housewife whose husband was a local official. The meal was usually stewed beetroot, rice and yogurt, which we ate with our hands, and afterward we all stretched out on mats on the floor and fell asleep in the afternoon heat. Jaya had a whole network of contacts among families and health workers in the area, and through them we were tipped off to couples who had put their daughters "to sleep." Belukkurichi was about one hundred miles from the area in Tamil Nadu that *India Today* had investigated for the "Born to Die" story. Officials at child welfare agencies in Madras told me they had heard rumors of infanticide in the area around Belukkurichi, but they did not expect anyone to admit to it. But by the end of the week, after combing the large valleys around the village, Jaya and I eventually met the four couples who told us, after long conversations about the problems in their lives, that they had murdered their baby girls. In the interest of telling the most complete story, I asked them if I could use their names, and they agreed. I am still not sure why. I told them I wanted to publish the information in a book I was writing, and perhaps the prospect of appearing in print in a land as vague and distant as America did not worry them. Maybe the couples thought I was going to help them; my questions had been sympathetic, and Jaya, whom they all knew and liked, was a reassuring presence. She was horrified by what these parents had done, but she too saw the deaths as symptoms of much larger problems beyond the parents' control. She knew that the couples, despite their guilt, felt that their actions had been justified. Whatever the reasons for their admissions, I will protect the parents—on the remote chance that they might be prosecuted—by not naming the areas of the large valleys around Belukkurichi in which they lived.

All four couples worked on the land for a living, but only Chinnaswami and Karuppai, an uneducated Harijan husband and wife who made less than a dollar a day between them, were desperately poor. They were thin, dark and sinewy, and most days they worried that they would not have enough to eat. I remember when I took their picture that they stared straight into the lens with intensely serious expressions, even more than other villagers, as if believing that the camera might uncover their souls. Karuppai, the wife, wore a thin cotton sari, and Chinnaswami, her husband, had on a Western-style shirt and a worn, faded lunghi, the traditional cloth that men tied around themselves like a skirt. Both husband and wife were barefoot, and no one could doubt that they had worked in the fields all of their lives. Eight years before, they said, they had hired an old man who lived in the hills to kill their fourth daughter. He gave the day-old baby the sticky white milk of what the villagers called the erukkampal plant, a spindly, light-green bush that grew along the roadside. For his services, the parents gave the man a free meal. "We felt very bad," said Karuppai, the child's mother, who was nineteen years old when her daughter died. "But at the same time, suppose she had lived? It was better to save her from a lifetime of suffering." She spoke in a quiet, flat tone as we sat on the floor of a local doctor's house. I had expected a dramatic, anguished revelation; instead her admission was made in grim, simple detail. I think this was partly because she was talking about an event eight years past, and also because she was nervous and terrified. Karuppai's face was expressionless, and she sat very still. Jaya was herself uneasy interpreting my questions. By the end of the interview, the tension in the room was suffocating.

A second couple, Muthuswami and Rajeshwari, were from a slightly higher caste and made more money. But three years before, they had their second daughter killed. "Abortion is costly," Rajeshwari, the child's mother, explained, almost defiantly. "And you have to rest at home. So instead of spending money and losing income, we prefer to deliver the child and kill it." I honestly don't know if Rajeshwari saw no difference, other than the expense, between abortion and infanticide. Her words were shocking, and would be powerful fuel for an antiabortionist. Perhaps the harsh economics of her life had made her as callous as she sounded, but I suspect she was putting on an act and was too proud to let an outsider like me feel sorry for her. Her manner continued to be lively as she explained, as we sat at a local landowner's house, that she had waited twenty-four hours before killing her baby. "I was of half a mind to bring up the child," she said. "I couldn't decide. But because of the problems she would face at a later stage, I decided to do it. And everybody else was in favor of putting the child to sleep, so I decided to go along." But it was the mother-in-law, not the mother, who gave the child the milk from the erukkampal plant.

A third couple, Mariaye and her husband, Natesan, both illiterate and from a low caste, had also stood back while Mariaye's mother-in-law had administered the milk to their third daughter two and a half years before. We were talking at the same landowner's house. "The child had breathing difficulties, and then froth came from her mouth," Mariaye told me slowly. "She became pale, and then she died." I didn't know what to say, so I said nothing. Mariaye's husband, Natesan, filled the silence. "It was a peaceful death," he said.

Of the four, the last couple I met, Muthaye and her husband, Mohanasundaram, were the parents I understood the best, to the extent that I understood any of them at all. Or maybe it was just that I saw a glimmer of their tragedy that the others had not allowed me to see. They were low-caste field laborers, and they too had killed their second daughter. We spoke first at the doctor's house where we had talked with the first couple. Muthaye was twenty-four, a slip of a woman in a yellow cotton sari, with her hair in a simple ponytail that made her look like a schoolgirl instead of a mother who had been through the kind of trauma she had. Like most village women, she was wearing her wealth: two nose studs, a pair of diamond-and-gold earrings, several gold toe rings. She remained utterly silent, with a serious, worried expression on her face, while her husband and mother-in-law did most of the talking. Her husband could have been any one of the thousands of young Indian men I had seen on the streets of small-town India: thin, with a little mustache, and an open, cheerful face that displayed an innocence mixed with a hard-learned savvy. He was twenty-nine years old and wore a Western short-sleeved shirt and a lunghi. His mother, Nallamma, had a wiry build, white hair, sun-leathered skin that crinkled around her eyes and the take-charge look of mothers-in-law across India. As she talked, her grandson, a little ten-month-old boy in a T-shirt that said "Freeport, Bahamas," gurgled and played on the floor.

Muthaye and Mohanasundaram had been married six years. Mohanasundaram had a fourth-grade education and made a dollar a day harvesting rice, peanuts and the tall stalks of the cassava plant, whose roots were dried and made into small, starchy granules of tapioca. His wife, because she was a woman, made fifty cents a day for the exact same work. They could not find jobs every day, but in a good year, with rain, the couple could bring home about $350 between them. Mohanasundaram's parents owned an acre of land, and this brought them about $250 a year, putting the total annual income of the family of four workers at $600. Although the four made less than India's average per capita income of $250, the family was not desperately poor. Everyone ate two meals a day—a warm cereal before leaving for the fields at eight in the morning, and a dinner of rice and perhaps cooked vegetables when they returned at five in the evening. They lived in a collection of smooth mud huts with thatched roofs, all very clean, under a cluster of coconut palms at the edge of a peanut field. They had a fresh-water well and several animals, including a cow, which Muthaye milked in the mornings. Life was hard, but the family was not living a hand-to-mouth existence. The acre of land gave them security, and unlike so many other villagers in India, they seemed to have a plan for the future.

This, in fact, was what had driven them to murder. Three years before, Muthaye had delivered her firstborn, a girl. A year later, when she was pregnant again, the family decided—although it was not clear exactly who Mohanasundaram meant by "the family"—that should the second child be a girl, they would "put her to sleep." The reason, the mother-in-law and Mohanasundaram said, was that "we wanted a male baby." When Muthaye felt her first labor pains, about noon one day, she was taken to the home of a dai in a nearby village. She delivered a little girl at four that afternoon. Three hours later she returned home with the child. The next morning at dawn, "the family" gave the newborn some cow's milk mixed with five sleeping pills they had bought from a pharmacist in town. This was done inside one of the huts as the mother-in-law and both parents watched. The baby, they said, fell fast asleep. Two hours later she had stopped breathing.

A few relatives were called for the funeral that day, and were told simply that the little girl had not lived. No other explanation was given, and the relatives asked no questions. Possibly they suspected what had happened and knew not to press; possibly they really thought the girl had died a natural death, since it happened all the time. Ten days later, a government health worker came by on her usual rounds and asked about the child. The family said she had died because she refused her mother's milk. The health worker noted it down, made no accusations and left.

Through Jaya, I then asked Muthaye and Mohanasundaram how they had felt afterward. Like that of the first couple I met, their story had so far been unemotional and straightforward. "For a month, we cried every day," Mohanasundaram, the husband, said. "We felt bad, but bringing up girls is very difficult nowadays." Then the mother-in-law chimed in. "It was not wantonly done," she said. "We were not in a position to bring up the child." Muthaye, the mother of the dead child, said nothing and stared into space with a strained expression on her face. It was impossible to read her mind, but I had the feeling that bringing up the murder of her daughter—which had happened only slightly more than a year before—was a nightmare for her. I wondered if she played the death over and over in her mind, or if she had forced herself never to think of it again.

Sensing my uneasiness, her husband moved on to explain the family finances. As part of a local bank savings program called the Marriage Saving Scheme, he had deposited 3,000 rupees—2,000 of his own, 1,000 borrowed—when his first daughter was a year old. This was the equivalent of about $250. The bank had promised, he said, that when his daughter was twenty-one, an age when he expected her to be ready for marriage, it would give him 22,000 rupees, or $1,700, an adequate dowry for his caste. Mohanasundaram explained that he would then ask for the same amount in dowry at the time of the marriage of his son, the ten-month-old who was gurgling at our feet. This was the common way that people like Mohanasundaram afforded dowries at all. Mohanasundaram felt that a second daughter would have ruined his financial plans and the family's future as well. Another 3,000-rupee deposit in the Marriage Saving Scheme for another girl would have been almost as much as he and his wife earned in a good year. They would have had to borrow all of the money, which would have put them in debt, probably for life. And yet without a dowry, Mohanasundaram almost certainly could not have married off the second daughter, which was his chief responsibility as her father, and a duty Hindus like himself believed was an essential part of a meritorious life. As an unmarried woman in rural India, his daughter would have been shunned for the rest of her life. Mohanasundaram told me he didn't like dowry, but that he felt he had no other choice.

Jaya and I went from the doctor's house with Muthaye and Mohanasundaram to their collection of huts, first piling into the car and then walking along a red dirt road under a blazing sun. When we got there, the family insisted we sit down on a charpoy in a patch of shade and have something to drink. The mother-in-law then directed a man who appeared to work for them to climb the trunk of one of the palm trees. The man scampered up, and with a big knife cut off several green coconuts, which came thudding down to earth. The man climbed back down, lopped off the heads of the coconuts, then presented Jaya and me with two each. Jaya took the first one, leaned back her head, opened her mouth, and poured the milk in directly from the coconut. I followed her lead. The milk was sticky and warm, but clear and not too sweet. I found it an oddly pleasant moment, sitting there in the shade enjoying the bounty of nature, as if I had not spoken to the family an hour before about what they had done to their second daughter. Jaya continued to talk to the family while I took pictures. Muthaye told us she was using no form of birth control, and that she was afraid of a sterilization operation because she was convinced it would mean a month away from her work.

As Jaya and I were leaving, I asked the husband where his daughter was buried. He pointed in the direction of our car, and then walked us down to the grave. It was an unmarked spot right along the road, with a beautiful view of the peanut fields and the hills above where the temple stood. The scene was so lovely that when I saw two women walking along the road carrying bags of rice on their heads, I got out my camera to take their pictures. One of the women was obviously pregnant, and Jaya went up to talk to her. She soon came back disgusted. "That woman has one son and two daughters," Jaya said. "She told me that if this one's a girl, she'll kill her."

SIX HUNDRED MILES FROM BELUKKURICHI, BOMBAY RISES UP ON THE other side of India, a fetid megalopolis of twentieth-century skyscrapers, crumbling Victorian gentlemen's clubs and wooden shacks jostling for breathing space on a narrow island that extends south into the Arabian Sea. Calcutta has long been India's internationally famous urban disaster, but I came to feel that Bombay is catching up and in sight of surpassing it. The stench of Bombay's poverty is particularly hard to take because nowhere in India is there such an abyss between those who have and those who do not. Bombay is the nation's financial capital, industrial engine and the home of its film industry—in short, the source of most of India's wealth. A sliver of the population, the very rich, inhabit apartments overlooking the sea for which they pay five thousand dollars a month, yet more than half of Bombay's ten million people live in squatters' slums. Bombay is the chic woman in the latest silk salwar kameez, but also the beggar who thrusts his leprous stump through her open car window when she stops at a light. Bombay is the "Queen's Necklace," the twinkling lights along the dramatic sweep of Marine Drive, and also the reeking swamp of raw sewage that greets visitors as they leave the airport after arriving on a direct flight from London. Bombay is the new industrial baron who hurries by the oxcart, and the elegant French restaurants not far from the street food of Chowpatty Beach. While Delhi is a political capital, like Washington, that goes to bed early, Bombay is up late, drinking imported Scotch on marble terraces open to humid breezes and the ripe smell of fish. Bombay is glamorous, exciting, decadent, appalling. Nowhere in India is money more important.

It didn't surprise me that Bombay had become, by the mid-1980s, the center of two new medical techniques used by the city's business class to avoid the birth of unwanted daughters. Both procedures were commonly referred to as the sex test; in the United States they would be recognized as either amniocentesis or chorionic villus sampling, two prenatal tests developed for the detection of genetic abnormalities in a fetus. In the Bombay of the mid-1980s, however, the tests were most often used to determine only the gender of an unborn child. Most people did not even know that the tests could diagnose birth defects.

In India, between the years 1978 and 1982, estimates put the number of abortions of female fetuses after the "sex test" at 78,000. That, at least, was the figure presented at a 1986 government hearing on the subject and widely quoted in the press. I was never able to determine how the figure was calculated or its original source, and it seemed to me another Indian statistic that could never be verified. Undeniable, however, was the fact that the majority of Bombay's private gynecologists (84 percent of those surveyed, according to one apparently reliable government study) conducted the test solely to determine the sex of a child. Even those doctors with misgivings said they performed the test because it was the wish of their patients. This led to all kinds of philosophical arguments to justify the practice, usually couched in such lofty concepts as "the will of the people" and "freedom." "Democracy should permit one to have a child that one wants," said Shirish Sheth, who was the incoming president of the Bombay Obstetrics and Gynecological Society. Sharad Gogate, a gynecologist with a busy middle-class practice, told me that "once a woman finds out it is female, in 80 percent of the cases she is hell-bent on an abortion." He estimated that he had aborted one thousand female fetuses. I gave him a look of alarm. "Yes," he said. "I have to accept that."

I always linked the "sex test" and Belukkurichi's female infanticide in my mind, and my pursuit of both subjects overlapped. I first went to Belukkurichi in January 1987 but arrived in the village already sick with stomach problems and had to turn back the next day. Four months later I went to Bombay to talk to women and doctors about the "sex test," and only after that did I finally return to Belukkurichi for the week-long stay. There are of course fundamental differences between the two practices—the most obvious being the use of technology—but the root of the problem is the same. Although that does not mean that they are equally deplorable, I found myself torn. Infanticide is one of the most heinous of crimes, and yet, although I have always been pro-choice, I was more appalled by the abortions. Most of the educated, well-off women of Bombay were of course trying to avoid the astronomical cost of dowries in India, but among the rich, who could afford the cost of any number of weddings, a stronger motive seemed to be to avoid the social embarrassment of having daughters but no sons.

Bombay feminists in any case settled on the sex-determination tests as one of their most important causes. In May 1988, when the legislature of the state of Maharashtra, of which Bombay is a part, passed a law that banned the tests for the use of sex determination, they claimed their biggest victory—raising all sorts of questions in my mind about how one controls the practice without infringing on a woman's right to abortion. The cause had been led by the Women's Centre, the leading feminist group in Bombay, which in 1982 had brought out its first report on the use of amniocentesis for sex determination. Although feminists in other Indian cities sometimes dismissed prenatal sex determination as an elitist problem confined to Bombay's business class, the Women's Centre countered that the tests were common in other areas as well, most notably in Punjab, India's breadbasket. In fact, Punjab's rich farmland and Maharashtra's industry made the states the two most prosperous in India, and it was a depressing irony that the "sex test" proliferated amid such plenty. Prosperity, as in the case of the sati in Rajasthan, had not eliminated old customs but seemed to be promoting them in alarming new ways. If nothing else, the sex-determination tests were a powerful example of what can happen when modern technology collides with the forces of a traditional society.

Feminists also warned that the tests were seeping down to the middle class and the poor. Although private Bombay doctors charged as much as $125 for the test, clinics had sprung up in working-class areas and slums that offered amniocentesis at cut-rate prices and played on the fear of dowry with such slogans as "Better 500 rupees now than 500,000 later." As far back as 1977, Bombay's Hurkisondas Hospital, a private institution catering to the middle and working classes, began offering amniocentesis at one of the cheapest rates ever, eight dollars, in its new Prenatal Sex-Determination Clinic. "This is the only institution in our country which is carrying out this humane and beneficial test with such a high accuracy of the results," the clinic's information sheet said. In the years 1978 to 1982, a study of the hospital by a Bombay women's organization found that of 8,000 women who came from all over India for the test, 7,999 wanted a son.

One muggy April morning in 1987, a year before the state legislature banned the tests, I found Assumpta D'Sylva, a thirty-one-year-old Bombay housewife, quietly waiting outside a Hurkisondas Hospital examination room for her "sex test," in this case a chorionic villus sampling. For CVS, as it is called, doctors use a catheter to extract a few milligrams of placenta tissue, which is then analyzed for any genetic defects. In amniocentesis, doctors extract cells from the amniotic fluid by inserting a catheter into the sac surrounding the fetus. Amniocentesis is normally performed from the sixteenth to seventeenth week of pregnancy, CVS around the tenth. Both procedures invariably disclose the sex of the unborn child. CVS, though considered less accurate than amniocentesis, has the advantage of predicting a child's sex at a much earlier date and thus eliminating the need for a difficult second-trimester abortion.

Assumpta D'Sylva already had two daughters, and if the child she was carrying turned out to be female, she would have an abortion. Her husband, Osbert D'Sylva, ran a family business, installing industrial boilers, that he said was worth $400,000. Assumpta D'Sylva said it wasn't that she and her husband couldn't afford another girl, and it wasn't that they didn't love their daughters. She even insisted that her husband was "not so keen" on her decision to have the test because "another girl wouldn't make any difference to him." The decision, she said, was hers alone. She simply wanted a boy.

Assumpta D'Sylva was in fact the woman who had first described to me the standard exchange that a mother without sons often heard from her friends. "Our society makes you feel so bad if you don't have a son," she told me before the doctor called her in. "Especially when I go out for parties, people say, 'How many children?' and I say, 'Two girls,' and they say, 'Oh, too bad, no boy.' And I feel very bad." She was well dressed and not shy about talking to me. From her point of view, she was doing what was best. She felt she was to blame, after all, for producing two daughters. When I reminded her that it is the man who determines the sex of a child, she said yes, she knew that, but "I still feel sometimes that it's my fault. I just feel a lady has the capacity for carrying a boy." Her parents and gynecologist were against the abortion she might have; her husband, she insisted, remained "neutral," although he seemed to me to be in complete agreement with her decision. He listened quietly as she spoke. "We do feel bad about it," he said, when I asked if he did, "but things have to go this way. You do feel looked down upon if you have two or three girls." Amazingly, she and her husband were Roman Catholics. "Being a Catholic, it's the only sin I commit," Assumpta D'Sylva said. "When this test is here and everybody is doing it, why shouldn't we have what we want?" Her tone was apologetic but casual. I could only think that her pregnancy was still so recent that it was not quite real to her, and that the technology had somehow sanitized the decision she had made. As I had with other women in India, I tried to put myself in her place and summon up the feelings that her society had forced upon her. But our worlds were too different, and her thinking was unfathomable to me.

In any case, "Why shouldn't I have what I want?" was the refrain I heard all week at doctors' offices in Bombay's pockets of affluence. Nowhere was this attitude more in evidence than at the clinic of Rustom Soonawala, a gynecologist for women from Bombay's leading business families. His patients also included some of India's top actresses, as well as Americans, Europeans and Saudis. His waiting room was like no other doctor's office I had seen in India: a marble floor, leather banquettes, recessed lighting, tennis magazines on the coffee table. It was a Sunday afternoon, and yet there were several pregnant women in his waiting room. One had arrived in a red Standard sports car, which was selling in India for $20,000. After a short wait, I was ushered in to see the doctor himself, a handsome and elegant middle-aged man whom I could easily imagine on one of those marble terraces overlooking the sea. He was a member of the country's most exclusive religious minority, a Parsi, one of the 90,000 people in India who worshiped the god Zoroaster. Dr. Soonawala seemed almost British in manner and outlook. He gave me a soft drink in a glass engraved with his initials, and he listened carefully to my first question about his use of amniocentesis. He thought for a moment, then began very slowly.

"Until the attitude of the whole Asian community changes, where a male issue in the family is a must," he said, "we as scientists can help out the poor mother who year after year produces a baby until a boy is born." Dr. Soonawala said he performed "fifty to seventy" sex-determination tests per year, using either amniocentesis or chorionic villus sampling. Of those, he aborted about "twenty to thirty" female fetuses, simply because they were female.

"I'm not very happy about it," he said. "But you have to think that the child is not wanted." The desire for male children, he explained, was stronger among the business community—the very people who could afford to have girls. "I wouldn't completely blame them," Dr. Soonawala added, "because if they've established a business, they need somebody to carry on the business after them." I asked why a father could not turn a family business over to his daughter. That was not an option, Dr. Soonawala said, because the daughter must be given away in marriage to another family. He then offered another reason for the necessity of sons: "Amongst the Hindu community," he said, "the funeral pyre has to be lit by a male." I thought about asking why a daughter could not light the pyre but decided that questioning thousands of years of Hindu tradition would be of no use. "It's a very peculiar situation," Dr. Soonawala admitted. "If you don't do it, you are creating an unhappy situation for the mother and child. And if you do it, you are discriminating on the basis of sex."

That morning I had gone to a regular meeting of the Bombay branch of the Indian Medical Association because I had heard that the discussion for the day was going to be whether there should be "sex determination for the termination of pregnancy." The prevailing opin-

ion among the thirty or so doctors appeared to be yes, with reservations. It was hard not be cynical; for many doctors in Bombay, the
sex-determination tests were a lucrative part of their business. About
halfway through the meeting, a young woman came to the front of
the room and introduced herself as Jayshree Patel, a gynecologist. She
began by asking her colleagues to think about why sex-selective abortion had become so popular in India. I settled in for an emotional
speech opposing the sex test but was soon startled to hear Dr. Patel sum
up by saying she was in fact in favor of sex-selective abortion. "It is
the lesser of two evils," she said. "The worse of the two evils is the
state that a woman is going to face until the day she dies."

The meeting continued with a presentation by Dr. Gogate, the
obstetrician and gynecologist who later told me he had aborted one
thousand female fetuses. Dr. Gogate spoke on the technical aspects of
amniocentesis, concluding that the test should be used, but "judi-
ciously," whatever that meant. After the presentation, I introduced
myself to Dr. Gogate, and he invited me to come to his office to see
a chorionic villus sampling he was performing the next morning. I was
there at eight, in time to see a thirty-six-year-old mother of three
daughters laid out on an examination table. She was eight weeks
pregnant with a fourth child. She could afford another girl, she later
explained to me, but then repeated what I had heard so often. "In
India," she said, "every parent must have one son."

The room where the test was to be performed was hot, run-down
and sour-smelling. Nurses and technicians crowded around the woman
and made last-minute adjustments in the medical equipment. Someone
gave me a surgical mask and asked me to take off my shoes. I found
a spot behind the bustle, where I stood, feeling out of place and queasy
from the strange odors and heat. Dr. Gogate inserted a thin wire tube
up into the woman's uterus in order to suck a few milligrams of
placenta tissue, which would then be transferred for analysis to a petri
dish. As I watched the wire's journey on the screen of the ultrasound
machine, I slowly became disgusted. It had been building all week, but
I think seeing this woman with her legs spread on the examination
table, so exposed and, in a sense, so violated by the forces of her society,
caused something to snap in me. What right did India have, I thought,
to take the newest technology from the West and use it for something
as reprehensible as the slaughter of female babies?

"Slaughter" is an explosive word, and it was something of a dilemma to find myself suddenly thinking of the abortion of a female

fetus as "slaughter" when I had for years believed in a woman's right to end her pregnancy. If I thought of the abortion of a female fetus as "slaughter," then what was I to call the abortion of a male fetus? Was it intellectually consistent to be in favor of a woman's right to abortion yet opposed to sex-selective abortion? I honestly did not know what I thought. For the rest of my time in India, I made a small career out of posing the question, whenever the topic came up, to feminists, doctors, lawyers and friends. It would often provoke heated arguments, and there seemed no way out of the moral dilemma.

It annoyed me that although the feminists were doing the right thing in opposing sex-selective abortion, they were so unaware of the philosophical traps. They tended to be more emotional than rational in their arguments, and the paradox was that some of their rhetoric could easily have been borrowed by right-to-life groups in the United States. Some Indian feminists routinely referred to sex-selective abortion as "female feticide," which made me wonder why they were not opposed to "male feticide" as well. Reports by the Women's Centre included incendiary phrases such as "large-scale killing of the female fetus." One 1986 magazine article about sex-determination tests they distributed from their files was entitled "The Silent Scream," which also happened to be the title of the 1985 pro-life propaganda film in the United States claiming to show a twelve-week-old fetus writhing in pain as it was surgically aborted. The feminists argued that sex-selective abortion was illegal because it violated Articles 14 and 15 of the Indian Constitution, which guarantee no discrimination against women. They also argued that the unborn female fetus had "the right" to be born. (Indian courts have not ruled in general on whether a fetus has rights, although the law does recognize certain inheritance rights in favor of an unborn child.) Whatever the case, if the female fetus had "the right" to be born, should not the male fetus have the same?

What I eventually concluded was that the feminists' sloganeering was aimed more at emotional effect than at logical persuasion, and that it reflected the differences in the issue of abortion in India and the United States. Bombay feminists could freely make outrageous statements that seemed to threaten a woman's right to terminate her pregnancy because the right to abortion was not under siege in India as it was in the United States. Interestingly, India had never engaged in the debate over when life begins, perhaps because the Hindu classical texts had expressed three views on the subject: life begins at conception; life begins with the first movement of the fetus; and life begins with the first breath of the baby after delivery.

Abortion in India was illegal in most cases until 1971, but in August of that year the law was liberalized after only two hours of tepid debate at the end of the monsoon session of Parliament. This was a year and a half before the U.S. Supreme Court in *Roe v. Wade* legalized abortion in America. Although I found in my research that it was never stated as such on the floor of the Indian Parliament, the reason for the easy passage of the Indian abortion law was widely acknowledged to be the government's desperate desire for another method of family planning in a country whose population was expected to reach one billion by the year 2000, with the result that India would eventually surpass China as the most populous nation on earth. The current Indian law in fact permits abortion only under certain conditions, but these are so broadly interpreted as to make abortion available on demand before the twentieth week of pregnancy. (For example, as the law is written, an Indian woman may have a legal abortion if she says that her method of contraception has failed.)

Since then, Indian feminists have generally supported a woman's right to terminate her pregnancy by abortion but have criticized what they believe is the government's callous view of abortion as a tool of the state in carrying out population control. Abortion in India has become a symbol—rightly—for the neglect of women's health. For example, the Women's Centre says that 90 percent of abortions in India are performed by unqualified doctors, and that on average there are 68 deaths for every 1,000 abortions performed in India. This is a much higher death rate from abortion than in other poor countries, but my instincts told me it was not an exaggeration. (In the United States in 1987, there were a reported 4 deaths following the 1,588,000 abortions performed.) "A woman's health isn't taken into consideration," said Vibhuti Patel, one of the leaders of the Women's Centre. "Our major issue is safe abortion." The same feminists also opposed the mass use of the birth-control pill, criticizing it as another example of the government's desire to control women regardless of health. Feminists complained that village women were commonly given oral contraceptives without adequate examinations or follow-ups, and were largely unaware of the pill's side effects. Many feminists were also opposed to the methods of the government's population-control program in general, arguing that the program was motivated solely by the desire to bring down the birth rate and not by any desire to better women's lives.

As I spoke to the feminists, I began to wonder if sex-selective abortion had ever been debated in the United States, where the ethical issues raised by advances in technology—such as genetic engineering—are more fully developed. I had noticed some references to American essays on the subject in the library of a medical research foundation during my trip to Bombay, and when I returned to Delhi I wrote a friend in Washington and asked her to try to locate the material for me. What she sent was fascinating: In the late seventies in the *New England Journal of Medicine,* in what was apparently one of the first explorations of the subject, a research group of the Hastings Center, a think tank for biomedical ethics in Briarcliff Manor, N.Y., concluded that amniocentesis for sex choice should be discouraged. But in a subsequent article in the same journal, John C. Fletcher, a specialist in bioethics at the National Institutes of Health and a codirector of the Hastings Center research group, changed his mind, apparently because of the same moral dilemmas I was experiencing. He argued that although "sex choice was not a compelling reason for abortion," it was nonetheless "inconsistent to support an abortion law that protects the absolute right of women to decide and, at the same time, to block access to information about the fetus because one thinks that an abortion may be foolishly sought on the basis of the information." It was a persuasive point of view, but one that is easier to hold in the United States than in a culture where tens of thousands of fetuses are aborted simply because they are female. After I returned from India, *The New York Times* discovered the issue in a front-page story on Christmas Day, 1988. Under the headline FETAL SEX TEST USED AS STEP TO ABORTION, Gina Kolata reported that in the United States, "many doctors are providing prenatal diagnosis to pregnant women who want to abort a fetus on the basis of sex alone." The story at first seemed to suggest that sex-selective abortion was taking root in America but later explained that the practice was chiefly confined to women from India and other parts of Asia who had settled in the United States and who were "most likely to ask openly for sex selection." If so, how could the United States stop the practice without infringing on abortion rights, as well as rights to certain medical procedures?

Ultimately, I decided that the question of whether it was intellectually consistent to be in favor of a woman's right to abortion yet opposed to sex-selective abortion had, for me, a different answer in the United States than in India. I can't resolve the contradictions and can only conclude that there are no universally applicable answers in this world. In the United States, although the principle of *Roe v. Wade* is under attack, abortion is still generally available until the twenty-eighth week of pregnancy; in effect, a woman does not have to give her doctor a reason for her decision. Although the idea of terminating a pregnancy simply because the fetus is female is morally repugnant to me, I believe that outlawing such a practice would fundamentally infringe on a woman's right to choose.

In India, I felt, the situation was different. The Indian abortion law, although broadly interpreted, did not, as it was written, give a woman an unconditional right to abortion. An Indian woman was permitted to have an abortion only under certain conditions, usually if her doctor determined that her pregnancy would cause "grave injury" to her "physical or mental health." Pregnancy as a result of rape was presumed to constitute grave injury to a woman's physical or mental health, as was a failure of contraception—the most frequently stated reason for abortion in India.

More important, I think the shocking number of aborted female fetuses in India constituted so serious a problem that the state had an obligation to step in and protect its interests, as the legislature of Maharashtra had done in banning sex-determination tests. The language of *Roe v. Wade* may help explain what I mean. In the majority opinion, Justice Harry A. Blackmun wrote that although an abortion should be considered part of a woman's right to privacy, that right was not absolute, and at the third trimester, when the fetus had the potential to live outside the mother's womb, "the state interests as to protection of health, medical standards, and prenatal life become dominant." Laws are not made in a social vacuum but reflect the societies they govern, and in India, I think, the rights of the state became dominant when prenatal tests developed for the detection of genetic abnormalities in an unborn fetus began to be so widely and grotesquely abused.

Not all Indian feminists agreed with this point of view. Some argued, as I had in the beginning, that any law to ban sex-determination tests infringed on a woman's freedom of choice. "I would not be surprised if some women do challenge the law on the grounds that they have a right to abort a female fetus," Indira Jaising, one of Bombay's leading lawyers, told me before the Maharashtra law was actually passed. Others thought India's population problem was the more important issue and saw an aborted female fetus as at least one less child. A few even argued, like the woman obstetrician I had heard speak at the meeting of the Bombay branch of the Indian Medical Association, that it would be more humane to abort a female fetus than to allow the child to enter a world full of such hardship for women.

Ultimately, the feminists sidestepped the abortion-rights issue by pushing for a ban on the "sex test" and not a regulation of abortion itself, even though the ban did, in effect, limit a woman's abortion right. But most feminists eventually came around to this approach. As it was written, the Maharashtra law permitted a prenatal test only if a woman was at least thirty-five years old, or had a medical or family history suggesting the possibility of a baby with birth defects. The law prescribed prison sentences for both doctors and patients, but only if a panel of health professionals or other "appropriate authority" found the test to be a violation of the law—which, feminists admitted, made the ban virtually impossible to enforce. "So many people congratulated us, but it was a limited victory and the task now is very complex," said Vibhuti Patel of the Women's Centre. She was hopeful, how-ever, that the law would at least have a deterrent effect. "It has taken away the respectability of the test," she said. "There won't be any more advertisements on trains." Although a number of doctors com-plained that an unenforceable law was not the best path toward reform, D. T. Joseph, the state health secretary, insisted it was an important first step. "Laws don't necessarily change society," he said, "but why can't a law occasionally lead the way?" He estimated that the ban had stopped 85 percent of Bombay doctors from performing sex-determination tests, and that the rest had gone underground. He also expected thou-sands of women to travel to other states where the practice was still legal. But by the time I left India, the Maharashtra precedent was increasingly seen as a qualified success, and a nationwide ban was under consideration in Delhi.

I was in Bombay again a few months after the ban was enacted, and so I stopped by to see how Dr. Soonawala's upmarket practice had been affected by the new law. Dr. Soonawala was as polite as ever, although more direct than before. "I would love to do the test," he said. "But at this stage, when it's all too hot, I don't want to put my foot in a mess." Dr. Soonawala told me his office turned down three to four requests a week for the test, and he assumed the women then turned to doctors who were willing to perform it illegally.

Dr. Soonawala found the situation unsafe and unfair, even though he insisted that he personally was not comfortable aborting a fetus on the basis of sex. "Emotionally, I don't accept it," he said. "No one emotionally accepts a war. But still there are wars where people slaughter each other. So it's sort of a similar situation. There are so many instances when we read in the newspapers of infanticide, but I think it is much more cruel to sacrifice a child after it is born than at a stage where there is hardly any format. Abortion *has* been accepted in this country."

DR. SOONAWALA WAS RIGHT. OF COURSE IT WAS INFINITELY MORE CRUEL to murder a day-old infant than to abort a ten-week-old fetus. But having been to Belukkurichi and met the four couples who had murdered their daughters, I found myself judging the situation a little differently. Those couples could afford neither dowry nor abortion, and they had no access to any prenatal tests. Although killing a baby because she was a girl could never be considered another version of aborting a fetus because it was female, the uneducated people of the valleys around Belukkurichi were doing what they felt they had to do, and what they saw as their right. Mariaye, the woman who had allowed her mother-in-law to kill her daughter, put it bluntly. "Abortion at the fourth month is legally accepted in India," she said. "Instead of killing the child in the womb, I killed the child when it was born. If that is accepted, why can't I do this?"

I could never agree with her reasoning, and yet I thought no better of the affluent women of Bombay who aborted their female fetuses. Although the Bombay women had all of the benefits of modernity, their values remained as backward as those of the villagers. Some of them were from families with enough status in the community to set an example by refusing to pay any dowry at all, but this option did not occur to them. It was especially depressing to me that educated women apparently valued themselves so little as women that they were willing to prevent a female child, just because she was female, from coming into the world. To those women who argued that this was their "choice," I would counter that "choice" is not made in a social vacuum, and that their "choice" had in fact been determined for them by thousands of years of prejudice and discrimination. Ultimately, the "sex test" was proof that education and material progress alone cannot alter traditional attitudes. I learned that there has to be a place for political action—as in the case of the feminist movement to ban the "sex test" in Bombay—that raises people's consciousness as it tries to change the system from outside.

CHAPTER 6

TOWARDS EQUALITY

The Indian Women's Movement

IN THE EARLY 1970S, VINA MAZUMDAR WAS A FORCEFUL, OPINIONATED and well-known university professor with two children, a doctorate in philosophy from Oxford and sixteen years of teaching political science behind her. Like most Indian women of her class and sensibility, many of them educated far beyond the dreams of their mothers, Mazumdar had looked around her comfortable world and assumed that the problems of the Indian woman had been solved at independence. The Indian Constitution guaranteed women complete equality with men. Not only could women vote and sit in Parliament, but the highest office in the land belonged to a woman, Prime Minister Indira Gandhi. The rest of India's women, it appeared, only needed a little more time. "We hadn't a clue," Mazumdar recalled.

So when the Indian government appointed a commission to investigate the status of the nation's women, Mazumdar thought it was, in her words, "a joke." She and her friends used to ask each other, she said, "What is the government of India up to that they want to investigate the status of women? Is that still a problem? Equality is a state of mind. If we are not yet equal, it is our failure." The government had in fact commissioned the study as a reaction to new thinking within the United Nations, which during the height of the Western women's movement in the early 1970s had begun prodding developing countries to improve the status of billions of forgotten women—the uneducated, rural poor who made up the vast majority of the world's female population.

The Indian government, like everyone else, had no clear idea how the changes at independence had affected, if they had at all, the lives of the women in the villages. The inquiry was to take three years, but halfway through, when it became clear that the commission was lagging far behind in its task, the government asked Mazumdar to take over. Most of her friends told her to turn down the offer, arguing that the timetable was impossible and, more important, that the work would narrow her focus, diverting her from the larger concerns of her academic career. Mazumdar was not particularly interested in women's issues, but she took the job anyway, accepting the limitation that there would be little time for new research in the eighteen months she had left. The committee worked mostly with existing data, but Mazumdar got intelligent people to analyze it, and the result was the first comprehensive compilation of material on the subject of India's women.

Its conclusions were shattering. The committee found that the majority of Indian women, far from benefiting from the country's material gains, were actually worse off in significant ways than they were before independence.

"The first thing I felt was shock," Mazumdar remembered, sitting enveloped in clouds of cigarette smoke one afternoon in a cramped, cluttered office at her research institution in New Delhi. She was a blunt and commanding woman, in her middle fifties, with a husky voice and stylishly short hair, in an unadorned sari she seemed to wear as an afterthought. "The second thing I felt," Mazumdar continued, "was a tremendous anger—'Something has to be done.' Then I began to question why even a social scientist can remain so damn ignorant. Not only about the situation of women, but even our knowledge about our own society is so appallingly unequal."

The 480-page report, "Towards Equality," published in December 1974, was the first thunderbolt announcing what is so well known today. Social change, development and other trends under the heading of "progress" had in many cases made the lives of women worse. The percentage of women in the labor force in India, rural and urban, had declined to less than 10 percent. Although most experts agreed that the official statistics ignored many women who did in fact work, particularly the millions of self-employed, the figure was still alarming. Industrialization and new methods of agriculture had improved the lives of men, but women were not trained to acquire the new skills demanded by modern industry. In factories, they had been displaced by technology, and the work they had once done for an income at home—spinning, oil pressing, tobacco processing—could not compete with factory-made goods. The literacy rate of women was half that of men, and the custom of dowry, which had once been confined to the upper castes, was sweeping the country. Concerns about women's problems, which had been central to the freedom struggle, seemed completely forgotten. "Our investigation has revealed that large masses of women in this country have remained unaffected by the rights guaranteed to them by the Constitution and the laws enacted since Independence," the committee concluded. The report would change Vina Mazumdar's life. "My earlier work," she told me, "was only earning a living."

Today, Vina Mazumdar is one of the matriarchs of the current women's movement in India. Her work with the report led her to establish the Centre for Women's Development Studies, a small but influential research institute in New Delhi that has forced the government to change important policies affecting women and to admit where it has failed. Mazumdar's group has also worked to organize and train women in villages. "What those women have taught me I did not learn in fifty-five years of my previous life," she told me. "They cured me of my feeling of guilt, that all this involvement was detrimental to my family. They gave me new insights into a woman's relationship with the environment and nature, of which I was totally unaware. They taught me that the achievement of equality does not necessarily mean giving up being a woman. These women taught me that I should not be ashamed of being different."

But Vina Mazumdar's metamorphosis is, more than anything else, a reflection of the unique problems that face the present women's movement in India. Like the feminist movement in the United States, the Indian movement was founded by an elite; most of its leaders are from the English-educated ruling class. Devaki Jain, for example, whose time-allocation studies of village women led to her evolution as the other matriarch of the women's movement, is from one of the leading political families of south India. As she admitted of her own background, "It's not a clear case of emerging out of what you would call feminist struggles." But unlike American feminists, whose first-hand experience of economic and personal injustice influenced the movement to focus largely on such middle-class issues as job discrimination and equal pay for equal work, Indian feminist leaders have come to the realization that their effort is meaningless unless it attempts to change the lives of the 80 percent of Indian women whose most basic concerns—access to clean water, animal fodder and cooking fuel—remain alien to their own privileged world. "We knew so little about India," Madhu Kishwar told me, describing the first few years of publication of *Manushi,* the feminist magazine she edits. "To talk about Indian women, and women's movements, is ridiculous unless you systematically attempt to understand who these Indian women are." The problem is also one of overwhelming numbers. "You are talking of four hundred million women," Margaret Alva, Minister of State for Youth Affairs, Sports and Women, told me with some exasperation. "The one thing I have realized is that whatever you do, you feel you're still just scratching the surface. For every woman who sits in Parliament, or has done a Ph.D. or goes to the Supreme Court to argue a case, you have thousands in the villages who don't even know about their basic rights and that they are equal citizens."

It was partly my work in Khajuron that prodded me into an exploration of the Indian women's movement. After my time there I was skeptical that any movement would ever make much of a difference in the lives of India's rural women. Was it possible that a smattering of upper-class women could ignite millions of poor villagers to rise up against repression when the village women themselves did not think they were particularly repressed? Were there any rural-based movements organized by the poor? How much, if at all, was the current Indian women's movement influenced by the American and European feminist movements?

It took me the better part of three and a half years to try to sort out a jumble of theory and action that spanned regions, political parties, class and caste, embraced both Mahatma Gandhi and Karl Marx, worked at often divergent purposes, encompassed elite groups and mass struggles and did not, in most cases, even think of itself as a collective movement. Indian feminists were always debating exactly what constituted "the movement," and were intensely self-critical about the gains they had made. "There is still no clarity, despite a great deal of enthusiasm," Vina Mazumdar complained. Ela Bhatt, a pioneer who founded the most powerful women's trade union in India, was also far from satisfied. "We are able to come together on a particular issue and raise our voices," she told me, "but beyond that, we are still scattered. We still have not learned to work together." Many Indian feminists frequently criticized the women's groups that accepted money from Europe and the United States, arguing that funding organizations like Oxfam and the Ford Foundation were trying to buy control of the Indian groups. I never saw any evidence of this, but India was still so sensitive to its colonial past that the funding issue was heatedly debated at women's conferences. Within the Indian government itself, where feminists had begun to have a voice in development policy, thereby making the women's movement a livelihood for a growing number of people, quarrels and disputes were routine. In the summer of 1988, when a government-appointed committee released a preliminary draft of a national plan for Indian women up to the year 2000, there was an uproar from those feminists who had not been included in the planning. They retaliated by denouncing the report in the press. When I went to see Margaret Alva, the minister who had overseen the report, she was fuming. "There are many who ask, 'How did you draw it up without involving us?' " she said. "But my point is, unless you have a draft, you can't have a debate. I can't just go and announce I want a national debate on women's programs. I would get ten thousand or twenty thousand letters saying 'You do this.' That's not the way to draft a plan."

Occasionally a troublemaker would question whether the women's movement in India even existed. In 1988, Madhu Kishwar of *Manushi* infuriated feminists when she asserted at a conference in the southern city of Trivandrum that there was in fact no women's "movement" in India at all, but rather "mobilizations" and "sporadic struggles." I myself would certainly describe all the activity that is occurring on behalf of women in India as a "movement," but one with three separate parts: first, the urban feminist groups; second, the larger, more rural-oriented voluntary organizations; and third, mass peasant struggles. In the following pages, I will take a brief look at these three segments of the movement and then explore in more depth the Self-Employed Women's Association, or SEWA, a trade union that I would classify as belonging to the second part of the movement. SEWA emerged in the 1980s as the premier women's organization in India and a model of what was possible in the development of the poor.

Like most foreign journalists, I made my initial contact with the Indian women's movement through the first group, the urban feminists, since they were the most accessible to me. These were young, articulate, highly educated and contentious women in New Delhi, Bombay, Madras and Calcutta who had begun to form feminist groups in the mid-1970s. The atmosphere in the country was ripe for them. "Towards Equality," the report of Vina Mazumdar's committee, had just been released to a flood of dramatic coverage in the press when the United Nations declared 1975 to be International Women's Year and the beginning of a UN "Decade for Women"—giving Indian feminist leaders a context for their actions and later, through international conferences, opening up a worldwide network of contacts for them. In 1977, after the lifting of the Emergency, the suspension of civil liberties imposed by Indira Gandhi, there was an "explosion," in the words of Vina Mazumdar, "of people wanting to participate." The women's movement—vocal, critical, focused on social issues—became a natural part of the new era. The current Indian women's movement is also, of course, propelled by the American and European feminist movements, although Indian women's leaders continue to debate the extent of the influence. Those women working with rural groups argue that the Indian movement is unique and indigenous, and from their point of view, they are right. Westernized feminists in the big cities, however, have established ties. Devaki Jain is a friend of Gloria Steinem's and stays with her when she is in New York. Ritu Menon, who cofounded Kali for Women, a feminist publishing house, received a master's degree in American Studies at Vassar and then worked at Doubleday in New York in 1970, the year that Doubleday published Kate Millett's *Sexual Politics*. "There was the excitement of the moment, of being there when something really significant was happening," Menon remembered of her time at Doubleday. In India, she founded Kali in part because "in the long term, there are few activities that are potentially more subversive than writing."

The urban women's groups took several forms. Some were in effect the women's wings of the major political parties in New Delhi, most notably the All India Women's Conference, the fifty-year-old establishment organization that had been part of the independence struggle and had longstanding ties to the Congress party. The more confrontational Mahila Dakshita Samiti was linked to the Janata party. The National Federation of Indian Women was the women's wing of the Communist Party of India, while the All India Democratic Women's

Association was closely associated with the Communist Party of India (Marxist). (India's Communist party split apart in the 1960s into two factions, one favoring the Soviet Union and the other favoring China; when the Soviet leader Mikhail Gorbachev came to India in 1986, he had to meet with both. One of Gorbachev's aides confessed at the time that he was "bewildered" by the existence of the two parties and stated with a certain irony that in the Soviet Union, one Communist party was considered sufficient.) Other women's organizations were small, independent, generally leftist groups whose activities centered on demonstrations. Much of their protesting was aimed at dowry deaths, but they also took on anything—such as the sati in Deorala—that might be considered violence against women. In New Delhi, the group Saheli grew out of a demonstration to protest the burning of a young woman in her in-laws' home; in Madras, members of the militant group Pennurimai Iyakkam threw eggs and cow-dung cakes at lurid movie posters to protest what they termed obscene portrayals of women in south Indian films. The groups also operated centers that helped poor women find jobs and housing and provided legal and medical aid.

And yet the scope of the groups was highly limited. Although some insisted that their membership included thousands of slum women, in truth there were rarely more than two dozen upper-middle-class women who were active in each organization. Each group wasted time on quarrels over ideology and personalities—conflict whose real source, I think, was the frustration they felt because of their inability to cross the boundaries of class and affect large numbers of women. "The purpose for which we had come together and had started Saheli does not look anywhere within reach," Amiya, a Saheli member, wrote in a collective diary that she and her colleagues kept and then excerpted in a booklet about the group's first four years. "Actually, no woman has been coming to us needing assistance . . . to me it looks as if gradually Saheli is becoming a place (a lovely club) where middle- and upper-middle-class women come and talk about their experiences, which are of no earthly use to anybody excepting themselves perhaps." The urban groups were easy targets for feminists more interested in rural development, who saw them as cliques of elitists involved in the women's movement because it was the fashion of the moment. Inevitably, the different urban groups squabbled among themselves, dismissing one another as "middle class" when, in fact, even the most militant women were from bourgeois, well-connected families. "They don't like us because they think we're elitist," Radha Sridhar, a member of the Madras Joint Action Council for Women, said of Pennurimai Iyakkam, the egg-throwing group. "But I don't think I serve the cause any better if I take a bus instead of a car."

The urban groups, however, served a purpose. If they did not represent the bulk of the movement, they certainly articulated the movement and molded feminism into a live, respectable issue in the government and the press. Without the urban groups, dowry deaths would never have received the attention they did. The sati in Deorala would not have become a national issue. In Bombay, the use of prenatal diagnostic tests to determine the sex of a child might still be a legal, socially accepted practice.

My next exposure to the women's movement came in visits to the large voluntary organizations, most of them outside Delhi. These groups, too, were run by elite women, but the leaders had succeeded in breaking the bonds of class and caste and reaching the grass roots. There were perhaps two hundred such groups doing significant work relating to women in India—no one was sure of the number—and international funding agencies estimated that some sixty of these were doing outstanding work. One of the leaders in this voluntary movement was Jaya Arunachalam, an official of the Congress party in the state of Tamil Nadu, a Brahmin, who had become disillusioned with politics as a means of helping the poor. In 1978, in Madras, she founded Working Women's Forum, an organization that arranged for small loans to poor women who sold vegetables, fruit, flowers, cloth and other goods in the streets. The organization had begun with loans of about twenty-five dollars each to thirty women; by 1987, the Working Women's Forum claimed more than sixty thousand members in three states. It had its own bank and had expanded to include an unusually successful family-planning program. When I visited the organization in 1987, Jaya Arunachalam had just received an invitation to speak at a forum in Washington to discuss how to implement a bill that would provide three-hundred-dollar loans to small enterprises owned by poor people in the United States. "Rather than taking the charity-from-above approach," Arunachalam told me, explaining her philosophy, "we must develop people instead."

I have categorized as the third part of the women's movement the mass peasant struggles—in some cases uprisings—in which women played leading, militant roles. These women would never have considered themselves connected with any urban feminist group, yet their actions were studied and celebrated by feminists in Delhi, Bombay, Madras and Calcutta.

The Chipko Movement, for example, one of the developing world's most famous grass-roots environmental campaigns, was an inspiration for urban feminists because of the unusually prominent role that women played in it. The movement was born one morning in March 1973, in a remote hill town on the edge of the central Himalayas, when several contractors arrived, on orders from a sporting-goods store, to cut down ten of the village's precious ash trees. The villagers asked the contractors to leave the trees standing, and when the men refused, the villagers stopped them by literally hugging the earmarked trunks. (*Chipko* means "hugging the trees.") The following year, it was the women—the gatherers of fuel, fodder and water who suffer the most from soil erosion—who brought the movement to its dramatic climax. On a day when the men of the village of Reni were away in town to protest the auctioning of a forest near their homes, contractors with axes arrived in Reni to begin cutting down 2,415 trees. Two dozen women of the village, led by Gaura Devi, a poor and illiterate widow of fifty, successfully barred the path to the forest and sang, "This forest is our mother's home; we will protect it with all our might." One of the contractors spat in Gaura Devi's face, but she and the other women refused to move.

In the southern state of Kerala, it was the women who were in the forefront of a struggle for the rights of fishermen and women, demonstrating in the streets and sending protest groups to the government long before the men became involved. In rural areas of the state of Maharashtra, during a movement in the early seventies to organize agricultural laborers, Gail Omvedt, an American academic and feminist activist now living in the area, reported that male organizers of the leftist parties said that women were "the most ready to fight, the first to break through police lines, the last to go home." In the small town of Nipani in the state of Karnataka, seven thousand women working in the tobacco industry rose up in March 1980 to strike for a minimum daily wage of fifty cents and an eight-hour working day. For the first time the owners of the tobacco factories were forced to the negotiating table, where they met the workers' demands. The strike set off a continuing struggle between the factory management and the workers' union, and although the union leadership was male, the initiative and militancy came, once again, from the women.

Sometimes more specific struggles for women's rights have evolved within the larger struggles. This was the case in a brutal battle over land in central Bihar, a bleak state in the plains of the northeast, the poorest in India, where thousands have died in recent years in clashes between militant peasant militias and "armies" fielded by wealthy landlords. In the late 1970s and early 1980s, in the villages around the town of Bodh Gaya, a group of educated young activists, inspired by the late revolutionary leader Jayaprakash Narayan, led poor villagers in a fight for redistribution of twelve thousand acres of land controlled by one local religious leader. Some of the activists were feminists from the city of Patna, Bihar's capital. Their initial goal was land reform, but in meetings with the villagers, the feminists asked why the women had to do all of the housework, although they labored in the fields as hard as their husbands—and why their husbands, as a matter of routine, felt they had the right to get drunk and beat their wives. After these discussions, one village woman went home and told her husband that from that day onward, he could wash his own plate after dinner. His response was to fling the plate in her face and beat her brutally. Yet the discussions had some positive effects. For example, one woman who was beaten by her husband for having a sterilization operation was rescued by her neighbors, something that might not have happened before. Later, when it became clear that a portion of the religious leader's land was to be redistributed to the men only, even though the women had been in the front lines of the demonstrations, the feminists led the village women to object. Eventually, only one thousand acres were given to the villagers, but some women did receive land in their own names. Many more had at least been made aware of rights they had never known before.

That was apparent when I visited Bihar in late March of 1987, at a time when the fields were already dry and brown, stripped of their harvest of wheat. In Shekhawara, a relatively prosperous village, I met Kunti Devi, a poor woman who had fought in the Bodh Gaya struggle. Unlike the shy, terrified women of Khajuron, Kunti Devi looked me squarely in the face, smiled and invited me into a mud house to talk. She wore a printed orange sari and was thin and muscular, with a tattoo on her arm. Her face was pretty but weathered by the sun; she might have been twenty, thirty or forty. We sat down on a charpoy. "Before the struggle," she told me, "I had to work all day in the fields and then come home to do all the housework while my husband did nothing." It wasn't clear whether her husband had now been reformed, but what amazed me was how openly she talked. Unlike the women of Khajuron, she was aware of the unfairness of her life. Kunti Devi told me that she owned land jointly with her husband, another breakthrough, and that when she and her friends heard of any man who was beating his wife, they rushed as a group to stop him. When I asked her to which caste she belonged, she refused to tell me. "I don't believe in it," she said. Coming from a villager, this was a remarkable statement. The raising of women's consciousness, here in the middle of Bihar, had accomplished an extraordinary thing: qualifying this village woman to be considered part of the larger movement in India.

WHEN I FIRST WALKED INTO THE MAIN OFFICES OF SEWA IN THE GUJARATI city of Ahmedabad one hot October morning in 1987, I was met by a cacophony of clamoring women, all of whom seemed to be having a good time. Crowds of them were noisily milling around tellers' desks with small handfuls of coins; others were eating chapaties and nursing babies along the sides of the room. It turned out that I was in the middle of the SEWA bank, a growing financial institution of nineteen thousand depositors, all women, some of whom had received loans for as little as four dollars. The Self-Employed Women's Association—the acronym SEWA corresponds to the Indian word *sewa,* or "service"— was a sprawling organization for the economic empowerment of women. It had organized poor women into unions of garment makers, cigarette rollers, vegetable vendors and tobacco processors, and had enabled them to open their first accounts in the SEWA bank. Every day, three hundred women walked through the doors to deposit a dollar or take out thirty cents, and every day the excruciatingly patient tellers had to fill out the deposit and withdrawal slips for their mostly illiterate customers. Frequently a depositor would forget that she had made an earlier withdrawal, and when a teller read out her passbook balance, she would become angry and complain. "So lots of explaining has to be done," sighed Jayashree Vyas, the bank's managing director, who had been lured away by SEWA from a high-paying job at the Central Bank of India.

Vyas talked with me in her office, a glassed-in cubicle that looked out on the pandemonium. On her desk were stacks of loan applications, and when I asked her about them, she selected one from the pile. The form said that Maniben Parmar, a seamstress who made petticoats and dresses for a living, had just been approved for a $400 loan. Maniben Parmar bought her cloth from a middleman and made thirty cents a day; she had eight dollars saved in the SEWA bank. She was the mother of four children and belonged to a low caste. Her husband, who worked at the telephone office, made the relatively impressive sum of $120 a month. Maniben Parmar wanted her loan to make house repairs. A friend, Ashaben, had recommended her. "It's not for a productive purpose," Vyas admitted. "But it's for improving their living standards." Even though her husband's income had helped her secure the money, the loan would be in Maniben Parmar's name alone. Her husband could not make withdrawals from her savings account, nor could he apply for a loan of his own.

For years, women had been treated "like dirt," in the words of SEWA founder Ela Bhatt, by traditional bankers. As Chandaben, a dealer in used clothes, explained in one of SEWA's reports: "We were not used to going to the big banks, and the sahibs would insult us. . . . We also wanted to open savings accounts, because though we sometimes manage to save some of our earnings, we have nowhere to hide it in the house. Our husbands or sons find it and use it up." With the SEWA bank, Ela Bhatt explained—in a gentle tone belying the boldness of her thinking—"we will be able to nonviolently, in the most Gandhian way, eliminate the husbands."

Ela Bhatt was an unlikely revolutionary. Small, shy and unobtrusive, she was a fifty-five-year-old woman with a little girl's voice who dressed simply in handspun cotton saris and had learned to overcome a stammer she had as a child. All of the SEWA members added *ben,* for "sister," to the end of each other's name, so Ela Bhatt was simply "Elaben." The women were in awe of her, and her reputation was such that Rajiv Gandhi had appointed her to the upper house of Parliament. As far as I could tell, she was a person devoid of egotism, and her manner was invariably sweet. When I told her, before I left India, that I would eventually be moving to Japan, she mentioned that she herself had once been to Tokyo. I asked her what she thought. "Too much neat," she said in her tiny voice. "One is always afraid of making a mess." I don't know whether she meant this literally or metaphorically, but I now know she was right either way. Another time I sat near her at a dinner in Delhi, at a table with a dozen of the city's most obstreperous intellectuals, all of them arguing in the usual flamboyant fashion about the failings of Rajiv Gandhi's government. But Ela Bhatt was mostly silent; even so, when I looked around the table I realized that of all the guests, she was the one who had most successfully challenged the status quo. Parliament, however, had terrified her at first. "The first week I was quite dazed," she remembered. "So many facilities, so much access to information, such easy access to power, so much respect. I was feeling like the fate of millions was there. And all the big names I've heard were sitting right next to me."

Her humility, of course, hid the formidable personality that she was. When Barber Conable, the president of the World Bank, was visiting Delhi in November 1987, his office had arranged a meeting between Ela Bhatt and Conable's wife, Charlotte, a specialist in women's issues. Ela Bhatt politely told the World Bank office in New Delhi that she would be very happy to meet with Mrs. Conable, but wouldn't it be nice if Mr. Conable were also available to discuss women's development issues, which should not be of concern only to wives?

Ela Bhatt's determination seemed to have come from her mother, a woman whose formal education had stopped at the age of ten but who had insisted that her daughter go to college, despite the reservations of Ela's father, a High Court judge in Gujarat. Ela, who was from a strict, well-to-do Brahmin family, promptly did the very thing her parents had most feared—she fell in love, with a Brahmin, but a penniless one. It took her parents seven years to agree to the marriage. While Ela and her future husband waited for permission, they soaked up the exhilarating atmosphere on a campus stirring, in the early fifties, with Gandhian thought and plans to build a new nation. Finally they were married, and Ela received a law degree and decided to live and work in a manner Mahatma Gandhi would have approved. "I was very saturated with high ideals, and I wanted to work for the poor," she said. "I never thought of women as such."

Ahmedabad's Textile Labor Association, or TLA, the oldest and largest trade union of textile workers in India, was a natural outlet for her. The union had been born out of Mahatma Gandhi's first fast, in 1918, in behalf of striking workers who labored in the city's textile mills, which had been responsible for the city's economic growth. Ela Bhatt knew that the union was involved in extensive social welfare work among its members, and that its belief in Gandhian ideals of nonviolence and women's equality would ensure that there was a place for her. "But there were no other women," she said. "So working amongst men, all men, and doing the union work was quite difficult. I was very shy. Also, our people are not so kind, so they make all kinds of stories. I had to travel with them, and as I came up slowly in the leadership, I had to travel to all the places in Gujarat. I had to go by car, and with men. Then you also stay overnight when you go. So it was not much approved. So I had to fight a lot and I used to feel, What am I doing? Am I doing the right thing?"

But by 1968, Ela Bhatt had taken over the women's division of the union. Historically, the leaders of the women's division had focused on social work among the union members' wives. Ela Bhatt would soon demolish the assumption that what the wives really needed was handouts from well-meaning people like herself. Many of them were in fact workers themselves, laboring as vegetable vendors in the streets or as seamstresses in their homes, yet, typically, what they did was not viewed as work. That began to change in 1971, when Ela Bhatt went to one of Ahmedabad's markets and met a group of "head loaders"— the women who carried cloth on their heads between the wholesale and retail markets—who complained that the cloth merchants routinely cheated them. The merchants, it turned out, did not keep proper records of the number of trips a woman made each day, or of the distance traveled and weight carried. Clearly these women needed organizing, not welfare. Ela Bhatt helped them form a group so they could collectively demand better wages, and then she wrote an article about their plight for one of the Ahmedabad newspapers. When the merchants countered with an article of their own, asserting that they were paying the women fairly, Ela Bhatt printed the merchants' claims on cards and distributed them to the women.

Out of that effort grew SEWA, a trade union for self-employed women based on the Gandhian principles of nonviolence and the need to uplift the poorest members of society first. Gandhi believed that India's economy should be based on agriculture and small-scale cottage industry—a conviction that India's leaders immediately discarded after independence but that Ela Bhatt reinterpreted as a Gandhian basis for her work among the self-employed. Her first battle, however, was for the right of her union to exist. Until that time, Indian labor laws had recognized trade unions only in situations where there was a formal affiliation between employer and employee. The self-employed had no such relationship, but SEWA argued that the self-employed, like other workers, should have the right to organize. The state government finally acquiesced by agreeing to accept a broader definition of the law.

Over the years, SEWA learned that with the power of numbers, women could agitate for higher wages and better working conditions and against exploitation from middlemen and corrupt police. Women were organized into what SEWA hoped would become self-reliant cooperatives of weavers, block printers, basket weavers, patchwork quilt makers and kerosene vendors. Their goal was to take over the production and marketing of their own products, eliminating the middlemen who had cheated them in the past. SEWA also expanded, with mixed success, into the most drought-stricken rural areas of the state of Gujarat.

The organization, which had a $200,000 annual operating budget, was funded by the Indian government, the Ford Foundation, the International Labor Organization, Oxfam, the Unitarian Universalist India Fund and other donors. Ela Bhatt was also chairwoman of a government-appointed national commission investigating the status of self-employed women throughout India. She often said that nearly 90 percent of the labor force in India was self-employed (only twenty-five million out of eight hundred million Indians draw a paycheck), and of that 90 percent, at least 40 percent were female. It was these women, she argued, who should be leading the movement. What they most needed was a sense of their own worth. "The moment a woman is associated with a group on the basis of her work, and outside her role as a mother and a housewife, two things happen," she told me in an interview in the sparse New Delhi flat she had been allotted as a member of Parliament. "One is that for the first time in her life she perceives herself as a worker. She realizes that she is doing something important and making a contribution. And when that happens, that leads to integration with other communities, and the distances of caste and religion are gradually cut down."

Some of SEWA's most important work occurred among the twenty thousand Harijan women who picked up waste paper for recycling from Ahmedabad's streets. The story of the paper pickers is a dramatic example of how women's organizations like SEWA have had to fight government corruption as well as poverty, and how strength comes from numbers. In telling it, I have relied on a report by Elisabeth Bentley, a Harvard student I met in Ahmedabad, who was on a year-long fellowship to work with the paper pickers in their struggle to organize.

In Ahmedabad, as in the rest of India, nothing is unused. Visitors to India learn quickly that if they buy vegetables from a vendor in the local market, he will hand them over in a bag made of last Saturday's feature section from *The Times of India;* the cardboard cylinder inside a roll of toilet paper will be covered with a discarded office memo from the Ministry of Agriculture. The women paper pickers of Ahmedabad were crucial to this large recycling industry. Much of the reprocessing was very profitably performed by machine, but for the women the work was low-paying, exhausting and dangerously unsanitary. More than half the paper pickers roamed six miles during the course of a twelve-hour working day, carrying on their heads sacks that when full weighed forty pounds. Their wanderings took them into the city's most squalid garbage dumps, where they came in contact with raw sewage, dead animals, empty chemical containers and jagged glass. The women suffered from frequent infections, cuts and poisonings and made little more than a half dollar a day. Forced into the streets over several generations, they were classic victims of the kind of industrialization that had benefited men and marginalized women.

The story of their displacement began sometime after the turn of the century, when many of the paper pickers' grandfathers, originally weavers by trade, left their villages in search of work in Ahmedabad. Once there, they moved their families into the city's slums, where there was no room in the cramped huts for the large handlooms they had once used in the villages. Fortunately, the men were able to find jobs in Ahmedabad's textile mills, but their wives, who traditionally had done the pre-weaving and post-weaving work—spinning, preparing the yarn and removing the cloth from the looms—were left out. Some wives did manage to find work in the mills, but after 1930, when new technology and a changing world market forced the mill owners to cut back on labor, the women were the first to be let go. By the 1980s, when 70 percent of Ahmedabad's mills shut down, the crisis in the industry forced ever more women into the streets, a source of enormous humiliation for them. As one of the paper pickers explained in a study written by a SEWA leader: "When I was in the mill, we used to look down upon the paper pickers. We would say, 'We are the mill workers, we earn a good salary. These paper pickers, they wander around everywhere without shame. They are dirty.' Today, I am degraded too. When I first had to start picking paper, I would try to make my [veil] long so no one could see my face. I was so ashamed. How low I have fallen."

SEWA's involvement with the paper pickers began in 1975, when it secured contracts that allowed a group of women to pick up waste paper directly from the textile mills. By 1981, internal turmoil had split the paper pickers into two factions, but those still with SEWA won the right to collect waste paper in bulk from government offices and warehouses. This meant they were able to shovel chest-high piles of paper into the sacks rather than scavenging for trash piecemeal in the streets. Naturally this reduced their working hours and improved their wages, but it also interfered with an elaborate system of secret deals between longtime paper contractors and low-level government officials. When the paper pickers began to suspect that one contractor was stealing paper that belonged to them, they complained to government officials, who promised to look into it. Not willing to take the government's word, the paper pickers decided to stake out a warehouse where they made their pickups. One night, just as they had suspected, a large truck pulled up. Several men got out and began rapidly loading bags of paper. When the truck was half full, the women came out of hiding. Umbabehn, a SEWA paper picker, was one of those leading the confrontation. "Whose orders are you following in taking this paper?" she demanded of the men. But the men refused to tell her and instead challenged SEWA's own right to the waste. "But we were not fearful," Umbabehn recounted. "I said, 'You show your papers. Who are you to ask me?' " The women went to the police, but the police did nothing. SEWA then charged that the police inspector, the contractor and the government official who controlled the release of the paper were acting as a united front. SEWA's action might have reached a dead end, were it not for the power of the media. In 1983, Doordarshan, the government-owned television network, broadcast a show about the paper pickers' struggles, in which Luxmibehn, one of the youngest of the paper pickers, made sure to mention the full name and position of every man involved in the illegal pickup. There do not appear to have been any arrests, but the public humiliation was apparently enough. Within a week, the women were once again collecting the paper they were due.

The paper pickers were not the only women whose lives were changed by SEWA. On a hot November afternoon in a slum in central Ahmedabad, I met two sisters, Assammaben and Chandraben, who had been making bidis, the rough Indian hand-rolled cigarettes, for twenty-one years. As they sat outside their mud house, their legs crossed under them, Assammaben cut the leaves and Chandraben rolled. Between them, they averaged one thousand bidis a day. Before SEWA, they had made twenty-five cents a day, but after joining the SEWA union, which had argued for increased wages, they made almost a dollar a day. SEWA had also transformed illiterate women into video producers who made instruction tapes for the rest of the membership. It started when the United Nations University in Tokyo provided SEWA with some video equipment. Jyoti Jumani, one of SEWA's college-educated leaders, found herself having to explain to poor women how to operate a camera, use sound equipment, conduct an interview and edit tape. Her task was further complicated by the fact that the equipment was labeled in English: *play, rewind, fast forward, volume, eject, microphone, headphone* and so forth. The women could not read and write even in their own language, Gujarati, so Jumani decided the easiest course would be to teach them to memorize the English words on the machines. "I felt bad about teaching them in English, but otherwise we would have had to invent Gujarati words," she said, apparently unaware that she was recounting another chapter in the story of how English became the world's language of technology. By the time I visited SEWA, a dozen women knew how to use the video equipment properly; particularly skillful was Lilaben, a former vegetable vendor, who was working full-time at SEWA's video unit. "She's a very good producer," Jumani said. Lilaben had made a tape about the vegetable vendors and how they organized, and another about women who made their living transporting sand on the backs of donkeys. I saw a video on the SEWA bank, of very good quality, which included an interview with a garment maker who had received a loan for a sewing machine. Other videos taught women how to speak in court, or how to make the kind of mud stove that did not give off suffocating clouds of smoke in the house. "We started using the video to organize our members," Jumani explained. "But as I continued to use it, I started understanding the potential of the medium. Then I started using it to teach people."

Perhaps the truest measure of SEWA's success was the pressure it had come under in recent years to admit men as members. When SEWA went to court to secure licenses for its vegetable vendors, for example, it also argued on behalf of a number of men who sold vegetables in the streets. The subsequent ruling stipulated that all SEWA members should be granted vegetable licenses. The men, who could not be members of SEWA, were left out. This put the organization in an awkward situation and forced its leaders to rethink its purpose and goals; as Ela Bhatt admitted, "When we are talking of social change, it can't be separate." But this was not the consensus of the membership. "Every time we talk about it, our members clearly say, no, we do not want men," Ela Bhatt said. "I understand that, and I also realize that as soon as there are men sitting in a meeting, they in all good faith will want to dominate. Even if we did not give them the right to vote, or any right at the decision-making level, even then the very presence of men will make women withdraw, including myself." I expressed surprise at this. "Yes, I think all women feel it," she said. "My husband is a great supporter, so his expectations are much, much more than what I have been able to perform. It's a very subtle thing, and of course never has such a situation come that he is there in my official meetings. But maybe in the meeting I would be always unconsciously thinking, Will he approve of this? or, Is he of the same opinion or not?"

SEWA, of course, was not without its problems. At the time I was there in the fall of 1987, many of the cooperatives had financial troubles. The handblock printers, for instance, could not sell everything they produced, and the quilt makers had found it difficult to get cloth scraps since most of the textile mills had shut down. Two years before, after much internal debate and some resistance, SEWA had brought in "committed professionals" from the outside, all of them women, to manage the cooperatives, the bank and the union activities. This ran counter to the organization's philosophy of bringing people up from the bottom, but as Renana Jhabvala, one of SEWA's leading organizers, admitted: "There is no substitute for twenty-four years of study and experience. We came to the realization that if we didn't hire professionals, the co-ops would all be at a dead end."

SEWA's rural wing also had problems. Encompassing sixty-five villages in several districts in Gujarat, the rural operation trained women to weave, spin, plant fruit trees, make roof tiles and raise milk-producing water buffalo. Many women had been organized into their own dairy cooperatives, eliminating the middlemen who routinely cheated them of a fair price for milk. But the problems in establishing the dairy cooperatives were enormous. The men left out of the co-ops became bitter and alienated, which SEWA claimed drove them to sabotage. In some cases, SEWA organizers said, the men poured water into the cooperative's milk. These were just a part of the larger problem that SEWA had yet to solve in its village operations, which was a serious lack of qualified personnel. In order for any kind of rural development project to work well, it needed, at least in the beginning, intense supervision from the organizers. SEWA simply did not have enough trained people willing to leave their homes in Ahmedabad and live full-time in a mud hut in a village.

The organization tried to deal with the problem by sending its top organizers in for a day or two at a time—work that was both rewarding and colossally frustrating, as I learned the day I went with Anila Dholakia, the director of SEWA's rural wing, to several villages in one of the most drought-stricken regions of Gujarat.

Dholakia, a former university professor who was never at a loss for words, had joined SEWA after she had lost patience with the women's groups in town that held meetings to make needlepoint pillows. Like a number of other Indian women's activists I met, Dholakia assured me that she was opposed to "radical Western feminism" and that in India "we do not end our marriages, we do not burn our bras, we do not want to deglamorize ourselves." (This reaction to Western feminism used to puzzle me, but I finally concluded that for many Indian women, no more recent development in the American women's movement had been nearly so graphic as the reports of bra burning were.) Yet Dholakia was more of a feminist than she realized. As we drove an hour and a half southeast from Ahmedabad into a dustbowl of ochre-colored sand, Dholakia told me about an overseas trip she had been offered because of her work with SEWA. Everyone in her family, including her own mother, reacted by heaping praise on Dholakia's husband for his generosity in allowing his wife to go. Dholakia herself felt completely left out. "If I had been a man," she said, "people would have praised me instead." As it was, the neighbors clucked that she was neglecting her children, her husband and her house. I asked her how she lived with this. "I rationalize," she said, then shrugged. "People can't help the way they think. They're all prisoners of their own environments."

As we drove along the highway, we passed streams of people walking south with bundles of clothes and little children, all part of a migration in search of water and work. In the sand were the drying skeletons of water buffalo, just some of the thousands that had died that summer. There had been no rain in four years, and if there was no monsoon in the coming year, people too would start dying. We were headed for the district of Dholka, where SEWA, in an effort to save the livestock that had so far survived, had begun distributing cut sugarcane grass for the cattle owned by its members. The purpose of Dholakia's trip that day was to check on this fodder distribution in several villages. She knew from experience that sometimes the truck drivers who brought in the grass would sell it for a good profit, instead of delivering it to the right hands.

Our first stop was the village of Baldana, a sad little place surrounded by a flat horizon in tones of brown. The leaves of the few trees were coated with a thick film of dust, and there was virtually no green in sight. Dholakia went into what appeared to be the village council building, greeted the village pradhan, then found herself in the middle of a protracted argument. The gist of it was this: Ten days earlier, the pradhan had tried to buy one fourth of SEWA's fodder for himself, but the SEWA worker in charge had become angry and told him to go away because the fodder was for the women only. The pradhan and his minions now wanted the SEWA worker removed from the village. Dholakia, in an effort to appease the pradhan, whose ill will could have ruined SEWA's work in the village, first apologized for the behavior of the woman and agreed that she should not have become angry. But then Dholakia pointed out that the pradhan should not have tried to buy the fodder since it was, after all, for the members of SEWA. The pradhan countered that he knew of a pradhan in another village who had been allowed to buy SEWA's fodder. Numerous village elders joined in, and the discussion continued in heated Gujarati for more than an hour.

Dholakia—who by this time had discovered that in any case there would be no fodder distribution that day because no trucks were available—finally left Baldana in order to drop in on a few other villages. Inevitably, this meant she spent the rest of her day troubleshooting. In the village of Dev Dholera, a group of weavers told her they didn't want to allow some families they didn't like into the weaving cooperative because they were sure they would cause trouble. "There will be more trouble if you leave them out," Anila told them. "Do you want your looms to be set on fire one night?" The weavers agreed to talk to the families the next day. "No," said Anila. "You talk to them now." Toward the end of the day, Dholakia made a courtesy call on a local official, another whose goodwill was crucial to SEWA's rural operations. After the preliminary tea and pleasantries, Dholakia began complaining that the people digging ponds as part of the district's drought-relief work were not getting paid. She also wanted to know why additional drought-relief work, promised months ago, was not yet under way. The official offered a vague excuse, then promised to look into it. As an offering at the end, Dholakia gave him a large brick of what looked like gooey dark chocolate, telling him it was a high-vitamin diet supplement for livestock that she wanted him to try out on his cattle. The official thanked her, then looked at the brick with some suspicion. "Cadbury it is not," Dholakia admitted.

During the ride back to Ahmedabad, Dholakia talked about her work and the problems that SEWA faced. "Maybe we're too ambitious," she said. "We just don't have the infrastructure in the villages." She told me it took her up to six months of visits every few days just to build up trust among women in the villages. Only then could she begin to think about starting a project that might improve their lives.

Most of the day I had been with her had been spent in the car, in transit between stops. It was obvious that she was spread much too thin.

The truth was that SEWA, for all its success, had not yet been able to clone itself. There were nine other SEWAs in India, all of them for poor women and all of them independent, but none had been able to achieve the stellar results of the original in Ahmedabad, where much of the organization's strength came from Ela Bhatt. She herself said, "I know realistically that we are not going to have many SEWAs, although I would very much like to. We work together as sisters, and I thought we would have been able to bring up a joint force, but so far it hasn't happened so much."

And yet, it was SEWA that proved to me what potential there was among the women of India. In the beginning, partly because my exposure to Indian feminism was limited to a few urban groups, I had been doubtful that the women's movement would ever make much of a difference. By the time I left, my feelings had begun to change, and after I returned to the United States and had the time to review three and a half years of work, I realized, in pulling it all together, how much vital activity in behalf of women was occurring in all parts of the country. Yes, it was true, the movement was not unified, but I don't know if it ever could be or should be in a country as diverse as India. And yes, the movement had so far affected only a minuscule minority of India's four hundred million women, most of whom lived in complete ignorance of its existence and goals. Voluntary organizations doing work for women involved only two hundred thousand women at most, and some of the groups worried that they had reached a plateau of ideas. But to my mind the movement was a strong, vibrant beginning, even if in many cases it had so far only identified what was wrong. SEWA, the Working Women's Forum, the peasant struggles and even the urban groups taught me it was possible to make a difference in at least some women's lives.

"INDIRA IS INDIA, AND INDIA IS INDIRA"

Mrs. Gandhi and Her Legacy for Indian Women in Politics

ONE OF THE GREAT PARADOXES OF MODERN INDIA WAS THE RISE AND tumultuous rule of Indira Gandhi, one of the most powerful women in the world, in a country where most other women were among the most impoverished and neglected on earth. How did Indira Gandhi win election as prime minister four times, and dominate the subcontinent for almost two decades, while the majority of women in her country remained unaware of the basic rights that Jawaharlal Nehru, Indira Gandhi's father and the nation's first prime minister, had insisted be written into India's Constitution for them? Why did Indira Gandhi, in many ways a surprisingly feminine woman, largely ignore those of her own gender?

Loved, feared, admired and despised, Indira Gandhi was a woman whose sensibilities were shaped by one of the most extraordinary dramas of the twentieth century. The story of her life was no less than the story of the traumatic, inspirational birth of India, in which one of the poorest nations in the world, moved by the ideals of democracy, secularism and nonviolent disobedience, wrested its independence from one of the greatest empires in history. Indira Gandhi was part of a family that not only drove the course of events but also left her convinced that her destiny was to have her own place in history as well.

She was born in 1917 during the last days of the British Raj, into the aristocratic Nehru household, which became a headquarters for the civil disobedience campaign. As a child she never knew when her parents might be sent off to jail. After an erratic education in India and Europe, she struggled in an unhappy marriage and served as her father's reluctant hostess at Teen Murti House, the prime minister's residence. By 1966, less than two decades later, the shy, tag-along daughter had become prime minister herself. She emerged as a shrewd, forceful politician, one who silenced her critics and increasingly took on the role of dictator after she suspended civil liberties and declared a state of "Emergency" in June 1975. Two years later, Indian voters turned her out of office in a massive political defeat, but in 1980, in the most astonishing political turnaround in modern India, the same voters returned her to power. Her death four years later seemed a tragic commentary on an almost mythic life. Indira Gandhi, the leader whose consuming interest had been keeping India together at a time when people thought it was splitting apart, was finally assassinated by two men linked to the nation's most threatening separatist movement.

Even before her death, Indira Gandhi's life had taken on the status of myth. In 1971, when she led India into its most successful war against Pakistan, the swift military victory seemed to place her in the tradition of powerful Indian goddesses, an image that persisted throughout her subsequent years of political victories and defeats. In the minds of many Indians, Indira Gandhi was like Durga, the goddess of war, who had single-handedly vanquished hordes of demons and the forces of evil.

Yet I needed to move beyond the myth to understand Indira Gandhi the woman, and her relationship to the women of India. This was not easy. The conventional wisdom in political circles in New Delhi, especially among those who had been close to her, was that Indira Gandhi's womanhood was largely irrelevant to her political life and that, much like Golda Meir and Margaret Thatcher, she transcended sexual categories, becoming, in the popular imagination, not man, not woman, but leader. As an adolescent, Indira Gandhi once recalled, she wanted to be a boy, and Rajiv Gandhi told me that in her adult years his mother never particularly thought of herself as a woman. "She thought of herself as a human being," he said. "We were never brought

Top: A street in Calcutta, 1987.

Middle: Arun and Manju Bharat Ram with their daughter in New Delhi.

Bottom: Rajput youth groups guarding the sati site in Rajasthan, 1987.

Top: Bhabhiji.

Middle: The women line up to vote in the elections in Khajuron, July 1988.

Bottom: Muthaye, the woman who put her second daughter "to sleep."

Top: Ela Bhatt.

Bottom: A member of the
Self-Employed Women's
Association weaving textiles
at a handloom in the village
of Dev Dholera.

Elisabeth Bumiller

Elisabeth Bumiller

Elisabeth Bumiller

Top: Mandakini *(right)* on the
set of *Dance Dance* in
Bombay.

Middle: Smita Patil on the set
of *Dance Dance* in Bombay.

Bottom: Shabana Azmi *(left)*
on location for the film *Sati*.

Top: Veena Bhargava,
Calcutta painter.

Middle: Nabaneeta Dev Sen,
Calcutta poet.

Bottom: Aparna Sen,
filmmaker.

Top: Shah Bano Begum.

Middle: A vegetable seller with the Working Women's Forum, Madras.

Bottom: Gayatri Devi, the former maharani of Jaipur.

Top: Three Muslim women
in purdah.

Middle: Kiran Bedi.

Bottom: Arvindar Rana
(*right*) presiding over her kitty
party in New Delhi.

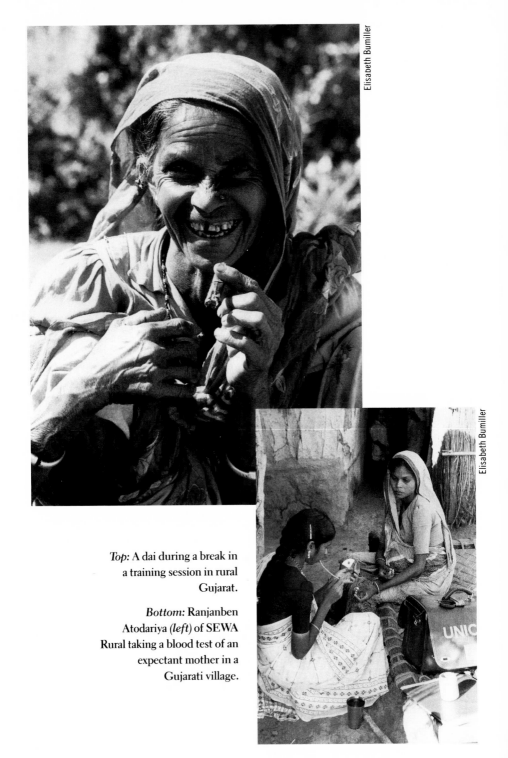

Top: A dai during a break in a training session in rural Gujarat.

Bottom: Ranjanben Atodariya *(left)* of SEWA Rural taking a blood test of an expectant mother in a Gujarati village.

Elisabeth Bumiller

Elisabeth Bumiller

up thinking that men and women are different species." Margaret Thatcher, the British prime minister and grocer's daughter, once mentioned to Mrs. Gandhi that women generally had to work twice as hard as men, and added that in her own career she had encountered special obstacles as a woman. Indira Gandhi agreed, according to her press secretary, Sharada Prasad, that women had to work harder than men. But she said that she herself, the child of modern India's greatest political family, had never felt particularly handicapped by her sex. It was an attitude that reflected her background of unusual privilege and thus made her something less than a role model for other women politicians in India. "She was typical of nothing," one young woman member of Parliament said to me. If anything, Indira Gandhi was typical of the dynastic politics of South Asia, where women have risen to prominence as daughters or wives of powerful men, many of whom have been cut down by violence. Benazir Bhutto of Pakistan inherited the political mantle, organization and popular loyalty of her father, the late prime minister Zulfikar Ali Bhutto, who was overthrown in 1977 and executed two years later. In Sri Lanka, Sirimavo Bandaranaike was swept into power after the assassination of her husband, W.R.D. Bandaranaike, in 1959. In Bangladesh, the two most prominent opposition leaders are also the daughter and widow of assassinated former presidents.

Certainly, by most definitions, Indira Gandhi was never a feminist. Although she was more strong-willed and ruthless than most men, she insisted that motherhood was a woman's greatest fulfillment and often held up the mythical Sita, the long-suffering wife of Rama, as the exemplary Indian woman. She counseled women not to rebel but to feed their children a balanced diet and to grow more vegetables in their gardens. And although she once wrote, "Since I was a little child, I have watched with growing pain and horror the maze of barbaric customs and superstitions which envelop the women of India so tightly as almost to smother them," as prime minister she expressed the view that the problems of poor Indian women were fundamentally no different from those of poor Indian men. "She was not a suffragette," Pupul Jayakar, one of Indira Gandhi's closest friends, once explained to me. "Nor did she believe in the way the problem is being presented today—as gender. She thought the problem of women was the general problem of poverty and unemployment."

I never met Indira Gandhi. She was murdered by two of her own Sikh bodyguards in the garden of her home in New Delhi on the morning of October 31, 1984, and by the time I arrived in India nearly three months later, her memory had been upstaged by the attention focused on her eldest son, who had become prime minister upon her death. The early part of 1985 was a time of almost euphoric hopes for the young prime minister, a man who then impressed Indians with his conciliatory style and modest demeanor. In that atmosphere, I readily accepted the notion that Mrs. Gandhi's gender neither affected her prime ministership nor allowed her a special relationship with other women in the country. There may have been amazement abroad when Indira Gandhi in 1966 became the first woman to serve as prime minister of India, but at home the press, reflecting the view of the educated elite, merely remarked that this was a sign of modernity and progress. Women, after all, had been involved in Indian politics since the civil disobedience campaigns of the 1930s. To Indians, it was not surprising that Jawaharlal Nehru's only child should become prime minister.

But as my stay in India lengthened, I heard and read things about Indira Gandhi that altered my earlier view, or at least added new dimensions to the legend. Although Americans might remember Mrs. Gandhi, not incorrectly, as the fiery and disheveled political leader with unkempt hair who traveled by jeep through mud and dust to India's villages, in New Delhi, I learned, she was seen as the epitome of style, an elegant, immaculately groomed woman whose silk saris were the envy of all the society matrons in town. The Nehru family's "ugly duckling," with her beak nose, hooded eyes and wiry build, had become a striking middle-aged woman with a dramatic streak of white in her hair. Imperious and aggressive in her public life, in private she pursued the traditional interests of a woman of her class. She once told a reporter, "If I had the time, what I really would love to do is design saris and jewelry." When she traveled to Washington to meet with Ronald Reagan in 1982, one of her first requests of the State Department's protocol office was to find her a good hairdresser. She loved arranging flowers and decorating the rooms of her Safdarjung Road home, a colonial-style white bungalow which became her sanctuary of understated sophistication: spare Western furniture, Indian sculpture, Tibetan religious paintings, a wall of books in her study. "The pattern of her life was that of an upper-class Indian society woman," recalled Khushwant Singh, the journalist, novelist and historian who was for a time a friend of Mrs. Gandhi's. In another life, he mused, "she might have married an army officer and become a social figure."

Nor was her conversation confined to politics and affairs of state. Khushwant Singh said that Mrs. Gandhi "thoroughly enjoyed the scandals of other people's private lives," and Elizabeth Moynihan, the wife of Senator Daniel Patrick Moynihan, the former American ambassador to India, remembered that Mrs. Gandhi once told her to ignore those in the Delhi diplomatic corps who complained that Mrs. Moynihan was not attending official parties like a proper ambassador's wife. "Well, that was the first I'd heard of those complaints," Elizabeth Moynihan said. "She knew all the gossip." Mrs. Gandhi's confidant and press secretary, Sharada Prasad, told me that the prime minister would work on the seating plans for important dinners during cabinet meetings, and her longtime social secretary, Usha Bhagat, recalled Mrs. Gandhi's sensitivity to talk among other upper-class mothers in Delhi who clucked that she never spent enough time with her children.

From these stories it became apparent to me that Indira Gandhi the woman could not be separated from Indira Gandhi the prime minister. As she herself once told an interviewer, "I think that political life, personal life, or outdoor life, or life of any other kind, is all one and the same thing." In a larger sense, it was impossible not to see that Indira Gandhi had left a legacy for other women in Indian politics. While it was true that she made no special effort to promote other women, her life in itself was a potent influence on the careers of others and on the consciousness of all Indians. Even Ela Bhatt, who was no fan of Mrs. Gandhi, told me once that her leadership in a subtle way made women more aware of their rights. "Consciously or unconsciously," Ela Bhatt said, "every woman, I think, feels that if Indira Gandhi could be a prime minister of this country, then we all have opportunities."

And so I came to realize that Indira Gandhi was inextricably linked with all of the other women who had succeeded in Indian politics. To understand her, I also had to understand them. Her assassination, after all, set off what Indian political analysts said was an emotional wave of sympathy for other women political candidates in the parliamentary elections just after Mrs. Gandhi's death. Women won in unusually large numbers, and partly as a result, by 1988 women accounted for almost 10 percent of the membership of Parliament—the largest proportion since independence. As I met these women, I discovered that most of them, like Mrs. Gandhi, were from the upper class and were far better educated than many of the men in Parliament. They also shared some of the advantages and disadvantages that Mrs. Gandhi had encountered along the way. Almost all of the seventy-four women members had come to power, like Mrs. Gandhi, because of their relationships to important men; most were widows, daughters, grand-daughters or daughters-in-law of former members of Parliament and powerful state political figures. Parliament was filled with men who were also there because of famous fathers or families, but they were not seen as undeserving inheritors who had to struggle to prove themselves. The fact was that most of the women, like Mrs. Gandhi at the start of her political career, had little influence over substantive issues and party politics. Only one woman, Sheila Dixit, was consid-ered a power broker on the level of the men, and only a handful of others, Margaret Alva and Mohsina Kidwai in particular, had authority because they were ministers as well as members of Parliament.

Not very many young professional women ran for Parliament, and the experience of one of the more impressive of them, Jayanti Natara-jan, illustrates why this was the case. Natarajan was the thirty-four-year-old granddaughter of a former chief minister of Tamil Nadu. She had left a lucrative law practice in Madras to spend more than half of the year in Delhi, earning $160 a month as a member of Parliament and worrying about her young son back home. "Today I feel terribly guilty that my son's alone," she told me during a summer session of Parliament. She was an up-and-comer in the Congress party, striking and well connected. She was also the subject of rumors linking her to a male politician. She denied the stories but they took a toll. "I finally decided it was inevitable," she said, "but it bothered me a lot. I was naïve to expect that my private life would remain private. If I wanted money or the good life, I would have continued in my profession."

Despite the difficulties, gossip and torn families, there were enough women in Indian politics in the late 1980s to develop a certain solidar-ity, and to make the point that, as women, they brought special gifts to politics. Perhaps that was why statistics in recent years showed that women candidates, even the many token candidates put up for office by the political bosses, were as successful in elections as the men—or more so. In the state legislative assembly elections of 1983, for example, 18 percent of the women candidates won, compared with 17 percent of the men. "Women tend to be much more accessible to their elector-ates," said Margaret Alva, the minister in charge of the government's policy and programs for women. She explained to me that when a man was elected to Parliament, he usually moved his home and his wife to Delhi. But a woman member of Parliament traveled to Delhi only during the sessions and most often kept her home in her constituency; it was unthinkable that the typical Indian husband should uproot himself because of his wife's career. Consequently, the woman member of Parliament went home to her constituency most weekends and for important festivals. "So the people feel she's more there than the men," Alva said. "She wants to get things done in her constituency, like work with schools, hospitals, crèches, a lot of the social welfare kind of support. This has an impact on the community, much more than a big industrial project."

Of course, none of these women, however successful, could ever be "Durga," the woman who in 1975 inspired the Congress party refrain "Indira is India, and India is Indira." The slogan was derided by Mrs. Gandhi's critics as a symbol of her megalomania, but the words nonetheless tied her to the soul of the country as mother, as daughter, as woman. Her story, and in essence the story of all other women in politics in independent India, begins one November day in 1917 in the northern city of Allahabad along the Ganges River.

———————————————

MOTILAL NEHRU, INDIRA GANDHI'S FLAMBOYANT, LARGER-THAN-LIFE grandfather, was a prosperous lawyer and a grandee of Allahabad who lived in Anand Bhawan, or "Abode of Happiness," a sprawling villa filled with Victorian furniture, Persian carpets and Venetian glass. Motilal, like most upper-class Indians of his time, admired things English, and for years his house was the site of lavish parties for British officials and Indian princes. In 1912, his son, Jawaharlal, returned from Trinity College in Cambridge to the grand family home in Allahabad, where he frequented the gentlemen's clubs and took up the pursuit of law. Like his father, Jawaharlal Nehru had a warm regard for the British; he would later describe himself in those days as "a bit of a prig with little to commend me." In 1916, Jawaharlal was married to Kamala, a shy, deeply religious young woman intimidated by the worldly Nehrus. The following year she produced the couple's only child, Indira. At the infant's birth, Indira's grandmother was said to have exclaimed, "Oh, but it should have been a boy!" This prompted Motilal, a member of the liberal school of nineteenth-century reformers who believed in women's emancipation, to snap at his wife, "For all you know [Jawaharlal's baby daughter] may prove better than a thousand sons."

That outburst, of course, became one of the more famous prophecies in the life of the infant girl who would one day rule over one sixth of the world's population. In recounting that life in the following pages, I will tell other such anecdotes, many of them well known to Indians, which seem to me to provide revealing insights into the psyche of the woman, and into the psyche of India itself. I have culled the stories principally from three biographies: Zareer Masani's excellent, even-handed *Indira Gandhi: A Biography,* Dom Moraes's respectful *Mrs. Gandhi,* and Nayantara Sahgal's scathing *Indira Gandhi: Her Road to Power.* I have also relied on Mrs. Gandhi's letters to her American friend Dorothy Norman, published by Weidenfeld and Nicolson in 1986; Linda Charlton's 7,000-word obituary of Mrs. Gandhi in *The New York Times;* and *My Truth,* a collection of Mrs. Gandhi's interviews with the journalist Emmanuel Pouchpadass.

By most accounts, Indira Gandhi led a turbulent and intensely lonely childhood, one which—depending on the point of view of the source—either inspired her or forever hardened her. By the 1920s, when she was still a young girl, her father and grandfather had set aside the English trappings of their lives and allied themselves with Mahatma Gandhi and the fight against the British. The palatial Anand Bhawan evolved into a bustling political headquarters for Congress party leaders, who crowded the spacious lawns for around-the-clock meetings. Indira could only watch from afar, a forgotten child in the chaos. Once when a visitor arrived he was met by a solemn Indira, who told him in a very grave tone, "I'm sorry, but my grandfather, father and mummy are all in prison." The struggle in many ways robbed her of her childhood. One of Indira's earliest memories was of the day when the Nehru family, in response to Mahatma Gandhi's appeal, gathered up their European clothes to burn them as part of a boycott of all foreign-made goods. "What fun for a toddler to jump on, play hide and seek in the heaps of velvets and satins, silks and chiffons!" she said. A short time later, a relative returning from Paris brought a beautiful embroidered dress for Indira, but Nehru's dutiful daughter, repeating the arguments she had heard from the adults, told the woman she could not wear it. "All right, Miss Saint," the relative replied, "how is it that you have a foreign doll?" The doll was Indira's favorite—"my friend, my child," she called her—and for days afterward she struggled with her conscience, unable to decide, she said, between her love for her doll and what she saw as her duty to her country. "At last I made my decision," she said. "Quivering with tension, I took the doll up on the roof-terrace and set fire to it. Then tears came as if they would never stop and for some days I was ill with a temperature."

Although the adults in the household doted on Indira when they had the time, very little in her life was normal. One of her favorite activities was to climb up on a table and deliver thunderous political speeches to the household servants. Once an aunt found her with her arms outstretched on the veranda, talking to herself; Indira said she was Joan of Arc being burned at the stake. Years later, Mrs. Gandhi told one of her biographers that her life in the household "was really all very unsettled. There was no regularity about meals, and I never knew where my parents were or when or if they would come home. By that time my mother was also involved in the freedom fight. I used to want to be with them whenever they went out, but I was never allowed to." Indira's aunt, Vijaya Lakshmi Pandit, who later became a bitter political rival of Mrs. Gandhi, wrote in her autobiography, *The Scope of Happiness,* that for her niece, "the long years alone gave her strength of character, but they took away from her some of the qualities a settled home helps to develop—tolerance and a kindred spirit. Instead of compassion she developed hardness—a feeling that life had not been fair, therefore she would have her revenge."

Adding to Indira's unhappiness was the scornful treatment of her mother by the more sophisticated English-speaking women in the Nehru household. "She thought her mother had been wronged," Sharada Prasad told me. Kamala became a passionate feminist within the freedom struggle, urging women to revolt against domination by their husbands and their lack of education, but her daughter, who had never been stifled, did not follow her mother's path. "She said, 'My mother was a feminist, but I am not,' " Prasad recalled. "By her time she felt it was so much easier." And yet Kamala taught her daughter one painful, important lesson. "I saw how my mother was hurt by people," Mrs. Gandhi once said, "and I made up my mind never to let people hurt me."

Indira's formal studies began at boarding schools in India and Switzerland, none of them as educational as the Nehru household, where history was unfolding every day. "It just seemed to me that what they were trying to teach had nothing to do with life," Mrs. Gandhi said years later. After boarding school she spent a brief but happy year at the university at Shantiniketan in West Bengal, founded by Rabindranath Tagore, the Nobel Prize–winning poet and freedom fighter. Nehru, in a letter to Tagore's secretary, informed the university of his requirements for his daughter's education, revealing what were radical views about women in the India of the 1930s. "I dislike the education which prepares a girl to play a part in the drawing room and nowhere else," Nehru wrote. "Personally if I had the chance I would like to have my daughter work in a factory for a year, just as any other worker, as a part of her education." In a background report sent with Indira's application, Nehru further instructed: "Her parents would like her later to specialize in some subject or subjects which would enable her to do some socially useful work . . . and at the same time enable her to be economically independent, so long as the present structure of society lasts. She is not likely to have an unearned income and it is not considered desirable by her parents that she should depend for her subsistence on a husband or others." Such expectations, as forward-thinking as they were, put enormous pressures on Indira. As Prasad said, "She always felt that she had to be worthy of her parents."

In 1936, after battling tuberculosis for nearly two decades, Kamala Nehru died, leaving Indira, at eighteen, in despair. The following year, still suffering from her mother's death, she became an indifferent student at Somerville College at Oxford. A shy young woman, she was intimidated by the intellectuals she had entrée to as Nehru's daughter. The widow of Harold Laski, the British political scientist and economist, remembered Indira as a "mousy, shy little girl who didn't seem to have any political ideas." Indira returned to India in 1941 without finishing at Oxford, and brought with her Feroze Gandhi, an exuberant young socialist from the London School of Economics who had been active in Congress party politics and had known the Nehru family for years. Shocking everyone, Indira announced that she intended to marry Feroze, who was no relation to Mahatma Gandhi. Letters poured in from across India, most of them abusive and threatening objections to the union of Indira, who as a Kashmiri Brahmin was considered to be among the most racially pure Brahmins in the country, and Feroze, a Parsi. Even the open-minded Nehrus were opposed to the marriage, although not on religious grounds; they worried instead that Feroze's lower-middle-class background would not be compatible with Indira's aristocratic roots. Finally Mahatma Gandhi himself gave the couple his blessing, and the two were married in March 1942.

That summer, in a dramatic turning point in the battle for independence, the Congress party adopted its historic "Quit India" resolution against the British, and by September both Indira and Feroze were in prison. Indira had been arrested while addressing a public meeting in Allahabad, and in later years she would refer to this as the most dramatic event of her life. Certainly it legitimized her; a stay in jail, for Congress party members, had become a credential that one needed in the nationalist struggle. The well-educated went so far as to see it as a chance for reflection and intellectual improvement. As Indira's aunt, Vijaya Lakshmi Pandit, wrote: "Popular jail reading among the educated were the French and Russian revolutions and Gibbon's *Decline and Fall of the Roman Empire*." For twenty years, Indira had stood on the sidelines while her elders were taken to prison, but now, at the age of twenty-five, she could at last feel a part of the movement. "I had made up my mind that I had to go to prison," she said. "Without that . . . something would have been incomplete."

Indira was taken to Naini Prison in Allahabad and shared a squalid barrack with her cousin and her aunt. Since childhood, she had visited her parents in jail, but as she once said, "What a world of difference there is between hearing and seeing from the outside and the actual experience. No one who has not been in prison for any length of time can ever visualize the numbness of spirit that can creep over one." The roof leaked, chunks of plaster fell periodically from the ceiling, a small corner of the barrack served as a bathroom and there was grit in the food. She was permitted to see Feroze only once before he was transferred to another prison. She was released nine months later—an internment that can scarcely be compared with her father's total record of nine years. But unlike Nehru, who used his years in prison to write his best books and formulate his political ideas, Indira, a doer rather than a thinker, came to a dead end during her time in jail. As she said years later: "It was only when I left prison that I suddenly found I had cut off my emotions and intellect, and I had been living only at a surface level."

A few months later Feroze was also released from prison, and the couple settled down for a period of relative stability in Allahabad. Rajiv was born in 1944 and Sanjay in 1946, the year that Nehru became prime minister of a provisional government in anticipation of full Indian independence. Kamala had been dead for ten years, and Indira became her father's official hostess in New Delhi, a job she later said she "hated," and which forced her to split her time between a famous, charismatic father living in the excitement of the prime minister's house and a resentful husband smoldering back home in small-town India. The marriage, which had always been difficult, began to fall apart. Invariably, when Indira returned to her husband, she would receive a telegram from her father, telling her that important guests were arriving and she should come at once. "My father would feel so hurt if I didn't come that it was very difficult to say no," Mrs. Gandhi said. Yet in Delhi, she claimed, she was "simply terrified by the so-called social duties. Although I met a large number of people, I wasn't good at 'socializing' and small talk and that sort of thing." There were always overnight guests at the prime minister's residence, and meals to be served from breakfast to dinner. Indira planned the menus, supervised the housekeeping, looked after heads of state and, for nearly two decades, submerged herself in her father's life. In 1951, she wrote to Dorothy Norman that "if someone asks me at the end of the week what I have been doing, I can't really answer but moment by moment the odd jobs seem important and urgent. On the whole it is a frustrating life. Long ago when I was a student in England, I went to Harold Laski for advice about my studies. He said, 'Young woman, if you want to amount to something you had better start on your own life right now—if you tag along with your father you won't be able to do anything else.' But there doesn't seem to be any choice, in the sense that I *felt* my father's loneliness so intensely, and I felt also that whatever I amounted to, or whatever satisfaction I got from my own work, would not, from a wide perspective, be so useful as my 'tagging along.' "

Yet Mrs. Gandhi was active behind the scenes in social welfare work and the women's wing of the Congress party, traditionally a political graveyard that restricted women to those do-good tasks that bored the men. The hard work of Nehru's daughter, however, did not go unnoticed, and by 1955 Mrs. Gandhi, now familiar to millions of Indians, who had seen her at her father's side, was elected to the twenty-one-member Congress Working Committee, the party's powerful national executive council. Although she remained quietly in the background, it was a small step toward a political career in her own right. In 1959, she was named president of the Congress party, a move widely seen as engineered by Nehru, who apparently needed an absolute loyalist to oversee the infighting among the membership. His daughter knew the party regulars from her days as her father's hostess and had already begun to display some acute political skills.

During her eleven months as Congress president, Indians got a first look at the emerging politician, whose maneuverings in those months to dismiss a popularly elected Communist government in the southern state of Kerala indicated that she was willing to put the fortunes of the Congress party above Indian democracy. The next year Mrs. Gandhi turned down the offer of another term as president in part because of her concerns about her father's failing health, but it was her own husband who died nine months later, leaving his estranged wife in stunned anguish. "We quarrelled over every conceivable subject, but the strong bond of affection never weakened," Indira Gandhi wrote to Dorothy Norman. "I feel as if I were all alone in the midst of an unending sandy waste." In 1964, when Nehru died of a stroke, Indira Gandhi withdrew for weeks, bursting into tears whenever anyone offered condolences. The new prime minister, Lal Bahadur Shastri, made Mrs. Gandhi Minister of Information and Broadcasting, an undistinguished cabinet post that did not meet her expectations. Indeed, for the first time she seemed to be nurturing serious political ambitions. She had no husband and no father and seemed aware that she had to start developing, as Harold Laski had told her, a life of her own. She made speeches across India, invoking the dreams of her father, and complaining in private about what she saw as the aimlessness of Shastri's government. She stumbled upon a chance to prove herself during a brief holiday in Kashmir, when several thousand Pakistani troops crossed the border into the state, igniting what became the 1965 Indo-Pakistan War. Mrs. Gandhi's refusal to leave until the situation was stable helped maintain Indian morale and later earned her praise as "the only man in a cabinet of old women."

When Shastri died of a sudden heart attack in 1966, the leading Congress party bosses, a group dubbed "the syndicate," turned to Mrs. Gandhi as their choice. In their eyes, her main advantage was that she could be easily managed and manipulated; many women had held political positions in India, but always at the behest of men, and no one thought a woman capable of independent leadership. Mrs. Gandhi was also a Nehru, a name that still stirred the nation. After her election in Parliament as prime minister, the dramatic expectations inherent in that name were made evident by the excited crowds who greeted her as she emerged from the building after her victory. They shouted not only "Long live Indira" but also "Long live Jawaharlal"—causing one of Mrs. Gandhi's biographers, Dom Moraes, to observe that it was as if her father had been reincarnated in his daughter's body.

The India that Mrs. Gandhi encountered upon taking office was a vastly different country from the one her father had led. By 1966, the post-independence euphoria had been replaced by a severe economic crisis; drought and the costs of the 1965 war with Pakistan had caused rampant inflation and the threat of famine. Mrs. Gandhi had a tentative first year, but the syndicate soon learned that the malleable "dumb doll," as one opposition leader had called her, had no intention of doing their bidding. Less than six months after becoming prime minister, under pressure from the World Bank and the United States, Mrs. Gandhi infuriated party elders with her surprise decision to devalue the rupee, which theoretically would have made Indian exported products cheaper and thus more competitive on the world market. Party leaders had been consulted only at the last minute, and she had ignored their objections that the devaluation would make India a pawn of the United States. The bosses of the old guard, who as contemporaries of Nehru felt that they were the true heirs to power, increasingly came to think that they had created a monster. They broke away from Mrs. Gandhi, and in 1969, following a battle over the choice of a Congress candidate for the figurehead post of Indian president, the party split. It was widely believed that Mrs. Gandhi had cleverly set the stage for the battle for her own political gain, and her critics were appalled. Nayantara Sahgal, whose mother, Vijaya Lakshmi Pandit, was Mrs. Gandhi's aunt and a bitter political rival, wrote that "her strategy to gain control of her party had displayed a militancy foreign to Congress tradition. She represented something ruthless and new. She had astonished people with her flair for cold assessment, shrewd timing, and the telling theatrical gesture; above all, with her capacity for a fight to the finish, even to bringing the eighty-four-year-old party of liberation to rupture." As Mrs. Gandhi later said: "My father was a saint who strayed into politics. I am a tough politician." Her power was complete in 1971, when she was reelected in a landslide. That same year, civil war broke out in Pakistan. India invaded East Pakistan to help the region defend itself against West Pakistan, and East Pakistan consequently emerged victorious as the independent nation of Bangladesh. India became the supreme power on the subcontinent, and Mrs. Gandhi the paramount leader.

But power in India is volatile, and two years later, as Mrs. Gandhi's government struggled to contain an economic crisis brought on by inflation, two severe droughts and increases in the price of oil, her popularity had sunk to an all-time low. An uprising against her leadership was gaining force in the state of Bihar, led by Jayaprakash Narayan, a populist Gandhian-inspired reformer. Mrs. Gandhi's critics charged her with mismanagement and corruption and closely followed the court case filed against her by a socialist member of Parliament, alleging irregularities in her 1971 election. In June 1975, the High Court ruled against the prime minister, convicting her of two counts of electoral corruption and declaring her election to Parliament invalid. The opposition immediately cried for her resignation, but Mrs. Gandhi responded two days later by arranging power failures at Delhi's newspapers and then sending the police to arrest opposition leaders in predawn raids at their homes. When the capital awoke later that morning, on June 26, 1975, the government-controlled radio was announcing that a state of "Emergency" had been declared. Mrs. Gandhi, invoking a law left over from colonial days, said a period of authoritarian rule was necessary because of "a threat to internal stability" and a fear of insurrection. Over the course of the next two years, some fifty thousand people were reportedly jailed, many without knowing the specific charges against them. The press was censored, constitutional guarantees of civil rights were suspended and the democracy that India had so long fought for seemed destroyed. Mrs. Gandhi continued to insist that "if we have these curbs today, it is because democracy was in danger. A handful of people were trying to stop the functioning of the will of the majority." The West watched aghast as the leader of the world's largest democracy moved increasingly closer to the role of despot. She installed her brash younger son, Sanjay, to run an aggressive slum-clearance and population-control program, and rumors of forced sterilizations led to sometimes violent protests.

Early in 1977, Mrs. Gandhi surprised everyone by calling for elections at a time when she was apparently convinced that the Congress party would win easily. But the voters turned her out of office, and Morarji Desai, an opposition leader whom she had imprisoned two years earlier, became prime minister. The *Indian Express,* one of the leading opposition newspapers, editorialized that no government such as Mrs. Gandhi's could assume that it could "drive a coach and four through the Constitution and the laws, make inroads on the liberties of the people and hope to escape nemesis from an outraged people." Over the next three years, Mrs. Gandhi spent a brief time in prison, formed the breakaway Congress-I (for Indira) party and exhaustively toured India in an attempt to return to power. The failures of Desai's government and her own popularity with the masses of Indians, despite her obvious flaws, paved the way for victory. In the 1980 elections, the Congress party won two thirds of the seats in Parliament; afterward, Indira Gandhi said that the triumph had been achieved "entirely on my name."

Her last years in office were a time of improved relations with the United States, and also of personal tragedy. When Sanjay, her favorite and heir apparent, died in a plane crash in June 1980, she kept tight control of her emotions in public, but in private, friends recalled, she was a devastated mother, deeply depressed and adrift. A year later, Indira Gandhi wrote to her friend Pupul Jayakar that sorrow "can be neither forgotten, nor overcome. One has to learn to live with it, to absorb it into one's being, as a part of life." It surprised no one in Delhi, however, when Mrs. Gandhi quarreled with Sanjay's widow, Maneka, and eventually threw her out of the house because, she said, she had discovered that Maneka was attempting to form an opposition party under her own roof. In fact, she had never liked the shrewd Maneka at all, and she seemed to be reacting less like a politician than like a typical Indian version of the aggrieved mother-in-law. "They both really behaved like rustic village women," Khushwant Singh recalled.

Throughout her private travails she remained preoccupied with what she saw as constant threats to Indian unity, and she worked to bring down a number of state governments—Kashmir, in particular— with which she disagreed. Fatally, she clashed with radical secessionists among the Sikhs, who wanted to create an independent Sikh nation in the strategically and economically vital border state of Punjab. In June 1984, in a move that would set in motion her assassination, Mrs. Gandhi sent in Indian troops to flush out Sikh terrorists holed up in the Golden Temple in Punjab, the holiest shrine of the Sikh religion. After a thirty-six-hour battle, as many as twelve hundred were reported dead, including Jarnail Singh Bhindranwale, the most militant of the secessionist leaders. The Sikhs never forgave her. Four months later, as Mrs. Gandhi was walking from her residence to her office on the grounds of the compound, two of her Sikh bodyguards turned their submachine guns on her, riddling her body with bullets. She was declared dead the same day at the All India Institute of Medical Sciences, and her only surviving son, Rajiv, was immediately sworn in as prime minister. The Nehru legacy had passed from father to daughter to son, and the family had become independent India's first political dynasty.

During my years in India, I often went to Mrs. Gandhi's Safdarjung Road home, which had become a museum after her death. It was close to our own house in Delhi, and as I walked with the crowds of Indian tourists past Mrs. Gandhi's old study and dining room, I tried to imagine what she might have been like. Even by Indian standards, it was a modest house for a prime minister, no larger than the bungalows the government provided for important cabinet members and judges. But unlike so many of those houses, whose drab, bureaucratic furnishings gave one the feeling that their occupants were just passing through, Mrs. Gandhi's residence, even as a museum, reflected the personality of a woman who cared about the small things—the flowers, the carefully selected art, the combination of subtle colors—that turned a house into a home. In back of the house there was a large well-tended garden of lush grass and rose beds, with a curving cement path that led toward the building she had used as an office. She had walked that route on the morning when her bodyguards turned their guns on her, and I always had an eerie feeling as I followed it. At the end of the path, in what I thought was one of the more macabre memorials to the fallen prime minister, were several brownish spots of what was said to be Mrs. Gandhi's blood. The stains were preserved on the path under a plastic covering and were watched over by guards with submachine guns. It was the last stop on the tour, and all of the Indian visitors soberly took pictures. To me, the brutal memorial of blood was a final counterpoint to the gracious woman of the well-kept household, revealing the defiant, warlike part of her psyche that Indians knew as Durga. Every time I left the house, I regretted that I had not had a chance to meet the world's most famous Indian woman—and, indeed, one of the most remarkable women of the twentieth century—but I also realized that one of the most explosive eras in modern Indian history had come to an end.

IN THE MONTHS AFTER MRS. GANDHI'S DEATH, A NEW AGE FOR WOMEN dawned in Indian politics. Pollsters determined that women in particular supported Rajiv Gandhi in the December 1984 Congress party elections, in part out of sympathy for his mother, but also because they seemed willing to put their faith in a young man who was a symbol of both continuity and change. Rajiv, eager to prove that he would be a progressive prime minister as well as Indira's son, responded by creating a new Ministry for Women and Social Welfare and selecting a woman to run it. While his mother was prime minister, people seemed to have been blinded by her power and position to the absence of women in government. Rajiv named Mohsina Kidwai, a veteran of Congress politics, to his cabinet, as the union minister for health and social welfare. Under Mrs. Gandhi, not a single woman had been a member of the cabinet. Rajiv appointed another woman as deputy chair of the upper house of Parliament, named two others to top positions within the party, selected a third as a minister of state and said that 20 percent of the seats in the legislative assemblies should be reserved for women. None of these were radical steps; like most politicians, Rajiv Gandhi was an incrementalist rather than a revolutionary, and later he would enrage feminists with his slow response to the sati in Rajasthan and his handling of legislation relating to a controversial Muslim divorce case. But there was no question that the climate had changed. In October 1985, in response to criticism that the new women's ministry might become a ghetto where women's problems would be shunted off from the larger concerns of government, Rajiv Gandhi reorganized it as a separate department within the Ministry of Human Resource Development and put one of the women stars of the Congress party, Margaret Alva, in charge. Alva was forty-three, straightforward, a lawyer who had successfully argued before the Supreme Court of India that Indian Airlines stewardesses should be subject to the same employment conditions as stewards; earlier, a stewardess had had to quit when she married or became pregnant. More than anyone else, Margaret Alva represented the new kind of woman who had come into power at the invitation of Rajiv, but who had risen in politics both because of and despite Indira Gandhi.

I first met Margaret Alva one hot summer day in her office at the Parliament building in Delhi, the majestic, circular red sandstone monument designed by an assistant to the English architect Edwin Lutyens and built on a scale that clearly indicated that the British intended to remain in India forever. Margaret Alva was a woman who bustled competence, but she was harried that day, having sandwiched me in between other appointments, and I remember watching as she gulped a cup of coffee in fifteen seconds flat. She was dressed in a simple cotton sari, and had a scrubbed, attractive face. She told me that she had been active in student politics in college, but after her marriage she began raising a family of four and settled in comfortably at home. "I refused to budge," she said. Her husband's parents, however, had been the first couple to serve together in the Indian Parliament, and Violet Alva would have no slouch for a daughter-in-law. "She kept telling me," Alva said, " 'You're wasting your time sitting at home. You have so much talent. Why don't you do something?' " She became active in local politics in the southern city of Bangalore, and in 1974 Indira Gandhi appointed her to the upper house of Parliament. Margaret Alva left Congress amid party infighting with Mrs. Gandhi in 1979, but Rajiv brought her back in 1982. By the summer of 1988, the last time I spoke with her, Alva had become one of the most powerful women in Rajiv's government. The official biography put out by her office concluded with this: "She combines many roles but is proud to be a wife and mother—devoting a good part of her time to domestic duties." It was standard boilerplate for a woman member of Parliament—the unwritten assumption was that Margaret Alva was perfectly welcome in Parliament as long as she did not neglect her responsibilities at home—but it also happened to be true. "You're doing two full-time careers, unlike the men," Alva said with an air of resignation. "And yet we women are always told we're the weaker sex."

Margaret Alva's influence over women's issues ensured that she would be both a sounding board and a favorite scapegoat for the feminist groups and women's organizations frustrated over their efforts to change government policy. There was constant quarreling and making up; both sides knew they had to live with each other. "Very often the groups tell me, 'We have to criticize the government; we are after all women's groups and we have to fight,' " Alva said. "But then they'll come and sit with me and talk about things and say, 'Well, how can we do this together?' " Yet inevitably there were complaints that Margaret Alva was merely a toady of the Congress party. This charge was made during the Muslim divorce case in 1986, which exploded into one of Rajiv Gandhi's biggest political disasters. The prime minister's stand on the controversy cost him crucial support among women and India's Hindu majority. In retrospect, Gandhi's aides agreed that the case was the beginning of the educated urban elite's disaffection with a man they had initially elected as one of their own. For Margaret Alva, the issue created a dilemma that forced her to choose between her personal views as a woman and what she saw as her duty to her government. "Very often our opinion as women activists and our commitment to the larger interests of the party do create situations," she admitted.

The case was so important to the cause of women that I decided I needed to know more about it. In the spring of 1986, I traveled to the town of Indore in India's dry central plains to meet the source of the controversy: Shah Bano Begum, a seventy-two-year-old middle-class housewife, who described herself as just another good Muslim woman trying her best to please her husband, Mohammed Ahmad Khan, a well-to-do lawyer. Years before, when her husband had taken another wife, as allowed by Islamic law, Shah Bano's upbringing taught her not to object. The result was that for next three decades, the two wives of Mohammed Ahmad Khan raised their children, ten between them, in the same uneasy household. The husband claimed he had tried his best to maintain the peace. "I bought them the same clothes and the same jewels," he told me with exasperation. "I took my evening meals with Shah Bano, and my morning meals with my second wife." But the relationship with Shah Bano was never smooth, and in 1978, when her children were grown, Shah Bano's husband finally divorced her, which Muslim law permitted him to do simply by making a unilateral declaration. "I felt enormous grief," Shah Bano told me, "but I also hated him." She was by then living around the corner from her former husband, in a small house that he owned, and was supported by her two sons. She was thin but not frail, with almost mischievous eyes in a lined, sunken face. After the divorce, she sued her husband for maintenance, similar to alimony, and then waited seven years as the case made its way through the lower courts.

In 1985, the Supreme Court of India finally ordered Mohammed Ahmad Khan to pay Shah Bano the equivalent of forty dollars a month, on the grounds that Indian law provides for maintenance payments for a destitute divorced woman. But Shah Bano was not destitute, and she even admitted to me that she wanted the maintenance as "prestige money" for pocket expenses. More important, the ruling disregarded another provision in the law, which holds that in some family matters Muslim "personal law"—based on the Koran and other texts—may take precedence for Indian Muslims. This personal law covers marriage and divorce and was guaranteed to Muslims at the time of independence to ensure that Muslims would not feel that a "Hindu Raj" would replace the British Raj under which they had suffered. Hindus and other religious groups had their own personal laws for marriage as well. Meanwhile, over the decades, various civil laws governing marriage and divorce were enacted, including one guaranteeing alimony. These laws were open to couples of any religion.

The Supreme Court decision, by a Hindu chief justice, set off a rampage across India. In what now seems a foretaste of the Islamic demonstrations against Salman Rushdie's novel *The Satanic Verses,* millions of Muslims took to the streets, demonstrating against the judge's ruling and burning him in effigy. Fundamentalist Islamic leaders made fire-breathing speeches about "Islam in danger" and denounced the decision as a Hindu attack on their culture and "blatant interference" in the affairs of their religion. What had begun as a simple question of whether all women should be given rights in modern India had evolved, for the Muslims, into nothing less than a debate over their future in a nation that is 80 percent Hindu.

With an estimated one hundred million Muslims, India is one of the largest Islamic countries in the world. To the fury of feminists and the dismay of some in his own party, Rajiv Gandhi yielded to Muslim pressures, and his government introduced a bill in Parliament to reverse the Supreme Court decision. The prime minister's advisers characterized the bill as an attempt to safeguard India's always tenuous national unity by protecting the rights of the minority; critics said that the bill was in fact undermining national unity rather than strengthening it. Clearly, Rajiv Gandhi's motives were complex. Muslims had long been a vital part of the Congress party constituency, but as one of Rajiv's advisers told me: "Grubbing for the Muslim vote is the reverse of the coin that says you are being sensitive to Muslim feelings." Such a distinction was of course rejected by the feminists. "We were shocked," said Zoya Hassan, one of the educated Muslim women who led an agitation against the bill. "One does not expect a secular government to introduce a bill based on distinctions in religious communities and which denies rights to women." Certainly, the condition of many Muslim women in India was already deplorable. I will never forget the first time I saw a Muslim woman in purdah as she walked on the hot streets of the Kashmiri capital of Srinigar, covered from head to toe in a heavy black burkha, like a moving tent with little holes made in the cloth for her eyes. I could never accept in my mind that under Muslim law a man can simply divorce any of his allowed four wives by writing "I divorce my wife" on a piece of paper and submitting it in court.

After an acrimonious floor debate, the bill passed in Parliament. Two years later, when tempers had cooled but the issue still lingered, I asked Rajiv Gandhi about his thinking behind the decision. We were in the conference room at the prime minister's residence on Race Course Road, and Gandhi, who had said very little publicly during the controversy, was suddenly eager to justify himself. Initially, he said, he had felt "very strongly" that "we must not bend at all, and take a hard stand, what we call a secular stand, and let the Supreme

Court ruling stand." But the prime minister said that as he spoke to Muslims—"I'm not talking about fundamentalists, I'm talking about educated Muslims," he insisted—he came to understand that they saw marriage not as a religious sacrament, as Hindus and Christians do, but as a contract. He explained that this gave Muslim marriage a "totally different" character, involving different values. "You cannot put the value based on a sacrament into a contract," he said. "Now, the real question is, in the Muslim contractual system of marriage, does it give the woman her rights?" The prime minister was convinced that Muslim women did indeed have "rights" guaranteed by their personal law. Under Muslim law, for example, a woman receives a lump-sum payment, called mehr, from her husband at the time of her marriage; in theory, although not always in practice, this is entirely hers should there be a divorce. Shah Bano had received her mehr before she filed her case for maintenance, but the judge did not accept the payment as a valid one, according to his interpretation of Islamic law. "It's very difficult to put things objectively into place," Gandhi said, "because most of us, including me, are Western-educated, and Western-educated really means, no matter how secular the education is, there is a basic Christian moral values background."

It was clear that Gandhi was still struggling with the issue, and that it seemed to wound him that he, of all people—a Western-educated person—should be accused of pandering to religious fundamentalism. He then digressed by telling a story about how "a staunch leftist" in India had remarked that Bangladesh became "secular" after its first ruler, Sheikh Mujib, changed the Muslim holiday, traditionally Friday, to Sunday. "So I said," Gandhi continued, amused, " 'I find it fantastic that you could think Sunday is more secular than Friday. Maybe Tuesday, which is nobody's holiday, perhaps it would be secular. But Sunday is Christian.' " In any case, the new divorce bill, which was a codification of the Muslim personal law, required a husband to pay his wife mehr plus maintenance for three months. Then the financial responsibility for a divorced woman fell to her family or her local Muslim community board. "In our system," Gandhi said, meaning in Hindu marriage practices, "the girl, once she leaves the home, goes to the husband. And that's also in many ways the Christian system. The family washes its hands of their responsibility. The Muslim system is the opposite. The family never washes its hands of the responsibility for the girl. Now you have to view it from that perspective, and it's totally different. You can't try and take one set of values and put them in the other one." Gandhi further reasoned that since Muslims were guaranteed their personal law at the time of independence, "that guarantee cannot be withdrawn, unless it is withdrawn by consensus." He pointed out that Muslim couples are also free to marry under civil law. "Anybody who wants out can have out," he said.

Even before I interviewed Rajiv Gandhi I had agreed with this point of view. My feeling put me at odds with most of my friends and acquaintances in India, and I frequently found myself disagreeing with educated "secular" Hindus and supporters of women's rights. Their arguments were undeniably correct: that the bill was bad for women because in effect it prohibited a Muslim woman from going to court to seek a maintenance payment from the man who divorced her—which was an apparent unconstitutional discrimination against women on the basis of religion. It was also true that the bill was seriously flawed: many mehrs were negligible; and it was hard to see how a local Muslim community board could provide financial support to a destitute divorced woman, since the boards generally had no money. And finally, it was undeniably true that fundamentalist Muslim leaders were inflaming the controversy for their own political gain. But it seemed to me that if Muslims were guaranteed their personal law at the time of independence, and if modern India had interpreted its status as a secular country to mean that the personal laws of all religions should be respected, then the prime minister had to abide by that interpretation—at least until the country could agree on a uniform civil code, which theoretically would combine elements from all the religious laws into one. No one expected a consensus on a uniform civil code to emerge any time before the next century. Some of Gandhi's less rabid critics admitted that he in fact had no other choice but to do what he did, although they argued that the prime minister should have stalled by turning the matter over to a commission so as not to appear to be caving in to the Muslims. Maybe so. But however it might have been handled, it did not seem right to me that a "secular" Hindu majority should impose its will on the personal law granted to a religious minority. Every indication was that most Muslims supported the supremacy of their personal law. Although I felt that change in their law was desperately needed, the change had to come from the Muslims themselves.

Among the many women who disagreed with the prime minister was Margaret Alva, although she made her views known only in private. "I made my own opinion on the bill very clear with the prime minister," she told me, explaining her view that allowing the Supreme Court decision to stand "would gradually help us move toward a uniform civil code." She gave up when she saw she had lost. "Once the majority in the cabinet takes a decision, this is a decision of government," she said firmly, as if expecting an argument from me. "I have no independent views here." The women's groups were appalled, but Alva felt she had no other option and apparently did not feel strongly enough about the matter to resign from the party, as did one liberal Muslim member of Parliament who disagreed with the bill.

Margaret Alva was the first of a number of women I met in Indian politics, from the aristocratic Vijaya Lakshmi Pandit, one of the political grandes dames of the subcontinent, to K. R. Gouri, a Marxist from a low-caste family who had risen to become the most powerful woman in the southern Indian state of Kerala. These women represented a multitude of social and political forces in India—the independence movement, former royalty, the popular cinema, the left. They were interesting to me because they had moved out of the shadows of powerful men and had established identities and to some extent political bases of their own. I met them in palaces, bungalows and cramped government offices. For me, their lives were a rich part of the tapestry of India.

By far the most exotic political women I encountered were two former maharanis, Vijayaraje Scindia of the old princely state of Gwalior and Gayatri Devi of Jaipur. Both had become members of Parliament as the wives of once-influential maharajas, both had written as-told-to autobiographies about extraordinary lives (Gayatri Devi's was *A Princess Remembers,* published in 1976; Vijayaraje Scindia followed nine years later with *Princess*), and both had been imprisoned as members of the opposition by Indira Gandhi during the Emergency. The two were in Tihar jail, Delhi's infamous hellhole, where they shared a bathroom. Scindia described the experience in *Princess:* "Gayatri Devi and I may have been ex-Maharanis, but Tihar had its own 'Queen,' an under-trial prisoner who had twenty-seven registered offences against her, including as many as four murders. She went about with a razor-blade concealed in her blouse, threatening to 'carve up the face' of anyone who dared to cross her path." There were flies, filth, stench and disease which made it, Scindia wrote, "depressing beyond words. Gayatri Devi, who was ill and in need of major surgery, had convinced herself that she was going to die in Tihar. 'Only my body will be taken out,' she used to say, and she had given her family instructions about where and in what manner she wanted to be cremated."

When I met Scindia in 1988, she was still a member of the opposition and had become active in the cause of the right-wing Hindu religious revival movement. She had split bitterly with her son, who had surprised many by becoming a minister in the Congress party government of Rajiv Gandhi—who was of course the son of the woman who had put the former maharani in jail. The Scindias' most recent public quarrel had been over the marriage of the son's daughter to the son of the former maharaja of Kashmir, in an extravagant, ostentatious celebration at the Gwalior palace. Vijayaraje Scindia used the occasion to score a political point against the prime minister and her own son as well. "When the country is going through all these difficulties, you shouldn't have this grandeur, this show," she said.

By contrast, Gayatri Devi, the onetime maharani of Jaipur, had quit politics, but her election to Parliament in 1962, which she had won by a majority of 175,000 votes, had earned her a place in the *Guinness Book of World Records* for the largest majority won by any candidate running for any election in any democratic country in the world. Her life is important because she represents one kind of woman—and, in fact, man—who made it in politics in independent India: the former ruler whose still-loyal onetime subjects voted their candidate into Parliament with a massive majority and then served as a potent power base. But I am also mentioning her here because I cannot resist dipping into the storybook life of India's most alluring former princess.

The Jaipurs were among the richest and by far the most glamorous clan of the nation's royalty, and even more than the others, whose combined kingdoms once made up one third of the country, they lived in the India of glitter and excess: tiger shoots, polo matches, party weekends at hunting lodges surrounded by the golden desert of Rajasthan. Gayatri Devi's grandfather kept trained parrots that rode little silver bicycles; her mother had a gold tongue-scraper and also a live turtle encrusted with diamonds and rubies that she used as a good-luck charm at the gambling tables of France. Gayatri Devi had grown up as the daughter of the maharaja of Cooch Behar, in a palace in northeastern India with four hundred servants. She shot her first panther when she was twelve, went to finishing school in London and Switzerland, and then fell in love with the young maharaja of Jaipur, "Jai" to his friends. He was one of the world's finest polo players and liked a good party. She became his third wife and had to adjust to life in Jaipur with the other two. "I think it's much easier to get on with your husband's other wife, who has an official position, and a status, than his mistress, who is usurping you," she said. Her husband died in 1970 of a heart attack during a polo match.

In late 1986 I went to see the former member of Parliament at her home in Jaipur. She received me at the Lillypool, the name of the large sun-filled house on the grounds of her former residence, the Rambagh Palace. Three decades earlier the family had turned Rambagh into a luxury hotel to pay for the upkeep, and at the time of my visit, tourists could stay in Gayatri Devi's old bedroom suite for $250 a night. At first she had treated the guests as interlopers and had stationed her maid outside the door of Rambagh's indoor swimming pool so she could do her laps without disturbance from unseemly American and European tourists. Her husband put a stop to that, and over the years she had learned to adjust. The Lillypool, after all, wasn't so bad. The house was airy and spacious, with yards of paisley, tables of polo trophies and a signed photograph of Prince Charles in a silver frame. When I arrived, a servant directed me to a plump white chair in the living room, and soon a cup of tea materialized. After some time, so did Gayatri Devi, still striking at sixty-seven, walking briskly forward in an unregal outfit of dark brown slacks and a plaid cotton shirt. She took a seat on a sofa with her elbows on her knees. "I was always a tomboy," she said in a throaty English accent that made her sound like an Indian Tallulah Bankhead. "If I got up in the morning, it was 'Rush, rush, I've got to go riding.' There was no time to look in the mirror and pluck an eyebrow." In her youth, *Life* magazine called her one of the most beautiful women in the world. She had an athlete's figure, dark eyes, full lips, lustrous hair. She almost never wore makeup. But for all her style, she was never particularly interested in clothes, and her friends in India still sighed that she wore her saris too high off the floor. In New York and London, she was an otherworldly addition to the social circuit; she liked to collect people, and she was much collected herself. Jacqueline Onassis stayed with her at the Lillypool in 1983, and in 1985 Mick Jagger dropped by her stepson's house. I found the former maharani magisterial, haughty, entertaining and no doubt capable of great charm. But on the morning I spoke to her, she seemed under strain; for months she had been engaged in a long-running feud with her stepson over rights to the Jaipur estate, estimated to be worth $400 million. The stress showed in her tired, lined face, although she was still a trim, elegant woman who had kept her hair brown and who still favored, for the evenings, a double strand of pearls.

In the old days, before the princely kingdoms became part of independent India, twenty or thirty guests would come to stay at Rambagh, spilling from the marble veranda onto the dance floor and into the gardens, where two hundred kinds of roses grew. By Indian standards, the one-hundred-room Rambagh was a small, cozy palace. The fun never stopped. "Quite a lot, we went riding in the morning," Gayatri Devi remembered. "Then we came back and had breakfast in the big dining room. Guests did whatever they liked—some went riding, some went for an early morning shoot, some might get up late. After breakfast, I had a bath, changed, then went to my office. In those days there was quite a lot of Red Cross work to be done, and I had started a ladies' club. Then after the partition of India there were all the refugees who came in, and I started schools for them and all that. Then we'd all sit in the front veranda of Rambagh before lunch and have a drink, and there'd be lunch, and most people went for a siesta afterwards. In the afternoon there would usually be a polo match; then there would be tennis on the lawns here. And after that a lot of people would go play squash—really athletic we used to be, come to think of it. Then there would be time to change again for the evening. We would have drinks, and dinner different places—sometimes in the summer it was on the lawn, and now and then we would go up to Mooti Doongri, that little fort in front there. It was a nice life."

By independence, in 1947, that life had ended. The new Indian government officially abolished the princely states, and in the following years her husband was a maharaja in name only, with no kingdom left to rule. In 1962, in an attempt to gain political influence while appearing to remain neutral, he allowed his wife to be put up by an opposition party for election to Parliament. For the former maharani, this was a journey into an India she had never known before. As she explained in her biography, written with Santha Rama Rau: "I had never before heard of electoral rolls, did not know the names of the different constituencies, and did not realize that there were special seats reserved for Harijans and the tribal people. I knew nothing about election agents, nominations, withdrawals, or parliamentary boards." She campaigned by jeep for thousands of miles across Rajasthan and struggled to make speeches in her rudimentary Hindi. "The whole campaign was, perhaps, the most extraordinary period of my life," she wrote. "Seeing and meeting the people of India, as I did then, I began to realize how little I really knew of the villagers' way of life." She spent the next fifteen years as the member of Parliament who wore chiffon saris and French perfume, but she emerged as a formidable power because of her enormous base of support among her husband's former subjects in Rajasthan.

Another woman whose relationship with an influential man led her to politics was Nehru's sister, Vijaya Lakshmi Pandit, who had a brilliant career as her brother's ambassador to Moscow, London and Washington, and who in 1953 was elected as the first woman president of the United Nations General Assembly. The international press at first did not know what to make of her. "How would you describe the sari you are wearing?" one reporter asked at the U.N. news conference following Mrs. Pandit's election. Mrs. Pandit would not sink to this. "Did you ask my predecessor to describe his suit?" she retorted. In her autobiography, *The Scope of Happiness,* she noted, "I was very put out that in this age of women's emancipation, and after all the years I had been in public life, such inane inquiries should be put to me simply because I was a woman."

In 1986, I went to see Mrs. Pandit after my editors at the *Post* asked me to write a story with an Indian angle about the Public Broadcasting System's Masterpiece Theatre series *Lord Mountbatten: The Last Viceroy.* Mrs. Pandit had been a personal friend of Louis Mountbatten's, or Dickie, as she called him, so in search of reminiscences I found my way up to her house on a road lined with jacaranda trees just outside Dehra Dun, a resort town 125 miles north of New Delhi. "I'm awfully amused that someone should want to interview me," Mrs. Pandit announced when we sat down on cane chairs in the cool winter sunshine of her garden, which looked out toward the tree-covered hills that announced the beginning of the Himalayas. "I'm not interviewable." Her view was that as a retired eighty-five-year-old woman she was no longer news, but I spent the morning enchanted and fascinated by her memories, anecdotes and political opinions. Mrs. Pandit was one of the great figures of modern India, and like her niece, Indira Gandhi, she had seen it all: the grandeurs of the old Nehru home in Allahabad, the freedom struggle, Mahatma Gandhi, prison, her brother's rise to the position of prime minister. She had broken with Mrs. Gandhi during the Emergency, when she spoke out against her, and the rift between the two women, who were said not to trust each other, never healed. But in a larger sense, it seemed to me that rivalry between Nehru's daughter and sister over who should inherit the family political legacy was inevitable.

On the morning I met Mrs. Pandit, I noticed immediately that she had the deep-set eyes and wide mouth of her brother, and it was startling to see so much of his face in hers. She was dressed elegantly in a blue silk printed sari with a navy cardigan, and age had brought a certain softness and sweetness to her. This did not mean she had lost her sense of humor and a predilection for saying whatever she pleased. She casually referred to Queen Elizabeth II, another old friend, as "not a great intellect, of course, but a warm person of many interests," and also spoke her mind about the relationship between her brother, a romantic and impassioned man, and Mountbatten's dazzling and difficult wife, Edwina. As the last British viceroy, Mountbatten had been thrown into a relationship with Nehru by the forces of history, and their goal was nothing less than the creation of modern India. Edwina was an important part of the chemistry that made it work. When things seemed to be at their worst, she was able to charm and provide solace for the moody Nehru; whether the close friendship became more intimate than that is something that has fascinated the Indians for years. In 1985, the especially juicy parts of *Mountbatten,* a well-received official biography by Philip Ziegler, were serialized in Indian newspapers, creating a brief flurry of fresh gossip about the threesome, but Ziegler in the end evaded the issue, describing the relationship between Edwina and Nehru as "intensely loving, romantic, trusting, generous, idealistic, even spiritual," and adding that "if there was any physical element it can only have been of minor importance to either party." The journalist M. J. Akbar, in his biography of Nehru, took the speculation a step forward when he quoted an Indian politician's son who said he walked into Nehru's bedroom to announce dinner one night and came upon Edwina and Nehru in what the politician's son described as a "clinch."

Mrs. Pandit had her own ideas. "Edwina was a great friend of my brother's," she said. "A man and a woman can be great friends. I've had many good men friends, but I haven't been to bed with them. I think Edwina was an extremely fine woman who was drawn on many levels to my brother. I pity a woman who wouldn't have been. And he found in her a woman with whom he could exchange many thoughts." If the relationship did become intimate, she said, "I'm glad. What can I say? I've seen many of the letters, and I've found they are some of the best literature I've read. But that's my brother."

Oddly, for all her time in public life in India—as a member of Parliament and the cabinet, and as the governor of the state of Maharashtra—Mrs. Pandit claimed in her autobiography that "I am not a politician. The ways of modern politics are not my métier; the slippery road of intrigue that politicians have to climb is not for me, even though the prizes at the end may be considerable." The morning I was with Mrs. Pandit, she looked back on her life and concluded, not unhappily, that the years of "great fun" and "great moments" had come to the last chapter. "You read the papers, and one by one the people I've known are no more," she said. "It makes one feel rather lonely. It's almost a desolate feeling. I feel it every morning when I get up. This is the biggest argument I have with my daughters, but I say this from the depths of my feeling. I honestly feel that having outlived everybody, it is high time for me to go on to a better world."

As moving and inspiring as Mrs. Pandit was for me, it remained undeniable that she owed more than a measure of her success to her brother. After I spoke to Mrs. Pandit, I began to wonder: Was there any woman in Indian politics who had succeeded without a relationship to a powerful man? Was there one woman who had been able to succeed on her own? I hoped that education and social change might have created such a woman, but instead modernity seemed to be taking the political tradition of "bahu-beti-biwi"—that is, daughter-in-law, daughter and wife—down bizarre new roads. In the state of Tamil Nadu, for example, there were actually two women, a wife and a mistress, who publicly fought over the right to succeed one of India's most popular politicians, the former matinee idol and Tamil Nadu chief minister M. G. Ramachandran. Both women had costarred with MGR, as he was called, and over the years they had maintained an uneasy coexistence. Their leading man's death in 1987 set off a political circus that began while his body was still lying in state. On one side was what the press and those in the controversy dubbed the J-1 camp, for Janaki Ramachandran, the sixty-four-year-old long-suffering wife, who had appeared with MGR in three films; on the other was the J-2 camp, for Jayalalitha Jayaram, the clever, wildly popular forty-year-old "sultry siren" of the Tamil Nadu cinema of a decade before. She was universally described as MGR's lover, although she preferred "protégée." As Tamil Nadu watched transfixed, Jayalalitha kept a vigil by MGR's body for twenty-one hours, withstanding fatigue and a group of women from the J-1 camp who, she told *India Today,* "started stamping on my feet, driving their nails into my skin, pinching me, and so on." When Jayalalitha tried to climb alongside MGR's body for the funeral procession, she was assaulted by a nephew of MGR's wife and forced to retreat. "I was disgusted with this uncouth behavior," Jayalalitha complained to *India Today*. MGR's wife was soon victorious as the new chief minister, but only temporarily, and by early 1989, neither of MGR's women was in power.

The fact was that in three and a half years, the only woman I met who had achieved real political stature without the benefit of a man was K. R. Gouri, the minister of industries in the Communist state government of Kerala. Gouri was sixty-seven, a tough, outspoken Marxist who had been drawn into politics with the peasant rebellions against a local maharaja in the 1940s. Although she was the daughter of an influential social reformer who owned a coconut plantation, the family was of a low caste, and Gouri had not been elected on anyone's coattails. She did, however, have the advantage of living in Kerala, where historically women had been treated with respect. Before independence, there had been a matrilineal system of inheritance among at least one important caste, and in recent years the state had both the highest literacy rate among women and the lowest birth rate. Gouri was an unusually powerful woman whose independence, competence and honesty had given her a massive following among the lower castes. Had it not been for the men in the party leadership, she might have become chief minister after the recent state elections.

Even in Kerala, of course, men and women were far from equal. In 1957, when the Communists first came into power in Kerala, Gouri was made a minister in the new government. But when she fell in love with another government minister and married him, the talk among her colleagues was that the party leadership had hastily arranged for the wedding for propriety's sake. If Gouri had not married, they said, she would have lost her ministership; the man with whom she was involved, however, would have been permitted to remain on the job. When the Communist party split in 1964, so, too, did the marriage. Worse, there had been no children, a terrible thing for a woman in India. Gouri was viewed by the male members of the local press as bitter and argumentative, made forever miserable by her childless state, and while I resented the sexism in their remarks, I have to say that I found her, for whatever reason, as unpleasant as promised when I caught up with her at her home in the town of Trivandrum one evening. When I arrived as scheduled at eight-thirty, she was absorbed in a popular television show, composed of silly but wholly mesmerizing song-and-dance numbers from Hindi films. Without saying a word, she motioned for me to sit down and watch. I was a fan of the show myself and soon became engrossed in it. When it was over, Gouri turned from the screen and spoke her first words. "What do you want from me?" she gruffly demanded. The interview went downhill from there, although Gouri did answer my questions. She insisted that her marriage had not been arranged by the party. "We decided we loved each other, so we decided to marry," she said. "As disciplined party people, we asked for their sanction. The party people were just like my family." The marriage broke up, she said, "not because of the party but because of personalities. We had some personal differences."

Whatever the case, the reality for women in Indian politics was the same as for women in politics everywhere: It was a dirty, expensive game run by men. Although the Indian independence movement had theoretically made a place for political women, the fact was that forty years after independence, the men still controlled the party leadership, patronage, money and the selection of candidates for office. The Congress party was probably the worst offender, but K. R. Gouri's story proved that the Communists, too, were reluctant to allow a woman into the highest level of the hierarchy. It was no surprise that most women, from Indira Gandhi to a first-time candidate for a state legislative assembly seat, needed connections to men. Once in power, they needed unusual reserves of strength. Sheila Dixit, the minister of state for parliamentary affairs, put it succinctly. "The going is rough in politics," she said. "Most women say the hell with it. They would rather do something else that will give them more security and stability." Dixit, the daughter-in-law of a powerful man, was one of the few who qualified as a power broker. "I think once we get into it," she said, speaking of herself but also, I am sure, of Indira Gandhi, "we are forces to be reckoned with."

CHAPTER 8

REKHA, DIMPLE, SRIDEVI AND FRIENDS

The Actresses of Bombay

OUTSIDE, THE SUMMER MONSOON WAS TURNING BOMBAY INTO AN IMPASS-
able swamp, but inside, on the set of the Hindi film *Dance Dance*, they
were busy making dreams. I had watched all day as one of India's top
actors, a slim-hipped, blow-dried heartthrob, gyrated to a disco beat
in a kind of subcontinental *Saturday Night Fever*. His costar was
Mandakini, a seventeen-year-old newcomer, who had made her movie
debut the year before in a wet sari scene that male audiences and
outraged feminists had still not forgotten. But the actress I found more
interesting was the "dramatic" female lead, Smita Patil, at that moment
stretched out in her dressing room, bored and exhausted. She was thirty
years old, one of India's biggest stars, sensuous and striking, and a
favorite of the highbrow art cinema. Yet there she was, at ten on a
Sunday night, working on schlock so she could make a living. What
was worse, lately her personal life had become more interesting to her
fans than her films. The big news was that she was five months pregnant
with the child of Raj Babbar, a well-known actor whom she called

her husband. But Babbar, as anybody who read the movie magazines knew, was married to someone else.

"When we got involved, he never promised to leave his wife," Patil told me calmly. "However difficult it was for me to accept certain facts, I still had to." I was talking to her in twenty-minute segments between shots. Despite the seeming contradictions in her personal life, Patil was one of the more intelligent actresses in Bombay, college-educated, with a feminist conscience and an awareness of the world beyond the studio gates.

For the day's scenes, Patil's costume designer had managed to create a dress that hid her growing stomach, but the strain of standing in front of the camera for hours in high-heeled pumps was evident in her face. "My back," she said, grimacing. She was sitting on her bed, feet propped up on a pillow, with a front section of her hair in an electric roller. She nibbled at a piece of toast covered with an unappetizing mound of melted cheese and tried to fend off a director's assistant who came in to tell her they needed close-ups. "Close-ups?" she said, horrified. "When I'm looking like a dead cat?" The room, a mess of costumes and makeup, smelled stale. From this vantage point, her life did not appear to be a glamorous one, although it had led to the kinds of entanglements for which Patil was now famous. "Women who work in this industry have no time for any kind of normal life," she said. "You're working ten or twelve hours a day with different men all the time. You're constantly demanded to emote, and it tends to become a very high-strung existence emotionally, which leads into your personal involvements. The line is very thin."

In between her comments, the director's assistant walked in with Patil's lines for an upcoming scene. They had just been written on the set, which was standard procedure for Indian films. Patil had only a vague idea of the story line, but this was not a matter for concern. She knew that *Dance Dance* was essentially about a brother-and-sister song-and-dance act and that she played the sister, who got raped. It was not the sort of plot that would have impressed her feminist friends, but Patil had already done a half dozen rape scenes in her career—a modest number in an industry that regularly spiced up its films with battered women for the heroes to rescue. "Because, you see, the man has to be the savior," Patil said sarcastically. "It's all for the sake of the man. The women have to continue being beaten." The rest of *Dance Dance* was a mystery to her. "If you ask me, I honestly don't know what happens," she said, shrugging. "It's a normal Hindi film."

Smita Patil worked in what was without question the largest and nuttiest film industry in the world. Every year, the Indian "dream factory" churned out close to nine hundred feature films, almost all of them frothy romances and bloody shoot-'em-ups, in Hindi and other regional languages, for an annual paying audience of no fewer than five billion. That was five times the number of people who saw the 230 feature films produced in 1988 in the United States. And even though Bombay, like Hollywood, had been hurt by video piracy and television, the dream factory remained in full production. This was one of the great ironies of an industry that always appeared on the edge of collapse. India's literate upper classes had for years avoided the lowbrow entertainment of Hindi films in the country's run-down cinema halls, and by the late 1980s, more movies were failing than ever before. And yet more movies were being made than ever before. This of course made no sense. A theory in the industry, virtually impossible to prove, was that accountants altered the books so that the films seemed to lose money, enabling producers to avoid the high Indian taxes on profits. Certainly the stars were notorious for receiving "black money," or cash fees paid under the table. Whatever the case, real-estate speculators, diamond merchants and expatriate Indians continued to finance new films with enormous sums of money from outside the industry. Like the tycoon in America who buys the local baseball team for the prestige and the chance to make friends with the players, the investor in Indian films was not completely rational. The glamour of Bombay was hard for many investors to resist, and they seemed willing to gamble that lush, big-screen movies would survive by offering escape in a country where most people struggled through impoverished lives on the edge of survival.

The industry was a good story in itself, but I was more curious about the actresses. They were the country's goddesses, appearing in lurid color, twenty times their actual size, on movie billboards in big cities and small towns all across India. Naturally they pouted regularly in the film magazines that they were not getting sufficiently serious roles to show off their talents. They seemed as self-absorbed, volatile and diverting as actresses anywhere. They were also among the most successful women in India, with the money and power, I thought, to break the rules and set their own agendas at a very young age. The actress Farha, for example, was only eighteen, but she had a bigger income than most business executives in India, swore like a camel driver and had an explosive, well-documented romance with a young director.

"Why do I love and hate so intensely that I want to either kill myself or him?" she asked *Movie* magazine one month. "I am now determined to make his life one big hell." Behind the gates of Bombay's Film City, a sprawling production lot of rolling hills and picturesque lakes, I found a less tempestuous Farha, dancing with a young costar in a soft-focus garden shot as technicians worked the fog machines. Farha, who, like most actresses in Bombay, used only one name, had already played the part of a woman who discovered that her husband had another wife and a set of children. Her character did what any proper Hindi film heroine would do in such a situation, which was to commit suicide out of shame. But Farha told me she had different ideas. "I would have killed him," she said.

Within the industry, however, it was the actors who were considered the big stars and commanded the large fees because they pulled in the audiences. The actresses merely played backup roles to the men. "Women are not looked upon naturally, as having faults and complexity," complained Deepa Sahai, a serious actress who had made a name for herself in a television series about several families caught up in the 1947 partition of India and Pakistan. "Even if a woman has walked out on her husband, it's always because he has gotten involved with another woman. She never has any ambitions of her own. She's reacting to betrayal rather than her own aspirations."

Yet the secondary roles of the actresses were a powerful influence on the standards of behavior for women in the country. Although I sometimes thought the feminists were overreacting when they complained about the portrayal of women in commercial Indian films, in essence they were right. On-screen, the actresses were the guardians of the country's conservative traditions, often playing women who were raped because they had committed such suggestive acts as working in nightclubs or wearing Western clothes. Only the good girls in saris lived happily ever after with husbands and children. "The cinema tells us that women who wear pants and play tennis are wicked," said India's leading film critic, Chidananda Das Gupta. "It tells us they may ride in a motorcar, but inside, they mustn't change."

During the ten days I spent one summer talking to Bombay's actresses about their careers, costars and love affairs, I learned that most of them, like Farha, led a schizophrenic existence. Offscreen, in the beach cottages and high rises of Bombay's film colony, Indian actresses were part of a culture that collided head-on with the conservative values of "Mother India" presented on film. Here there were love affairs, love triangles, love children, love nests. This was the real entertainment the stars provided for the fans, all of it breathlessly reported by the film magazines each month. KIMI DUMPED! announced the cover of *Cine Blitz* one summer. JAYAPRADA WEDS HER LOVER! gasped *Star & Style*. Every star in every article lamented that she just wanted to be happy, but this was an elusive goal since even in Bombay divorce and living together were still cause for shame. So the film colony managed by making its own rules. One recent trend, as in the case of Smita Patil, was the husband with two "wives." The pioneer of the custom was Hema Malini, once known as the Ice Maiden of the industry, who decided, just before giving birth to her lover's child, that she had "married" him in the eyes of God and that his other wife was acceptable to her. "It's not legally all right," she admitted to me. "But in my conscience, I married him and then had the baby." We were talking in the living room of her suburban Bombay home, an expanse of marble, mirrors, servants and guards. Her "husband" was Dharmendra, the Indian he-man, who divided his time between his wife and her. "At least I'm open," Hema Malini said. "I'm not saying, 'We're just friends.' "

A spate of similar "marriages" followed, all carefully documented by the film magazines. The trend hit a new high, or low, when a well-known director, Mahesh Bhatt, converted to Islam in a half-hour ceremony that immediately preceded his second wedding—enabling him to marry wife number two without divorcing wife one. "It was the best solution for the three of us," he told me in utter seriousness. "For me, divorce would have been the final rejection of a person I couldn't amputate from my life. And I had to give my second wife some kind of legal respectability." Under Hindu law, however, his marriage was illegal. "If my first wife contests it, I'm dead and gone," he admitted.

I never understood how the stars found time for such extracurricular activities, given that some of them worked in as many as fifteen movies at once, often rushing frantically to play two different lead characters in two different films on two different sets in a single day. Farha, for example, told me that she had recently worked twenty-four hours straight. First she did studio shots for one film; then she stayed up all night performing stunts in an underground train station for another. Clearly, this was not Hollywood. No commercial actress in Bombay ever spent months studying the soul of a character, not least because the character was almost always the same. As Das Gupta wrote in

Talking About Films, a book of his essays: "What passes for acting is a game between the producer and the audience, played with well-established types—the crying mother, the doting father, the dancing, singing, dewy-eyed heroine, the sad-faced or epileptic hero, the comic, the precocious child—in which a few mannerisms of the actor are enough for the audience to take the details for granted. . . . Similarly the situations are stock situations, with stock responses too ready-made to require any exploration of why or how something has happened; the sooner the rest of the action springing from a situation (in a nightclub, a swimming party, a sentimental scene between father and daughter) can be taken for granted, the better."

The Hindi commercial movie should not be confused with art films by directors like Satyajit Ray that are shown by film societies in New York, Paris or Rome. About fifty of these films used to be produced each year in India, most of them explorations of the dark side of the human character, intended for the urban intelligentsia. They almost never made money. What the motor rickshaw drivers and tea shop owners of India wanted was essentially a musical, loud and garish—a genre that would have baffled most Americans. Chandra Barot, a Hindi film director, certainly found this to be the case. "When I visited 20th Century-Fox, they asked me, 'Why do you have songs in every film?' " he told me. "But basically we're very simple people. All the films have the same story." The story usually was about a young girl and a young boy who loved each other but encountered problems, often because the girl's father opposed her marriage. It all usually worked out in the end, but not before a series of violent fights, car chases and, of course, the elaborate songs and dances, in which the hero would put his arms around the heroine, maybe give her a kiss (permitted only recently by the censors) and then dissolve with his loved one to, say, a meadow of buttercups in Kashmir, where the couple would suddenly be seen bursting into song. The meadow would have nothing to do with the locale or story line of the film, but the audience never cared. "The main difference between American films and Indian films," said the actress Rekha, "is that American films make sense, and Indian films don't."

The dancing mixed Western disco with Indian classical and folk dance and was often punctuated by aggressive pelvic thrusting that was more vulgar than anything I ever saw in an R-rated American movie. The songs were lilting and undeniably catchy—I heard them coming from radios in back alleys all over India, and sometimes found myself singing them for days afterward—but the women's voices were pitched so high that it sounded to me as if Alvin and the Chipmunks had done the soundtrack. In fact, the female vocals in nearly every Indian commercial film were dubbed by either Lata Mangeshkar, the undisputed empress of Indian film singing, or her sister, who had an identical high-pitched voice. The result was that when every woman in every Indian film opened her mouth to sing, she sounded exactly the same. No one in India thought this was at all peculiar.

THE THREE LEADING COMMERCIAL INDIAN ACTRESSES THROUGHOUT THE mid- and late 1980s were indisputably Rekha, Dimple Kapadia and Sridevi. Although their positions as numbers one, two and three shifted according to their most recent box-office hits and failures, no other commercial actress came close to touching their star quality. When I was in Bombay in the summer of 1986, Rekha, the longtime queen of the Hindi screen, who had been number one for years, had recently been surpassed by her younger rival, Sridevi (pronounced Shree-day-vee). Dimple, as everyone called her, had recently reentered the film world after a disastrous marriage and was not yet in the running. Two years later, after Sridevi had suffered a few box-office flops, Rekha was back on top as number one and elder stateswoman. Dimple had come roaring back as well and had at times threatened to take the number-one spot for herself. This was all sometimes very hard to follow, even for those who made a career of it. "We find it difficult to keep up as far as the girls are concerned," admitted Nari Hira, the publisher of *Stardust,* the leading film magazine.

The first actress I met was Dimple, who was shooting one afternoon at a bungalow in a high-rent section of Bombay. This was in the summer of 1986, when she was still down on the lower rungs of the film industry. Even so, most men, even intelligent, professional men who never went to the Hindi films, used to go into raptures over Dimple. When I first saw her on the set, I could see why. She was beautiful—tall, shapely, with enormous eyes, swollen lips and a dramatic cleft in her chin. She was wearing a curly long-haired red wig and a green-and-cream silk sari. The film was called *Insaaf,* or "Justice," and Dimple played twin sisters, one a nightclub singer, the other a doctor. Naturally the singer was raped, then jumped off a building out of shame. When I arrived on the set, Dimple was in the middle of a scene, shot in a bedroom, in which the nightclub singer was telling her lover, a former college professor, that she had just aborted his child. When the lover asked why, she replied that it was because they were not husband and wife. The lover, by now extremely agitated, declared his love and asked for her hand in marriage, at which point the singer admitted that she had made up the abortion story and that she was still carrying his child. At the melodramatic conclusion of the scene, Dimple burst into real tears.

"It just happens sometimes," she said afterward in her dressing room, still sniffling. "That scene was from within. Until yesterday, I didn't know where this character was at. But now I'm getting it. She wanted to be an actress and she couldn't make it, so she got into this nightclub scene." I asked her about her attempt to make a comeback after her failed marriage. "The comeback has been no comeback," she said flatly. "I don't know what people were expecting from me." Dimple had the straightforward, no-excuses manner of someone who had been through too much to put up a front. At least her life had provided abundant material for the scene she had just played. At the age of fourteen she had starred in *Bobby,* a love story that became one of the industry's all-time hits. The film made Dimple into a sensation, but instead of using it to launch her career, she married, at the age of fifteen, the country's most popular leading man at the time, Rajesh Khanna. He promptly told his new wife that her acting days were over. "My husband believed that my place was at home," Dimple said. "It was not a husband-wife relationship—it was father-daughter." After two children and ten years of marriage, she finally walked out. "It's a big stigma to leave a man," she said. "I didn't expect to be accepted. But after I left him, it made a tremendous difference to me. The best part was that I was earning my own bread." I could see by now that Dimple was clearly pleased with her outburst of tears in the previous scene. "That one shot gave me a lot of pleasure," she said. "That kind of high I've never been able to experience with anything else in my life. And if I can get that high twice or thrice a year—I just love it." Another marriage was not in her future since she, too, was involved with an actor who she said would "never" leave his wife. I asked her why she stayed in the relationship. "I don't owe anything to anyone," she said. "If I'm happy, I'm going to do it."

Some days later I met Rekha, a stunning thirty-two-year-old beauty who that summer had seen her career eclipsed by her young friend Sridevi, in a widely discussed Indian version of *All About Eve.* Even worse, the dreaded Sridevi had the effrontery to be linked romantically with the leading man, who was said to have been Rekha's lover of many years. I decided it would be best to bring up a less incendiary topic first, so in Rekha's dressing room one muggy evening I began by asking her about one of her favorite subjects—Rekha, a mythic being she had come to see as larger than herself. "Nobody can take my position, not even myself," she announced to me as she draped her forehead with jewels for an upcoming scene. "Not even the human being that I am can ever take Rekha's position. No. That is only for her. She has taken that position for life." Although she viewed herself as a deity, Rekha was warm, friendly and so talkative that it was difficult to guide the conversation to a new topic. Listening to her voice, however, was lovely. She had learned to speak English with a smooth, almost musical upper-class Indian accent that veered toward the British.

The goddess had arrived in Bombay from south India more than a decade before as "a round ball of flesh," as Rekha herself said. But she had ambition, she had street smarts and, most important, she had the quality called *oomph* in Bombay, which was the powerful sex appeal necessary for success. So her movies did well. As the years passed, Rekha slowly transformed herself, changing her makeup, learning how to dress and slimming down with the help of Jane Fonda's workout videos. Soon she was starring in movies with Amitabh Bachchan, the male megastar. Even upper-class housewives went to their beauty salons and said they wanted to look like Rekha—full lips, dark, dramatic eyes, lustrous black hair. At the same time, the gossip magazines were chronicling Rekha's depressions, tantrums and periods of Garbo-like reclusiveness, which merely added to her appeal. When she did speak, she had the unfortunate habit of saying whatever came into her head, revealing on several occasions that all she read was *Cosmopolitan* magazine and *Archie* comic books. But then Rekha hit thirty and was immediately branded as "aging" by male audiences, who preferred, she said, "a child-woman, impish, bubbly, voluptuous." Rekha insisted to me that she still had that kind of appeal, but the talk in the industry was that she had in fact become, after all her workouts, much too sleek for the tastes of the masses. This set the stage for Sridevi, the more recent arrival out of south India, who was every bit as plump, popular and savvy as Rekha had been a decade before. Suddenly it was Sridevi's face that appeared on movie posters across India. Only twenty-one years old that summer, Sridevi had already signed up for more movies than Rekha, which had earned her the title of Miss Number One in Bombay.

"She's *one* of the number ones," Rekha corrected, with a tiny frown. "There are a lot of number ones." Both she and Sridevi continued to insist that they were friends, and they made a big fuss of greeting each other in public. A year before, when I had been on a plane from Madras to Delhi, I had watched as Sridevi and Rekha unexpectedly ran into each other on the same flight. They squealed with delight across the cabin, throwing the rest of the passengers into an uproar. Such behavior was great entertainment for their fellow actresses in Bombay, who believed that the two were obsessed with each other and actually imitated each other in their films. The friendship, these other actresses told me, was more like détente—Sridevi was so afraid of Rekha's venom and Rekha was so fearful of Sridevi's success that the two refrained from clawing at each other in public. Rekha, though, had her moments.

"She's a cute kid," Rekha said when I finally got around to raising the issue of Sridevi's success. "She came into the industry at a time when I was thinking of stepping out. People missed me so much, and she almost had perfect timing in filling that gap. She is very intelligent. Of course, she's much more immature than me, but in no time she'll learn."

I found Miss Number One at another studio in Bombay, impatiently waiting for her next scene on the set of *Mr. India,* a big-budget special-effects film with a bizarre plot twist in which she played a reporter for a newspaper called *The Crimes of India* who falls in love with an invisible man. The set, a futuristic grotto of aluminum foil that looked like *Star Wars* run amok, appeared to be the headquarters of a diabolical villain. The producers had hopes for a blockbuster, and when *Mr. India* was released a year later, it quickly became a big summertime hit. I dragged an Indian friend, Bim Bissell, to see it with me. Bim worked at the World Bank in Delhi, had a son in an American university and was one of the many Indians who had stopped going to the cinema halls years before. I think she looked upon our excursion as a minor adventure. "I haven't been in this theater since I was in college," she told me as we took our seats. The theater was hot, gritty and smelly, but the movie, which had received something better than the usual disdainful reviews, turned out to be absurd fun. Much of its success was due to Sridevi, who was charismatic on-screen, especially in one memorable song-and-dance number when she was costumed Bombay-style in a clinging gold lamé gown with a matching gold headdress and fingernails.

Back on the set in Bombay, however, the *Mr. India* star had been in a bad mood, annoyed with her director for keeping her until eight at night when she had been up since dawn. But when I asked Sridevi about her rival Rekha, the irritation gave way to a little-girl innocence. "We don't have any problems between us," she told me with a wide-eyed look. She was collapsed on the bed in her dressing room, a dusty refuge filled with costumes and half-eaten sandwiches, and up close had none of the seductive magic she projected on-screen. She was merely a young girl, pretty and plump, who had become an object of fantasy for her fans in the south who liked her that way. "I hate being a fatty," she sighed. "But if I were skinny, my fans in the south would kick me out." Most Indian actresses were equally fleshy, and even those viewed as slender were twenty pounds overweight by Hollywood standards. Only Rekha worked out at a health club. The others spent lots of time telling film magazines about the exercise programs they followed at home, but I had my doubts. The desired look for an actress in the film industry was soft and luscious, which implied leisure and wealth, and separated her from the lower classes in the villages, where the women were muscular and thin.

Sridevi began acting when she was five and had appeared in more than one hundred films. She routinely worked fifteen hours a day, seven days a week, and insisted she never tired of it. "I love this profession," she told me sweetly. "It's such a beautiful thing. Sometimes I feel I should take a day off, but by the afternoon, I get restless." It was only in recent years that she had learned English and gained some independence. "Now I talk to the press without my mummy," she informed me. Clearly she had picked up a few tricks since then, because when I asked her again about Rekha, Sridevi was as evasive as a Congress party politician. "She's very interested in her work," she said of Rekha. "She has a very lovely face."

In order to find out what was really going on between the two women, I made an appointment back in Delhi to see Amitabh Bachchan, the star who was at that time also a member of Parliament. At forty-four, he remained the single biggest phenomenon in the history of Indian film. I found him in his subtly decorated beige-and-cream office, all six feet of him folded into an expensively upholstered chair. He had bedroom eyes and a gentle manner and in person turned out to be nothing like the Rambo he played on-screen. He had grown up in cultivated surroundings as the son of a well-known poet and scholar in Allahabad and was a close childhood friend of Rajiv Gandhi. Despite his privileged background, he had risen to stardom as the quintessential cinematic "angry young man," whose swaggering manner and contempt for social niceties made him a symbol for an alienated generation of moviegoers who had left the villages and struggled to find work in the cities. "My fan is the man on the street who's looking to make it in life," Bachchan said. "I've always played the underdog who has single-handedly risen above all obstacles."

At the height of his success, Bachchan was making so many movies at the same time that he had had to "die" three times in one day—shot twice and stabbed once. ("It was deadly," he said.) Several years before, when he really almost died performing a stunt on a set, the nation went into mourning. Prime Minister Indira Gandhi paid her respects at the hospital, and All India Radio broadcast bulletins on Bachchan's vital signs as people fasted and prayed nationwide. "It's something I can never forget," he said. When he recovered, he found he was a bigger star than ever. In 1984, his friend Rajiv asked him to run for a Parliament seat against a particularly powerful and entrenched incumbent. Bachchan won easily, but after the election he never had the political impact that people expected, and by 1988 he had resigned amid allegations, never proven, that he was evading taxes by using his brother, a resident of Switzerland, to funnel his fortune out of the country. His health had also suffered, and he was undergoing treatment for myasthenia gravis, a muscular disease. But throughout it all, he had continued his acting career, for fees that were estimated as high as $1 million per film. (Sridevi, the highest-paid actress, made only about $150,000 per film.)

I talked with Bachchan in his office for an hour, and he seemed happy to hold forth on the subject of films, Rekha and Sridevi, rather than discuss his political headaches. For years, Rekha and Bachchan were the unbeatable couple of Indian films, and the gossip magazines continued to write that the on-screen electricity between them was crackling offscreen as well. Bachchan was said to have exerted a sophisticating influence on Rekha, helping to polish her to her present sheen. Bachchan, who was married, casually denied any relationship with her. "Why only Rekha?" he asked me. "Why not the rest of them?"

Rekha had rather unconvincingly denied the relationship too, although she did say, "I wish I were" involved with Bachchan. She had never married. She also spoke very passionately about the married man who had been in her life for years, but whom she never named. "It's a lot of pain, no matter how independent you are," she said. "It's all very nice to live in a dream sequence and say, 'Oh, you are the mistress and you're having the best, you're more enticing and desirable to your man.' No, no, no. You're giving up a lot."

That summer, Rekha was no longer making movies with Bachchan. Sridevi was. "She has a lot of talent as an actress," Bachchan said enthusiastically of his new costar. "There's something that excites people when she comes on-screen. There is much more to her than just legs and body." Somewhat incredibly, when Sridevi did not have the time to do the dubbing for one of her recent films with Bachchan, Rekha offered to do it for her. Afterward, the gossip press quoted Rekha as saying that now "he" has "my voice and her body."

———————————

IN THE END, BACHCHAN OFFERED NO REAL CLUES TO HIS PERSONAL IN- volvements. The fact was that any actress, and not just Rekha and Sridevi, knew that appearing in a film with Bachchan offered a possible ticket to stardom. One of those hoping for such a break was Neelam, an eighteen-year-old ingenue. Her prayers were answered one day when she was cast in a film with Bachchan, although as his daughter, not his costar. But since Bachchan was old enough to be her father, Neelam was, as she put it, "thrilled" about the part. I met Neelam before she was to start the Bachchan film, on the set of *Mud and Gold,* a standard Hindi love-triangle in which she was cast opposite Chunky Pandey, a slim, long-legged teen idol in black leather pants. The details of the plot were, as usual, obscure. "I'm in love with the hero, Chunky," Neelam explained, "whereas he's in love with another girl. She's a prostitute, and I'm a prostitute's daughter, but I don't know it. The other girl dies, but I don't know how. I haven't heard the whole story, actually."

Neelam interested me because she was a darling among the new crop of teenage stars who might or might not make it to the superstardom of Rekha, Dimple and Sridevi. Neelam was also a nice girl from a prosperous family who refused to "reveal," which was the film indus- try verb for appearing in bathing suits and wet, see-through saris. "I feel that once I start revealing," Neelam told me in her dressing room, "there will be no end to it." Neelam had been born and raised in Hong Kong as the daughter of an Indian diamond exporter and had acquired an English accent from the British schools she attended there. She had good manners, a lovely face and a healthy complexion. She might have grown up to marry an international financier had she not been discovered at the age of thirteen. During one of her summer visits to her grandparents in Bombay, the father of one of her playmates, a successful director, was so struck by her fresh beauty that he insisted she appear in his next film. Neelam's parents were appropriately appalled and said no, but they eventually gave in under pressure. "We were never for it," sighed Neelam's mother, Parveen Kothari. "Neelam said, 'Let me try one.' Well, it's never one, really. You get stuck." Neelam, too, had at first been horrified by the film world. "I was like, oh, these people are so uncouth, so ill-mannered," she said. "I couldn't adjust. But after two or three films, I started getting used to it. Now it's become a part of my life. It's something totally different. It's hard work, but it's nice."

Neelam appeared to have adjusted quite well the day I watched her work on the *Mud and Gold* set. We were at the decrepit Natraj Studios, and the scene was a big dance number in a disco. Neelam and Chunky were leading fifty other dancers through bumps, grinds and a Bombay version of the shimmy. Rock music throbbed over the set, which was sweltering and crowded with technicians, hangers-on and little men serving tea. Neelam's mother, who accompanied her starlet to all her shootings, sat on the sidelines in a tasteful salwar kameez, as unhappily as if she had suddenly found herself in the middle of a malodorous village bazaar in Punjab, yet determined to be a stoic chaperone for a daughter who was having the time of her life. Neelam threw herself into her dance steps with great enthusiasm, wiggling and shaking in take after take. In between she talked with Chunky, who responded by whispering in her ear. The two then shared a secret giggle. Chunky had told me in his dressing room that he had a "crush" on Neelam, and love did seem to be blooming. The fan magazines were of course on the case, although previously they had linked Neelam with another of her costars. "But now it's starting with Chunky," Neelam complained about the gossip in the magazines. She seemed amazed at how the press could jump to such conclusions.

ONE OF THE CHIEF PEOPLE RESPONSIBLE FOR MONITORING THE JOYS AND torments in the love lives of the stars was Bhawna Somaya, a kind of walking all-news radio station who edited *Movie,* a popular and entertaining film magazine. She was as crucial an element in the film industry as the stars themselves and in many ways was even more amusing to watch. I was waiting for Somaya in her office when she arrived one morning shortly before ten, an hour that passed for dawn to Bombay's stars, who normally slept until lunch. Unlike the people she covered, Somaya, thirty, was dressed in a subtle, conservative sari and wore her long hair in a braid down her back. She greeted me warmly, then set aside the lunch that her mother had packed for her at home. She did not seem the gossipmonger I had expected, but that impression changed a few moments later when she sprang into action. In an authoritative staccato, she dispatched a staff member to a studio with strict instructions to bring back fresh news, consulted another about a design problem in the magazine's next issue, then turned her attention to her real area of expertise, the phone. For the rest of the morning, I listened as she coddled, coaxed and bulldozed the stars into interviews and information.

"Yes, I was deeply moved by your film," she purred to an up-and-comer.

"We want to talk to you because you are *the most* important actress today," she said a short time later, then hung up and sighed. "You have to tell everybody that they are *the most* important," she complained. "At the end of the month I get exhausted."

Later she took another call, this one from her coeditor. "Oh, God," said Somaya. She put her hand over the phone and explained: "She's just thrown me a bomb." It appeared that the new wife of a well-known actor had just walked out on him, baggage in hand. "So much happens," said Somaya. "Somebody is always breaking up, somebody has a miscarriage, somebody snatches somebody else's boyfriend. We try to get in as much as possible." But space was always tight. That summer, Somaya had had a terrible time trying to fit in a crucial late-breaking development just as she was closing an issue. "My coeditor called me up and told me about some star who was having an affair," she told me, "and I said, 'Oh, *please*, can't he do his cradle-snatching next month?'"

Fan magazines, I came to realize, were a pervasive subculture of India, with a large number of readers who never even went to the films. Collectively they served as a combination of *People* magazine and the *National Enquirer* and were the staple of secretaries, office clerks and shopkeepers across India. I bought them on newsstands all the time, and while I could tell myself that I did so for "research," the truth was I loved them. After my trip to Bombay, it was impossible to resist *Cine Blitz*'s cover story, headlined SPITFIRE SRIDEVI ON HER AFFAIRS, HER "SEX FILM" AND JEALOUS RIVAL or *Movie*'s enticing story on the reunion, in a film, at least, of Dimple and her former husband, Rajesh Khanna. It was through the film magazines that I followed the pregnancy of the actress Zeenat Aman, and learned that Sunjay Dutt, the former bad boy of the industry, had settled down to marry a nice girl, the actress Richa Sharma, who promised to leave her career to be a full-time wife and mother. The stars complained about the magazines, but they needed them for publicity and were fascinated by something that so powerfully defined their world. The magazines, for example, never had any trouble enlisting starlets to play journalists for a day. When *Movie* magazine asked Khushboo, a sixteen-year-old starlet, to interview her colleagues, she eagerly set off with pen in hand. Her questions, however, revealed some confusion on her part about who was supposed to be the subject of her interviews.

"I think you are a great artiste," she told one actor. "How do you find me as an actress?"

"Good," the actor responded. "Very good. Except sometimes, of course, when you are asked to do scenes that you have never experienced, you go off the mark."

Somaya, the editor of *Movie,* was an unlikely candidate for the gossip trade. After graduating from college with a degree in psychology, she fell into a job with a film magazine, much to her mother's dismay. At first, Somaya was aghast when she saw the liquor, cigarettes and carryings-on at a film party, and she told her editor she would not do interviews after dark. By the time I met her, eight years later, she was a veteran. "It's like a bad marriage," she said. "I keep telling myself that I should do more serious writing. I go through months of hating it. And then I walk into a studio, and that studio smell gets in my nostrils, and I feel this is where I belong." *Movie* always reported with great relish and detail, yet the magazine retained a mothering approach toward the foibles of the stars. "I don't want to say that what they do is right, but I don't want to pass moral judgments," Somaya said. "What they're looking for is their own happiness, however short-term it is."

Nari Hira's *Stardust,* on the other hand, gave Bombay's actresses no such allowance. *Stardust* was the number-one film magazine, with a circulation in English, Hindi and Gujarati of 250,000, second only to *India Today* in magazine readership. It had a wicked, catty tone, best personified in "Neeta's Natter," the widely read gossip column. Every month Neeta sharpened her claws on such stars as Kimi Katkar, who was famous for "revealing" her body in modest bikinis, but who had caused a stir on one recent occasion when she shooed away still photographers who were trying to get shots of her cleavage during a swimming-pool scene. "I wonder why Kimi Katkar makes such a big noise about being photographed in a swimming costume, considering she wears them in her films for the entire population of India to see," Neeta meowed. "Well, excuse me, Kimi darling, apart from the fact that the photographers were only doing their job, there is hardly anything left to be shown in your case." The column was jointly written by the *Stardust* staff, and "Neeta" did not actually exist. But she was a creation of Nari Hira, the gossipy magazine mogul, who was responsible for much of her tone. "We came in with a kind of frivolous irreverence," he said of the first issue of *Stardust* in 1972. "We wrote about the stars as human beings. We were like the Hedda Hoppers of the fifties in Hollywood."

In person, Hira turned out to be an elegant, rather formal bachelor in a well-pressed dark business suit. Because of his busy Bombay schedule, we talked at his residence in Delhi. Hira had multiple homes: a house and a beach house in Bombay, an apartment in New York, Michael Caine's former townhouse in London. His house in Delhi was, disappointingly, a standard suburban box, dark and gloomy. It might have been a way station for a traveling businessman—which was, in fact, what Hira was. Besides *Stardust,* he owned two other glossy magazines, a travel agency, a video film production unit, a cosmetics company and a suburban Bombay country club. But above all, Hira was known as the *Stardust* man, and the reason was readily apparent when he opened his mouth. More than anything else, Hira loved gossip, which he delivered in a rapid-fire tumble of words. I would throw him a name, a movie, a subject—and he was off. *"Shahenshah?"* he said, repeating my reference to Amitabh Bachchan's recent film with the actress Meenakshi Seshadri. "Didn't do that well. Amitabh will be okay, though. It's Meenakshi who has to pay. She didn't get a hit with Amitabh; therefore she won't be paired with Amitabh in the future. Now she's being written off. But just wait."

Hira was pleased that in seventeen years his magazine had been the subject of only six libel suits, four of which he had won. One was pending, and one he had lost. That was when *Stardust* printed that a certain married actress was pregnant with her lover's baby. Incredibly,

Stardust's source was her husband's doctor, who informed the magazine that the husband was impotent. "Since she didn't deny she was having the affair," Hira reasoned, "we thought that two plus two made four." The actress saw the arithmetic somewhat differently. She threw a fit and, as a Muslim, swore on a stack of Korans that the child was her husband's. Then she called her lawyer. "It was our biggest mistake," said Hira, who nonetheless chuckled as he recalled the episode. "I'm not convinced that we were wrong," Hira said. "I'm convinced that we should not have published it." For Hira, a certain amount of friction with the stars was inevitable. "Sure we fight with them," he said. "But then we make up. We're never mad at anybody for more than three months."

Hira counted among his friends many of the people found on the pages of *Stardust,* including Bombay's flamboyant society decorator and hostess to the stars, Parmeshwar Godrej. The last time I was in Bombay, I was invited to a small party to celebrate the opening of Khyber, a tony new restaurant that Parmeshwar had recently finished decorating with marble columns, arches, mirrors and potted palms. Khyber served mutton kebabs, heavy meat curries and other Moghul-style favorites, but the real attraction was Parmeshwar's two dozen guests gathered around tables laden with imported cheeses, Chivas Regal and champagne. Aside from the usual members of the famous Godrej clan, an industrial family whose business kept India supplied with soap and shaving cream, there were plenty of film stars, male and female, all of whom were dressed in either all white or all black. Pritish Nandy, the editor of the racy and politically hip *Illustrated Weekly of India* and a fixture on the Bombay social circuit, wore tight black pants and a body-hugging black shirt unbuttoned to his sternum. So did a famous director who first made a name for himself directing Amitabh Bachchan in a "tandoori Western," as the genre was called in Bombay. The talk was about new films, the box office and marital splits. In New Delhi, such an evening would have been dominated by gossip about who was in and who was out of Rajiv Gandhi's ruling circle, but at Parmeshwar's, the subject barely came up. The hostess was in a tight-fitting black minidress and had that thin, brassy and hyperactive inter-national-socialite look. "I was just in Beverly Hills staying with some good friends," she told me when I was introduced to her, mentioning the name of a well-known Hollywood studio executive. The hostess spent the rest of her evening circling animatedly among her guests, taking time out at one point to curl up in the lap of Vinod Khanna, the square-jawed, dimple-chinned leading man, who was dressed all in white. After hours of drinking, dinner was finally brought in by a small army of waiters at Bombay's typical dinner hour, midnight.

ONE ACTRESS WHO KEPT SOME DISTANCE FROM THE PARMESHWAR SCENE was Shabana Azmi, the winner of more acting awards than any other female star and, in my mind, the reigning feminist conscience of Hindi films. More than most others, she had the ability to look at the curious world of the Indian actress with a degree of perspective and irony. Azmi was a serious artist who began her career in India's highbrow art films, then crossed over into the commercial cinema because, she said, "I saw it as something that would get me stardom." That it did, and her fees increased, although Azmi could never command the prices of Sridevi. Instead she shuttled between the serious cinema and shlock and argued that the name she made for herself in her popular movies brought more attention to the small-budget films in which she played strong women who fought back. In recent years, Azmi had worked much less than the other actresses, but her few well-chosen roles helped spread her reputation in the West, where she was a favorite choice of directors who needed Indian women in their films. Azmi was cast in *Bengali Nights,* a French film shot outside Calcutta, and played the doting mother of a brilliant young piano student in *Madame Souzatska,* which starred Shirley MacLaine. Azmi also had the time, and inclination, for using her status as an actress to further her political interests. Although the press sometimes criticized her for trifling with serious political causes as a hobby, in some instances she had the influence to make a difference. In 1986, for example, Azmi went on a hunger strike that moved the Maharashtra state government to make some concessions to find housing for slum dwellers whose paper shacks and hovels had been callously razed by Bombay authorities. "I knew there was absolutely no way they were going to let me die," she said of the strike, which lasted only a few days.

I first met Azmi at her beach cottage, a small house of dark wood that was decorated not in the usual Bombay style of gilt and chrome but with Indian textiles and other folk crafts. Azmi was thirty-four and had an intelligent face, striking but not classically beautiful. She was in many ways India's version of Meryl Streep, and Meryl Streep was in fact her favorite actress. Her status as an "artist," however, had not made her insufferable, and she turned out to be lively, gossipy and no more narcissistic than anyone else.

Azmi, like so many others, had fallen in love with a married man. But because she was a "serious" actress who espoused feminism, the gossip press made more of the affair than usual. Some fans even called her a hypocrite. "Here is a woman," Azmi said of herself, "who believes in liberation and women's rights, and then she just goes and snatches a man away from his wife?" Her case was more convoluted than most. The man, one of the industry's top screenwriters, was a lifelong Muslim who ended his first marriage by making the simple unilateral declaration prescribed by Muslim law. As a feminist, Azmi said, she found it difficult to accept his divorce because she felt Muslim religious law was unfair to women. But love triumphed and she married him anyway. "I went through hell," she said. "It was only in the final analysis that I felt that nothing was worth giving up my man for." Azmi had been able to ignore social conventions because of the unique culture in which she lived. "Actresses come into power, and then they have the ability to make choices, which most women in India don't," she said. This was the real advantage of being an actress in India, I thought, and Azmi was one of the few with a star's status who had the intelligence to articulate it. "An actress is treated like a real person," she went on. "She's handling her finances, she's employing people. In a sense, she's totally equal to a man. And you realize you have this in you, despite your sheltered existence and your cultural heritage. And you say, 'All right, if men have the freedom, why can't we?'"

A year later I ran into Azmi again, this time in a remote corner of the state of West Bengal, where she was on location for *Sati,* a film set in a village 150 years ago. *Sati* was an art film, and Azmi had a role that even for her provided an unusual challenge: that of a mute nineteen-year-old rural Brahmin girl who is forced by her family to "marry" a tree. The family feels it has no other choice, because an astrologer has told them that any man the girl might marry will die. This kind of "tree marriage" really used to occur during the last century in rural parts of western Bengal. *Sati* was written and directed by another favorite of the feminists, Aparna Sen, a former actress who had become one of India's leading film directors. She had taken the title from a sati that occurred at the beginning of the film, and also from a more mystical kind of "sati" at the end.

I was there on the day the wedding scene was shot, a torturously hot afternoon in mid-May. The film unit had set up under an enormous banyan tree on the banks of the Ganges, in a village that was a seven-hour drive north of Calcutta. A knob of the tree had been draped, like a groom, with a garland of hibiscus flowers. Azmi wore a red-and-white wedding sari as she was led around the tree seven times and then sat down in the shade by its trunk for the marriage ceremony, led by a Brahmin priest. In front of him, on a large banana leaf, were offerings: flowers, papayas, chilies, coconuts, cucumbers, potatoes. The scene was bizarre, but Sen and Azmi were working hard to make it both credible and tragic. I stood transfixed, as did more than five hundred present-day villagers, roped off behind police lines. A scorching wind and an intermittent sun made filming difficult, so there were long breaks between shots when I could talk to Azmi about her feminism, her career and her family. Like Amitabh Bachchan, she had come from a privileged background. Her father, like Bachchan's, was a poet, and both her parents had been active in India's Communist party.

"When my mother came to Bombay," Azmi said, "she was told that a Communist wife didn't just hang around but went out and got some work. So she went out and got a job with All India Radio. I come from a house where there were no great cries of feminism, although it was certainly practiced. But, you know, women, particularly in India, feel very guilty about being successful. There's the feeling that somewhere you're losing out on your femininity, so the woman tries to compensate in the home by playing second fiddle to everybody, because she's guilty of being successful. It was my husband who pointed that out to me. Now the feminists will say that even that had to come from a man." After another scene the conversation continued, this time on the subject of motherhood. "I want to have a baby immediately," Azmi said, "but I want to get this film over with first." She would be thirty-six in a few months. "I don't feel like an incomplete woman because I haven't had a child," she said. "But everybody keeps pushing it into my head." Smita Patil, the pregnant actress of *Dance Dance,* had told me much the same thing. "This is a very hypocritical society," Patil said when I interviewed her in Bombay. "For centuries we've been told that to be a good woman you must be a good mother."

The reality was that Indian actresses, even those as independent as Shabana Azmi and Smita Patil, could not ignore the rules that had been set down for women in India. Although their unusual status gave them the freedom to reject those rules, they paid a high price for that in

India. Most actresses, particularly the younger ones, were not as self-aware as Azmi or Patil. Despite their money and love affairs, they were culturally still very Indian, reacting to life as daughters and wives. "Most of them are still very dependent on what their parents say," said Nari Hira of *Stardust*. "Their parents control their money, and when they get married, the husbands take over. They're not exposed to the outside world at all."

The plots of the films themselves showed that the country was even more conservative than it seemed on the surface. Chidananda Das Gupta, the film critic, took this a step further and said that the Indian commercial film was not just a passive reflection of society but also an active "moral guide" for the working classes struggling to hang on to traditional values in a world that was changing too fast. In one of the more persuasive arguments of his book, Das Gupta maintained that the Indian commercial film, in its condemnation of the sinful twentieth-century woman and endorsement of the traditional wife and mother, "paradoxically becomes the most effective obstacle against the development of a positive attitude towards technological progress, towards a synthesis of tradition with modernity for a future pattern of living." Ironically, it was the actresses, in their screen roles, who were the chief promoters of the regressive values by which their personal lives were so harshly judged.

The melodramas in the actresses' private lives didn't stop anyone from buying tickets to see them, of course. In a country as poor as India, the stars were so fantastically out of reach that they really were idols, allowed to behave in ways that would not be accepted among ordinary mortals. The movies may have been moral guides, but the lives of the stars proved that people in India liked to have it both ways. The fans delighted in the scandals of the actresses in the same way that Indians had always loved the legends of their promiscuous deities. In that sense, the stars were simply continuing a tradition as old as the Hindu myths. "Clandestine relationships have existed from time immemorial," Amitabh Bachchan said. "Most of our gods have had two wives."

CHAPTER 9

POETS AND REVOLUTIONARIES
Three Women of Calcutta

CALCUTTA HAS BEEN FAMOUS FOR AT LEAST TWO HUNDRED YEARS AS ONE of the most appalling places on earth, and on initial impression it lives up fearsomely to that reputation. The city is one of the largest and most densely populated urban areas in the world, overflowing with more than ten million people, many of whom live in such miserable conditions that I often felt as I walked through the streets that I ought to do something, anything, to help, and not just stand there observing another human being's degradation, or worse, taking notes. For as long as anyone can remember, hundreds of thousands of people have lived, died and procreated on the city's pavements. Some had been there since World War I and were still unable to afford better shelter. One family that I came across in 1987 was camped out on a noisy traffic island and was forced to subsist on meals of chicken skins thrown out by a butcher. Six million people were crammed into mud huts and tarpaper shacks, many built along gutters rippling with raw sewage. Traffic choked the streets, crawling at an average rate of five miles an hour and spewing forth noxious black fumes. During the monsoon motor transport did not move at all. Then only barefoot rickshaw pullers waded knee-deep through fetid, flooded streets, past pigs that rooted through piles of reeking garbage not far from the city's most expensive hotel.

Widespread summertime power failures, euphemistically referred to as "load shedding," routinely threw homes and businesses into sweltering darkness for hours each day. Calcutta's businesses were regularly crippled by strikes, a testimony to the city's tradition of worker consciousness and leftist politics. To use the telephone in Calcutta was to plunge into the unknown; calls usually ended in busy signals, strange clicks or dead air. During one of my visits, the city announced that 55,000 dead phone lines would be down for two years. Although some services did improve over time—by the late 1980s there were fewer power failures, and a new subway had cut down on the gridlock in Calcutta's affluent neighborhoods—the city still seemed to me to be in a permanent state of cardiac arrest. Even the state government tourist guidebook observed, with the kind of literary reference much prized by the city's educated residents, that "Calcutta appears to lie helpless, like a prostrate, disembowelled Gulliver."

In 1985, Rajiv Gandhi casually referred to Calcutta as a "dying city" when he responded to a question in Parliament about why most major airlines no longer flew there. This provoked an uproar in Calcutta and an angry demand for a retraction from the state government, which was controlled by one of India's two Communist parties. The *Telegraph,* the city's most literate newspaper, quickly conducted a poll and reported that two thirds of Calcutta's citizens felt the city was not dying at all but merely "decaying," a distinction perhaps best appreciated by the residents themselves. In fact, Rajiv Gandhi was only the most recent notable to continue a long tradition of denigrating the city. Rudyard Kipling once referred to Calcutta as "the city of dreadful night" and Winston Churchill, in a letter to his mother, observed, "I shall always be glad to have seen it—namely, that it will be unnecessary for me ever to see it again."

And yet, I eventually came to love Calcutta, in a complicated, guilt-ridden way. For all of its troubles, Calcutta remained India's thriving center of culture and thought, the nation's largest and most alive city, more proud to have been the home of India's three Nobel laureates than of the merchants and industrialists who had made Calcutta a thriving commercial center at the turn of the century. Once the capital of all of British India and in recent years of the state of West Bengal, the city was a crazy, appealing mishmash of architectural styles. The English imperialists had erected near-replicas of the government buildings they remembered from home. Calcutta's rich had displayed a weakness for Italianate arches, domes, turrets, pilasters and porticos, and built hundreds of "palaces," most of them now decrepit but still so romantic that parts of the city looked like a stage set of old Southern mansions from a Tennessee Williams play. Calcutta was also the headquarters for Mother Teresa's worldwide network serving the poorest of the poor. Every day at her home for the dying, the sisters tended rows of twisted, emaciated forms; in the evening they returned to the simple walled complex known as Mother's House, and softly chanted prayers as they knelt on a cement floor in a candlelit room.

But what I loved most about the city was its people. Calcutta was defined by the Bengalis—creative, passionate, deeply intellectual, sensitive—a stereotype accepted by the Bengalis themselves, and one I found in many ways to be true. Within the city lived one of the world's greatest concentrations of poets, artists, filmmakers, novelists, actors and thinkers. Very few actually made a living from their creative activities, but that was beside the point. When I met a Calcutta accountant, he told me he was really a writer; a surgeon invited me to his latest play. A rickshaw puller knew how to find the home of Moni Sankar Mukherjee, one of India's most successful novelists, because Mukherjee, he informed me, was his favorite author. Calcutta had also produced Satyajit Ray, one of the few Indian filmmakers with an international reputation, who told me that his work "has been possible only because I have lived here, and have loved Calcutta." Bikash Bhattacharya, an important young artist whose paintings of the city were haunting in their satire and desperation, said simply, "Calcutta is my mother."

Calcutta had been the home of many unusual women, too. The nineteenth-century reform movement in Bengal that sought to ban purdah, sati and child marriage had elevated the status of wives in the middle class, and a hundred years later, Calcutta's women were still better off than those in the north. Dowry deaths were rare in Calcutta, and women were not as afraid of harassment and verbal abuse in the public streets. Calcutta's women had also benefited from the legacy of Rabindranath Tagore, the city's poet laureate and its most famous Nobel Prize winner, who had been one of India's greatest supporters of women's rights.

Calcutta was a place of a thousand revelations, but I was especially struck by the way it worked as a leitmotif in the lives and the work of three creative women: a filmmaker, a painter and a poet. All of them worked under adverse conditions unimaginable in the West, and yet all said they could not be as creative living anywhere else. They alternately romanticized their lives and felt guilty about Calcutta's squalor, and simultaneously loved and hated their city. But they seemed to blossom not in spite of but because of the misery around them, and the city always appeared in some startling form out of this tension in their work.

I also found in the subtleties of their creations some of the most impassioned statements and sentiments I had encountered about women in India, and women anywhere—even though not one of these women considered herself a feminist, associating the word with politics and single-minded groups that they saw as ineffective and uncreative. They wanted their work to speak to a much wider audience, in a voice that was strong, angry and even accusatory, but still tempered by irony and a sense of life's ambiguities and biological contradictions. In the end, the three women taught me not only about Calcutta, but about the relationship of an artist to her environment, and why women who thought and created in the India of the 1980s found it impossible not to rebel.

APARNA SEN'S FIRST FILM, *36 CHOWRINGHEE LANE,* UNFOLDED IN AN almost magical world of narrow, intimate side streets, soft afternoon light and lovers' quiet walks across the lush green expanse of trees and grass of the city's central park, or maidan. This was a Calcutta of solitude, without crowds, beggars and traffic jams, a city drawn more from the director's imagination than from the reality in the streets. Written and directed by Sen, *36 Chowringhee Lane* told a semiautobiographical story of a lonely Anglo-Indian teacher of Shakespeare in a school for upper-class girls. The film, though widely admired by Calcutta's intelligentsia, was also criticized for its nostalgic view of a city that no longer exists. And yet that forgotten Calcutta seemed to me an important supporting character in the film, a poignant setting for a schoolteacher whose hybrid ancestry had made her feel an outsider in both modern India and England. She seemed at home only in the old Calcutta of wrought-iron gates and palm-shaded balconies, or of silent Italianate mansions, stained and crumbling after years of monsoons. "This is the Calcutta of my childhood," Sen remembered when she talked about the film. "It was greener, much greener, and it had a sort of lazy quality about it. I have a strong nostalgia for closed shutters and summer afternoons, neem trees, and these deserted streets, and hawkers' calls. To me, Calcutta is not the dirtied-up place it is now. There is no point in showing that."

Aparna Sen was one of India's finest directors, male or female, making the kind of intelligent, serious film that her mentor, Satyajit Ray, had helped inspire with his own classics. After *36 Chowringhee Lane* came *Paroma,* a daring look into the layers of social pressures surrounding an upper-middle-class Bengali housewife who has an affair. Sen's third film, still in production when I left India, was *Sati,* the one in which Shabana Azmi played the mute Brahmin girl who "marries" a tree. Sen's work was among the best and most interesting I had ever seen. I interviewed her three times in as many years—twice in her flat in Calcutta, once on the location of *Sati.* At the first interview, in the summer of 1985, I arrived at Sen's apartment in Alipore, Calcutta's affluent neighborhood of tea traders and industrial barons, to find the director, very much amused, on a chair in her living room surrounded by a half dozen schoolgirls. For years, Sen had been one of West Bengal's most popular actresses, and the girls had come on a school field trip to ask awed questions about how to become actresses themselves. Sen was nearly forty, but she still had a smooth, dreamy face, with large, slightly almond-shaped eyes and a full, sensuous body built for saris. When the girls had left, she apologized for keeping me waiting, then agreeably settled in for my questions about an artist's relationship to Calcutta.

"I hate Calcutta," she began, in a clipped, upper-class accent. "Even posting a letter is difficult. Transportation is difficult. Drying clothes is difficult. Even if you have a dryer, you often don't have the electricity to run it." Professionally, she said, Calcutta was even worse. "Our studios are very ill equipped, and the equipment itself is ancient. We have some antique Moviolas which are rejects from God knows when. The film tears and you can't rewind. But it does tend to make your work technically simpler, which is not necessarily a bad thing."

I remember thinking that evening that Sen presented a warm, self-possessed mix of glamour and brains, although anyone who wrote and directed the kind of emotionally tumultuous film she did could not have been as collected as she seemed. Later, when I watched her work on location for *Sati,* I saw another Sen, a high-strung perfectionist who was so tense at the end of a long day of shooting that she would relax with a glass of whiskey, or, alternatively, by weeping. "I do burst into tears, yes, but not in regularity," she admitted, explaining that she was especially possessive about the few moments she had to herself. "For instance, when I am having my tea in the morning, and dunking my biscuits, which I like to eat all soggy, if there are any telephone calls or if anyone bothers me, I can even start crying, I get so upset," she said. "Yoga helps, although I don't do it regularly. I wish I could sing. I think singing could really release the tension, but I am completely tone deaf."

Sen's father, Chidananda Das Gupta, had, with Satyajit Ray, founded the Calcutta Film Society in 1947 and would later become Ray's biographer and a great champion and critic of film. Aparna Sen grew up in a house where the Russian classic *Battleship Potemkin* was shown on the veranda wall after dinner, and where Jean Renoir, the greatest filmmaker of his day and the idol of all Bengali intellectuals, came for dinner one evening and asked her, a precocious two-year-old, to sit in his lap. By the age of ten, the young Aparna was seeing the films of Ingmar Bergman and Akira Kurosawa, and at thirteen she starred in Ray's *Two Daughters* as the village tomboy who is married off against her will and escapes from her husband on the night of her wedding. Making the film, she has said, "was like a prolonged picnic." At fifteen, her rain-spattered face appeared on the cover of *Life* magazine for a story about the Indian monsoon, and by her mid-twenties she had become Calcutta's number-one actress in Bengali commercial films. These films offered the same lowbrow entertainment as the ones made in Bombay, but in Bengali rather than Hindi. Sen, with her intellectual background, was an unlikely star, but the money and fame were irresistible. "I used to count on my hands the number of films I had at a time," she said. "I was quite determined to prove myself as a box-office star. But once I had them I started feeling, Well, if this is what it is all about, then it's not all that hot. I wanted to do something better. And then I started writing."

The plot of *36 Chowringhee Lane* grew out of a short story that Sen had written about a teacher she had known in school. Released in 1981 and starring Jennifer Kapoor, an English actress who was married to Shashi Kapoor, the Indian film star, Sen's first movie instantly established her as a brilliant new talent.

Four years later came *Paroma*, named after the film's protagonist, a Bengali housewife imprisoned within a decorous but unexamined life. Again, Sen had written the story, basing the housewife on a friend who had excelled in college but had then become trapped by children, in-laws and domesticity. "She's a very beautiful girl to look at," Sen said, "and she told me once that whenever she got a compliment, which were then coming very few and far between, she nurtured it, and turned it over and over in her mind. 'I can live on it for a month,' she said. Which I found very sad and very revealing." The film was itself a powerful look at Sen's view of the conflicts surrounding women's identity and consciousness.

The story begins when a photographer for *Life* magazine, a handsome young Indian-born rake from New York, visits Paroma's home for a picture story about Calcutta. This was a plausible enough development, and echoed what had happened in Sen's own life years before. In the film, the photographer becomes the first person to treat Paroma as a woman independent of her family, one who is sexually attractive and interesting in her own right, and he inevitably draws her into a relationship forbidden by her culture and conscience. The affair erupts during Calcutta's steaming summer monsoon, at a time when the withering heat that has been building with great tension for months finally bursts into showers—an obvious sexual metaphor Sen could not resist. The Calcutta of *Paroma,* though more textured than the city of *36 Chowringhee Lane,* nonetheless struck me as an almost imaginary playground for the two lovers, who discover its temples and charming alleys during their illicit afternoons. Paroma's apartment evoked the languorous mood of a spacious home with high ceilings, fireplaces, polished black-and-white-tiled floors and verandas that looked out toward the falling rain.

At the end of the monsoon season, the photographer abruptly moves on to another assignment, cruelly abandoning Paroma. Months later, Paroma's husband discovers the affair when he opens the mailbox and finds a copy of *Life* with a stunning full-page picture of Paroma, seductively drenched by the monsoon showers—a touch that was obviously inspired by Sen's own photograph on the magazine's cover twenty-five years earlier. A suggestive note scrawled by the photographer across Paroma's picture makes everything clear.

Paroma's husband, children and mother-in-law, horrified by the scandal in their household, virtually excommunicate Paroma from the family, bringing her to the sudden realization that all her relationships within the household have been based solely on the contract and structure of marriage, and not on an understanding of the person she feels she is inside. In despair, she attempts to kill herself. While recovering in the hospital, she undergoes a small but profound change and takes a first step toward acceptance of herself, thus bringing the movie to a poignant and very real conclusion.

Such complicated women did not often appear in Indian films, and *Paroma* created a sensation. Some viewers were offended by its unusually explicit—for India—bedroom scenes. Others were confused about why a woman who was not desperately unhappy, and who had money, a nice home and a husband who did not beat her, would object to her life. At its core, the film questioned what Sen called "the very pillars of our society," which were the family and a woman's role within it. An especially subtle but revolutionary message was conveyed in an early scene, when the photographer was setting up his equipment at Paroma's home. The photographer's American assistant, hearing Paroma's family referring to her by a number of different names, becomes confused, unaware that family members in India traditionally address the people within the household not by their given names but according to their relationships with each other. (The practice takes the use of "Mother," "Father," "Aunt" and "Uncle" in the West to an extreme. In Hindi, a child calls her maternal grandmother Nani and her maternal grandfather Nana, but refers to her paternal grandmother as Dadi and her paternal grandfather as Dada. There are specific terms for addressing siblings, parents-in-law, brothers- and sisters-in-law, and maternal and paternal aunts and uncles. Sociologists theorize that these titles bring order to the chaotic life of an extended family in India, but that they also impose limits, especially on the identity of a woman.) That was why the scene in the film was so powerful. The photographer's assistant finally turns to Paroma, who until then has been addressed only in terms of her role as wife, mother, daughter-in-law and sister-in-law, and says: *"But what is your name?"*

Scenes like that one had made Sen a favorite of Calcutta feminists, yet she refused to ally herself with any women's causes because, like most serious artists, she saw her films first as stories about people and not as political tracts. She also turned down requests to speak to women's groups, explaining, "I feel whatever I have to say, I have to say it through my films." Despite the themes of her films, Sen insisted that none of their feminist spirit had been derived from any personal feelings of being repressed. "Somehow I never in the least felt fettered as a woman," she said. "I felt that I was at an advantage, because I could either have a career, or get married and do nothing—whatever I wanted. Either one was okay." And yet, I felt her films were feminist in the very broadest sense, especially *Sati,* which she also wrote and directed. But when I spoke to Sen on the film's location, she refused to see it as a vehicle for any point of view. "I really don't like making statements," she said. "It has nothing to do with a social message. Although I think it's rather obligatory for me to tell my audience *why* a woman is getting married to a tree."

This time we were talking in a rural northern corner of West Bengal, on a small boat that was waiting to ferry the *Sati* film unit across the Ganges to the banyan tree on the opposite bank. It was only seven-thirty in the morning, but the mid-May sun was already hot and high in the sky, and members of the film crew had not yet turned up. Sen was in charge of eighty people in all—actors, cameramen, production crew, sound technicians, makeup artists, seamstresses and caterers. "I'm officially responsible for everything that goes wrong," she explained, growing impatient as the sun grew hotter. Since *Sati* was financed by the Indian government's National Film Development Corporation, Sen was also forced to handle many of the film's day-to-day business and accounting problems herself. Sen had spent five months searching riverbanks in West Bengal for the perfect tree, in essence her film's leading man. She finally settled on an enormous gnarled banyan with a trunk, thirty feet in diameter, that split into three muscular main branches; the art department later extended its roots with plaster and paint for a more dramatic look. The tree stood at the edge of the small village of Neemtolla, about 150 miles north of Calcutta, but to enhance the atmosphere of isolation, the film crew had to demolish a large group of nearby huts and plant grass and vegetation in their place. The villagers were compensated, but seizing the opportunity, they also were charging the rich interlopers the equivalent of six months' wages for any number of small tasks. "If we want two sailboats, they want a thousand rupees per day," Sen complained, explaining that this was eating up her limited budget. "Then they want a thousand rupees more just to move out of a field." Meanwhile, more than five hundred of the villagers had to be kept away from the shooting behind barricades erected by the local authorities. A few regularly slipped out to wander into shots and walk on the newly planted grass. "My precious grass!" Sen cried out at one point.

An even bigger problem, however, was the weather, which was showing no sign of developing into one of Bengal's famous premonsoon storms for the climactic finale of the film. Sen had organized her shooting around the storm's expected arrival date of May 20, and in between shots she anxiously looked up toward completely clear skies. A few days after I left the location, a storm did come, but at seven in the evening, when it was too dark to register anything on film. The storm was so fierce that it blew down one of the tree's branches, which fell on a member of the film crew, nearly killing him.

"Everything seemed to go wrong," Sen said when we spoke again in Calcutta. Then she startled me by saying that, as a woman, she didn't think she had the strength or the aggressive sense of command to direct a big-budget commercial epic like those churned out by the men in Bombay. "When I have to choreograph more than three people in a shot I start getting panicky," Sen admitted. "Whereas I can see male directors doing it all the time with these huge vistas. I would love to do something like that, but what I think I can bring to a film well is intimacy." She mentioned a scene that she had once conceived but never shot for *Paroma,* in which Paroma would have recalled in a flashback a time when she was giving her daughter a bath. "You know how mothers give their daughters baths," she said, "and how they love to feel the softness of the child's body, and how children like touching the mother, and smelling the mother. So these things like smells are very important, and I have never come across them in a man's film."

There was one particularly intimate moment that I remember from *Sati,* when Sen was directing Azmi in a scene in which the mute girl was weeping against the trunk of the tree. The girl had just been beaten by her aunt and had come to the isolated riverbank to seek solace under the banyan. As she lay among its massive roots, it was almost as if she were crying on the tree's shoulder for comfort. Sen hoped the scene would help to build toward her nearly impossible goal of establishing a mystical kind of sexual relationship, using the heat and shadows of the riverbank, between the girl and the tree. Now I watched Sen step back from the banyan and look at the shot from all angles, studying it silently. It was dusk on the Ganges, and the light was softening the hard edges of what had been a suffocating day. Speaking very quietly, Sen asked Azmi to pull up her sari a bit tighter across the shoulder, then told her cameraman to stand aside as she peeked through the lens. "This just looks, I can't tell you how it looks," she said excitedly to Azmi. "I'm not even going to describe to you how it looks." Sen had created this character and was now, despite the overwhelming difficulties of making a film, at last bringing her to life.

In the midst of her success as a director, Sen had surprised everyone in 1986 by taking on another job, as the first editor of *Sananda,* a Bengali women's magazine that combined beauty-and-fashion tips with more serious articles for the middle-class housewife. Feminists accused the magazine of catering to bourgeois attitudes, but *Paroma* had shown how well Sen understood the concerns of her middle-class readers. "A woman gives her entire life to bringing up her children and looking after the house, and then at parties, when her husband is asked what his wife does, he says, 'Oh, nothing, she's just a house-wife,' " she said. "But being a housewife and a working woman, I know what it takes to manage both things at once. These men don't seem to realize that, and it maddens me." Interviewers from other Indian women's magazines were always asking her how she managed to cope as a wife, mother and filmmaker, and her answer was that she did not cope very well. "If you asked what is the most important thing about me, the answer is guilt," she told me. "Every time I am knitting I feel I should be writing a script, and when I am writing the script I feel guilty because I haven't finished the cardigan for my father. When I am at work I feel, 'Oh, my poor daughters, they are always deprived,' and when I am looking after my daughters I think, 'All these other people are working on their careers, and what am I doing?' "

Sen's married life had been disordered. At the age of nineteen, she had fallen in love with the nephew of a family friend, and against her father's advice she skipped her final exams at Calcutta's elite Presidency College for her wedding. A year later, when the young wife had become a star in her first commercial Bengali hit, the marriage began to falter, although it officially lasted ten years. Sen seemed to feel that the marriage died a natural death because of a loss of romance. "Maybe I became a difficult person after my success," she said. "But you see, I feel a marriage and a love affair are two different things. I tend to get confused between the two. Marriage and romantic love don't necessarily go together, except in the first few years. I think being married is like being able to get on with your sisters and your mother. You have to give each other a lot of room and space." When I first met Sen in 1985, she was living with her second husband, the magazine editor and columnist Mukul Sharma, whom she had cast, after a fruitless talent search, as the roguishly good-looking photographer who opens up the world to Paroma. "I was really desperate," she told an interviewer after the film was released. "Of course, this decision to try him out was very painful—I took photographs, made him diet, the works." Sharma turned out to be a fine actor and perfect for the part, but the last time I saw Sen, two and a half years after the film was released, she and her husband were living separately and Sen was talking in the abstract about the problems of women who are more successful than their husbands.

"You can idealize about a man who is kindly and indulgent about his famous wife," she said, "but it doesn't happen often in real life. And it's difficult for the wife because women like me are conditioned into wanting their husbands to be more successful. And you're constantly trying to contain yourself. Ultimately, it ends in fights, because if you are married to an intelligent man, he can see through it all, that you are underplaying yourself. And so it's a mess." The social conditioning about men that she had received as a woman in India was, she said, "very, very contradictory. Sexually I like to be dominated, but intellectually I like to be at par. That creates a tremendous problem inside me. I am attracted when I can depend on someone, because I think everyone has some sort of child in them who wants to be cosseted and pampered. But when you have someone who pampers and cossets, he also wants a certain amount of obedience." She said she wasn't sure she would ever marry again but added: "I'll tell you something—it's very difficult to live without a man. Very difficult emotionally, physically, socially." Directing small-budget films every few years did not provide enough income to support her and her two daughters, the elder of whom wanted to go to college in the United States. Sen was forced to take roles in a traveling theater group to make ends meet. "I am doing these awful plays," she said, complaining about how her daughters' education was entirely on her shoulders. "My daughters feel that they have no one to fall back on but me," she said. "Though I don't manage very well as a mother and a housewife and a career woman, I feel that in one area I have been successful. And that is that my daughters have complete faith and trust in me. I am so terrified of falling in their esteem."

At the end of our last interview, I asked Sen once more about the city that had shaped so much of her work. "I hate Calcutta," she said again. "I hate the traffic, I hate the fact that the phones don't work, I hate the power cuts. These three. And the lack of dustbins." But was that all there was to it? No, it seemed, and Sen's tone softened. "I don't want to get sentimental," she said, "but it's really like hating your own family. You can have a nasty mother, or a nasty sister, but they are still family. I don't think I could live away from it without a lot of pain." The film she wanted to make next was based on a gruesome

Bengali short story in which three college girls on a picnic end up murdering a schoolmate. Like *Sati,* this story would not be set in Calcutta, and Sen did not know if she would use the city again in her work. "I think I have exorcised Calcutta, really exorcised it," she said, laughing. "Now it's art."

————————•—————————

VEENA BHARGAVA'S PAINTINGS AND DRAWINGS HAD LITTLE TO DO WITH the leafy courtyards and spacious interiors of Aparna Sen's early films. Instead, they evoked the urban disaster that had been created by the millions of refugees who flooded across the border during the 1971 Bangladesh war, and by homeless and impoverished peasants driven by desperation from villages all over India to seek some kind of job in the city. In the "Pavement Series," a collection of thirteen large oil canvases and forty pen-and-ink drawings that received great praise when it was exhibited in 1976, Bhargava captured, in a way that photographs could not, the wretched lives of these immigrants who lived on the city's streets. There were no faces in her paintings, only tense limbs stretched across broken pavements. In the accompanying catalogue, Bhargava wrote that her work was meant to explore "the underlying estrangement of man in a city" and his responses of "hope, despair, tolerance, indifference, frustration, apathy, acceptance, and, at times, a contentment that ignores the reality around him." She was determined not to shrink from the reality that she saw every time she walked out her front door. "In Calcutta, nothing is tucked under the carpet," she said. "The well-to-do and the poor are living side by side. It's all out in the open, and you can't run away from it."

Bhargava was one of Calcutta's most sensitive and socially conscious painters. Although not a Bengali—her family came originally from the province of Sind in what is now Pakistan—she had enormous compassion for those who suffered in the city. She was also one of the angriest voices I encountered in India, even though her medium was pictures and not words. Her paintings were like screams of pain, brutal in their honesty; this was how she related to her urban environment. But I felt there was also an anger that derived from her struggle to become an artist and discover her own identity in a world of men. She did not call herself a feminist and was restrained and even resigned about the conflicting pressures that she faced as a woman. But the rage was there for anyone to see, boiling over in her uncompromising work.

Her first exhibition, in 1972, had included "Victim," a pen-and-ink drawing of a corpse, inspired by a newspaper photo of seven dead bodies discovered during the reign of terror of the Naxalites, the Maoist peasant guerrillas who murdered and pillaged across West Bengal in the sixties and seventies. After gripping the Indian art world with her "Pavement Series," Bhargava built on the same themes of alienation and despair six years later in a show that included "Man on a Bench" and "Onlookers," two large oils of faceless, listless forms that seem lost in the world around them. This show also introduced the beginning of a feminist consciousness. In "Woman on a Lounge Chair," a desolate, older female form, a widow perhaps, slumps on an old wooden chair, one bare foot resting on a black-and-white tiled floor. The picture evokes a sad feeling of time past. Bhargava took her explorations of the female sensibility a little further with "A Man and a Woman," completed in 1986, in which a silent couple sit back to back on either side of a bed. There seems to be an invisible wall between them, and the woman's stomach and womb are both empty.

Toward the end of my stay in India, an art critic I respected told me about Bhargava, so I telephoned her and asked to see her work. Bhargava was agreeable, and soon I arrived at her apartment in a group of three buildings called Roy Mansions. When I first walked in the door, the high ceilings and formal dining room gave me an odd sense of déjà vu. It turned out that I had seen the flat before, in the interior scenes of *Paroma,* shot in a neighboring building in a flat identical to Bhargava's. The artist had grown up in yet a third Roy Mansions flat, with the same floor plan; she was living in this one with her husband, a senior partner at the Calcutta office of the Price Waterhouse accounting firm. Although Bhargava's physical setting resembled Paroma's to some degree, the artist's flat was distinguished by the signs of a quiet rebellion. "Victim," her pen-and-ink drawing inspired by the Naxalite killings, put a damper on any conversation in the sitting room, and in the apartment's entranceway stood a dark, ominous assemblage that Bhargava had constructed out of a shuttered, dilapidated window roughly nailed to some old pieces of wood.

Bhargava herself was a tall, angular woman, self-contained and serious, although in later conversations I uncovered a warmth and a wry sense of humor. She had short hair and was dressed in slacks, definitely not the traditional look of a Calcutta businessman's wife. "You came to see my work, so should we go have a look at it?" she said right away, abandoning the usual half hour of small talk and tea. Bhargava led me to her studio, a spacious room in which stood a large oil painting in progress. Entitled *"Baarat,"* the term for a groom's wedding procession toward the home of his bride, the work was in the style of a lurid Hindi movie poster, but devoid of all happiness. The groom was faceless, and a musician joylessly played his trumpet, as if he wished he were elsewhere. "I find this sort of celebration very forced," Bhargava said. "You have to perform, you have to dance, you have to let your hair down whether you like it or not." She next showed me "The Sun Moon Beauty Parlor," another large oil, depicting an overfed middle-aged woman in a gauzy green sari, leaning back to have her hair washed in the beauty parlor chair as if submitting to something vaguely sexual. She had an air of hopelessness about her. "In this woman, I see a great deal of pathos," Bhargava said. "At this age, you see women wanting to transform themselves into something they're not."

There was little in Veena Bhargava's background to suggest that she would develop into an artist whose work would question some of the more fundamental social mores of her class. Her father had worked as an executive for the Indian railway system under the English, and Veena, the second of his three daughters, was born in the British summer capital of Simla. After living in Delhi, Karachi and then Lahore, the family settled in Calcutta shortly before independence in 1947, when Veena was nine. Her father eventually became the general manager of the Calcutta-based Eastern Railways, culminating a career that had ensured Veena a place in elite English-language schools, tennis and piano lessons, and summers at fashionable resorts in the Himalayan foothills. After college, she entered medical school in Calcutta, thrilling her father by training for one of the few professions then acceptable for girls from good families. There she particularly enjoyed the dissections—her knowledge of anatomy would later turn up in such works as "Victim"—but quickly realized that she was not meant for medicine. She dropped out of school and took an examination to enter an art college, which devastated her father. "That was a difficult phase for me, because art has never been considered one of the more stable careers," she said.

By the time she completed her five-year course of studies, including one year spent in New York, she had married and had given birth to a daughter. When her second child, a son, was born, Bhargava turned her back on her art and settled into a "domestic hibernation" lasting five years. "It was not that I did nothing," Bhargava said. "But I feel it was a total blank as far as my artistic career is concerned. I don't really know why it happened. Possibly because of the children, but I had no one to blame but myself. I felt very frustrated by the end of it. I realized a lot of time had been lost." I asked her if she didn't think of her "hibernation" as natural when her hands were full with two children. "No," she answered, "I think I could have done more with myself during those few years." She had found it especially difficult to work at home. "It's not a healthy arrangement," she said. "The house is like a public thoroughfare, friends drop in, the family is there and no one takes you seriously." Things finally began to change after Bhargava ran into a young woman who had just graduated from art school. "She was full of beans, and only a year younger than I was, and I felt, What have I been up to?" Bhargava said. So she collected her courage and, with another friend, called on Paritosh Sen, one of the city's most celebrated painters, to ask if they could study with him. "He didn't know us, and we didn't know him, and he wasn't too keen about doing it," Bhargava said. "But it worked wonderfully, and it was a real springboard into finding myself." Two years later, Bhargava had her first show.

Bhargava and I talked again on a mild winter evening a week later, sitting in her flat next to some enormous old windows opened to the roar of traffic, honking horns and shouts from Calcutta's streets. The sounds made me think of one of Bhargava's paintings, "Chowringhee Crossing," in which a massive, angry bull surged forward across the city's busiest and most famous street. Bhargava described the work to me as "an anthropologic reaction to the aggression of the city." But I saw that the city wasn't the only source of conflict in her life. We were frequently interrupted by phone calls, questions from servants, and, at seven, Bhargava's husband, a mild-mannered man who quickly passed through on his way to change for a wedding that evening. Bhargava herself wasn't going. "I have never been one for socializing and I don't have much patience with it," she said curtly, acknowledging that she had "developed a bad reputation for being antisocial and cutting out people, but it was the only way to do it. You have your own career, your own personal views on life, and at the same time your social setup demands other things from you. This is expected, or that is expected. Either you conform, or you don't conform, or you strike a balance. I try to strike a balance."

Her voice remained even and she insisted she wasn't bitter, but her paintings told a different story. I remember in particular one canvas of an Indian housewife, naked except for her sari blouse. A vague kind of discharge trickled from her vagina, giving the entire painting a feeling of desperation. "I think the reason why women have been appearing in my work is that I feel that Indian women are cloistered and shut in," Bhargava said. "This hemmed-in existence, this very protected existence, is rather sapping and unhealthy." She said that she herself had never felt restrained, even during her years of domestic hibernation, but it seemed to me that she had been caught, like all women, in the multiple roles demanded of her. Her grown children still required attention, and Bhargava recently had organized her daughter's wedding. Bhargava's parents still lived in Calcutta, and as a good Indian daughter, she tended to them, too.

I told Bhargava that of the Calcutta women I was interviewing, she was the only one who was still with her husband. "Really?" she said, interested again in talking about the pull of professional and personal demands. "It's a juggling game. You keep your husband and kids happy, you keep your parents happy, and you try to keep yourself happy. At this point, my priority is time, time to work. If there has been any resentment, it may be that I haven't had as much time as I would like. But then you look at it in another way. Artist friends of mine tell me that I'm very pampered. Well, perhaps I am quite pampered. If I lived alone, I don't know if I could support myself on the sale of my paintings. Nothing's ideal in a sense, is it? There are always compromises. And I don't look back anymore. In some ways I feel as if I'm starting a new life."

At the end of our conversation, I asked her if she felt any larger responsibility toward Calcutta, and how she rationalized painting the homeless rather than directly helping them. "It's difficult," she said. "It's very difficult. It's something which does affect me. You can only do your own little bit, you know, in your own personal way. In this building, a number of people come to me for medicines. I'm not a doctor, but something simple like a flu or a cold or a fever, they come, I help them. This is a very small thing, but one tries to . . . to . . ." Bhargava stopped, struggling. "I'm not a social worker, right? And at times I feel, What the hell am I painting for? But then, these problems do not exist only in Calcutta. They exist in many other countries. I rationalize that I can only do what I am fit to do."

And yet, the city had been her muse, and its poor had provided the rich material for her work. "My experience is here," she said. "I felt it, I feel it, therefore I paint it. It's got to come from within. I don't know that I could paint what I'm painting here, living in Delhi, for instance. Or let's say I was up in the hills, in the mountains. I think I'd be doing something quite different. Sometimes I feel like escaping. Maybe I'll go up to the hills and experience a different environment. But I know it will be temporary. I'll come running right back."

———————————•———————————

THE IMAGE OF CALCUTTA IN "RETURN OF THE DEAD," ONE OF NABANEETA Dev Sen's most moving poems, differed from the cruel reality of Veena Bhargava's work and the pastoral scenes of Aparna Sen's. Calcutta appeared instead as a metaphor for abandoned childhood love. Written in the rhetorical tradition of Bengali literature, "Return of the Dead" directly addressed a city laden with images of motherhood, fertility and the threads of the poet's own life. Dev Sen wrote it upon her return to Calcutta in the early seventies, after her marriage dissolved in London. She had lived overseas for more than a decade and now suddenly found herself on her own, with two daughters, memories of two sons lost in childbirth, and fears of what the city would think of a woman whose husband had left her. Like most of Dev Sen's work, the poem was originally written in Bengali. What follows is her own translation.

> *Receive me then, Calcutta*
> *I am your first love,*
> *your childhood sweetheart*
> *Here I am, an aborted mother, I have*
> *brought the ocean with me instead*
> *My arms are empty, yes, but my breasts*
> *are heavy, overflowing with milk*
> *look at the fathomless salt water.*
>
> *Come, watch me, then, virginity*
> *glows on my brow once again, naked*
> *as the setting sun*
> *Touch me, Calcutta, my buttersoft flesh belongs to you now*
>
> *belongs to you now*
> *receive me in your waiting arms*
> *No more loneliness for you*
> *I have returned just as you would have liked me to.*

Why, then, this stunned silence?
Lift up your chin, don't shift your eyes, speak to me
here she is, returned from the dead
just as you had wished
yes, look at me, I am her,
your world of passion, your old flame
your very own
Nabaneeta.

Although most creative Bengalis considered themselves granted a muse by birth, Nabaneeta Dev Sen had risen above others to become one of Calcutta's preeminent voices. (She was no relation to Aparna Sen; Sen was a common Bengali name.) Raised as the only child of the famous Bengali poets Narendra Dev and Radharani Devi—"I was conceived in the womb of one poet and sired by another," Dev Sen once wrote—she published her first collection of verse, *First Confidence,* when she was twenty-one. A dozen years, two children and a doctorate later, she brought out her second collection, *Welcome, Angel.* After that came four novels, two books of short stories, three travel books, two volumes of literary criticism and three hundred more poems. She shared the prestigious Rabindranath Tagore prize with her mother in 1986, the same year she appeared as part of the Festival of India poetry-reading series in New York. In Calcutta, her days were spent as a professor of comparative literature at Jadavpur University, and also as hostess for the constant stream of friends and followers who dropped by her house.

In fact, the house was itself a character in her life, famous in Calcutta and among some feminists I knew because of what it once was and what it had become. Dev Sen came of age when the house overflowed with the intellectuals and writers who sought out her parents, but in recent years it was known for the three generations of strong women who coexisted uneasily on separate floors. The first floor was rented out to office tenants, Dev Sen lived on the second, her mother lived on the third, and one of Dev Sen's two daughters lived on the fourth. Dev Sen's father had died, and she had no plans to remarry, so there were no men to temper—if that was at all possible—the passions that were said to simmer between mothers and daughters.

One warm March evening in Calcutta I made my first trip to the house, in Hindustan Park, a lovely, once-elegant neighborhood that had clung to some of its gardens and quiet side streets despite the surrounding high rises and decay. Dev Sen's house, a narrow four stories of yellow brick, was named Bhalobhasha, which means "love" in Bengali. She had been born in the house and had lived there for most of her life. I walked up to the massive front door, rang the bell, then waited. Nothing happened, so I rang again. This time, the door opened so slowly it seemed to be moving on its own. I peeked behind it, only to discover that no one was there. Unsure of whether to enter or wait, I looked up a steep flight of stairs and saw a woman smiling down at me. "You can come up," she called, introducing herself as Nabaneeta and explaining that she had long since saved herself the trouble of the trip downstairs by attaching a long rope to the door, which opened it from above. "It was my cousin's idea," she told me, adding that the device had its risks, "because we never know who is coming in."

Dev Sen was a handsome, comfortably disheveled woman of fifty, bundled that evening into a traditional Bengali silk sari with intricate folk designs on the borders. Her dark hair was long and loose, and she had a pretty, amused face. I did not notice a discrepancy she had once complained about in an essay: "My right eye always seems to smile. My left eye, on the other hand, does not twinkle at all. Its very shape is mournful, as if I have stolen it from the mask of a Greek tragedy. Even when I am splitting my sides laughing, my left eye does not take part and retains its melancholy identity." With no trace of a poet's melancholy that evening, Dev Sen led me to what had been her father's study, then arranged herself cross-legged on a mattress on the marble floor, in the middle of a nest of files, books, magazines, newspapers, medicines, papers and pens. Dev Sen wrote, slept and received all her guests in this room. None of her visitors called before they dropped in, and no one seemed worried that she might have work to do. "This is India, and it is a sin to be busy," Dev Sen said dryly. Gregarious and entertaining, with a self-deprecating sense of humor, she loved literary talk and had taken the art of disorganization to unparalleled heights. Poems written over the last fifteen years were scattered uncollected throughout her papers, and she had abandoned a half-finished historical novel about women in Calcutta, awaited by fans and feminists, because, she claimed, she had lost the manuscript in the chaos of the house. It was not hard to imagine this happening: the walls around her mattress were lined floor to ceiling with an alarming jumble of ancient files, dusty notebooks, souvenirs from trips abroad and a portion of what Sen said were the fifteen thousand books—in Bengali, English, German and French—that crowded the bookshelves, tables and floors of most rooms in the house.

Dev Sen's approach to love seemed equally free and easy. When I asked her if she had been in love since her marriage, she immediately replied, "Oh, every day. How can you not be in love?" Some of her most vivid verses were love poems, such as "The Other Tongue." Translated by Paramita Banerjee and Carolyne Wright, it was a fervent invitation to a lover to

> *Come, kiss me,*
> *with your tongue, lips, arteries and veins*
> *let me teach you that language*
> *that's eternally elusive in the ear,*
> *that whispers in the blood.*

"I am falling in love all the time," Dev Sen went on happily, although it was difficult to tell whether her statement was literal or whimsical. The day before she had told me that her two daughters were twenty and twenty-four years old, "and I am twenty-five, so we have all become the same age, and we try not to fall in love with the same men." Dev Sen said the two "official" loves in her life were her former husband and an earlier fiancé, who had broken off the engagement. "The others are unofficial," she said. "Only my daughters must know about them, because I must tell them everything. My mother knows one. The other two I think she knows, but she is more intelligent than I am, so she does not bring it up."

This seemed a good time to ask about the house, and what seemed to be the totally dependent if tempestuous relationships among its women. Dev Sen warmed to the subject, pointing out that she was the only woman in the house who worked for a living—a sacrifice that in her opinion did not adequately impress her mother, her daughters and her female servants. She complained that the servants rarely stirred themselves to pull the rope for the front door when callers arrived, leaving Dev Sen to interrupt her own writing to let in and out the guests. "You see, I am everybody's servant," she said, both exasperated and amused. "I drive the car, I do everything that is necessary, but nobody takes me seriously in this house. Nobody thinks my work is important. My mother doesn't work and she is taken seriously. But it's my fault. I don't think."

I soon learned that the normal wear and tear of mother-daughter ties had run riot in the household, in a way that was comically and somehow uniquely Bengali. Although I never met Dev Sen's mother, Radharani Devi, because she was not well, Dev Sen described her to me as "an extraordinarily ambitious person who knows that I am not doing anything." Her mother, she said, had a brilliant mind and "two personalities—one for the outsider, and one for me." Her elder daughter, she continued, "has a very complicated relationship with me and is overprotective of me. She was eight when I came back to Calcutta and she always felt that she had to take care of me, that I was not grown-up enough. Even this morning she was telling me, 'Your problem is that people can see through you. If you hate a person your eyes tell it, and if you like a person your eyes tell it. The other person knows what you think, so the other person is always at an advantage. This is why you have so many friends, because you don't know who your enemies are.' " Dev Sen sighed. "My mother thinks I am underdeveloped."

Dev Sen went up to the third floor to visit her mother only once a day, but in between, the two poets communicated by notes passed through the servants. "All day long the notes come from her," Dev Sen said, "saying do this, do that." This absurdity reached new heights when Dev Sen's elder daughter was in the United States for her first year at Smith College, "calling up every week, every day, as if she were around the corner," while Dev Sen's mother, upstairs, sent her five-page letters in the morning and evening. "This is a really crazy household," Dev Sen said, laughing. Most of the notes from her mother were unsolicited, although occasionally Dev Sen made requests, such as one on this day asking about a line from a poem or an essay by T. S. Eliot. "My mother has a fantastic memory about everything that she learned fifty years ago, so she sent the correct line back down," Dev Sen said. The next day, Dev Sen's mother asked her why she had wanted the line, and Dev Sen replied that she needed to use it for a point she was making in her writing about whether a reader needed to know the background of the poet in order to understand his or her verse. Dev Sen's mother told her that knowing about the life of the poet was essential to understanding the poem, but Dev Sen replied that Eliot thought the work should speak for itself.

It was amazing to hear about these elevated carryings-on between mother and daughter, but to Dev Sen it was just a matter of routine. "I don't see my mother very much," she said, "because sometimes she is wonderful, and sometimes not at all wonderful." In a poem called "Game" that was part of the *Welcome, Angel* collection, here translated by Paramita Banerjee and Carolyne Wright, Dev Sen had written of her mother:

You come on rounds to look daggers at me.
Whenever I sit hidden
I think that after playing for this one last time
I'll definitely put my mind to work—
Somehow you figure out everything.

Dev Sen began writing verse as a child, inspired by her parents and their poet friends, who gave her the impression that "the whole world was writing poetry all the time." Her first two poems, one about sugar and salt, another about a frog croaking during the Calcutta monsoon, were published in her school magazine when she was seven. She grew up mesmerized by the sounds of certain words—especially the words *Binapani Bipani*, which she saw on the signboard of a shop that she used to pass on her way to school. "The name used to play in my mind like the humming of a line from a song," she once wrote. Although it was Rabindranath Tagore, Calcutta's greatest poet, who had suggested the name Nabaneeta to her parents, she had never liked it very much and one day scratched it out on the covers of her schoolbooks and replaced it with "Miss Binapani Bipani Dev." In Bengali, Binapani was the name of a goddess, but *bipani* meant "shop." "When my mother saw my handiwork, she fell into fits laughing," Dev Sen once wrote.

In addition to speaking Bengali and English, Dev Sen learned to read French, German, Greek, Hindi and later Oriya and Assamese, the languages of the Indian states of Orissa and Assam. She studied English literature at Calcutta's Presidency College, earned a master's from Jadavpur University, worked a year toward a doctorate in comparative literature at Indiana University, but then returned home to marry a young Bengali economist she had first met in Calcutta. After a wedding for 1,200 guests, she and her husband left for the United States to embark on the enviable life of a gifted couple with what promised to be two stellar careers. Dev Sen's husband had a job teaching at the Massachusetts Institute of Technology, and Dev Sen transferred the credits she had earned toward her doctorate from Indiana to Harvard. When her husband's work moved him the next year to Cambridge, England, Dev Sen continued her doctoral work long-distance with Indiana University, mailed in her thesis, and was able to take her oral exams in England because four out of five of her examiners from Bloomington turned up in Cambridge for a comparative literature conference. They were especially lenient, she believed, because Dev

Sen was pregnant with her first child. "So when I was twenty-five, I had my Ph.D. and my daughter," she said.

But the next decade would drag her down as the tag-along wife of a rising academic star, a situation that provided the material for some of her finest and most deeply feminist poetry. As her husband moved like an academic vagabond between the great universities of England, America and India, traveling to the University of California at Berkeley, then to Delhi University, then to Harvard, then back to Delhi again, and finally to the London School of Economics, Dev Sen followed as a post-doctoral researcher. Although she continued to write poetry, had a second daughter, and published *Welcome, Angel* to critical acclaim in Calcutta, all this did not seem to matter in her husband's world. "I did not have my own friends or my own existence," she said with some bitterness. "My husband's friends did not know I was a poet. Nobody knew. They didn't know anything apart from the fact that I was a good cook." Most of her husband's friends were economists, and in Dev Sen's view, "They thought I was not a very intelligent person because I couldn't understand what they were talking about. In fact, they thought I was very dumb." Her husband, she said, never read her poems. "That was one thing that upset me, although it was very silly of me," she said. "I wanted all his attention. I think I kind of crushed him with my attention, because I was interested in him and in nobody else."

The worst year was 1965, spent at Berkeley with her husband, who persuaded her to concentrate solely on her work and leave their ten-month-old daughter with her parents in Calcutta. "He said she would be happy, and in fact she was," Dev Sen recalled. But the separation, she said, "was too much for me." Before departing for Berkeley, Dev Sen wrote "Dismissal," a poem addressing her husband about her anguish. It is translated by Paramita Banerjee and Carolyne Wright.

> *What can't I do for you? My dear,*
> *whatever is mine is all set neatly out for you.*
> *Just to see you happy, what can't*
> *I do, my dear!*
> *You said you couldn't stand the smell*
> *   of bakul flowers,*
> *   so I chopped down my great-grandfather's*
> *   bakul tree*

in the yard. Just to see
you happy.
Thinking that jewels might please you,
just look how I've uprooted
my child's heart from my bosom, for
your jewelry box. (Where would I get
any jewel more valuable than this!)
*   Just to see*
you happy.
But, how weird, my dear, is the play
*   of the human heart!*
In spite of all this, you've dismissed me.

"I don't know why I felt that way," Dev Sen said, reflecting twenty-four years later in Calcutta. "Nothing had happened. He was very sweet to me, although probably I knew he was going to leave me someday. My poetry knew, but I didn't know."

At Berkeley, Dev Sen's husband had spent most nights in his cubicle, working on the research that would advance his career, and Dev Sen, afraid to go home alone, would sleep on the floor next to him until he finished. "He wrote eleven articles, and they made him what he is today," she said. That summer, she wrote "On That Invisible Tower, You," the lament of an anxious wife who knew that a more successful husband was "climbing up to the neighborhood of the sun" and leaving her behind. Translated here by Sunil B. Ray and Carolyne Wright, it too became a part of *Welcome, Angel*.

From my grassland
I watched how you climbed
step by step up the air
onto an invisible tower.

I watched you on the tower top
brush your cheeks with golden clouds
and touch the sun's fingers, binding yourself
*   to a promise.*

And suddenly I, on the mountain track,
as if riding disaster,

was falling at an unbearable speed,
spiralling into a bottomless pit . . .

As I fell, I watched
how gently you stepped upon the air,
climbing up to the neighborhood of the sun.

In 1972, Dev Sen returned alone to Calcutta, found her present job at Jadavpur University a year later, and then, for a time, stopped publishing her poetry. "When I was writing all these poems, suddenly I discovered that it was a very personal and confessional view, and because it was a small world, Calcutta, everybody knew what was happening in my life, and people were full of pity," she said. "I felt that this must stop. So I started writing humorous stuff, about my family and making fun of myself and things happening around me. I didn't want people to think, Oh, this soulful, sorrowful woman has been spurned by her husband." I had read the occasional prose she had written in English and found it light and amusing, but Dev Sen herself knew it could not measure up to her earlier poetry or her subsequent work, most of it untranslated, that appeared in the city's Bengali magazines. "When I retire, should I say I am a retired professor of comparative literature?" she asked rhetorically. "I don't think so. I would probably say I am a poet. I would say I was a poet before anything else." As she had once written, "Poetry is entwined in the very nerve-center of my being. It is my guard, it expresses my hurts, my prayers, my aloneness. It is my companion, my fulfillment, my frustration."

Dev Sen, like the other women I met in Calcutta, did not call herself a feminist, although in her case I think it was a matter of semantics. She seemed to know that her fate in life was to shatter traditions. "In 1988, a woman who thinks and writes—is it possible for her not to break some shackles?" she asked me. Knowing that I was interested in her as a woman writer, she would frequently pull one of her poems out of a messy pile and say, "This is a very definite feminist poem." She flipped through *Welcome, Angel,* too, and when she came upon a poem called "Space to Graze," which she had written in 1964, she loosely translated it for me on the spot. "This is about the meadow that is meant for the grazing of cows," she said. "It says, 'There is no point in chewing on the cud'—there is a Bengali word for it, for cows keeping their cud in their mouths and chewing it again and again—and so it says, 'I want room to graze, although I like this cow shed, and it is very clean, and there are no mosquitoes. But, you see, the jaws get tired. Although I have calves, the heart gets tired, there is no fun in regurgitating. Dear Cowherd, let me go.' " She looked up from the book. "I was thinking of myself as a cow with a calf in a very nice, clean and well-taken-care-of cow shed. I never thought consciously of working or becoming a working woman or teaching or anything. It is very strange. I still didn't even have my second child."

Like much of Dev Sen's most moving work, that poem was written in Calcutta. Although the city itself appeared directly in only a handful of her poems, it clearly pushed her toward creativity, and its intellectual tradition seemed inseparable from who she was. "I am glad that I came back to Calcutta," Dev Sen said. "Every day I get fan letters from unknown people, from old people, from young people, from schoolboys. And that makes me feel good. It makes me feel wanted and useful. I have gotten used to receiving fan mail now, but when it started it was very exciting. It was a good thing for me because my confidence is very low in myself." Both "Dismissal," her poem about leaving her daughter, and "On That Invisible Tower, You," the poem about being left behind by her husband, were also written in Calcutta, when she returned home from the States to visit her parents during the summer monsoon. Although she pointed out to me that Calcutta's actual rains are not like those in *Paroma*— "The Calcutta monsoon is not at all beautiful; all the roads get blocked, and life becomes very hard," Dev Sen said—the weather seemed to inspire her.

"I don't know why," she said. "Once the heat goes, one feels more relaxed. It must be the sound of the rain falling that has a physical effect on your nerves. Calcutta always has a very strong effect on one's nerves."

CALCUTTA ALWAYS HAD A STRONG EFFECT ON MY NERVES, TOO. THE THREE women I met there unraveled many of the city's mysteries, taught me about the relationship between an artist and her environment and eventually made me feel at home. But the truth was that in a half dozen visits, I never really came to terms with the suffering of Calcutta. On my first trip I had been overwhelmed. I felt as if a war had recently been waged in the streets and somehow no one had noticed. For a time I decided I should not talk about Calcutta, let alone visit it, unless I was prepared to do something to help. But the city inevitably drew me in, as it had so many others. I eventually met Satyajit Ray, found painters and poets living on grimy, charming back alleys of one-hundred-year-old row houses with hanging flowerpots, and meandered past the bookstalls on College Street with their copies of Nietzsche and Kant. I spent many long hours in conversations about artists, and about India. In short, I was seduced, all the while nurturing my own guilt that talk was cheap, and that the rest of India had no patience with the greatest talkers of them all, the Bengalis, famous for spending too much time in the city's crowded coffeehouses and not enough time doing something—anything—about the squalor around them.

During one of my interviews with Aparna Sen, I asked her how it was possible for affluent Bengalis like herself to rationalize making intellectual films when there were so many hungry people on the streets. Her reply was typically direct. "We don't rationalize," she said. "Periodically we feel guilty. But we don't like to think about it too much, because you can't live like that." Of course I could have asked any New Yorker the same question, but it always seemed to me that Calcutta's poverty was qualitatively different because it was so pervasive. Every day, even the very rich and very isolated could not help but be engulfed by it, and be forced to think about it. When I asked Veena Bhargava the same question, how she rationalized painting the homeless rather than reaching out to them directly, I was really looking for an answer for myself.

All I know is that I will return to Calcutta and be as guilt-ridden as before. I also know that in the end, for me, Calcutta was a case study in how misery and oppression may produce creativity, and how they can sharpen an artist's insights into society and herself. But it was interesting, and not surprising, that the mightier influence on the three women's work came from the experience of simply being a woman.

The three Calcutta women I met identified themselves as filmmaker, painter and poet first, but it was undeniable that their experiences as women enriched their lives because they had to be, in a sense, both men and women—professionals, and mothers and wives. Although the partitioning of their lives took time and concentration away from the creative process, ultimately it brought enormous depth to their work. "Women are broken into little parts all the time," Aparna Sen told me. "It's very difficult to arrive at harmony, because in this kind of work, you need to give of yourself completely. At the same time, a woman has a tremendous emotional experience to draw on."

None of the women said they felt a larger responsibility toward improving the lives of other women in India; they hoped that their work spoke for itself. "I'll tell you in all honesty that I can't think of devoting my life to the education of women, because that's not my scene," Aparna Sen told me. "But I can make films. Perhaps I may sound awful to you, but I feel that by doing my own thing the way I believe, and not abiding by every single rule that is laid down, I am in a way holding myself up as an example. I don't presume that I am, but I don't see what else I can do." Nabaneeta Dev Sen had told me much the same thing. "Every feminist poem is one woman's way of speaking of all women," she said. "Even confessional poetry speaks about a group."

She paused and smiled. "Don't you think that every creative woman is a lover and a revolutionary?"

HER OWN PLACE
IN THE SUN

A Professional Woman and
a Housewife

EVERY OTHER WEEK, A NEW ISSUE OF *FEMINA* APPEARS ON THE MAGAZINE tables of India's beauty parlors and living rooms, bringing cheerful advice and a touch of glamour to the lives of eight hundred thousand housewives in the country's middle class. I always enjoyed it. As India's largest-selling English-language women's magazine, *Femina* offered such features as the baby-of-the-fortnight contest, an investigation into the quality of laundry detergent, and an interview with the tenacious wife of a philandering husband. That confessional—ZARINE KHAN: THE TIGRESS WIFE!—was one of my favorites. The tigress, featured dramatically but somewhat inconsistently on the cover in a blouse with leopard-style spots against a leopard-skin background, was the wife of Sanjay Khan, an aging movie star. Zarine had responded in exemplary fashion to her husband's well-known infidelities with pouty Bombay actresses: She bucked up, lost weight and started a business that transformed her into "the hottest interior designer in town." Nonetheless Zarine knew what came first in her life. "She works 'round the clock, but her children and her home are her number-one priority," *Femina* approvingly reported. Zarine herself concluded: "I think I am above all an Indian wife."

It will come as no revelation that such fare, irresistible to house-wives, and also to professional women, who pretended not to read it, thoroughly disgusted Indian feminists. One year a group of them turned up to demonstrate against the annual Miss India beauty pageant that *Femina* sponsored. They waved placards and chanted slogans outside the Bombay auditorium, which impressed the media but not the contestants. In that year and the following years, the pageant had more entrants than ever before.

Yet *Femina* had shifted perceptibly in tone, and its content no longer focused on the recipes for samosas and other snacks it had dished out a decade before. Any casual reader could see that the magazine, in its own fashion and in an attempt to ensure its own survival, was trying to wrestle with the dramatic changes in the lives of Indian middle-class women since independence. Admittedly, Indian middle-class women had not poured into the work force the way women had in the United States in the 1960s and 1970s, but the visibility of the relative few who had made it created a new standard and forever changed the way a middle-class woman looked at herself. Every affluent Indian housewife knew who the trailblazers were, and a supportive press reported on their exploits with much fanfare. *India Today,* in a July 1980 cover story on women entrepreneurs that was typical of the genre, fell over itself with such enthusiasm that it wound up producing some of the more amusing, and patronizing, prose I had read. "If life gives you lemons, make lemonade," began a miniprofile of a successful bee-keeper. "Well, life did not really give Sarparveen Kaur lemons. It gave her bees—and has she made honey!" The next page featured a sari and dress designer. "Nalini Sharma looks like your typical girl next door," that profile began. "But don't get fooled by those looks. Within there lurks a dynamic businesswoman." The message was clear. A middle-class housewife was left to feel defensive about the only role society had expected of her a generation ago. It was a familiar story I had watched unfold in America. In India, *Femina* was a particularly reveal-ing window on its permutations.

To learn more, I went to Vimla Patil, *Femina*'s editor in chief, who had helped put the first issue of the magazine on the stands in 1959. In chronicling three decades of the traumas and glories of the Indian housewife, she had become as much of an institution as *Femina* itself.

She turned out to be a savvy and charming mother hen. She received me in her modest office at *The Times of India* building in Bombay, behind a large desk covered with copies of *McCall's* and *Ladies' Home Journal*. To her left was a new word processor. "Next week I have to learn how to use it," she said, smiling weakly. Short, round and carefully made-up, dressed in a cotton summer sari, with her hair pulled back in a traditional bun, Vimla Patil might have been any well-to-do Bombay housewife with time on her hands. She ordered coffee for me, then answered a few questions about her background. She had grown up in upper-middle-class Bombay, and her father, a publisher of English and American medical textbooks for the Indian market, always told her that being a girl was no different from being a boy. After her marriage, her husband, a builder, was transferred to England for a year and a half; she stayed in India and had her second child. "I remember counting the pains and collecting my clothes to go to the hospital," she said. "When the baby was born I told the doctor to send a telegram to my husband. My state of self-reliance was born that year. I learned for the first time how to do banking, how to handle money, how to take care of crises. In a funny way, my husband never forgave me because I didn't need him in those days."

It was that experience that led naturally to *Femina*. "All along, I would say, it has been a middle-of-the-road magazine," Vimla Patil said. "It does not tell women to fight irrationally. There are all kinds of injustices, there are all kinds of hurdles. But no one with the stroke of a pen can change a country." The middle class in India was changing so rapidly, she said, that unreasonable demands were suddenly placed on housewives to be things they were not. The last thing she wanted was to add to those demands. "When there is so much pressure already on a woman, is it right to give her more insecurity? Is it fair to tell a woman that she has to become a doctor, or a lawyer?" The typical *Femina* reader, Vimla Patil said, was a middle- or upper-middle-class woman, educated in English at least through junior college. She was married to a banker, a businessman, a professor, a civil servant, a doctor, an engineer or a member of the military. Her husband made about three hundred dollars a month, a good middle-class salary. She had an awareness of Indian politics, wrote lots of letters to *Femina* and channeled her ambitions through her offspring. "Whatever she did not have, her children must have," Vimla Patil said. "She will struggle for an education for her children, and will tutor her children and will see to it that her children learn dance and music. She is shrewd and smart enough to entertain the right people for her husband. She is not at all an imbecile. But deep in her mind there is the envy of the woman who is self-reliant, a woman who has her own field of interest. She sees this woman as luckier." *Femina* never hectored, only gently encouraged. In doing so, it reached the kind of women—90 percent of *Femina*'s readers were full-time housewives—who never would have responded to the feminists who had demonstrated outside the beauty pageant. "I didn't want the magazine to be a constant cribber," Vimla Patil said. "So we found a manner by which women could taste success."

The June 23–July 7, 1988, issue of *Femina,* which had been on the stands the week before we talked, was a classic example of the Patil "You, too, can do more than the dishes" philosophy. Although there were the usual recipes (Chinese-style prawns), decorating tips (how to create better lighting for your home) and sewing features (make a bunny schoolbag for your toddler), there was also a much larger section called "Career Counseling," which included articles advising women on how they could find jobs in science, graphic design, textile design or as secretaries. The article suggested that women ask themselves a number of important questions before embarking on training for a career, including this crucial one: "Will your family permit you to work at night, or to travel frequently, or to live away from home? If not, will you be able to effectively deal with their resistance?" Anticipating that the answer in many cases would be no, the article suggested that there were many things a woman could do at home, such as designing pillow covers—"or if your home has a fairly large balcony, you can start screen printing of scarves." In the same issue there was a profile of a housewife who started her own bakery, and a story about another housewife, Malti Munsif, who "so desperately wanted an identity of her own, her own place in the sun" that she set up her own business selling silver-plated pots and pans. When the business dragged her into a lawsuit with a landlord, she learned, *Femina* told its readers, how to fight her own legal battle. "I coped with the case myself and gave no tension to my family," Malti explained. She was determined to do it all. At the end of the article she happily concluded: "It is a pleasure for me to meet customers from various well-known families and get to know them. I would have definitely missed out on this rich experience had I been a housewife satisfied with a life of luxury." Superwoman may have died in the United States, but she had been reincarnated in India. In another issue of *Femina,* a beauty makeover of a "busy career woman" had the headline HOW TO JUGGLE HOUSEWORK, CHILDCARE, CAREER AND STILL LOOK GLAMOROUS.

Femina owed its success, and in fact its very existence, to the emergence of the Indian middle class, probably the most important social transformation that has been occurring in the country. Not only was the magazine's editorial content designed for the middle-class housewife, it was also supported by pages of advertising that promoted Indian-produced middle-class products—casserole dishes, vacuum cleaners, sanitary napkins, nail polish, skin moisturizer, vacation re-sorts, aluminum foil, baby powder, quartz watches, refrigerators and instant french fries—which had flooded into the market in the last two decades. The middle class had risen out of the prosperity created by the "green revolution" in agriculture and modern farming methods, chiefly in the northern state of Punjab, and the industrialization that had been spreading in the country since independence. Much of the middle class was made up of the children of the first generation of Indian civil servants who assumed power in the government after the British left. Again, the term "middle class," as it is used in India, refers not to those in the middle but to the people in the top 10 percent, who can afford to buy the products advertised in *Femina*. But 10 percent of India is eighty million people, a consumer market the size of a European industrial country. Many in this elite are impatient with the socialism inherited from Nehru and the asceticism of Mahatma Gandhi and believe that the accumulation of wealth is in itself not bad.

As any reader could see from the pages of *Femina,* the women of this new middle class were beginning to face the dilemma of balancing career and family that had become so familiar to women in the United States. These Indian women had no new answers, and their husbands seemed to me Neanderthals when it came to sharing chores at home, but the women did have some distinct advantages over their American counterparts. The more affluent ones had full-time ayahs, or nannies, as had been the practice in upper-middle-class families for generations. These mothers, for better or worse, did not seem to be as filled with guilt as many American women were about leaving the baby with others. If there wasn't an ayah, there was often a live-in mother-in-law in the extended family who could look after a child. Neither, of course, was a perfect solution. A young working woman I met in Ahmedabad left her toddler all day with an ayah, but had to endure the busybodies in her apartment complex, all housewives, who told her it was very bad for her son that his mother was not at home. The young woman worried constantly that maybe these women were right. As in America, freedom had not come without difficult choices.

Two women I knew in Delhi, a housewife and a professional, had taken this freedom and traveled in different directions, neither without some misgivings. Both had children, and both illustrate the costs and the rewards of their choice. One was Kiran Bedi, the first Indian woman to wear a police uniform, a controversial thirty-eight-year-old celebrity famous for her drive, integrity and flamboyant nerve. She once charged a mob of sword-wielding Sikh demonstrators, disarming them with her long police stick, and on another occasion was so determined to crack down on Delhi's illegally parked vehicles that a subordinate actually towed away a car belonging to Indira Gandhi. In 1988, Kiran Bedi's refusal to back down in a skirmish with the Delhi Bar Association led to a sometimes violent ninety-day lawyers' strike that temporarily shut down the country's criminal justice system and caused her transfer, not for the first time, to a job that kept her out of the newspapers. What interested me about her case was that behind the headlines was a woman trying to balance career and family obligations like so many others.

The other woman was Arvindar Rana, a fifty-four-year-old New Delhi housewife, a friend of a friend of mine, who since her marriage in 1956 had quietly devoted her life to looking after her husband and raising her three daughters. She had a master's degree from Delhi University but had never gone to work for pay. It was more important, she felt, to send off her children when they left in the morning and to be there when they returned in the evening. Her husband worked as a program officer for the United States Information Service in Delhi, a prestigious job which allowed the family to live in one of Delhi's better housing colonies. Mrs. Rana filled her pockets of spare time with reading, household projects and friends.

Both women were products of the upper middle class, both were from Punjab—Mrs. Rana was a Sikh; Kiran Bedi was a Hindu—and both had seen their lives change with the new prosperity of the top 10 percent. Mrs. Rana was involved in the affluence of her class principally as a consumer. She had a videocassette recorder and in the last five years had been able to rent the pirated tapes of such American shows as *Three's Company* from the video shop in her local market. Kiran Bedi, on the other hand, found herself dealing, at least in part, with disaffected members of a new generation of young people, who felt left out of that prosperity and had turned to crime and terrorism.

Both women were familiar with *Femina*. Kiran Bedi had been featured in its pages, and Mrs. Rana regularly read it. Mrs. Rana had followed Kiran Bedi's career, and had carefully read the news of the lawyers' strike in *The Times of India*. She admired Kiran Bedi for her courage, although she would not have wanted that kind of life for herself. Essentially, the one thing the two women had in common was that each one, at the end of the day, was satisfied with the choice she had made. If nothing else, their lives showed the tremendous range in experience that had been made available to the privileged women of the middle class.

———————

I CAUGHT UP WITH KIRAN BEDI AT HER HOME ON THE MORNING OF INDIA'S Republic Day, January 26, when I arrived at eight to leave with her on her rounds. Kiran was not quite ready, so I sat down on the couch—Kiran lived in one of the drab, standard-issue one-story government houses in central New Delhi—and had a cup of tea while I waited. When Kiran emerged a few minutes later, I looked up, startled. In her police uniform and hat, high-heeled boots, diamond stud earrings and a smart, broad-shouldered trench coat, Kiran looked like some Bombay director's fantasy of a policewoman. She had, in fact, been the inspiration for a stunning, hard-charging policewoman in one recent Hindi film. Kiran had the sturdy body, short hair and healthy skin of an athlete, and out of uniform she looked more well-scrubbed than glamorous. I sometimes passed her running in the opposite direction as we both did our laps around the fifteenth-century tombs in Lodi Garden. Usually she dressed in slacks and an open-necked cotton shirt, even when she attended dinner parties in Delhi; she said she had worn a sari only four times in her life. It was her eyes—large, dark, glistening, with thick lashes—that made her face beautiful. "Good morning!" she said enthusiastically as she strode into the room. Kiran had been raised on the positive thinking of Norman Vincent Peale—one of the quirks in her otherwise Indian upbringing—and she was always enthusiastic.

Today, however, she was also tense. Republic Day, the annual celebration in honor of the day when India first adopted a constitution declaring itself a republic, was one of her biggest headaches. Every year, thousands of people stood in the brilliant winter sunshine to watch the parade of schoolchildren and armored tanks down Raj Path, or Road of the King, the grand boulevard that slices through the ceremonial mall of imperial New Delhi, and every year, the Delhi police hoped there would be no bombings, shootings or other violence committed by Sikh extremists agitating for an independent Punjab. As deputy commissioner of police in charge of the North District of Delhi, Kiran oversaw a territory that included the old walled city, one of the roughest areas in town. There were more than thirty thousand policemen and policewomen on the streets of the capital that morning, and in her district alone she was responsible for three thousand. Kiran had spent most of the previous night getting loiterers off the streets and checking out the reports of bomb threats, which always prolifer-ated before Republic Day. She had not gone to bed until two in the morning.

Since the October 1984 assassination of Indira Gandhi by her Sikh security guards and the subsequent anti-Sikh riots that killed at least twenty-five hundred people in New Delhi alone, visitors to the capital might have assumed that the country was at war. Barbed wire and guards with submachine guns surrounded the homes of cabinet minis-ters, government officials and others on the "hit lists" of Sikh terrorists. Police routinely stopped cars at checkpoints, and the road leading to Rajiv Gandhi's residence was completely blocked to traffic. The prime minister always wore a bullet-proof vest and was surrounded by rings of security guards whenever he went out. Not quite two years after his mother's death, Rajiv Gandhi had escaped one amateurish but serious attempt on his life during a ceremony at Raj Ghat, the memo-rial built on Mahatma Gandhi's cremation site. Today he would be on an outdoor viewing stand. Further adding to the jitters about security was the presence of the government's chief guest at the parade, Junius R. Jayewardene, the president of Sri Lanka, which had been ripped apart by a bloody civil war since 1983. Jayewardene had himself recently survived a bomb blast in the Sri Lankan parliament that had wounded the prime minister and several others, and authorities feared a possible new attempt on his life in Delhi.

"It's like adding agony to agony," Kiran said. Her own concern was focused on the parade route through the old city and up the main shopping street of Chandni Chowk to the ramparts of the Red Fort. She had fifteen hundred men and women on Chandni Chowk alone, spaced three feet apart, and yet she was nervous. Every single person on duty had to be alert to a potential disaster, and Kiran was well aware that the overall quality of the rank and file of the Delhi police force was poor. Problems of corruption, low educational standards and low pay have made the police in India a generally disaffected and in some cases despised institution. Kiran's promotion to deputy commissioner had in fact been part of an attempt by Rajiv Gandhi's government a few years earlier to clean up the police. Today, her hopes for an uneventful celebration were shadowed by a police tip that the parade might be attacked en route. "On Raj Path they can't do it," Kiran said, referring to the heavy security around the prime minister, "but elsewhere it will be easy."

The parade was not due in the North District until noon, but Kiran had been preparing for this day for a month and was too wound up to stop moving. She ordered her driver to take us on a round of the streets. The sun was behind a cloud, but a light wind had blown away the usual smog as thousands of spectators, wrapped in shawls and quilts, lined up behind the barricades to wait for the parade to start. Schools and businesses were closed, traffic was light and patriotic songs with the catchy, irresistible lilt of Hindi film music were playing through loudspeakers into the streets. The city was in a good mood.

As the car moved slowly past the gathering crowd, Kiran sat in the backseat and issued instructions to her constables through a loudspeaker on the roof of the car. "Separate yourselves!" sounded her booming voice when she caught several constables chatting. "Don't talk on duty!" she ordered another group of lollygaggers. Then she turned to me. "Some of our police are so lethargic," she complained. "They don't want to work. They just want to bask in the sun." Farther along she saw a group of mounted police clustered at an intersection, their horses at rest, enjoying the morning air. She ordered her driver to stop, rolled down her window and told the men to make a round of the parade route. "No rest for you!" she shouted in parting. As we continued our drive, she periodically looked up at the roofs and balconies of Chandni Chowk to check on the snipers stationed at dozens of positions along the route. Satisfied, she turned her attention to the crowd, asking them through her loudspeaker in polite and lilting Hindi to please report any "suspicious characters" to the police. Most of them seemed to recognize India's most famous policewoman and smiled.

Kiran continued to patrol the streets for several hours but by late morning finally seemed satisfied that there was nothing more she could do. She asked her driver to pull up outside the hulking 350-year-old Red Fort. We sat listening to the cracklings of the police radio as the day grew warmer and the crowd more restless. At eleven-thirty, with half an hour to go, Kiran decided she would walk down Chandni

Chowk. It was, on the surface, an unnecessary gesture, but I think the setting was irresistible to her: the wide street, normally packed with cars, buses, oxcarts, scooters, horsecarts, people, beggars and cows, had been cleared, cleaned and watered into a beckoning stage. The clouds were gone, and the brilliant sunshine and music made any danger seem remote. Kiran jumped out of the car and started to walk, a lone figure in front of a crowd of thousands lining the street. I scrambled after her, feeling foolish, but was soon swept up in a sudden wave of exhilaration brought on by the warm sun, sweet music and my unexpected role with Kiran as a parade warm-up act. The crowd had been waiting so long that anything would have satisfied them; Kiran Bedi and an American sidekick with a notebook weren't bad. When people waved at me, I happily waved back. Kiran waved at everybody, especially the little girls. "All potential lovers of the police," she said, pleased. We continued past the closed shops, which normally offered spices, mustard oil, pickles, coconut powder, brooms and ghee. "It's sending so many messages when I do this," Kiran said. "It's important for them to see that I will come down to their level." It was now almost noon, and we could hear the parade. "And besides that," she added, as if it weren't completely obvious, "I love it."

Kiran Bedi remains one of the more extraordinary women I have ever met. It was interesting to me that she admired Golda Meir, the former prime minister of Israel, more than any other woman, including Indira Gandhi, because "she was more self-made. I identify with a woman who is self-made. Indira Gandhi had a lot of things offered by destiny."

Kiran was intelligent, obsessively hardworking and capable of great charm, all desirable qualities in an Indian woman. She was also unusually self-confident, direct, impatient, uncompromising and confrontational. These are not desirable qualities in an Indian woman. I found it remarkable that she had turned out the way she had, and when I tried to find out why, Kiran directed me to her father. "He and my mother have molded us completely," she said. "They made us grow up as a mission. They invested everything of theirs into us. We were their walking goals, and still are."

Kiran's father, Prakash Peshawaria, had wanted to go to college and play competitive tennis, but his father, convinced that higher learning was unnecessary for a son who would inherit his business, had forced him into an arranged marriage and a job at the family starch mill. "My best years went by," Prakash Peshawaria said, huddled in a shawl one winter morning in Kiran's flat. "I should have gained more knowledge from books. That, I think, made me think about my own family. Whatever I didn't get, they should get. And they should get the best."

It did not matter that he and his wife produced no sons. Prakash Peshawaria saw in his four daughters more pliable beings in whom he could instill the positive thinking culled from his collection of books by Peale and other positive thinkers. "Women, I found, have some qualities which are rare in men," Kiran's father explained to me. "For instance, they are most persevering. They are hard workers. They are very much composed and cool thinkers. They don't lose their self-control. And most important, they are very obedient and loving." If he had had a son, he concluded, "he would never have listened to me." His goal was that his daughters should be entirely independent, because he hated seeing women ask their husbands for money. "It's like keeping them as slaves," he said.

Kiran was born in June 1949, in the heady days after Indian independence. The participation of women in the freedom struggle had committed its leaders to an India where men and women would have equal constitutional and political rights; in 1950, when Kiran was a year old, the new Indian Constitution put it in writing. Several acts passed in the mid-1950s liberalized marriage and divorce laws and provided for near-equal inheritance rights among the sons and daughters of Hindu families. For educated women, the world had opened. Kiran had not only the advantages of class but also a father like no one else's.

The Peshawaria girls were taught to read and write at home, before entering a convent school. Once they enrolled, they realized, according to their father, "that the other girls were not preparing for life. They were preparing for marriage." Instead Prakash Peshawaria taught his daughters tennis, spending three to four hours with them on the court each day. "Then immediately after tennis, they would go home, do their homework, take dinner and go to sleep early," her father said. "Then they would get up at five and study for two hours before leaving for school. They would study and play tennis and do nothing else. They never had time for movies."

His hard work paid off. One daughter became a clinical psychologist, another a lawyer, and another a painter. Kiran, who had been on the courts since the age of nine, had enough talent and drive to distinguish herself at first as a national tennis star. In February 1972, she won the International Lawn Tennis Championship of Asia, and a month later married a fellow tennis player, for love. She was twenty-two, the age when most Indian women settle down and start a family, but that was not the kind of life her father had planned for her. Instead, she was the first woman to enter the upper levels of the Indian Police Service, the elite national force that is one of the most competitive branches of the Indian Civil Service. Its discipline and organization greatly appealed to her father, and as for the widespread corruption of the rank and file, well, Kiran would set an example. "As an honest officer she would be valued more," her father said. But police officials, stunned by Kiran's application, were at first unsure whether to take it seriously. After passing her exam, she was summoned to the Home Ministry, where a panel of judges explained to her the problems a woman would encounter in the job. Some years earlier, another woman who had passed the police exam had been persuaded by these arguments to withdraw her application. But Kiran told the judges it was her "constitutional right" to join the Indian Police Service and refused to back down.

From the very beginning she attracted attention. Kiran, after all, had not been raised to remain in the background. Her first assignment was as an officer in charge of three police stations in the diplomatic enclave of Delhi, a highly conspicuous posting among embassies and official residences that was a security nightmare. She herself went out every night to check up on the patrolling of her men and make sure that suspicious people were rounded up. But it was not until she charged the group of Sikh demonstrators that she became a national celebrity and earned herself a gallantry award from the president. In 1980, when she was chief of a gang-infested West Delhi police district, Kiran was able to reform a number of bootleggers by arranging for bank loans and shop space so they could start new lives. Later, as deputy commissioner of traffic in Delhi, the zeal with which she ordered the police to tow away illegally parked cars with cranes earned her the nickname Crane Bedi. And yet her take-charge, self-righteous style, which critics always complained was the result of a reckless need to promote herself as an officer as tough as the men, inevitably irritated the people around her. In 1982, after her department denied a roadside franchise during the Asian Games to a businessman who was a close associate of Indira Gandhi, she was transferred to the state of Goa, a tropical backwater on India's western coast, where her fame was such that the local newspaper announced her arrival by warning motorists to be careful.

But by mid-1984 she was back in Delhi, and by the time I got to know her, Kiran was in line for another promotion, to additional commissioner, which would have made her one of the top dozen police officials in the capital. She seemed unstoppable. I watched her operate one morning in her office at Tis Hazari, the central court complex in Delhi, where as deputy commissioner she had taken it upon herself to lecture criminals about the futility of their ways. Her theory, perhaps naïve but typical of her thinking, was that a good scolding and sound advice were more effective in preventing a repeat offense than the trial, which in any case would take years to be heard. So all those from the North District who had been arrested and jailed the day before were brought from their cells, dirty, unshaven, in torn clothes and frightened, and lined up in a semicircle in front of Kiran's desk. An underling announced their cases while Kiran flipped through the files. In fast, forceful Hindi she told two men charged with brawling over a political argument to stay away from political parties, pointing out that while the men were getting arrested the party leaders were not. Another case was announced: "A suitcase lifter, under the influence of liquor." This defendant had his lawyer with him, but when the lawyer began pleading for his client, Kiran abruptly cut him off in English.

"The man doesn't have that clean a record," she snapped. "He has been arrested in the past."

The lawyer tried to object.

"The man has a damn bad record," Kiran shot back, then abruptly switched her attention to another case. The lawyer had no recourse but to scuttle out of the room, humiliated.

It was like that the entire day. Moving in Kiran's orbit, I felt as if I had passed through a looking glass into a topsy-turvy land where women had complete control over the lives of men. Male officers leapt to attention and saluted as Kiran sped through corridors. Supplicants waited outside her office with invitations for her to speak at meetings or attend festivals. A reformed criminal wanted her to recommend him for a loan to set up a vegetable stand. In a meeting at a police station, she asked the officers, as if they were students in an elementary school class, to stand and relate a news story from the paper that morning. At one of the six drug treatment centers she had begun in her district, she lectured the former addicts, in her best positive-thinking style, to begin improving themselves by reading the magazine *India Today*. I was standing around watching, and Kiran, seeing a body unengaged in productive activity, briskly ordered me to hand out a bag of apples to the men. I followed her instructions as obediently as everyone else. "When I started, I didn't wait to see if the men would accept my order," she said later. "I just gave it." At home, she almost never slept through the night. The phone would routinely ring at three or four in the morning; usually the call was an official one, but sometimes it was simply a private citizen—her phone was listed—calling to report a burglary at home, thinking, usually correctly, that reporting it directly to Kiran Bedi would get faster results.

It was not a life conducive to domestic tranquillity. Kiran's husband, who had become a textile engineer, lived in Amritsar, near the Pakistan border, 250 miles away, where he looked after his mother, his business and his farms. That had been the arrangement for all but the first four months of their marriage. Kiran said simply that it was impossible for her husband to leave everything behind and live with her in Delhi. They saw each other only about twice a year. When I asked her more about it after her lectures to criminals were over, Kiran started out cheerfully enough. "It's working all right, at least as far as I'm concerned," she said. "It was a choice we made. We knew what was coming. My husband knew he was marrying a very ambitious career-oriented woman. And it's been kept up. We didn't let it break, we didn't let it crack. And we didn't let a sulk come up. Both of us are in love with our jobs."

In Delhi, Kiran's parents had moved in with her to help take care of her teenage daughter and run the house. "I don't manage my home, I have it managed," she said. "I don't feel guilty because my parents are there. This is something special that I deserve—not only me, but my parents. We all worked for it, and we deserve it. And my parents continue to be my best friends. They're much more friends with me than my husband is. Because by the time I see him, so much has passed. Even if there was something that was important, by that time it's not important."

But as she continued to talk she began to sound bitter, and her thoughts fell into a jumble of justifications and regrets. "He's not willing to sacrifice his career for me, and I'm not willing to sacrifice mine for him," she said. "It's as simple as that. Just because I'm a woman—am I supposed to sacrifice? I said to him, 'I'll have a second child only on the condition that you be here and you participate.' But he said he couldn't move. So we have one child. My parents are not baby-sitters. They can do it for one, but I don't expect them to do it again and again. Having not moved, he's a big loser. He's missed out on seeing his daughter grow. But he doesn't understand the loss. So, he can be happy with his nonappreciation. And he could have moved, had he been slightly more enterprising. He could have bought some farmland here, or opened a textile mill. But I can't blame him. He's not enterprising. He's content. So what I've really lost out on is a mental companion back in the house. There are my parents, but I really don't have a mental companion of my own, someone who I could sit down with and share some of my problems."

And then, putting a positive thinker's spin on a sad situation, she brought the subject to an end. "But I've not let that loss be heavy on me because I've gotten used to a lot of self-analysis and self-help. It would be nice if I could have that person, but fine, I can't have everything. But what I've got in return—is it more? Is it to my heart's content? Yes. So I'm a happy person."

Three days after that conversation, an event occurred that would stall Kiran, at least temporarily, in her professional pursuits. Her critics said it was another example of her arrogance getting her in serious trouble; her supporters, including the feminist groups who demonstrated in her behalf, said the system was sexist and that the men at the courthouse could not tolerate taking orders from a woman.

It all started simply enough. A lawyer was arrested for stealing money from a woman's purse at Delhi University and then was brought on a bus to Tis Hazari by a police subinspector who thought it wise to handcuff the man while using public transportation. The president of the Delhi Bar Association, angered that a member of his profession had been handcuffed, asked Kiran Bedi to suspend the subinspector. She refused, saying the suspect had never informed the subinspector that he was a lawyer. "If he had declared he was a lawyer, we wouldn't have handcuffed him," she told me a few months later. "But after that it got blown up—every newspaper wrote about it in its own language." The Bar Association was in the middle of its elections, and Kiran became a political issue. The lawyers, many of whom were never fond of Kiran on a good day, went on strike to protest the police action. They had struck before over working conditions at the courthouse, but the walkouts had lasted only one or two days. This time the strike was to last three months.

In the first episode, a group of fifteen lawyers forcefully broke down the door of Kiran's office and ran toward her, only to be repelled by the police. Kiran later said that the lawyers had been shouting obscenities and threatening to rip off her clothes, and that her men may have reacted emotionally. "Had I not been a woman, things would have been different," she said. "An attack on a man would not have been viewed so seriously as an attack on a woman." But the next day, the lawyers charged that the police had used excessive force, and they demanded Kiran's suspension. The strike gained momentum. A few weeks later, hundreds of other demonstrators, this time in support of Kiran, had a rock-throwing fight with a group of lawyers outside the court complex. Two dozen people were injured before the police broke it up, and the lawyers charged that Kiran was slow to respond to protect them. They issued a call for a nationwide strike, which was effective, at least for a short time.

Delhi's commissioner of police cleared Kiran of any wrongdoing, but in April a two-judge panel appointed to investigate both incidents concluded in an interim report that there was some evidence of police lapses. It said, however, that it needed more evidence before it could hold Kiran personally responsible. The panel suggested that Kiran be transferred, and she was, to the Narcotics Control Bureau as a deputy director. It was a lateral move to a desk job designed to keep her off the streets and out of the press. The panel's investigation continued, and when the judges called Kiran to testify, she refused, taking an aggressive stance recommended by her lawyers that as the accused she had the right to hear the entire case against her first. The judges summoned the prosecution to make its case, but her lawyers balked, and the case went to the Supreme Court. The last time I saw Kiran, in early August 1988, she was waiting for the Supreme Court judgment, which she felt would be in her favor. After that, the panel's investigation would continue.

I asked her if this was the worst thing she had ever been through. "It's the most stupid thing I've ever been through," she said. She did not seem to me especially troubled; at most, she seemed subdued. "I'm feeling quite normal," she said, "but waiting for the day when I have something better to look forward to." She had just come home, at the unusually early hour of seven P.M., from the job at the narcotics bureau, which bored her. Although she was in charge of all investigations of illegal drug trafficking in India and coordinated her work with the U.S. Drug Enforcement Agency and Scotland Yard, the reality behind this dazzling job description was that she remained at headquarters analyzing field reports and passing them on. "It's all paperwork," she said. "I'm a total misfit." She planned to stay with it for another few months and then, if things did not improve, to take a leave to finish her doctoral work in drugs and crime at the Indian Institute of Technology. (Kiran had a master's degree in political science from Punjab

University and a law degree from Delhi University.) She also wanted to write a book about her work in drug rehabilitation. "I don't like marking time," she said. On the other hand she was pleased to have more hours for her family and friends, although Kiran herself admitted, "I don't have many friends. The ones I do have are from school, and they're not friends because of my status. They were good friends before I got into the police."

She claimed the panel was politically motivated and she worried that the proceedings against her would drag on for another five years. The government was paying for her legal defense. "This doesn't shake my faith," she said of her troubles. "I have, after all, been in the service with my eyes and ears open all along. I've been fighting injustice for others. Now I'm fighting a personal battle."

She was certain that the battle was so bitter because she was a woman. "I think that somewhere deep down in the subconscious mind this has bugged them," she said of the lawyers. "I don't think there would have been a personal vendetta to that extent if I hadn't been a woman. In a woman they found a common enemy. They had something to rally around. I think deep down they resented it that a woman did not surrender or concede. They have nursed it. Perhaps this is their first encounter with a woman in authority. It was getting too hard for them."

THE KITTY PARTY AT MRS. RANA'S WAS CALLED FOR SATURDAY AT NOON, and by half past the hour all the ladies had sunk comfortably into the sofa and chairs in anticipation of money and lunch. Mrs. Dharmaraj, Mrs. Nagpal, Mrs. Rihal, Mrs. Mathur, Mrs. Chabra, Mrs. Singh—that was how they addressed one another—wore cool summer saris and loose salwar kameezes and engaged in the desultory conversation of women who had lived in the same neighborhood and gossiped about each other for years. Mrs. Rana, a deft hostess who had held such parties for decades, was relaxed and attentive, looking slim in a flowered chiffon sari and a single strand of pearls. She had been cooking her special eggplant dish since the day before and had dusted her living room that morning. Modest by American standards, the room had a Bokhara rug, Moghul-style miniature paintings, Western furniture and a Sony television set, marking it as the home of an upper-middle-class woman who read the decorating articles in the women's magazines and entertained her husband's colleagues for dinner. The house, a single-story concrete-and-plaster-block structure with a tiny front veranda, sat on a quiet semicircular street in one of Delhi's affluent housing colonies, named by some literal-minded government bureaucrat, or so I always imagined, as the Safdarjung Development Area. Architects were always deploring the monotonous design of such projects, particularly the government-built and drearily named Delhi Development Authority Flats (that same bureaucrat again), yet Mrs. Rana's neighborhood looked better than it sounded. The clutter of Indian life had brought character to the streets. Mrs. Rana could go on a morning walk and see balconies crowded with pots of white summer lilies, children's tricycles overturned in driveways and outdoor chick blinds shading the cane chairs on her neighbors' verandas. A good monsoon that summer had turned the little lawns into lush swatches of green.

Mrs. Rana belonged to three different kitty groups. Each met once a month, and each member contributed about two hundred rupees, or sixteen dollars, to a kitty. Whoever drew the slip at the end of the party got the kitty and had to be the hostess the next month. Then she was excluded from the drawing until all the others had won. The kitty for this particular group amounted to more than two hundred dollars, a minor windfall. The ladies used it for special treats for themselves or their families. For Mrs. Rana, the parties were a chance to see people; otherwise she was home alone for most of the day. The kitties she won helped her save money on a budget determined by her husband. As one of the ladies, Mrs. Dharmaraj, explained to me: "Some people get a certain amount of money from their husbands, which is just sufficient to run a home. But this way, you know you'll have some money in the year." When Mrs. Rana built her house, she joined a kitty party, won at her first meeting and used the prize to buy her television set. "It's a savings," she said. It was somewhat illogical, though; why couldn't the women set aside two hundred rupees in a bank account each month and earn interest as well? Mrs. Dharmaraj gave me a patient look. "We cannot," she said, in a tone that implied there was nothing to be done to change this sad fact of life. "There is a temptation to spend the money you have at home."

I had been introduced to Mrs. Rana by Renuka Singh, the friend who had helped me track down the dowry case. Renuka's mother had known Mrs. Rana for years and lived down the street. I had told Mrs. Rana that I wanted to write about a "typical" middle-class housewife, and she had readily agreed to be interviewed. Like many Indians, she believed that Americans thought there were only poor people in India, and she felt they should also know that there were Indian women like herself.

Kitty parties are an institution among middle- and upper-middle-class women in India, so I was glad to be invited, even though the other women, all kitty-party veterans, were a little embarrassed, I think, that I had turned up to catch them in the act. Like Tupperware parties, India's kitty parties were easy targets. Professional women and husbands always made fun of them. Maybe the women thought I would do that too, or would think they did nothing else all day. Mrs. Dharmaraj, a retired gynecologist and apparently the only former working woman in the group, was introduced to me first and spent the party preliminaries describing her former practice to me. All the other women listened intently. When Mrs. Dharmaraj was finished, I looked up and found myself eye to eye with another woman. "I am just a housewife," she offered quickly, as if afraid I would ask her what she did for a living. Mrs. Dharmaraj then took it upon herself to put the kitty party in context. "Most of the women here are also members of the Hauz Khas–Green Park Welfare Association," she said, referring to two neighborhoods nearby. "Every year we give away wheelchairs and sweaters to the poor. That is not only for fun. This is for fun."

The fun began before lunch, when the women played two rounds of a game called Tambola; an American would recognize it as Lotto or Bingo. This also had a winner's kitty, to which everyone contributed five rupees. While the woman who sat next to me called out the numbers she pulled from a bag in a singsongy voice—"six-one, sixty-one, four-eight, forty-eight"—the other ladies intently marked off the numbers on their cards. "This is also a thrill, you know," Mrs. Rana said, suggesting, I guess, that it wasn't just money the women were after.

I had always been fascinated by the various permutations of the Delhi housewife, not least because the infrastructure in India that I had inherited—the house, the servants, the garden, the social schedule of the *New York Times* spouse, guests from overseas who stayed a month—was like that of an Indian general's wife. I often felt as if I were a secret visitor to her world. Sometimes I would cross paths with such a woman at parties, where she sat silently near the buffet, intensely bored by the official world of her husband. Other times, I watched her at one of the hotel beauty parlors as she was attended simultaneously by a manicurist, a pedicurist, a hair styler, a person to hold the blow-dryer, and a friend to advise. Most of all, I loved listening to her gossip in the sauna of a health club favored by Delhi's new money, where she would sit, with a fantastic belly and enormous glistening breasts, discussing the attributes of the grooms who had been found for the daughters of her friends.

This was usually the preferred topic of conversation in any group. I once went to a lunch at the home of a housewife where the talk centered on a woman whose daughter had agreed to marry a boy selected by the family after only fifteen days. Everyone marveled at the good luck of the mother of the bride but then became a little crabby when they moved on to discuss the engagement party she was throwing the next day. The family traveled in a fashionable crowd that liked European cigarettes and Scotch, but the bride's mother, in what was viewed as a craven attempt to impress the boy's more conservative family, had asked all her friends not to smoke and drink at the party. The ramifications of this were discussed at length until lunch, which wasn't served until two-thirty. When I left later in the afternoon, the bridge game was just getting started.

People, usually Indian men, were always telling me, in trying to explain the "complicated" situation of the Indian woman, that many housewives had attained considerable happiness and power within a family as chief manager, nurturer and behind-the-scenes decision-maker. I could see for myself that this was true, but the statement always annoyed me because the family, for the middle-class housewife, in most cases remained the only outlet for her energy and ambition. What was her alternative? Mrs. Rana had made her choice, or had the choice made for her, many years ago. Did she yearn for more? Was there enough to fill her day?

Mrs. Rana usually got up at five-thirty in the morning, when she and her husband went for a walk. Her husband was in the United States on business during the time I spent with her, but usually they would both be back in the house by six-thirty. She would make herself a cup of tea, glance at the headlines in *The Times of India,* then start preparing packed lunches for her youngest daughter and husband. They carried the food to school and work in tiffins, little aluminum containers that had separate compartments for a dal, or lentil stew, with gravy or cooked green peppers and potatoes. In the other compartments Mrs. Rana put homemade yogurt, a salad of sliced tomatoes and cucumbers, and several chapaties, the round Indian flat bread. Mrs. Rana, like most serious Indian housewives, would never send her family off in the morning without a properly cooked meal from home. Even Kiran Bedi's mother made sure that her daughter carried a tiffin to work.

By eight-thirty Mrs. Rana's maid had arrived to clean the kitchen, sweep the house and mop the floors, which had to be done every day. Grit and pollution from the air would settle all over a freshly cleaned house in a matter of hours, and in minutes during the dust storms of May and June. While the maid was working, Mrs. Rana had a bath, changed into a fresh sari, then prayed for fifteen minutes. Like most Indians, she wanted to be clean before worshiping God, and like most housewives, she was in charge of the family's spiritual life. As a religious Sikh woman, she fasted for her family's health on holidays and prayed for her husband's and daughters' well-being every day.

After her prayers, she dusted and cleaned up the living room, and, depending on her mood, did the laundry. It was really a job for the maid, but the maid could not always be trusted. "She doesn't do it properly, actually," Mrs. Rana said. "Sometimes I feel I need some exercise, so I wash the clothes. But if I get fed up, I give them to her." She had no washing machine, so everything, even sheets and towels, was done by hand.

By ten-fifteen the maid usually left, and by eleven Mrs. Rana was free. She loved the quiet. Her daughters were gone, and the kitchen and house were clean. This was her time to really read the newspaper— she considered keeping up with events very important—and to make some calls to friends. Then she usually went out, either to a kitty party, or to the bank, or to do some shopping, or to pay the water or electric bills, which always had to be taken to the office in person. On Tuesdays she went to a religious meeting. The Sikh women in the neighborhood would gather at someone's home, pray for an hour, then have lunch. Other days Mrs. Rana just went to a friend's house for coffee. "That is the time when I don't like to be home," she said. "That is the time I like to relax."

She came back to the house around two and had lunch, usually the same food she had cooked for the tiffins that morning. After lunch she took a half-hour nap, then got up, listened to music and read. She liked Sidney Sheldon and Mills & Boon, the English series of romance novels. The family subscribed to the periodicals that were required reading for the English-speaking middle class: *India Today, Business India* and *The Economic Times*. Mrs. Rana borrowed the glossy personality magazines and women's magazines, like *Savvy, Society, Eve's Weekly* and *Femina*, from her local lending library for a nickel a day each. She liked *Reader's Digest,* too; that cost seven cents. "Mostly I try to read one magazine a day," she said. She had read *Femina* for years, although she was less enamored of it now than she once was. "The recipes are all right, but not too great," she said. "The stories are bad. The decorating articles are good, although I feel most of them are just ads for people. Usually I can find one or two good articles, on laws affecting women, or investments."

This was hardly the life of a revolutionary, and yet the world that was available to Mrs. Rana was radically different from the one her mother had known. Her day, as unremarkable as it was, nonetheless reflected the progress that had occurred in the lives of urban middle-class women in India since independence. Mrs. Rana's mother never knew English, and even if she had, there were no magazines in her time that would have discussed such preposterous subjects as how women might best invest money. Mrs. Rana's mother spoke only Punjabi, and as the wife of an assistant commissioner in the Indian Revenue Service, dutifully set up a new household when her husband was transferred every three years. The family had lived all over the subcontinent's northwest: Karachi, Quetta, Bombay, Gwalior, Pune, Ahmedabad, Jalandhar and finally Delhi.

Mrs. Rana was born and reared in the undivided India that was the prize of the British Empire. In 1947, when she was twelve years old, the family was living in Quetta, a city in the mountains of Baluchistan near the Afghan border. In June of that year her father was transferred to the city of Pune near Bombay. He went ahead to find a house, saying he would send for the family when all was in order. History of course intervened. In August the British withdrew from the subcontinent, hastily dividing the empire into independent India and the new nation of Pakistan, which was created to meet Muslim demands for their own country. Quetta was part of Pakistan, Pune of India, and Mrs. Rana and her mother and sister suddenly found themselves, a Sikh woman and two daughters, on the wrong side of the border. When Quetta dissolved in the rioting that eventually killed hundreds of thousands of people, the mother and two girls were terrified they would never get out. It wasn't until September that they were able to obtain seats on a train, wearing just the clothes on their backs, fearful throughout the long journey that they would die. They tried to send a few possessions by rail car, but the train was looted along the way and the boxes were full of stones when they opened them. "It was only after we reached here," Mrs. Rana said, "that we realized we had nothing."

Her story was one I had heard dozens of times before, from friends and the parents of friends in Delhi. It was the story of an entire generation traumatized by some of the bloodiest partition riots in history, of millions of uprooted families having to start lives all over again. Four decades later the wounds were still healing. A friend of ours, knowing that Steve and I made trips to Pakistan, gave me the addresses of the two places her parents had lived in Lahore before partition and asked if I could take pictures of them the next time I was there. She had written "Our houses in Lahore" at the top of the directions, as if the homes had been frozen in time with all of the furniture intact. That was how her family remembered them, as home, and now it was impossible for her parents, as it was for most other Indians, to get visas into Pakistan, India's bitter enemy in three wars since partition. In 1988, when the government-owned television network broadcast a six-part television series called *Tamas,* or "Darkness," based on a novel about several families caught up in the carnage of partition, the country seemed to go through a national exorcism. The series had an estimated audience of fifty million. It showed how violence had been provoked deliberately by Muslim and Hindu extremist groups, some of which still exist today. Demonstrations against *Tamas* erupted in several cities across India. At one television station, police fired into a rampaging mob of Hindu political workers, injuring fifteen. A Muslim businessman from Bombay filed a lawsuit to halt the showing of *Tamas,* on the grounds that it would "poison the minds of the people," but the Bombay High Court supported the broadcast, saying, "You cannot whisk away history simply by brushing it under the carpet." Those in the older generation who had lived through partition wept during the series, or found it too painful to watch at all.

That was Mrs. Rana's generation, the people who had to resettle and rebuild. When she earned her bachelor's degree in economics from Delhi University in 1954, only seven years after the train trip from Quetta, it was a symbol of how far the family, and India, had come. Two years later, she received her master's degree and was married into another Sikh family that had resettled from Quetta. The parents knew each other from pre-partition days—Mrs. Rana's father-in-law, who sold Persian carpets, was a former secretary of the Quetta Race Club— and they were certain their children would be compatible. "It just struck them that this could be a suitable match," Mrs. Rana explained. "They asked us if we would meet, and so we met for a while. Then they asked us if marriage was okay with both of us, and it was." Her husband had a master's degree from Delhi University and was starting a new job at the U.S. Information Service. It was a stirring time. In the next few years, relations between India and the United States would reach a pinnacle, unmatched since then. The United States, certain that the best American intentions and technology could haul India into a prosperous future, was on one of its third world missions of goodwill, a mission that some historians—and Indians—would later judge to be as arrogant and naïve as it was well meaning. But at the time, Nehru was delighted to welcome the hundreds of American specialists and later the flood of John F. Kennedy's Peace Corps volunteers. India became one of the world's laboratories for testing the new development theories, and the atmosphere at the American embassy was electric. Indians still talk about the parties that U.S. ambassadors like Chester Bowles and John Kenneth Galbraith gave on the big lawn of the residence on the old Ratendone Road, where everyone knew they could find out what was happening in town.

Mrs. Rana spent those years at home raising children. Although she had toyed with working in a public relations office after her wedding, her first child was born within a year of the marriage and the job idea was put aside. Her two other children came soon after that. "Since my girls arrived quickly, I had no time," she said. "My husband always told me, 'You look after the girls first, and afterward you can take a job.' But I never did. You can't leave girls alone, and you can't leave them with the servants. You have to take care of them more than the boys." In India, even college girls are rarely left home alone for the weekend with servants. It is not just that something could happen, although the fear is certainly there, but also that leaving unmarried daughters unchaperoned is considered improper and bad for the girls' reputation.

Only one of Mrs. Rana's daughters still lived at home, although she was gone most of the day at a job working for an export house. Mrs. Rana could have gone to work herself, but she found that the habits formed when her children were young were difficult to change. "Somehow, I got so used to being at home," she said. But her daughters, like all their friends, had been educated to be professionals. Mrs. Rana's husband had insisted on it. One daughter taught grade school in Punjab, and another worked for a large company in Bombay. "Times have changed," Mrs. Rana said. "Things have become so expensive. With one person's earnings you can't maintain a house.

When I got married, you could make do with what your husband made."

Mrs. Rana's quiet afternoon of music and magazines usually ended at four-thirty, when she had a cup of tea and then started cooking for dinner. Her maid came to help in the kitchen, and by six-thirty her husband and daughter were home. Sometimes she made them a snack of samosas, plump, deep-fried dumplings filled with ground meat or vegetables. At seven, she and her husband would go for another walk, or drop in on friends, then return home to read or watch television. Sometimes people would drop in on them, always unannounced, and they would have to be fussed over and attended to with tea and biscuits. Dinner was at nine, usually a chicken, mutton or fish curry, with a vegetable, like cauliflower that had been cooked in spices. There was also dal, sliced tomatoes and cucumbers, and freshly made chapaties. Dessert was caramel custard, ice cream or fruit. Afterward, the family would settle in front of the television to watch a rented video or an Indian serial.

This was another departure from the life Mrs. Rana's mother had known. In the past decade or so, television and the consumer culture it helped spawn have exploded in India, forever changing the expectations of the middle class. In 1983, the government estimated that Indians owned fewer than three million televisions, but five years later the number was up to twelve million, with an estimated ten viewers per set. The programming had changed too, also reflecting the concerns of the new middle class. When I first arrived in India, the government-owned network, Doordarshan, was broadcasting only its standard fare: deadly documentaries on fertilizer plants and somnolent discussions by panels of experts on the outlook for the government's Sixth Economic Plan. (As wretched as the stuff was, I always liked Doordarshan's name. *Door* in Hindi means "distant" and *darshan* means "a show or a viewing.") Things improved in 1985 with the arrival of *Hum Log,* or "We People," an evening soap opera about an extended family that had left the village to struggle with a new life in the big city. It was the story of many of its viewers, and the show took off. It was soon followed by *Rajani,* a wildly popular hit about the somewhat implausible exploits of a crusading middle-class housewife who for a period of months became a national heroine. As Indians cheered every Sunday in front of their television sets, the young and pretty Rajani took on the daily injustices and petty corruption that plagued middle-class life. She went after fake astrologers, bribe-demanding cooking-gas delivery men, rude cabdrivers and pickpockets on buses. In one episode, when a rude taxi driver refused to take her on a short trip, she went, outraged, to the police, which immediately prompted an angry demonstration by five hundred real-life taxi drivers outside Doordarshan's Bombay offices. In another, Rajani discovered that her maid's husband was beating her, and that he was planning to take a second wife. Rajani bullied the husband into his senses. In another episode, when the police refused to do anything about the noise coming from the loudspeakers at a wedding, Rajani got her own loudspeaker and aimed it straight at the station. The police gave in, and Rajani won once again.

Although upper-class women found Rajani's loudmouth style unsophisticated, millions of middle-class women saw her as a positive role model. Meena Kaushik, a Bombay sociologist and market researcher, interviewed women about their attitudes toward the show and came to this conclusion: "Rajani is providing a catharsis for a number of women who are leading very repressed lives and who are not allowed to voice their opinions. I think she's a harbinger of change." Advertisers of consumer goods began to rethink the decades-old strategy of appealing to the Indian woman as a doormat whose self-image was provided only by her family. Meera Vasudevan, another Bombay market researcher, complained in an article in a trade publication that traditional advertising "pandered to this self-abnegation" by turning any product a housewife bought "into a 'badge' of her motherly concern and care." There was a billboard I used to pass in Delhi that advertised a product—I can't remember what now; possibly it was cooking oil—with a slogan to the effect that if you use it, "even your children will be proud of you." The reason I remember it at all is that my own mother noticed it on the road when she visited me in India, and wondered why the woman on the billboard was so desperate for approval from her children. Such advertising, Meera Vasudevan argued, was missing a new breed of woman "no longer willing to be trampled upon," typified in part by Rajani, who represented "a good Indian wife and mother, not very sophisticated, but a revolutionary nevertheless."

By eleven or sometimes midnight, Mrs. Rana was in bed. It was usually the end of an eighteen-hour day, and she was always tired. "There is so much work in the house," she said. "Being a housewife is a full-time job." On weekends she had to do the shopping at the local market, and there were always letters to answer from relatives and friends. Some years ago, she had thought of starting a nursery school, but that, like the public relations work, had been set aside. "I wanted to take up a part-time job, but I had no initiative, actually," Mrs. Rana said. "And I didn't want to be a saleswoman. Now I feel, Oh, now it's too late. But I'm satisfied. That time is past." Her new idea was voluntary work, and she had gone so far as to ask a friend at the All India Institute of Medical Sciences whether the patients needed someone to write letters or to read books to them.

When I first met Mrs. Rana, I had thought I might find a frustrated woman under the graceful housewife exterior. Maybe that woman was there, but I never saw her. What I did see was someone who had a few regrets but was, like Kiran Bedi, resigned to them. I think this made her more typical than the angst-ridden housewife I might have imagined. I suppose feminists would have called her repressed; certainly she was dependent. But her life, by anyone's standards, was rewarding. Her marriage had lasted more than thirty years and produced three fine daughters, of whom she was very proud. She had several grandchildren and was looking forward to more. She had a nice home and a respected place in the community. She had good friends, good health and activities that she enjoyed. Most important, she had some sense of control over her life. And if, compared with Kiran Bedi, she did not have a jam-packed day, no one could call her lazy. She liked what she did, and as she said herself, "This is a very fulfilling job." Her life may have lacked the edge of Kiran Bedi's, but it was far more serene, and I don't think it contained any less passion for the things that were important to her. It was a triumph for middle-class women in India that both Kiran Bedi and Arvindar Rana could find a niche and become, in their own ways, content.

CHAPTER 11

"SMALL FAMILY, HAPPY FAMILY"

The Lessons of Population Control

IN A PARCHED CORNER OF WESTERN GUJARAT, ALONG AN EMPTY ROAD that disappeared into the brown, scrubby plains, there stood a local government health center, nothing more than a drab, single-story cement building, where for twenty minutes one November afternoon I observed what India's population-control establishment bureaucratically, and somewhat inappropriately, referred to as a "laparoscopy camp." When I arrived for the "camp," shortly before two in the afternoon, I found four peasant women—Januben, Taraben, Nortiben and Manjuben, ranging in age from thirty to twenty-two, all mothers of two or three—squatting barefoot and huddled together with their backs against a wall in a small holding room, as frightened and wide-eyed as cornered small animals. The government nurses had removed the women's saris but had tied the waists of the women's full-length petticoats up over their breasts to create make-do surgical gowns, all soiled and greasy from cooking smoke and field work. Each of the women had come to the health center under pressure from local government health workers, whose pay would be docked if they did not meet strict annual quotas of sterilization cases. The health workers knew that the women, illiterate, poor and leading hand-to-mouth existences after another summer of drought had scorched the fields, desperately needed the twenty-four-dollar payment promised by the government to those who had the operation.

When the doctor was ready, three of the women were led into the "operation theater," a dark, dank, sour-smelling room with stained, peeling walls. There were three low operating tables, and to raise them up higher, the hospital staff had precariously stacked red bricks under each of the legs. The nurses instructed the women to climb up on the tables, which they did, as awkward in their petticoats as toddlers climbing stairs. Once the women had settled, the nurses flipped the petticoats up over their faces, spread the women's legs, then waited for the doctor in a far corner of the room. He was R. P. Raol, a laparoscopy specialist who was known for his fast work. He could usually sterilize twenty women in an hour and had once sterilized one hundred women in a single session at a "prestige camp," attended by a government minister. Today's small workload would be accomplished in no time. Dr. Raol gave the first woman, the one on the operating table the farthest from the holding room, an injection of local anesthesia in her stomach. With a small knife, he made a slit just below her navel, then inserted a thin tube that blew in carbon dioxide. This procedure pumped up her abdomen and pushed the large intestine away from the uterus to make his field of vision clear. Dr. Raol took the laparoscope, a shiny metal rod about an inch in circumference, inserted it into the slit, looked through a small magnifying lens at the top, and found one of the patient's fallopian tubes. He then pulled a triggerlike mechanism on the side of the laparoscope, releasing a tiny ring that wrapped around and tied up the woman's fallopian tube. Dr. Raol repeated the procedure on the other tube, instructed an assistant to stitch up the slit, then rapidly moved on to the other two women.

By twenty past two, all four women were sterilized and the "camp" was over. The speed of the operation explained why laparoscopies had become such a popular method of sterilization in India. The conventional method for a tubal ligation, or tubectomy, as the Indians called it, normally required a larger abdominal incision under general anesthesia and six days of hospitalization. But with the laparoscopy, these women were expected to feel only mild pain in their stomachs, and it was presumed they would be able to start normal activities after only twenty-four hours of rest at home. Dr. Raol quickly departed—he normally worked two camps a day—leaving the medical officer who ran the day-to-day activities of the health center, a polite, nervous bureaucrat named Dr. S. G. Gharia, in a sullen mood. He, too, was feeling pressure from his superiors to meet the annual sterilization targets sent down from Delhi. "This was a small camp," he said, annoyed and embarrassed by the low turnout. "We had an insufficient number of cases." The term "camp" more accurately applied to the weeks-long sterilization sessions in remote areas of India, where thousands of men and women journeyed to be sterilized by government doctors. But India's family-planning establishment also used the term for the smaller group sterilization operations at the permanent government health centers scattered in thousands of towns and villages across the country. Dr. Gharia normally held his camps twice a month, sometimes attracting dozens of patients by advertising with leaflets and passing the word through his nurses and midwives. "I am not satisfied with my workers," he complained. I asked him what he intended to do. "I will scold them," he said, explaining that he was trying to finish half of his yearly quota of sterilizations within the next few weeks. "I will say, you must achieve 50 percent target by the end of this month. Why are you not working?"

Before I saw Dr. Gharia's laparoscopy camp, it was easy for me to sit in New Delhi and think that part of the answer to India's population problem was simply to sterilize more people. But once I saw the operation for myself, my reaction was that treating women as if they were cattle could not possibly be the most humane or even the most effective method of population control. In 1988, *The Telegraph,* the Calcutta-based daily, reported that forty-four women had died during sterilization operations in Rajasthan during the preceding two years. The newspaper described the camp conditions as "unhygienic and filthy," which I readily believed, and reported that laparoscopes were used over and over without sterilization. In one camp the reporter discovered that a bicycle pump was used to pump ordinary air into the women's stomachs instead of carbon dioxide, which dissolves easily in the blood. Ordinary air bubbles in the arteries can block the heart or damage the brain.

And yet I also knew it was too easy to simply deplore the excesses and mistakes of programs like the laparoscopy camps. The truth was that something urgently had to be done to prevent India from over-populating itself toward self-destruction. At the very least, Dr. Gharia's laparoscopy camp introduced me to the dilemmas of population control in India. I also realized, after seeing how the population-control program worked—and did not work—in villages in Gujarat and other parts of India, that there could be no success without a significant improvement in the lives of India's women.

The nation's population statistics were well known, even to those who only casually followed the problem. At independence in 1947, the population of the country stood at 342 million; by 1988, that number had more than doubled to 800 million. Paradoxically, overpopulation was a result of progress and development. India's population had been virtually stationary at the beginning of the century, before the spread of penicillin and vaccines, because people died routinely from infections, plagues, cholera and malaria. Medical advances since the 1920s had succeeded in substantially lowering the death rate, but there had been no corresponding drop in the birth rate. Sometime in the next century, India is expected to surpass China as the most populated country in the world. (No one is quite sure about this; a number of experts think that China is underreporting its own population growth.) In any case, China's one billion people live in a territory three times the size of India. In 1988 one out of every six people in the world was an Indian, and every year the country grows by fifteen million people—the equivalent of the population of Australia.

It did not take a trained demographer to see that the country was already staggering through a nightmare. All you had to do was watch the commuters clinging to the outside of a packed bus as it groaned across a New Delhi intersection, or look at the masses of shacks in the streets, or gaze at the miles of northern Indian hillsides denuded of the trees and grasses that millions of villagers cut down for firewood and cattle feed. Such deforestation caused the soil erosion and floods that were destroying agricultural land faster than the government could reclaim new land by building expensive irrigation systems. Despite steady national economic growth, overpopulation helped to keep more than half of all Indians in a state of miserable poverty. In fact, nearly every major problem that India faced—from unemployment in the cities to scarce drinking water in the villages to violence among religious and ethnic groups—had its roots in the strains caused by overpopulation.

The government is hardly blind to the dilemma. Reducing fertility became part of the Indian government's official policy in 1951, and since then the country's population-control program has grown to become one of the largest and most complex in the world. Over the years, India relied on an array of nonterminal family-planning methods—intrauterine devices, the pill, condoms—but the core of the program was always the sterilization of men and women. It was chiefly sterilization, for example, that succeeded in bringing down the birth rate from 47.1 live births per 1,000 people in the 1960s to around 34 per 1,000 in the 1970s. At that point, Sanjay Gandhi, Mrs. Gandhi's younger son, began to assume increasing control of the Indian government and took on population problems as a personal project. But he used aggressive and coercive methods that everyone now agrees backfired disastrously. Particularly devastating were the widespread reports of forced vasectomies, a procedure many village men equated with castration. The issue led to the popular revolt that helped defeat Mrs. Gandhi in 1977 and also derailed any further effective program to control the country's population. Vasectomies are much simpler procedures than laparoscopies, but they became so unpopular in subsequent years that most of the sterilizations in India have been performed on women. Governments after the Sanjay debacle were forced to play down what was already a sensitive political issue. India, for example, always referred to population control by the more euphemistic term "family planning" and was critical of China, which had used coercion to greatly reduce its birth rate in a remarkably short period of time. As a result, by the early 1980s, India's birth rate was stagnating at around 33 per 1,000. (As a way of comparison, the U.S. birth rate hit a record high of 26.5 per 1,000 during the height of the postwar baby boom in 1947; in 1985, it was 15.7 per thousand.)

When Rajiv Gandhi became prime minister in 1984, India's population was growing by an estimated 2.1 percent annually, a rate at which it would double every thirty-five years. Fresh, impatient and confident that he would not repeat the mistakes of his brash younger brother, Gandhi was willing to declare, although not too loudly, that overpopulation was the most serious problem facing India. In the fall of 1986, after a long period of preparation, his government announced a five-year, three-billion-dollar "revised strategy" to promote the goal of a two-child family by doubling the money spent on health and family planning, and using television, radio and posters in an extensive advertising campaign. To improve literacy and health care for women, the program envisioned a "Women's Volunteer Corps" of two million members, to be selected from India's villages at the rate of one for every sixty families and then trained by the government to provide rural women with information about health care, immunizations, nutrition and birth control. The "revised strategy" was largely the work of Krishna Kumar, a highly respected and successful family-planning specialist. (In 1971, he had organized a "sterilization festival" in which more than 63,000 vasectomies were performed in a single month.) The overall strategy was praised by population experts at the United Nations as an intelligent, promising program, but as always, coordinating a master plan from Delhi through myriad ministries and state governments, each with its own intractable bureaucracy, was an onerous job—especially when Kumar, the person who might have had the skill, influence and determination to do so, was transferred to another job, apparently for political reasons, just as the new program was announced. Two years later, much of the program had not been implemented, and the "Women's Volunteer Corps" existed only on paper.

A more fundamental obstacle to population control was, as it had always been, the Indian family's overwhelming desire for sons. Surveys in the 1980s showed that 90 percent of the population was aware of the family-planning program, and that as many as 65 percent thought it was a good idea to limit the size of families. But the truth was that most couples preferred to have at least two sons, no matter what encouraging statements they might have made to a questioner hired from New Delhi. In the absence of a social security system, parents felt they needed someone to provide for them in old age—ideally an heir and a spare. In pursuit of those sons, parents often had five or six children. Bilquish Jahan, the woman who ran the government health program and was the chief advocate for population control near the village of Khajuron, where Steve and I had lived, told me that she herself had given birth to five children—first a son, then three daughters, and finally a second son. She admitted that she was not a good example in her efforts to encourage people to practice birth control. "Those who have only daughters—I never try to persuade them to adopt family planning," she said.

One of the main misconceptions of India's approach to population control had been the family-planning message "A Small Family Is a Happy Family," which was plastered on billboards and buses and in health centers and offices across the country. In fact, the slogan made sense only to the kind of people in Delhi who had devised it. Urban, educated families knew what it cost to raise, educate and find jobs for more than two children, but throughout the rest of the country, it was still the large family that was the happy one. For most families in India, more children meant more hands to help in the fields, and therefore more income. This attitude was changing among some of the poor families in the cities, who had no opportunity for field work, but in rural areas, experts such as Rami Chhabra, the media adviser to the Health and Family Welfare Ministry, told me that most families still thought the economic benefits of their children's labor outweighed the burden of feeding them. "Where there is work, two hands do amount to more than one mouth," she said. Another specialist, George Walmsley, who worked at the United Nations Fund for Population Activities in New Delhi, said that in some cases families did see that having six children was not to their benefit. "But that has been translated down to having four kids, not two," he said. India's family planners had learned these lessons too, and readily admitted that their "small family, happy family" message had failed. The government's revised strategy abandoned the whole approach and instead focused on improving the health of women and children. A barrage of new advertisements told women that it was medically risky to give birth as a teenager, or to have a fourth child, or to have one child right after the other. "We've shifted the communication," Chhabra said. "Now the approach is 'This is what's good for you.' "

But trying to change people's attitudes through an advertising campaign was an uphill fight. Even legislation had its limits. Although the legal marriage age for girls in India is eighteen, in rural areas this was almost completely ignored, and the government estimated that three million out of the four million marriages in the country each year involved an underage bride. The government also had tried offering incentives to families practicing birth control, such as preferences on loans for water buffalo. But there was fraud and cheating, and the program had a mixed success.

By far the most controversial aspect of India's family-planning program, both the revised strategy and those that preceded it, was the use of targets. Every year in New Delhi, the Health and Family Welfare Ministry set goals for the number of couples to be protected from conception by each of four methods: sterilizations, intrauterine devices, birth-control pills and condoms. For example, for the years 1980 to 1985, the ministry determined that it would protect one million women with oral contraceptives. By the end of the period, the ministry reported that it had actually surpassed its goal and had motivated 1.29 million women to use birth-control pills. It was an utterly meaningless statistic, and even family-planning officials admitted that most village women taking the pill did so erratically, sometimes only a few weeks a year. But taken together, the targets helped the government achieve a "couple protection ratio," or the proportion of couples of child-bearing age using some sort of birth-control method relative to the entire population in that age group. Over the years, India had consistently met its targets, and the couple protection rate had more or less steadily risen, at least according to the volumes of statistics churned out by the government. But the real problem of overpopulation persisted. Despite this stellar performance on paper, there was no corresponding drop in the birth rate.

Critics of the family-planning program for years had said that the misguided overreliance on statistics came from the "target fever" throughout the bureaucracy. The fever started in New Delhi, where the ministry dispensed targets to the states. The states then sent them down to the health centers, which distributed them among the health workers in hundreds of thousands of villages. Ultimately, each health worker in India had personal targets each year and would be docked pay or demoted if the targets were not met. Under this kind of pressure, health workers resorted to an amazing variety of distortions. They sometimes had both husband and wife sent for sterilization operations, or had the same person sterilized twice. More typically, older women with six or seven children—who had already done their damage to the birth rate and probably weren't expecting more children anyway—were sent for the operation. In other cases there was outright fraud. In 1983 and 1984, for example, the state of Maharashtra was apparently so eager to win a national family-planning award that, according to an estimate by the *Indian Express* newspaper, 180,000 of the state's claimed IUD insertions—25 percent of the total—were fictitious. In a statewide investigation, the *Express* alleged that medical officers had made up the names of IUD recipients and had entered in the books the names of real women who had never received IUDs at all. In one village, the paper reported, health workers had recorded three hundred IUD insertions for the year, twice the number of women who were eligible. In another village, *Express* staffers found that two current "recipients" of IUDs had been dead for more than two years. As one person involved in family planning had told me: "Things are happening in the files, and not in the field."

———————————•—•—————————

ABIGAYAL PATRIC CHRISTIAN WAS THE MOST PROFICIENT HEALTH WORKER in her area of Gujarat. I am sure of that, because otherwise her superiors would not have let me speak to her. I was usually able to interview anyone I wanted in India—it was not only the world's largest democracy, but also one that never stopped talking—but population control remained a sensitive subject. I had discovered in Tamil Nadu, for example, that village health workers were extremely nervous about talking to me without permission from district officials, who were themselves reluctant to grant approval without authorization from state officials and, ultimately, Delhi. This time I knew I had to start at the commanding heights of the bureaucracy. I sent the central government in Delhi a letter saying I wanted to interview health workers in Gujarat, specifically in a western area called Bharuch District, which I chose because I wanted to visit a rural hospital in the same area. My request made its way from Delhi through Gujarat's state capital and then down to a village in Bharuch District, where it landed on the desk of Dr. Gharia, the man who had overseen the laparoscopy camp. I told Dr. Gharia that in addition to observing the camp, I wanted to accompany a health worker on her rounds for a day, and to talk to her about her job and her targets. Clearly made nervous by instructions sent all the way from Delhi, Dr. Gharia obediently took me along with one of his subordinates to meet his star health worker, Abigayal Patric Christian. Then he and his subordinate sat in on the interview, and the four of us went together on her rounds. It was not, to say the least, a perfectly authentic experience. On the other hand, it gave me a hint of the quality of village health care in India and what life was like for the women who delivered it.

The day began shortly before nine in the morning, when Dr. Gharia and his assistant and I arrived by car in Jabugam, a village of mud huts and dry fields that was suffering, like most of the state, from a disastrous three-year drought. Jabugam and the surrounding district were populated largely by what India called tribespeople, villagers believed to be descended from the country's original tribes, who lived in India before the Aryan invasions of thirty-five hundred years ago. Although many tribespeople have darker skins, they look no different from other Indians. Yet they retain a separate ethnic identity, and although they are supposed to receive extra benefits from the government, they remain among the poorest and most backward people in India. Delivering health care to them was especially challenging, but as it happened, both the village and the surrounding district that we were visiting had a relatively low birth rate and a good "couple protection ratio." Local population-control officials thought the probable reason for the success of family planning was that the tribal families were more desperate for the money received for sterilization operations than most other people in India.

Christian ministered to the tribespeople from a small health subcenter in the village, which doubled as her home. It looked like the other health centers I had seen across India: a primitive one-story building of cement and plaster, although in this case there was a sign on the front saying U.S. AID ASSISTED, a reference to grants from the Agency for International Development that helped build it. Christian, a slight figure in the all-white sari of a nurse, was waiting for us at the door. She shyly said hello and then led us into a small sitting area, where Dr. Gharia explained to her what I wanted. She seemed too apprehensive to speak, so I began by asking a few simple questions that Dr. Gharia translated into Gujarati. Slowly, she told me that she was fifty-two years old, a widow, and the mother of three sons and one daughter. Her father had been a mill worker and her mother a primary school teacher. Her late husband had been a primary school teacher too, but she had only finished the seventh grade. Trained by the government as a nurse and midwife, she had worked in Bharuch District for twenty-five years, and now, from her base at the health center, was responsible not only for Jabugam, but also for the people in two other villages and five outlying hamlets. Her days followed a pattern: door-to-door village visits from nine to twelve-thirty, lunch and a nap during the heat of midday, then follow-up paperwork for her village rounds from four to six in the evening. She also delivered babies and held a health clinic for mothers and their children on Tuesdays. Her salary was $115 a month, and her biggest worry was making her targets.

I asked what her targets were, and she knew them by heart. That year, out of the three thousand people in her area, Christian had to persuade fourteen villagers to be sterilized, fourteen women to use IUDs, thirty-five men to wear condoms and five women to take birth-control pills. Not surprisingly, she had already met her condom and pill targets; it was easy, after all, to give them to villagers, who most likely would never use them. Her sterilization target, however, was a problem. She had persuaded only seven people—one man and six women—to have operations. With only four months left in the year, which ran from April 1 to March 31, Christian needed seven more cases. As it was, she had been forced to use part of her salary to bribe the first seven to have the operations. The government awarded her an incentive of fifty rupees, or four dollars, for every sterilization case she achieved, but inevitably she gave all of it to the people who had the operations, even though they were already receiving twenty-four dollars from the government. "There are poor people in the tribal areas," Christian said matter-of-factly. "They demand more money. They all know that I am getting fifty rupees, so they think they should get the money instead." Christian was actually fortunate. I had heard reports of villagers in some areas of Tamil Nadu demanding larger sums of money and jewelry before agreeing to the operations. Well aware of how health workers were held hostage to their targets, other villagers demanded that the workers take care of their children and do the family's cooking and cleaning while they rested after the surgery.

After explaining this dismal situation to me, Christian was ready to leave on her morning rounds. It was a pleasant mid-November day, not too hot, and all four of us piled into the car and headed for the hamlet of Vadafalia, another collection of mud huts, about a mile down the road. Normally Christian walked on her rounds, sometimes up to four miles a day, so a small commotion erupted when the inhabitants of Vadafalia suddenly saw their health worker arriving in a cloud of dust kicked up by the car. Christian got out, made her way through the clusters of gaping children and headed for a hut indistinguishable from the others. But this was an important stop for her. Inside was a potential sterilization case, a twenty-five-year-old mother of two. The woman had earlier told Christian that she would have the operation, and today, if Christian was lucky, she might get case number eight. Dr. Gharia, his sidekick and I followed Christian into the hut, where we found the woman sitting on the mud floor near the cooking fire, a baby at her breast and another half-naked child nearby. The air was damp, smoky and suffocating. The woman's mother-in-law, a gruff-looking woman, stood near the door. With no preliminaries, Christian asked the woman if she was ready to come with her for surgery. The woman looked up at us silently, expressionless, then stared back down at her baby. She must have been terrified, I thought, by four intruders who had just barged into her home, demanding that she come with them for a mysterious and frightening operation. After an awkward moment, the mother-in-law spoke up. "The baby has been vomiting," she said. "My daughter-in-law doesn't want to go." Dr. Gharia, speaking up for the first time, suggested that the woman bring her baby with her to the health center, but the woman refused. None of these health specialists, I noticed, went over to look at the baby, and no one offered help. After some more discussion, the woman's mother-in-law spoke up again. "My daughter-in-law does not have permission for the operation from her husband," she said this time. Conveniently, the husband was not home but out cutting field grasses. The mother-in-law, to bolster her case and take the onus off herself, then added that while she personally was in favor of the operation, the woman's own parents were not (although usually a woman's parents have little say over what happens to her in her in-laws' house). The mother-in-law had won, Christian gave up and the four of us went out, leaving behind an atmosphere of tension inside the hut.

The next stops, in the nearby village of Choramala, were uneventful. Christian gave a woman pregnant with her fourth child a supply of folic acid tablets to help prevent anemia, then listened to the woman explain that she had wanted to be sterilized after her third child but couldn't go for the operation because one of her children fell sick. Quickly moving through the village, Christian gave iron tablets to another pregnant woman and to the mother of a four-month-old. At still another hut, a woman approached Dr. Gharia about reversing her laparoscopy. One of her two children had died of an unexplained fever, she said, and now she wanted to have another. Dr. Gharia patiently told the woman about recanalization, a complicated operation that might or might not reopen her fallopian tubes. The procedure required eight days in a hospital and a month of rest afterward, and the government would pay. It seemed to me that the solution to problems like hers should have been sufficient medical care to ensure that Indian children do not routinely die of fever.

———————•———————

IN ANOTHER PART OF BHARUCH DISTRICT, ABOUT AN HOUR'S DRIVE FROM where A. P. Christian made her rounds, two Gujarati doctors, a husband and wife, were running an unusual project directly challenging the Indian government approach to population control that I had just seen. Based at a forty-bed hospital in the village of Jhagadia, this voluntary program was described by numerous experts as family planning at its best. It had won an award from the World Health Organization, a grant from the U.S. Agency for International Development and, most significant, the attention of the Indian government. The project was called SEWA Rural—the Society for Education, Welfare and Action, and was no relation to Ela Bhatt's SEWA in Ahmedabad. (SEWA was a popular acronym for rural-development groups across the country.)

This SEWA was the child of a group of seven Indians who had

known each other in the United States, chiefly a married couple, Anil and Lata Desai, and a friend of theirs, Dilip Desai. Anil and Lata Desai had met at medical school in India and then worked together at Brooklyn Jewish Hospital in New York. Inspired by the charitable works of the Hindu religious leader and teacher Swami Vivekananda, their plan had been to "earn and learn" in the United States and then return to work among India's poor. In 1980 they took over the hospital in Jhagadia and began working as doctors among the local tribal population in a way that few people had tried before. Four years later, the Indian government shut down its own health-care and family-planning operations around Jhagadia and turned the entire area over to SEWA Rural. In effect, the government was introducing a minor revolution by permitting a voluntary project to operate as a government agency, but almost entirely on its own terms. (Once SEWA Rural became an arm of the government, it did, however, have to agree to meet family-planning targets like everyone else.) By the time I visited SEWA Rural in the fall of 1987, the project had grown into a comprehensive rural health care program covering thirty-five thousand people in thirty-nine villages. Its success was best defined by its statistics. The infant mortality rate in the area covered by SEWA Rural had come down to 61 per 1,000 births, compared with a rate of 109 per 1,000 births in a neighboring area of similar size that was covered by the Indian government health services and where A. P. Christian, Dr. Gharia and their colleagues worked. (In the United States, the infant mortality rate at the time was approximately 10 per 1,000 births.) Most significant, SEWA Rural had brought the birth rate in its area down to 25 per 1,000; the neighboring area had a birth rate of 29 per 1,000.

SEWA Rural's method was deceptively simple: provide good health care first, worry about targets later. The Desais believed that the way to bring down the birth rate was not, for example, to pressure women into sterilization operations, but to monitor them carefully through their pregnancies, provide good follow-up care for the children and then, and only then, raise the sensitive issue of birth control by sterilization. One advantage of this integrated approach of delivering family-planning information with health care was that a mother, confident that her children would be properly cared for, might not feel the need to have more children as insurance. This "integrated" approach was also the official policy of the Indian government, but the reality was different. The government was still heavily dependent on health workers who were not from the areas in which they worked, and consequently the villagers did not trust them. Government health workers were also spread so thin that in many cases the only time they saw a mother was when they tried to talk her into sterilization, a situation that caused villagers to think that the government did not have their true health interests at heart. "They don't go to see a woman when she's pregnant," Anil Desai said to me. "They only go to see her when they want her to have an operation." Lata Desai, Anil's wife, agreed. "They are so obsessed with the targets," she said. "They don't ask the health workers about the problems in the field."

The biggest advantage that SEWA Rural had over the normal government health services in the rural areas was its resources. The forty-bed hospital was unusually large for the area and attracted people from four hundred villages. Private donations and grants from international development agencies allowed SEWA Rural to start additional projects, including a health outreach program that brought doctors and medicine directly to villagers by a mobile dispensary. The Desais also attracted a young, idealistic staff of health workers and doctors, some of them just out of medical school, who worked with a dedication that was rare in the government. But these advantages merely underscored the Desais' original point that quality of care and grass-roots work among villagers built up a sense of trust that brought results. One by-product of the trust, I discovered, was the collection of accurate statistics. In 1982, when the Desais were relatively new to Jhagadia, they organized a group of students and medical interns to survey the area. That group arrived at an infant mortality rate of 102 per 1,000. But a professional research agency, working in the same area during the same period, came up with an infant mortality figure of 60 per 1,000. To resolve the discrepancy, the Desais commissioned another survey a year later, making an effort to be more thorough and careful in their data collection. The Desais were hoping that the infant mortality rate would have gone down after their year of hard work, but to their dismay it had gone up instead, to a new level of 173 per 1,000— far worse than the Indian national average. As depressing as this finding was, the Desais suspected that the new figure was correct, since it had been gleaned by workers who had built up relationships with those surveyed. They also suspected that the Indian government statistics, much more favorable but collected by outsiders, were hopelessly optimistic.

One night, I watched SEWA Rural put its philosophy in action when I went along with the staff in the "mobile dispensary," a van carrying doctors and medicine to people who normally would have had to walk miles for medical care. In rural India, where 80 percent of the country's population lives, there is an average of only one doctor for every 15,000 people. The van pulled up about six in the evening at Ranipura, a village as dusty and drought-stricken as the others I had seen in Gujarat. Most of the doctors and health workers got out to tend to the people waiting at Ranipura's small health center, another dark little building, but I went with a health worker and a doctor, Nankishore, to see people too sick to leave their homes.

Our first stop was along a dirt road, where a little boy and a little girl lay motionless on two charpoys outside their hut. Both were dangerously sick with malaria. On a third charpoy lay an old man—either their father or grandfather, I couldn't tell—who was emaciated and wheezing from tuberculosis. Dr. Nankishore, a slight young man who had the earnest, cautious manner of someone just out of medical school, sat down on the charpoy alongside the old man, gave him chloroquine for the children, then made some notes. It was now so dark that it was nearly impossible to see, and the air had become heavy with the sweetly pungent smell of burning incense. Two oxen rumbled past, pulling their carts home from the fields, and in the distance I could see the flickering lights of small cooking fires.

Our next stop was to see a man with an oozing abscess on his thumb. Dr. Nankishore wrote out a prescription for antibiotics, told the man to go to the health center for the medicine and a tetanus shot, then moved on to check up on a mother who had recently given birth. She and the baby were healthy, so we quickly headed for another patient, this one on a far edge of the village. When we arrived at a sagging mud hut, Dr. Nankishore peeked inside and saw the outline of a young woman silhouetted against the flames of a cooking fire. When he called to her she came and leaned weakly against the door. Her face was only half lit from the fire inside, but I could see a pained, vacant look in her eyes. Her sari was dirty and torn, her hair tangled, and when she stepped out a bit from the door I could see that she was horribly thin. She began to cough and wheeze from deep in her chest. Dr. Nankishore told me she had pulmonary tuberculosis and then asked the woman to squat down in the dust by the door so he could listen to her chest with his stethoscope. Stepping away to leave the doctor alone with his patient, I wandered to the back of the hut and saw the view that the woman looked at every night: a flat, black plain, its bleakness broken only by a few lights in the distance. There were stars in the sky, but it, too, was so black and enormous that anyone who lived under it must surely have felt small and defenseless in a world of disease and death. Feeling desolate, I walked back to the door of the hut. Dr. Nankishore had finished his examination and was asking the woman's husband to get medicine for her. He wrote out a prescription, then headed back to the van, stopping first to see another young boy and a girl, these two with 105-degree fevers from malaria. "They will survive," Dr. Nankishore assured me. "It's amazing the kind of fevers that these people can tolerate."

That morning I had seen another part of SEWA Rural's outreach work when I went with Gayatri Giri, a supervisor of the health workers, to a meeting for village midwives, or dais. The meeting was held at another health center, this one in the middle of an arid plain ripped open by coal-mining fields. The dais had arrived by foot from across the barren landscape, all of them noisy and boisterous and dressed in the wildly colored saris—bright reds, blues, greens and pinks—of tribal women. Their ears were pierced in three places with big silver hoops, and they wore heavy silver bracelets on their ankles and wrists. With their leathery faces and gnarled, wrinkled hands, they reminded me a little of gypsies. They were at the bottom of India's caste hierarchy, and, as often happens, their low status had freed them from repressive village traditions. They never bothered to veil their faces, they often spoke their minds, they drank and smoked, and many of them had two husbands. In that sense, they were among the most liberated women in India. On that morning, in fact, one of the dais was already drunk by the time of the nine o'clock meeting; this represented a considerable improvement over previous meetings, when all of the dais had arrived drunk. The problem was that the earlier meetings had been training sessions, held at SEWA Rural's headquarters in Jhagadia, a two-hour walk for the dais, who had kept up their strength by drinking homemade liquor along the way. SEWA Rural finally decided it was easier to move the meetings closer to the dais, as they had on this morning, than to attempt to teach classrooms of drunken women the techniques of proper childbirth.

For thousands of years, dais had delivered all of the babies in India. In the 1980s, they still delivered most of the babies in the rural areas, using methods that were a grotesque distortion of the concept of folk wisdom. Katherine Mayo's description of dais in *Mother India* ("dirty claws," "vermin-infested hair") is overwrought, but the situation has not changed as much in sixty years as might have been expected. Most dais were untrained village women of the lowest castes, and as I have already described, many of them pushed on a mother's stomach the moment she went into labor, risking rupture of the uterus. Dais often cut a baby's umbilical cord with the nearest sharp implement, usually a dirty stone, knife or a sickle, and afterward smoothed the wound with cow dung, which they believed to be an antiseptic. Dais frequently told mothers not to give their babies milk until two or three days after birth, and also not to drink milk themselves during their pregnancies, since milk was believed to cause the baby to stick to the uterus during delivery. Dais further advised expectant mothers not to eat too much, saying that the baby would grow too big and not come out. Some dais told mothers that eating green vegetables caused miscarriages.

To counter these superstitions, and in an attempt to bring down one of the highest infant mortality rates in the world, the Indian government had in recent years sent trained midwives into the country's rural areas to displace the dais. But many village women would have nothing to do with the outsiders, most of whom were unmarried young girls. "They don't have babies, and the women won't listen to them," Lata Desai told me. "The dais have been in the community for years."

In 1977, the government of India decided to train the dais themselves in the proper techniques of delivery and hygiene rather than attempt to replace them. SEWA Rural's dai training program was more extensive than that of the government and was held once a week for a year. What I was attending on this morning was not a training session but a meeting to elicit information from the dais about expectant mothers and the couples who might be ready for family planning in their villages. SEWA Rural was forced to get the information this way because the woman who normally compiled such statistics had quit and not yet been replaced. While waiting for the meeting to begin, the dais sat down on the cement floor of the health center and directed questions at me. One asked if there were dais in my country. I told her there were midwives, but that most babies were born in hospitals. She then asked me why babies weren't born at home in the villages, and I told her that people thought hospitals were safer, and besides, there weren't many villages in the United States, and none like those in India.

When all the dais had arrived, we went outside to the veranda of a one-room schoolhouse for a laborious, time-consuming process that brought home to me once again how difficult it was to obtain basic information in India. The SEWA Rural staffers split the dais into groups, and then one staffer sat down with each group and began asking questions. Slowly, the dais told the staffers the names of the pregnant women they knew, their ages, the extent of their education and the number and types of injections they had received. The staffers wrote everything down on little cards to be distributed later to the people accompanying the mobile dispensary. The questioning took two hours and left the SEWA staff members mentally exhausted. At eleven-thirty, everyone took a break, and all of the dais went out to smoke hand-rolled cigarettes by a log in the sun. Fifteen minutes later, the SEWA Rural staff members called the dais back, this time to ask about the couples in their villages who might be willing to accept sterilization operations, IUDs or birth-control pills. The dais were founts of local gossip and seemed to know everything. One told a SEWA Rural staffer that a woman with three daughters was pregnant with a fourth child, and that her husband was threatening to divorce her if she had another girl. Finally, by twelve-forty in the afternoon, after more than three hours, the meeting was over. The dais lined up for a payment of five rupees each, the equivalent of forty cents. They acknowledged the receipt of the money with their thumbprints, then headed back home on foot across the scorching plain.

Even with all of the training, Lata Desai estimated that as many as 20 percent of the dais in the area still pushed on a mother's stomach from the beginning of labor—a practice that had caused the death of a woman while delivering twins a month before. I learned about the tragedy from a young doctor at SEWA Rural, Mukesh Dave, who was still haunted by it. As Dave explained it to me, SEWA Rural had known from the village health worker a month before the delivery that the woman was expecting twins, and also that it would be a breech birth. The woman had been asked to come to the hospital for the delivery, but she was frightened and refused. When her labor pains started, her mother-in-law called for a local dai, who pushed on the woman's stomach. The woman began to bleed profusely and went into shock, and the family at last called a village doctor. By the time he arrived, the woman's uterus had ruptured and she was dead of a postpartum hemorrhage. "We could have prevented it," Mukesh Dave told me. "If I could have gone to see her four or five times, I could have motivated her to come to the hospital. This is a bad incident on our part." The twins, though small, made it through the delivery. The SEWA Rural staff asked two mothers in the village who were already breast-feeding their own babies to take care of them, hoping that at least the woman's children would survive their mother's death. But most villagers do not want to bring up children who are not their own flesh and blood, and the twins, to no one's surprise, were not breast-fed at all and died.

My last morning at SEWA Rural was spent with a SEWA health worker, Ranjanben Atodariya, on her rounds. Gayatri Giri, Atodariya's supervisor, came with us. Atodariya, a pretty, talkative mother of two, set a good example for her patients: She was twenty-seven and had had a sterilization operation after giving birth to one boy and one girl. Her job was exactly the same as Abigayal Patric Christian's, although I noticed as Atodariya made the rounds of one of her villages that she took more time with each patient. Instead of simply handing out folic acid tablets, Atodariya took each expectant mother's blood pressure, measured her growing stomach with a tape and listened to the baby's heartbeat through a stethoscope. At the hut of an expectant mother who had had malaria during her pregnancy, Atodariya took a blood test and made notes for the hospital staff that there might be problems during the delivery. At another house, this one the prosperous home of landowners, Atodariya weighed a small girl—the seventh—who had just been born to a mother with no sons. As Atodariya went about her work, Gayatri Giri, the supervisor, gently brought up the subject of sterilization. This immediately sent the woman's mother-in-law into a tirade. "The eighth will be a boy," she said, then turned toward her daughter-in-law. "If you go for the operation," she threatened, "I will leave this family. You take care of your own children."

Giri dropped the subject but afterward admitted, as had Anil and Lata Desai, that even SEWA Rural was under pressure to achieve the targets set by Delhi. SEWA Rural had fallen short of its targets during its first year as a government agency and had learned that simply providing good health care was not enough to bring down the birth rate, at least in the short term. In subsequent years, the project easily met its targets, but the Desais admitted that they had to put pressure on their staff toward the end of each year to do so. Atodariya, for example, was well aware that she had to achieve thirty sterilization cases within the next four months. So far she had only sixteen. "Yes, she worries about her targets," Giri said. "But there's no scolding."

THE COASTAL STATE OF KERALA IS A LUSH, TROPICAL STRIP OF RICE paddies, coconut palms and white sand beaches, separated from the rest of India by a string of mountains called the Western Ghats. Over the centuries, Kerala's relative isolation allowed it to develop an indigenous culture in peace, while its 350 miles of coast along the Arabian Sea opened it up to the influences of European spice traders and Christian missionaries. With an unhurried and soothing way of life, Kerala in modern times seemed almost a nation unto itself. Historically, Kerala had always gone its own way. It had put one of the world's first democratically elected Communist governments into power in 1957, and its land-distribution system was more equitable than those of most other states in India. Kerala had one of the largest concentrations of Roman Catholics in India; Christians accounted for one fifth of the population. Kerala's people were poor, but because land was abundant, they did not suffer from the wretched poverty scarring so much of the north. Most important, Kerala was India's most spectacular success story in population control.

While the nation's birth rate stagnated at 33 per 1,000, Kerala's in the 1980s was 23 per 1,000 and was continuing to drop. Kerala had the distinction of being the only state in India where women outnumbered men: 1,032 females to 1,000 males. The mean age at which Kerala's women married was almost twenty-two, the highest in India, compared with eighteen for the rest of the country. Kerala's infant mortality rate was 33 per 1,000, the lowest in India, and less than a third of the nationwide rate of 105 per 1,000. These startling statistics were a subject of endless interest to everyone involved in population control, including Rajiv Gandhi, who often said that India had to figure out how Kerala had achieved its success and then duplicate its techniques. There were many theories, including one that the Communist government and the Catholic Church had influenced the state to spend generously on education, health and family welfare. But Kerala's per capita expenditures in those areas were not, I learned, higher than those in most other states in India.

In the end, the most persuasive solution to the puzzle was that Kerala treated its women differently than did other regions in India. More than 70 percent of the state's women were literate, for example, which was three times the national average. "In northern India, women just do the housework and have never learned to read and write," said Vijay Lakshmi, Kerala's director of public health services. "Here, women play more of a partnership role in the family. They have a higher stake in deciding how many children each family has. In Kerala, a male cannot just brush his wife aside and make her a child-rearing machine." Kerala also had more jobs for women, particularly in harvesting tea and coffee, weaving, making textiles from coconut fibers and processing fish. As K. Krishnamurthy, the state health secretary, said: "If women are the ones supporting a family, they recognize how pregnancy can interfere with their work."

But applying the lessons of Kerala was not as easy as it seemed. The state was unique in India in that it traced its respect for women to the once-prevalent matrilineal society practiced among the warrior caste of Nayars, in which women inherited family property. Before I came to India, I had never heard of this matrilineal system, and once I got there, it was not easy to learn about it because so many of its practitioners were dead. But I felt it was important to understand the history behind Kerala's population success. When a woman was married, for example, she remained in her parents' home, and saw her husband only when he came to visit at night. The woman made no effort to claim her husband's property because her parents gave her as many shares of family land as she had children. A son in a family received only one share of land for himself. The British outlawed these practices in the nineteenth century, and in recent years Kerala observed Hindu inheritance laws requiring all children to receive an equal share of family property. But the matrilineal tradition apparently continued to influence Kerala's women. Kamala Das, one of India's most well-known poets, once ran a quixotic race for Parliament on a platform of "gender justice," calling for the government to build a house for every girl when she reached adulthood. "By being provided a house, a woman would get a sense of security, which I believe is every woman's birthright," she told me. "I think a woman feels insecure without a piece of land."

Leela Damodara Menon was a more practical case in point. She had been a member of Kerala's first legislative assembly and continued to run the women's wing of the state's Congress party. She had entered politics as the wife of a famous Indian freedom fighter, but it was undeniable that the matrilineal tradition of Kerala had also contributed to her drive and success. One warm February morning, when I went to see her about politics in general in Kerala, I wound up spending hours instead on a more fascinating subject—her own childhood.

Menon had not grown up in a matrilineal household, but her father had, as the only son among five daughters in a large landowning family in the northern part of the state. When Menon's father married, he moved with his wife to a separate home, but his five sisters followed the matrilineal tradition and lived with their husbands in their parents' home. The sisters had their own rooms, where they slept on large platforms with their children and elderly aunts, sometimes a dozen women in all. As in most traditional Indian houses, all of the rooms opened onto a central courtyard. Meals were served in a dining room and were prepared by servants in an enormous kitchen. Menon came with her father for visits, which she recalled as the highlights of her childhood. "There would be food for everybody—some rice, some gravy curry, some dry vegetable," she remembered. "Then there were all the mangoes, and jackfruit and pumpkins and gourds—everything! Season by season it would change. There were a dozen cows, which gave milk to all. And then each family unit might want their own little items, which they made—some little stew, or some little item for the children. You had a sense of freedom; you had so much land. There was so much to do. Even running around the house took so much time. So many people, so much talking. You could never be lonely. Psychologically, we had a sense of belonging."

The husbands of the five sisters, however, were merely nocturnal visitors to the extended family. They kept separate rooms downstairs, where they received the sisters and performed their services as progenitors of the family line. Menon, for all her support of the matrilineal system, felt it would not have worked in modern-day Kerala. "Today, we want the husband to be living with us all the time," she said. "We want to be part of his life, his feelings. But there, they had arranged only for progeny and not for companionship. The family provided for that. Not that there weren't people terribly in love with each other— there were couples like that, and the family would make fun of them. Today, you want your husband to be the closest to you in your life. But that was not possible then."

Menon told me that the family house was now 250 years old, and that it stood locked and empty, a symbol, I suppose, of a system that had slipped into disuse even though its influence still lingered. Menon had no intention of ever living in the old home. "When there are not enough people in a house, there are echoes, and you feel scared," she said. "It had its place at that particular point in our history." She felt that Kerala's women had their own place in history, but that, too, was part of the past, and that there were signs that the equality of women was eroding. Although many women held jobs, their work was under- valued, and political power within the state remained in the hands of the men. "The status of even Kerala women is deteriorating," Menon said. "Society is willing to have a woman work, because she is augmenting the work of the family, but they are not willing to give her a place in society. We all joined the freedom movement, but after freedom, when it came to sharing power, the men were reluctant. Elections have become a very costly thing, and women cannot bear the cost on their own."

But the influences of the old matrilineal system and more recently of education had given Kerala's women something that many other women across India could not imagine: a voice within the family. As population-control officials had learned, that voice was loud enough for women to make family-planning decisions on their own. In the village of Peyard on the outskirts of Kerala's capital city of Trivandrum, for instance, a health worker named Gouri Indira had records which showed that 584 of the village's 791 families had undergone sterilization operations. Most of those operations had been performed on women, as was the case in India in general, but the fact that the overall rate of sterilization was several times the national average was significant. Gouri Indira said it was the women in the village who did the harder labor—carrying bricks to a construction site, for example, while the men merely mixed the mortar and baked the bricks in a kiln—and it was the women who were not afraid, as were the men, that the operation would leave them too weak to work. At the very least, the brick carriers had earned themselves the right to choose to limit the size of their families. In a much larger sense, Kerala had proved that educating and employing women was the most effective and far-reaching way to lower the birth rate.

No one in India disputed the notion that the status of women had to improve, and doing so was actually an official part of the government's population-control program. As the revised family-planning strategy stated: "Significant impact on fertility can be brought about when the status of women is raised and they become equal partners in decision making." The problem, of course, was that educating enough women to make a difference in the birth rate would take several generations, and India did not have that kind of time. "If we rely on standards of living improving, then it will be too late," one of India's leading family welfare officials explained. "We don't have one hundred years to experiment with."

Until then, the family-planning targets were seen, correctly I think, as a necessary evil. Population-control officials were well aware of "target fever" and its abuses and often said they would have preferred to drop the targets entirely if the family-planning program could have made progress without them. But that did not appear to be the case. The government had eliminated targets in the three years after the excesses of Sanjay Gandhi, and at the same time had increased the budget for family planning. But in the absence of a standard by which to judge their work, the performance of health workers was so poor that the "couple protection ratio" actually took a step backward. More important, the statistics showed that during that period the population growth rate increased.

India's goal is to arrive at zero population growth by the year 2050, when the population is expected to be an incredible 1.3 billion. To accomplish this goal, the family-planning program desperately needs to reach not the older mother, as it has in the past, but the women fifteen to thirty years of age, the ones causing most of the population problem. What is worse, this age group is increasing in size, so that even if these women have fewer offspring, the number of children will still be growing exponentially for years to come.

The problems and the work ahead remain overwhelming. Bilquish Jahan, for example, the government health worker for the village of Khajuron, was supposed to be responsible for five thousand people, but in reality she had to handle a population of twelve thousand spread out over three villages and dozens of hamlets. Worse, her medicines ran out four or five months before the end of the year—which wasn't surprising, since a family-planning official once calculated that the government was spending only $20 million a year on medicines for basic health care, or about twelve cents a person. The cost of an effective program, he said, would be fifteen times that. Where was the money going to come from? Certainly not from the international agencies, whose contributions to the family-planning program amounted to millions of dollars but covered only 10 percent of the program's budget. And even if the United Nations, U.S. A.I.D. and European foreign-aid agencies offered India great sums of money, a country historically wary of compromising its independence would likely reject the funding, seeing it as too much of an interference from outsiders.

"Our population problems are frightening," one of India's top population-control officials concluded. Although the $3 billion that India had allocated to family planning over a five-year period seemed an enormous sum, in reality it was only 1.5 percent of the government's annual budget. "You often hear people wonder why we are wasting so much money on population control," the official continued. "My own feeling is that we are wasting the money unless we spend a lot more. Only a massive effort will solve the problem."

By the time I returned from Kerala and Gujarat, I had learned that, at its heart, the country's population problem was the most profound symbol there was of the powerlessness of India's women. And yet it was these women who held the power to help India solve its greatest crisis. In the end, Indian women had to do more than just save themselves; in essence, they had to save India. To realize this was to discover a different dimension altogether to the problems and potentials of women in India, and also to my journey itself. I was depressed about the obstacles, guardedly hopeful about the possibilities, and ultimately moved that there was suddenly a reason, an incentive, for the ruling forces in the country to agree that India could not continue oppressing its women. The women of India had to be lifted out of their bondage, not only to reduce the shocking rate of maternal and infant deaths, or even to establish equality and justice. Women had to be recognized because no less than the future of India depended on it.

DEPARTURE AND CONCLUSION

STEVE AND I LEFT INDIA AT THE END OF THE MONSOON IN AUGUST 1988, on a drizzly, sweltering evening that promised three more months of heat. We were headed for California, where Steve would study Japanese for six months at an institute in Monterey before becoming the *Times* bureau chief in Tokyo, and where I would work on this book in a small house we had rented in nearby Carmel. California should have stretched before us like a promised land, but leaving India turned out to be more wrenching than I had ever imagined. During three and a half of the most exhilarating and difficult years of our lives, Steve and I felt we had made lifelong friends. A month before, we had left Sheo Singh and Bhabhiji for the last time in the village, promising to write and one day return. A few weeks later, a group of friends organized a good-bye train trip with us across the Rajasthan desert, made suddenly green by the monsoon rains. For three days we talked and laughed, stopping to wander through the deserted palaces and mighty fortresses of the maharajas who had once ruled India. Back in

Delhi, our final days deteriorated into a blur of good-bye parties and the exchanging of addresses as a team of movers packed up the house and dismantled our lives. By the time we arrived at the airport, I was in tears. Bim Bissell and Renuka Singh, the friend who three years earlier had helped me find the burned bride, came to see us off. As I said good-bye to them, I felt as if I were saying good-bye to a part of myself.

India, the country that once made me feel as if I were free-falling in space, was home. Delhi, once so foreign and overpowering, had evolved into a lovely, vaguely dull suburb to which I was always happy to return after my other adventures. The exotic had become the routine. Once, when an American friend asked what Steve and I planned to do for our vacation that summer, I had replied, offhandedly, "Oh, I guess we'll just go to Kashmir again." She pointed out that I had become alarmingly blasé about our annual trips to see dawn over the mirror of Dal Lake, or to ride horses through alpine meadows up to the snow line of the Himalayas.

I never have had patience with people who romanticized India, but as I write these last pages in Tokyo, in a modern, Westernized house, with all of the latest conveniences but none of the charm of our old place on Prithvi Raj Road, I am afraid I am perilously close to sinking into sentiment. When I look at our pictures of India now, of meals on the mud floor of Bhabhiji's house, or of peacocks on the ramparts of Rajasthan, or of our garden of dahlias, it does not seem possible to me that I lived there. India seems part of another time, as if it were a dream I had before awaking one morning. And yet, this nostalgia has overcome me only since I left. While I was living in India, the day-to-day irritants—power outages, water shortages, erratic phones, heat, dust, months of stomach troubles—always balanced out the romance. But I do not think I ever found myself in that love-hate relationship with India that is peculiar to foreigners, and which Ruth Prawer Jhabvala, herself a foreigner, described in her essay "Myself in India." As she wrote: "It goes like this: first stage, tremendous enthusiasm—everything Indian is marvelous; second stage, everything Indian not so marvelous; third stage, everything Indian abominable. For some people it ends there, for others the cycle renews itself and goes on. I have been through it so many times that now I think of myself as strapped to a wheel that goes round and round and sometimes I'm up and sometimes I'm down."

India was an up-and-down experience for me, too, but I see it more as a gradual journey in which I moved from utter confusion to a measure of understanding. I was too bewildered to love India in the beginning, although I felt that I somehow should. Nor did I love it at the end, when I realized that it is neither possible nor right to "love" a country where there still exists such widespread poverty and injustice. What I can say, selfishly, is that I loved my life in India. The country brought a depth and a richness to my experience that I had never known before and changed many of the assumptions that I had brought with me. I am a Christian but my husband is Jewish, and I occasionally used to worry about the difficulties of combining the two religions in our family. But in India, the all-absorbent nature of Hinduism helped to teach me that all religions are essentially one, separated only by cultural ritual, and that death is not necessarily an end to life. I found a richness, too, in my ordinary day-to-day existence, a joy that has always been difficult to articulate to puzzled friends. The chaos of India was in the beginning overpowering to me, but in the end I was amused by the anarchy it brought to my ordered life. The embattled Indian author Salman Rushdie, in *The Satanic Verses,* explains a little of what I mean when he imagines what a "tropicalized" London would look like: "Improved street life, outrageously colored flowers (magenta, vermilion, neon-green), spider-monkeys in the oaks . . . Religious fervor, political ferment, renewal of interest in the intelligentsia. No more British reserve; hot-water bottles to be banished forever, replaced in the fetid nights by the making of slow and odorous love. Emergence of new social values: friends to commence dropping in on one another without making appointments, closure of old folks' homes, emphasis on the extended family. Spicier food; the use of water as well as paper in English toilets; the joy of running fully dressed through the first rains of the monsoon."

I have been gone from India for nearly a year now, and the newspapers tell me that little has changed. It was 106 degrees yesterday in Delhi, as it often is in June. A few days ago a bomb went off in the city's busiest train station. Police suspect, as usual, that it was planted by a Sikh terrorist. The Delhi intelligentsia are still complaining about Rajiv Gandhi, and buses are still plunging off cliffs. But the India that touched me more directly has changed, sometimes in shocking ways. Smita Patil, the thirty-year-old actress who was five months pregnant when I interviewed her on the set of *Dance Dance,* died tragically of complications a few days after giving birth to her son. This past November in Khajuron, after Sheo Singh fell ill, the family decided to take him to a doctor outside the village. But he died of a heart attack on the way, somewhere along the road to Gurha. Dr. Singh will hold on to the family land, but I worry about what will happen to Bhabhiji. Dr. Singh sent us the news in California of his brother's death, and a letter from Shardul Singh, Khajuron's largest landowner, followed a few weeks later. Sheo Singh, he wrote, had been "complaining of pain in the chest for the last few days. But he, or anyone that he told, did not know that it was something serious. We could never imagine that he would leave us so soon." It was incredible to me that a letter should find its way to us in America all the way from the dusty paths of Khajuron, and it seemed, like our photographs, a voice from another time. Earlier, Shardul Singh had sent us a letter with a passage that nearly made me cry. "The thought that you will no more visit our village gives us pain," he wrote. "We feel that we are losing something which cannot be explained. My wife is remembering you both very much."

I also continued to hear from R. L. Verma, the lawyer I had hired to follow the bride-burning trial. The trial was moving at its usual glacial rate, and Verma dutifully kept me informed of developments. One incident of note occurred in September 1988, a month after I left India, when Verma wrote me that there was a "heated argument" in the courtroom between the bride, Surinder, and the husband who was charged with burning her. According to Verma, the husband threatened Surinder, and she hit him back. "She caught him by his beard," Verma wrote, "and his turban fell on the floor." The trial, and the letters, continued into 1989. Only a few weeks ago I again heard from Verma, who is now sending the news of the trial to Japan.

Over the past year, I have discovered that writing this book has been almost as much of a journey for me as India was. Women were my window onto the country, but also a window into myself. It was only as I was writing, for example, that I understood the real anger I felt in the beginning of the journey, when I followed my husband to India and abandoned my job, my family and a comfortable life that had given me a sense of myself. Friends wondered why I was not delighted to have a husband with an interesting job that took me to the far corners of the world. Their reactions made it seem as if feminist rage were no longer an acceptable emotion, at least not in the large part of American society that believed the women's movement was over because we had won most of our rights. Like Vina Mazumdar, the Indian feminist who once thought that "if we are not yet equal, it is our failure," I nursed the suspicion that if I was still angry, it was because I had somehow fallen short. India helped to teach me that this was not so, simply by allowing me to see that my reaction was a universal one that could not collectively be the fault of women. In India I learned that women from Aparna Sen, the accomplished director of *Paroma,* to Sheela, the uneducated wife of the Khajuron silversmith, were also angry, or at least well aware that life was at some level not fair. As Sheela had told me inside her mud house, with a reasoning that still echoes: "Men are not smarter. But they have been educated and go outside. Women stay in the house." Anger, of course, is not always a productive emotion, and over the long term it is not good for a marriage. I realize now what I did with mine. Like Katherine Mayo, who confronted her own indignation about the sexual exploitation of women by writing, however badly, about distant places, I took my own conflicts—some of which I did not even know I had—and looked for the answers through the lives of others, and through the writing of this book.

I feel less anger now, and I am not sure why. Writing this book exorcised some of it, but I also think that India made me come to terms with being a woman. I realize now that as the eldest of four daughters I had been raised, in a way, as the son. I grew up knowing that a girl could achieve as much as, or more than, a boy, and in later years I was determined to ignore the difference between men and women. In my mid-twenties, I ran four 26.2-mile marathons, placing in about the middle of the pack, and I remember with what pleasure I used to pass by some of the men. This would still give me pleasure, but I also know that my experience in India finally forced me to acknowledge the differences between men and women, and hold them as special. As I write these words, I have just learned that I am pregnant with my first child. It is time—I am thirty-three—but I am sure that India moved me in that direction as well. I remember how I used to walk into Indian villages and be struck by the incredible power of fertility. Out of the dust, against every obstacle of poverty, there emerged babies—human babies, baby chicks, baby goats, calves, colts, puppies, kittens—all of them created, it seemed, by the most mystical force in life. By far my most moving experience in India was seeing the birth of the baby boy in Belukkurichi, the village where I found the couples who had killed their daughters. The mother had walked to the health center at eleven in the morning, and by noon she had delivered her child with ease, without painkillers or complaints. She walked home with her baby that afternoon, leaving me in complete awe of her strength. I realized that there was a reason why Shakti, or female energy, was considered such a powerful force in the Hindu religion, and why goddesses like Durga were more feared than the gods. Indians knew that in the order of nature, it was the women who were powerful, who bled and did not die, who reproduced life itself. Later, when I read a speech the historian Barbara Tuchman once gave after accepting an award from Washington's men-only Cosmos Club, I realized that it summed up my feelings.

"I have never felt that I belonged to an inferior sex," she said. "On the contrary, I think that nature's selection of us as the sex that procreates the species and nurtures it through infancy—men's role being momentary and casual in comparison—is an obvious indication of superiority and privilege. I am glad to be female and I do not feel that my, or any woman's, sense of her own worth would be enhanced by membership in hitherto male precincts. Men's affairs, from what I can tell, are dominated by two primary components, aggression and alcohol. That is, fighting and drinking. Neither of which has any appeal for me still. . . . With regard to the Cosmos Club in particular, let me just say that if, as stated, the criterion of membership is 'achieve-ment,' then the exclusion of women is the club's loss, not ours."

A few years before leaving for India, I had interviewed Gloria Steinem, six months shy of her fiftieth birthday. She told me something then which I have never forgotten: that women may be the one group that grows more radical with age. "As students," she said, "women are probably treated with more equality than we ever will be again. The school is only too glad to get the tuitions we pay." But later, she said, come the important "radicalizing" stages in a woman's life. The first is when she enters the labor force and discovers that men, by and large, still control the workplace. The second is when she marries and learns that marriage is not yet a completely equal partnership. The third is when she has children and finds out who is the principal child-rearer. And the fourth is when she ages, which still involves greater penalties for women than for men.

By this measure, I am right on schedule, although I do not think it is only because I have reached certain stages in my life. I am less angry in my personal life, but I think I have also grown more radical—which is to say more acutely aware of the basic injustice that exists in the lives of most women—because I have spent the past four years interviewing and thinking about other women who have gone through these radicalizing stages themselves. I have learned that to write about women in India is to write about their problems of work, marriage, children, poverty and aging—problems that are not unique to India but are rooted in any society's definition of womanhood. The women I interviewed were part of a foreign culture but nonetheless members of the same world to which we all belong. Their reactions to their problems were human reactions, ones that all of us can understand. Infanticide may have been the most heinous of crimes, but I saw it not as the act of monsters in a barbarian society but as the last resort of impoverished, uneducated women driven to do what they thought was best for themselves and their families. As alien as their lives were to the lives in the world from which I had come, it was these women—and women like the poet Nabaneeta Dev Sen, and the policewoman Kiran Bedi, and Mrs. Rana, the New Delhi housewife—who convinced me that when life is pared down to its essence, there is a universality to each woman's experience. In the end, I did not feel so very different from them. As the Indian journalist Anees Jung wrote in *Unveiling India,* her lyrical book about her own travels among the women of India: "In the macrocosm of a vast land I find the microcosm of my own experience repeated and reaffirmed."

As I traveled throughout India, I often thought about another part of Ruth Prawer Jhabvala's essay "Myself in India," in which she wondered whether it was morally right for foreigners like herself to live so well amid such desperate poverty without lending a hand to help. This thought plagued me the most in Calcutta, where in asking Veena Bhargava how she rationalized painting the homeless rather than working among them, I had sought a justification for why I was interviewing interesting artists instead of helping out myself. But I realize now I was searching for a larger answer, for one that would have helped me define my whole purpose in India. I have come to the conclusion that if I did not work among the poor, I have at least told their stories and unveiled a part of their lives. This book was my mission—to inform, to enlighten, and to prove that the women of India are more like us than they are not.

This does not change the fact that the majority of women in India continue to live deplorable lives and are still held back by the overpowering forces of poverty, history, tradition, religion and caste. The country has not solved its most basic problem, overpopulation, which burdens women most heavily and makes all of the other problems worse. Men still control the power structure, and modernity has been a mixed blessing. Women have been displaced from traditional labor, and medical advances have ensured that discrimination against them can now begin before birth. And yet, in the four decades since India's independence, there has been a marked improvement in some women's lives. In the past decade, the women's movement has made some of the most dramatic gains of any group in India and has made the political leadership aware that there is a desperate need for reform. The work of people like Ela Bhatt among the poor women of Ahmedabad is a cause for optimism. I know I will not see major change in the lives of Indian women in my lifetime, but I am convinced that there will be progress.

Of India itself I am less sure. The statistics, particularly those predicting the horrific growth of the population into the next century, are not encouraging. To look at India compared with Japan, Korea, Thailand, Taiwan or Singapore is to realize how much it has fallen behind these newly prosperous nations of Asia. But India has had to face the obstacle of massive poverty, and while struggling with that problem it has at least managed to feed itself without deteriorating into a totalitarian government or a military dictatorship.

In the end, the country's three biggest challenges—maintaining democracy, secularism and national unity—cannot be accomplished without justice, including justice for women. In a sense, the country is a proving ground for whether humanity can tame itself, and whether we can eventually evolve into a world civilization. One reason to believe there is hope lies in India's resilience and spirit, but most of all in the strength of its women.

BIBLIOGRAPHY

BOOKS

Akbar, M. J. *Nehru: The Making of India.* London: Viking, 1988.

——. *The Siege Within.* Harmondsworth, Middlesex, England: Penguin Books Ltd., 1985.

Altekar, A. S. *The Position of Women in Hindu Civilization: From Prehistoric Times to the Present Day.* Delhi: Motilal Banarsidass, 1983.

Basham, A. L. *The Wonder That Was India.* New York: Grove Press, Inc., 1959.

Beauvoir, Simone de. *The Second Sex.* Trans. and ed. by H. M. Parshley. Harmondsworth, Middlesex, England: Penguin Books Ltd., 1987.

Borthwick, Meredith. *The Changing Role of Women in Bengal, 1849–1905.* Princeton, N.J.: Princeton University Press, 1984.

Das Gupta, Chidananda. *The Cinema of Satyajit Ray.* New Delhi: Vikas Publishing House Pvt. Ltd., 1980.

——. *Talking About Films.* New Delhi: Orient Longman, 1981.

Dastur, R. H. *Sex Power: The Conquest of Sexual Inadequacy.* Bombay: IBH Publishing Co., 1983.

Devi, Gayatri, and Santha Rama Rau. *A Princess Remembers: The Memoirs of the Maharani of Jaipur.* London: Century Publishing, 1984.

Erikson, Erik H. *Gandhi's Truth: On the Origins of Militant Nonviolence.* New York: W. W. Norton & Co., 1969.

Gandhi, Indira. Presented by Emmanuel Pouchpadass. *My Truth.* New Delhi: Vision Books, 1981.

Gandhi, M. K. *An Autobiography: Or the Story of My Experiments with Truth.* Translated from the original Gujarati by Mahadev Desai. Harmondsworth, Middlesex, England: Penguin Books Ltd., 1984.

Hobson, Sarah. *Family Web: A Story of India.* Chicago: Academy Chicago, 1982.

Indira Gandhi: Letters to a Friend, 1950–1984. Selected, with commentary, from correspondence with Dorothy Norman. London: Weidenfeld and Nicolson, 1986.

Jain, Devaki, ed. *Indian Women.* New Delhi: Publications Division, Ministry of Information and Broadcasting, Government of India, 1975.

Jhabvala, Ruth Prawer. *Out of India.* New York: William Morrow and Co., 1986.

Kakar, Sudhir. *The Inner World: A Psychoanalytic Study of Childhood and Society in India.* New Delhi: Oxford University Press, 1981.

Kakar, Sudhir, and John M. Ross. *Tales of Love, Sex and Danger.* New Delhi: Oxford University Press, 1986.

Kapadia, K. M. *Marriage and Family in India.* Calcutta: Oxford University Press, 1981.

Kapur, Promilla. *Marriage and the Working Woman in India.* New Delhi: Vikas Publications, 1970.

Kishwar, Madhu. *Gandhi and Women.* New Delhi: Manushi Prakashan, 1986.

Kishwar, Madhu, and Ruth Vanita, eds. *In Search of Answers: Indian Women's Voices from Manushi.* London: Zed Books Ltd., 1984.

Lelyveld, Joseph. *Calcutta.* Hong Kong: The Perennial Press, 1975.

Liddle, Joanna, and Rama Joshi. *Daughters of Independence: Gender, Caste and Class in India.* London: Zed Books Ltd., 1986.

Lloyd, Sarah. *An Indian Attachment.* New York: William Morrow, 1984.

Mandelbaum, David G. *Society in India.* Vols. 1 and 2. Bombay: Popular Prakashan, 1972.

———. *Women's Seclusion and Men's Honor: Sex Roles in North India, Bangladesh, and Pakistan.* Tucson: University of Arizona Press, 1986.

Masani, Zareer. *Indira Gandhi: A Biography.* London: Hamish Hamilton, 1975.

Mayo, Katherine. *Mother India.* New York: Harcourt, Brace and Co., 1927.

Mazumdar, Vina, ed. *Studies on the Political Status of Women in India.* Bombay, New Delhi, Calcutta, Madras, Bangalore: Allied Publishers Private Ltd. Copyright SNDT Women's University, Bombay, 1979.

Miller, Barbara D. *The Endangered Sex: Neglect of Female Children in Rural North India.* Ithaca, N.Y.: Cornell University Press, 1981.

Miller, Barbara Stoler, ed. and trans. *The Gitagovinda of Jayadeva: Love Song of the Dark Lord.* Delhi, Varanasi, Patna: Motilal Banarsidass, 1984.

Moorhouse, Geoffrey. *Calcutta: The City Revealed.* Harmondsworth, Middlesex, England: Penguin Books, 1984.

Moraes, Dom. *Mrs. Gandhi.* New Delhi: Vikas Publishing House Pvt. Ltd., 1980.

Mukhopadhyay, Maitrayee. *Silver Shackles: Women and Development in India.* Oxford: Oxfam, 1985.

Nehru, Jawaharlal. *Jawaharlal Nehru: An Autobiography.* New Delhi: Jawaharlal Nehru Memorial Fund, 1980.

————. *The Discovery of India*. New Delhi: Jawaharlal Nehru Memorial Fund. Copyright Rajiv Gandhi, 1982.

O'Flaherty, Wendy Doniger, ed. and trans. *Hindu Myths*. Harmondsworth, Middlesex, England: Penguin Books Ltd., 1976.

Omvedt, Gail. *We Will Smash This Prison! Indian Women in Struggle*. London: Zed Press, 1980.

Outhwaite, R. B., ed. *Marriage and Society: Studies in the Social History of Marriage*. London: Europa Publications Ltd., 1981.

Pakrasi, Kanti B. *Female Infanticide in India*. Calcutta: Editions Indian, 1970.

Pandit, Vijaya Lakshmi. *The Scope of Happiness: A Personal Memoir*. New York: Crown Publishers, Inc., 1979.

Panigrahi, Lalita. *British Social Policy and Female Infanticide in India*. New Delhi: Munshiram Manoharlal, 1972.

Paul, Madan Chandra. *Dowry and Position of Women in India*. New Delhi: Inter-India Publications, 1986.

Rai, Raghu (photographs), and Pupul Jayakar (text). *Indira Gandhi*. New Delhi: Lustre Press Private Ltd., 1985.

Rao, V. V. Prakasa, and V. Nandini. *Marriage, the Family and Women in India*. New Delhi: Heritage Publishers, 1985.

Rushdie, Salman. *The Satanic Verses*. New York: Viking, 1989.

Sahgal, Nayantara. *Indira Gandhi: Her Road to Power*. New York: Frederick Ungar Publishing Co., 1982.

Scindia, Vijayaraje, with Manohar Malgonkar. *Princess: The Autobiography of the Dowager Maharani of Gwalior*. London: Century Publishing, 1985.

Singh, Renuka. *The Womb of Mind: A Sociological Exploration of the Status-experience of Women in Delhi*. New Delhi: Vikas Publishing House Pvt. Ltd., 1990.

Spear, Percival, ed. *The Oxford History of India*. London: Oxford University Press, 1958.

Thapar, Romila. *A History of India*. Vol. 1. Harmondsworth, Middlesex, England: Penguin Books Ltd., 1976.

Walker, Benjamin. *The Hindu World: An Encyclopedic Survey of Hinduism*. Vols. 1 and 2. New Delhi: Munshiram Manoharlal Publishers Pvt. Ltd., 1983.

Wolpert, Stanley. *A New History of India*. New York: Oxford University Press, 1982.

Ziegler, Philip. *Mountbatten: The Official Biography*. London: William Collins Sons and Co. Ltd., 1985.

REPORTS

Balasubrahmanyan, Vimal. "Contraception As If Women Mattered." Centre for Education and Documentation. Bombay, May 1986.

Bentley, Elisabeth. "Struggle for Survival: Organizing the Paper Pickers of Ahmedabad." Mahila SEWA Trust. August 1988.

Chen, Marty. "The Working Women's Forum: Organizing for Credit and Change." In *Seeds,* No. 6, 1983, New York, N.Y.

Draft National Perspective Plan for Women: 1988–2000 A.D. Department of Women and Child Development, Government of India. New Delhi, February 1988.

Jain, Devaki, and Malini Chand. "Report on a Time Allocation Study—Its Methodological Implications." Institute of Social Studies Trust. Technical Seminar on Women's Work and Employment. April 9–11, 1982.

Jhabvala, Renana. "Closing Doors." SETU Publications. Ahmedabad, 1985.

Kulkarni, Sanjeev. "Prenatal Sex Determination Tests and Female Feticide in Bombay City." Study commissioned by the Secretary to the Government, Department of Public Health and Family Welfare, Maharashtra.

"National Family Welfare Programme." Chapter 11 in Annual Report 1986–87 of Ministry of Health and Family Welfare, pp. 121–141.

Ramusack, Barbara N. "Sister India or Mother India? Margaret Noble and Katherine Mayo as Interpreters of the Gender Roles of Indian Women." Paper prepared for presentation at the Seventh Berkshire Conference on the History of Women, Wellesley College, June 1987.

Ravindra, R. P. "The Scarcer Half." Centre for Education and Documentation. Bombay, January 1986.

"Recommendation of the Executive Director: Assistance to the Government of India: Support of a Comprehensive Population Programme." United Nations Fund for Population Activities, Proposed Projects and Programmes. Governing Council of the United Nations Development Programme. Thirty-second session, New York, June 1985. Item 6 of the provisional agenda.

"Revised Strategy for National Family Welfare Programme: A Summary." Department of Family Welfare, Ministry of Health and Family Welfare, Government of India. New Delhi.

"Saheli: The First Four Years." Booklet prepared by the Saheli Women's Organization. New Delhi.

Sebstad, Jennifer. "Struggle and Development Among Self-Employed Women: A Report on the Self-Employed Women's Association, Ahmedabad, India." Office of Urban Development, Bureau for Development Support, Agency for International Development. Washington, D.C., March 1982.

"Shramshakti: The Report of the National Commission on Self-Employed Women and Women in the Informal Sector." Ela R. Bhatt, chairperson. New Delhi, June 1988.

Singh, Renuka. "Status of Indian Women: A Sociological Study of Women in Delhi." Ph.D. thesis, Jawaharlal Nehru University, Centre for the Study of Social Systems, School of Social Sciences, Jawaharlal Nehru University. New Delhi, 1986.

Srinivas, M. N. "Some Reflections on Dowry." J. P. Naik Memorial Lecture, 1983. Published for The Centre for Women's Development Studies, New Delhi, by Oxford University Press. Delhi, Bombay, Calcutta, Madras, 1984.

"Towards Equality: Report of the Committee on the Status of Women in India." Government of India, Department of Social Welfare, Ministry of Education and Social Welfare. New Delhi, December 1974.

"Women in India: A Statistical Profile—1988." Government of India, Department of Women and Child Development, Ministry of Human Resource Development. Project Staff: T. K. Sarojini, B. K. Sharma, Y. D. Sharma. New Delhi, 1988.

"Women in Tamil Nadu—A Profile." The Tamil Nadu Corporation for Development of Women, Ltd., Madras. Madras, 1986.

INDEX

ABOUT THE AUTHOR

ELISABETH BUMILLER was born in Aalborg, Denmark, in 1956 and grew up in Cincinnati, Ohio. She graduated from the Medill School of Journalism at Northwestern University and the Graduate School of Journalism of Columbia University. She has worked for *The Washington Post* since 1979, in Washington, New Delhi and now Tokyo, where she lives with her husband, Steven R. Weisman, the Tokyo bureau chief of *The New York Times*, and their daughter, Madeleine.